THE I
RENAISSAN

James Hankins, General Editor

MANUTIUS

HUMANISM AND THE LATIN CLASSICS

ITRL 78

ALDUS MANUTIUS
✦ ✦ ✦
HUMANISM AND THE LATIN CLASSICS

EDITED AND TRANSLATED BY

JOHN N. GRANT

THE I TATTI RENAISSANCE LIBRARY
HARVARD UNIVERSITY PRESS
CAMBRIDGE, MASSACHUSETTS
LONDON, ENGLAND
2017

Printed in the United States of America

Series design by Dean Bornstein

Library of Congress Cataloging-in-Publication Data

Names: Manuzio, Aldo, 1449 or 1450–1515. | Grant, John N., editor, translator.
Title: Humanism and the Latin classics / Aldus Manutius ; edited and translated by John N. Grant.
Other titles: I Tatti Renaissance library ; 78.
Description: Cambridge, Massachusetts : Harvard University Press, 2017. | Series: The I Tatti Renaissance library ; 78 | This is a facing-page volume: Latin on the versos; English translation on the rectos. | Includes bibliographical references and index.
Identifiers: LCCN 2016011704 | ISBN 9780674971639 (alk. paper)
Subjects: LCSH: Latin literature. | Humanism. | Rome — Civilization.
Classification: LCC PA6163.H86 2016 | DDC 880.8 — dc23 LC record available at https://lccn.loc.gov/2016011704

Contents

Introduction

In the prefatory letter to his 1514 edition of Cicero's rhetorical works, Aldus Manutius complains how his work is impeded by, among other things, "numerous letters from scholars that come . . . from all parts of the world." In a similar vein, in his eulogy of Aldus[1] in the edition of Lactantius, published in April 1515, just two months after Aldus' death, Giambattista Egnazio asserts that "there is no nation in Europe, no matter how uncultured or remote, to whom the name of Aldus is not well known and famous."

Such widespread fame that Aldus was to enjoy as a scholar-printer-publisher contrasts strongly with our dim knowledge of his early life. He was born in the small hill-town of Bassiano in Lazio, the year of his birth being uncertain (his son Paolo gives it as 1452, his grandson points to 1449 or 1450). We know from his prefaces that he went to Rome for his university education and that he attended the lectures of Domizio Calderini when he was still a boy (*puer*)[2] and was a pupil of Gaspare da Verona, professor of rhetoric. In the late 1470s he extended his studies by moving to Ferrara and working under Battista Guarini. There he pursued or continued to pursue the study of Greek, the importance of which for serious work on the classical corpus Aldus must have already understood.

As was the case with other young humanists, one path to some financial security after his studies lay in finding a position as tutor to an aristocratic family, and this is the route that Aldus followed. He seems to have spent most of the 1480s in Carpi, in the employment of Caterina Pio, the widow of Leonello, the prince of that small principality, as tutor to her sons, Alberto and Leonello.[3] This was Aldus' last official teaching position that we know of, but

even when he had changed his profession, he retained a strong conviction concerning the importance of the teacher as the nurturer of the intellectual and moral development of the young. In the preface to his Latin grammar of February 1501, Aldus writes explicitly about this to grammar school teachers:

> And so we must strive with all our strength to see to it that our young are taught virtuous behavior at the same time as they are being taught classical literature, since in no way can one of these be done without the other. But if one were to fall short in one area, I think that how to live an honorable life is more important than how to acquire learning in the best possible way. For I prefer that upright youths know nothing of literature than that immoral persons know everything . . . but are as dissolute as can be.

In the previous month, in the preface to the first volume of the collection of Christian poetry, he had said something similar, but with an added religious component. He writes there that he was publishing these poems so that "young children of impressionable age . . . in their adolescent years . . . would not turn out to be morally corrupt and unfaithful in their beliefs . . . but rather upright men and strict adherents of the Christian faith."[4]

In 1489 Aldus had moved to Venice, which, apart from some breaks caused by the turmoil of the wars in northern Italy, was to be his base for the rest of his life and where he was to publish from his press, over a period of twenty years, the 130 or so[5] editions of works in Greek, Latin, and the vernacular, which brought him fame all over Europe.

Although Venice was already one of the great centers of printing in southern Europe at that time, we do not know whether Aldus was drawn to the city because he had in mind for himself a new career as printer and publisher. However, he may have begun

to think about printing editions of Greek works soon after he arrived there; in the preface to his *Thesaurus Cornucopiae et Horti Adonidis* of August 1496, Aldus says that he has been working on the printing of Greek for more than six years.[6] If he is not exaggerating, this would place the beginning of his enterprise as far back as 1490, almost as soon as he arrived in Venice and five years before the first datable publication of the press, the Greek grammar of Constantine Lascaris (February–March, 1495).

At first the main attraction of the city to Aldus may have been the presence there of many Greek exiles and the possibility of gaining access, through them, to manuscripts of the works of the ancient Greek authors. However, additional draws may have been the opportunity for further employment as a tutor to the Venetian aristocratic families and the existence of some fine private libraries in the city, such as those of Bernardo Bembo, Marino Sanuto, Ermolao Barbaro, and Domenico Grimani.[7] Aldus was soon acquainted with leading Venetian scholars, including Giorgio Valla, who was public lecturer in humanities at the school of San Marco, and with high-ranking members of Venetian society, such as Sanuto and Pietro Bembo, and we know that he met Angelo Poliziano when the renowned Florentine scholar visited Venice in 1491, as Poliziano includes his name in a list of Venetian patricians that he encountered there. It is clear then that he was mixing with fairly illustrious and learned members of Venetian society. His first major publication, however, was his Latin grammar of 1493, an indication perhaps that he was still engaged in tutoring. This was published by Andrea Torresano d'Asola, who had worked in Venice under the famous printer Nicolas Jensen and had bought much of the equipment of Jensen's press. By the time of the publication of Aldus' grammar, Torresano had built up a thriving publishing business that, in addition to an output of very salable products, including breviaries and the works of

such authors as Cicero and Livy, served the needs of lawyers with legal works and those of students with philosophical texts.[8]

His association with Torresano and his acquaintanceship with Giorgio Valla may be the keys to understanding the turn that Aldus' life took in the early 1490s. Valla was particularly interested in the scientific works of the Greeks in the areas of medicine, geography, mathematics, and natural philosophy and had translated into Latin many Greek works in those areas. Both Valla and Aldus must have felt keenly the need to have printed editions of the Greek originals rather than having to be satisfied with the Latin translations that were on the market. The threat that the wars in Italy posed for the survival of Greek manuscripts would have added to their concern.[9] It seems likely that Aldus was the driving force behind the formation with Torresano of a company whose initial aim was to safeguard and promote Greek studies. In whatever way it came about, the Aldine Press was formed in 1495 by the partnership of Torresano and Aldus with the Venetian nobl man Pierfrancesco Barbarigo, who held a 50 percent stake in the company, the rest being divided between the two printers, 40 percent to Torresano and a mere 10 to Aldus.[10] In the last six years of the century, a stream of Greek works issued from the publishing house, most notably, in the years 1495 to 1499, the famous five volumes of Aristotle (without the *Poetics* and *Rhetoric,* however, and containing much material from Theophrastus as well as some other items). The focus of the press was clearly on Greek philosophical and scientific works. The latter included Dioscorides' *De materia medicinae* and Nicander's *Theriaca* and *Alexipharmaka,* printed in one volume in 1499, while Aratus' *Phaenomena* and Proclus' *Sphaera* appeared in the same year. In comparison, there was very little by Latin authors, but even these publications had a scientific slant: Hyginus' *Astronomica* (1497); Varro's *De lingua latina* (1498); the astronomical/astrological works of Julius Firmicus Maternus and Manilius (1499), in the same volume as Aratus and

Proclus. Even the Lucretius of 1500 may have been chosen less for its literary qualities than for the philosophical content and the physical theories espoused in the poem.

Along with such works were the aids to learning Greek. In addition to the Greek grammar of Constantine Lascaris of 1495, already mentioned, that of Theodore Gaza appeared in the same year, to be followed in 1497 by Aldus' Greek dictionary and the Greek grammar of Urbano da Belluno. Hand in hand with these were the editions of Theocritus-Hesiod in 1496, Aristophanes in 1498, and the Greek epistolographers of 1499; these were authors that Aldus felt helped students to achieve all-round proficiency in Greek. On the Latin side, a new edition of Aldus' grammar appeared in 1501, but, at the other end of the educational spectrum, this had been preceded, in 1498 and 1499, respectively, by the extremely learned *Cornucopiae* of Niccolò Perotti and the *Opera* of Angelo Poliziano, works of enormous interest and appeal to scholars of the day.

If Aldus' publishing career had come to an end in 1500, posterity would still have thought that he had accomplished much, particularly in the areas of Greek philosophy and literature;[11] his editions of the works of Aristotle, Aristophanes, and Aratus were *editiones principes*. Some would have thought that any plan to print any work in ancient Greek at that time was a risky and foolhardy undertaking, and one that was in no way certain to be successful financially. The presence of ligatures and abbreviations, as well as of breathings and accents, in Greek handwriting made printing a work in that language quite complicated, and only a few Greek fonts had been used in the 1470s and 1480s. One way of circumventing the difficulty was devised by Janus Lascaris in Florence in the 1490s. He chose to print the text in an uppercase font, similar to the letter forms in ancient inscriptions. His text included diacritics, but there were no ligatures or abbreviations. In contrast, Aldus opted for a font that resembled the script of contemporary

copyists. He was fortunate to engage the services of a skilled punch cutter, Francesco da Bologna (identified as Francesco Griffo), to make the font.[12] But even with that hurdle passed, the production of a Greek text was bound to be more time-consuming than one printed in Roman type. Compositors would make more mistakes and more time had to be devoted to proofreading. Editions of Greek authors were inevitably expensive to produce. Moreover, there was no huge market for Greek texts that would offset to some extent the extra production costs. The Greek exiles in Venice may well have purchased the texts, but the number of even the well-educated and well-off members of the public who were able to read or were interested in reading ancient Greek was quite small, compared to the market for the Latin classics. We do not know how much of a commercial success these editions were, but since the 1513 catalog of Aldine books for sale shows that there were copies of the five volumes of Aristotle still available in that year, they do not seem to have been what we might call "best sellers." The financial status of the company after the first six years of its existence may well have been the impetus for a new accomplishment of Aldus as a publisher, for which he is also remembered.

In April 1501, the Aldine Press published an edition of Vergil in a pocket-book size (octavo), printed in a new font, which was very similar to the humanistic cursive script of the time, what we call italic. It is difficult for the modern reader to imagine the significance of what Aldus did with this presentation of the text of a classical author, unencumbered by any surrounding commentary and printed in an attractive font with familiar letter shapes, in a book whose size and weight allowed it to be carried and read when one was away from one's library or home (hence the name for such a volume was *enchiridium*, literally, "what can be carried in the hand"). The format of the volume was not in itself an innovation, as the octavo size had been used for some time, but primarily for devotional works, an obvious convenience for a worshipper.[13] The

novelty was in its use for the great authors of antiquity, "all the best authors," as Aldus describes them. Aldus may have been nervous about this initiative of his, as he makes very little of the innovation in the two very short prefaces of the Vergil. Perhaps he was uncertain about how it would be received because of the religious association of the format; Aldus writes there that he has not included in the volume the poems of what we now call the *Appendix Vergiliana*. This includes "obscene poems which are not worthy of being in an *enchiridium*." If Aldus held any doubts, they were quickly swept away. The Vergil edition was soon followed by volumes in the same format of other Latin authors: Horace (May), Juvenal-Persius (October), Martial (December), and Catullus-Tibullus-Propertius (January 1502), and Aldus becomes more expansive in the prefaces about the merits of this new presentation of classical texts, often stressing the convenience that the pocket-book format provided.[14] One unfortunate indication of the success of Aldus' innovation was the almost immediate appearance of counterfeit copies of his editions, in similar format and with a similar, if inferior, font. These were produced by printers in several cities, but primarily in Lyons.[15]

This deviation in 1501 from an almost exclusive focus on Greek works was probably prompted by financial considerations and pressure from his partners.[16] The Latin authors would sell, and sell well. The Catullus-Tibullus-Propertius volume of the following year had a press run of three thousand, and second editions of Vergil and Horace appeared in 1505 and 1509, respectively.[17] It is not surprising then that, in addition to the composite volume of the love poets, Latin authors were prominent in the publications of the press in 1502, with the appearance of editions of Cicero's *Letters to Friends*, Lucan, Statius, Valerius Maximus, and Ovid (in three volumes). Greek, however, and the initial mission of Aldus were in no way abandoned. Editions of Thucydides, Herodotus, and Sophocles appeared in 1502, and the next year saw the publi-

cation of the works of Lucian, Xenophon, and Euripides.[18] This list, not complete,[19] of the products of the press in the years 1501 to 1503 is quite astonishing, and it was not matched in later years. Indeed, there were subsequent periods when the press was inactive, mostly because of the unsettled state of affairs in northern Italy. Nothing appeared in 1506 and most of 1507, and the thirty months between April 1509 and October 1512 were also barren. But between this last date and the end of 1514, there was another stream of publications, both in Greek and in Latin. On the Greek side most notable were the editions of Plato, Pindar, Hesychius, and Athenaeus, on the Latin there were the *Commentaries* of Julius Caesar, Cicero's *Letters to Atticus*, Cicero's rhetorical works, a volume containing Columella and other writers on agriculture, and Quintilian. Aldus' final publication, in January 1515, was a new edition of Lucretius, in which Aldus talks of the severe illness that has afflicted him for several months. By coincidence, the addressee of the prefatory letter of that final edition was also the first person to be specifically named in a dedication: Alberto Pio, Aldus' former pupil, to whom Aldus dedicated the first of the five volumes of Aristotle in 1497. Aldus died on February 6, 1515, a man "whose industriousness neither our age not any earlier age has matched," as Egnazio states in his eulogy.

No one can doubt the veracity of those words of Egnazio. The output of Aldus' publishing house in the twenty years that passed from the time when the company was formed is outstanding, and it is little wonder that the Aldine press enjoyed considerable prestige, not simply from the quantity of the editions it produced but also from the typographical innovations and from the pocket-size format that it popularized. Fame and commercial success were not achieved, however, without the marketing skill and techniques that Aldus used.[20] The world of printing and selling books was an expensive and risky place to inhabit, but it was heavily populated

by a large number of companies. Many of those did not survive in a highly competitive market.[21]

Aldus employed more than one approach to boost sales of his publications. An obvious one was to advertise his wares, by publishing a list of the books for sale. Three of these lists of Aldine books survive, dated to 1498, 1503, and 1513,[22] and there may have been more. The distribution of such fly sheets was probably a common practice of publishing houses but, because of their nature, it is not surprising that few have been preserved. As far as can be seen, however, Aldus' list gave a much more detailed description of the books than was usual.[23] This at least is true for the Greek works, where he often listed many of the components of the volumes (for example, the individual works of Aristotle or Theophrastus in a particular tome), information that might have whetted a reader's interest enough to make a purchase.[24] How much in the way of sales these catalogs produced we cannot know; the fact that he published at least three of them suggests that he thought it might generate some income.[25]

A significant part of Aldus' marketing arsenal was the revival of the use of prefatory letters. The prolific editor of many of the first editions of Latin works, Giovanni Andrea de' Bussi, had prefaced the text of almost all his editions in Rome with a dedication, but this practice became less prevalent in the late 1470s and 1480s. Aldus, however, included prefatory letters in many of his publications. Some of these were addressed to the anonymous reader (*lector*) or to *studiosi*, a term which seems to embrace students, scholars, and all devotees of classical literature (*studiosi litterarum bonarum*).[26] In most of them, however, the recipients were particular individuals, many of whom were prominent members of their society.

In the early works, Aldus uses such letters to appeal directly to anyone who might browse through the edition with the intention

of buying it and thus ensuring other publications in Greek from his press, as in the preface to Musaeus (ca. 1495–97):

> So accept this little book, though it is not free; but give me the money so that for my part I may furnish you with all the best Greek books. If you give, I certainly will; I am unable to print without substantial funds.[27]

In a more subtle approach, Aldus chose to dedicate to academics and schoolmasters editions of appropriate authors, appropriate in that these were the authors they were expounding to their students. Battista Guarini, the former teacher of Aldus in Ferrara, is the dedicatee of the 1496 volume that included Theocritus and Hesiod, a text that Battista had requested from Aldus, because he was about to give public lectures on Hesiod's *Theogony*. Aldus probably hoped that Battista would recommend the edition to his students and that the prestige of the professor would be an inducement for others to consider its purchase. Similarly, in the prefatory letter of *The Greek Epistolographers* of 1499 (*Greek Classics*, Preface 14) addressed to Urceo Codro, professor at Bologna, Aldus expresses the hope that Codro will show the edition to his pupils.[28] At a lower level, Daniele Clario, the rector of a thriving school in Dubrovnik, is the addressee in four volumes, whose authors were eminently suitable for teaching: Aristophanes (1498), the two volumes of the Christian poets (1501 and 1502), and Demosthenes (1504). In the first of these, Aldus admits that he has never met Clario but is dedicating the volume to him because of regular favors Clario has done him. The most obvious kind of favor would have consisted of promoting the purchase by students or fellow teachers of Aldus' earlier publications, such as the Greek grammars of Lascaris, Theodore Gaza, and Urbano da Belluno, or perhaps Aldus' own Latin grammar of 1493.

Aldus cast his net further than Dubrovnik, however, and aimed higher than the schoolroom and the lecture hall. Cicero's *Letters to*

Friends was dedicated to Sigismund Thurzó, who was secretary to Vladislav II of Hungary, while the *Letters to Atticus* were directed to a successor of Thurzó's in the same court, Filippo Csulai Móré. Johann Kollauer, secretary to the emperor Maximilian I, was the addressee of the 1505 edition of Pontano's Latin poems, and Jan Lubański, advisor to the Polish king, was honored in the edition of Valerius Maximus of 1502. One cannot help but think that such men would have been happy to promote Aldus' work in their milieu in return for the compliment Aldus paid them.

Even more exalted recipients were persons of noble rank. In the prefatory letter of the 1499 edition of Iulius Firmicus, Aldus writes:

> I think it is well worthwhile for all the volumes that we undertake to print to reach the hands of the public with the protection of a preface that acts, as it were, as a shield, and for them to be dedicated to men who are highly distinguished by their learning or their rank (or by both of these) so that these books may carry more weight with our readers.[29]

It is not surprising, then, that in this context the addressee is Guido da Montefeltro, duke of Urbino, who clearly satisfies the criterion of rank and is addressed as "most learned prince."[30] Aldus' former pupil Alberto Pio certainly qualified in both respects and was the recipient of a dozen dedications. To him one may add Gianfrancesco Pico, Lucrezia Borgia, and Giovanni de' Medici.[31]

There can be no doubt that, despite all the difficulties it faced, the Aldine Press was a commercial success and that this resulted not just from its innovations in fonts and format but also from the marketing skills of Aldus. To those that have already been mentioned, we must add Aldus' adoption of what became the identifying trademark of books of the Aldine press — the symbol of the dolphin and the anchor, a pictorial representation of the proverb

Festina lente (Hasten slowly). The dolphin reflected the speed and tireless energy with which the publishing house worked, the anchor marked the delay in publication that resulted from careful checking and correcting of the texts. Aldus first mentions the proverb in the preface to Poliziano's *Opera* of 1498, crediting Marino Sanuto, the addressee, with providing the proverb as advice to him, but the symbol, based on a coin issued by the emperor Titus and given to Aldus by Pietro Bembo, did not make its appearance as a trademark of the Aldine press until June 1502, in the second volume of Christian poets. Thereafter, it was a staple component of the books Aldus published, becoming an acknowledged mark of excellence for the products in which it appeared. To its use in this regard, Erasmus pays tribute in his lengthy discussion of the proverb in the 1508 edition of his *Adagia:*[32]

> His trade-mark, the same which pleased Titus Vespasianus once, is now not only famous but beloved wherever Good Letters are known or cherished. Indeed I should not think this symbol was more illustrious [then] . . . than now, when it is sent out beyond the bounds of Christendom, on all kinds of books in both languages, recognized, owned and praised by all to whom liberal studies are holy.

Though Erasmus was not a disinterested observer,[33] the success of the symbol as a marketing tool can hardly be doubted.

From the perspective of a much later age, however, an inevitable question is whether the editorial quality of volumes deserves the same plaudits as Aldus' business expertise. In this regard, the works in Greek, a large number of which are *editiones principes,* must be looked at separately from those in Latin.

In the absence of earlier printed editions of Greek authors, Aldus and his editors had to rely on the manuscripts that they were able to procure.[34] It used to be thought that Aldus would have had access to the fine library of Cardinal Bessarion, which had been

bequeathed to Venice. There is no indication that this was the case, and there is good evidence to the contrary.[35] More often than not, the manuscripts used were poor witnesses to the text, and the result is often that a poor text in the press copy becomes an even poorer one in print. Even the readings of a manuscript of good quality did not always make their way into the printed text, and sometimes editors flitted in an unsystematic manner from one witness to another. The prefaces suggest that Aldus was involved in some capacity or other in the production of all the volumes that left his press. In some cases, however, the task of actually establishing the text fell principally to others. Demetrius Ducas had the prime responsibility for the volume of Greek rhetoricians of 1508 and Plutarch's *Moralia* of 1509, while John Gregoropoulos was the main editor of Sophocles (1502) and Euripides (1503). The star among Aldus' editors of Greek texts was undoubtedly Marcus Musurus, the leading Hellenic scholar of his day. He seems to have been the principal editor of Aristophanes (1498), the Greek epistolographers (1499), Plato (1513), Alexander of Aphrodisias (also 1513), Hesychius and Athenaeus (both appearing in 1514). These surpass in quality the other Aldine editions of Greek authors. This is particularly true of the lexicon of Hesychius, to whose text Musurus made many valuable improvements.[36] However, the unhappy result of the prestige that the Aldine editions acquired was that in many cases (Aristotle, Sophocles, and Euripides, for example) their text held a privileged position for three hundred years, though the shortcomings of some were immediately apparent to contemporary scholars.[37]

In the preparation of the texts of Latin authors, Aldus also made use of the services of fellow humanists: Andrea Navagero for Quintilian and Vergil (both in 1514) and Lucretius (1515); Giovanni Giocondo for Pliny (1508),[38] Caesar and Nonius Marcellus (both in 1513), and the edition of the writers on agriculture (1514); Girolamo Avanzi for Lucretius (1500) and the volume of the Latin

love poets of 1502; Francesco Negri for Iulius Firmicus Maternus in the 1499 edition of astronomical works. Again, as in the case of the Greek editions, we cannot be sure how significant a role Aldus played when it came to the question of the constitution of the text, but it is most unlikely that he did not have some input in that regard. His words in the preface to Catullus imply that he worked alongside Avanzi in improving the text of that author:

> Avanzi . . . expended much energy on correcting the text and restoring it to its pristine splendor, doing so for a long time on his own in the past and with great labor, and then together he and I applied ourselves with extreme diligence to the same end while the book was being printed.

On occasions it seems that Aldus may have been the prime editor, if not the sole one; this is suggested by the content of the preface to the Ovidian volume containing the *Heroides*. There he writes that *he* has removed two verses of *Heroides* 16 (ll. 97–98) on the grounds that they are spurious; he also points out other instances of non-Ovidian intrusions into the manuscripts.[39]

Unlike the Greek authors, however, almost all of the Latin writers had a history of more than thirty years of printed editions that preceded Aldus, with only a few exceptions, such as the *Mathesis* of Julius Firmicus Maternus and the *De prodigiis* of Julius Obsequens.[40] It is not surprising, then, that Aldus, like many contemporary printers, often stresses in his prefaces that his editions surpass in quality those already in circulation,[41] claiming that many errors in the text have been removed.

In support of this, Aldus frequently adduces the evidence that the finding of new manuscripts has brought. Giovanni Giocondo's discovery in Paris of a very old codex of Pliny provided a large number of letters that were omitted in most previous editions, and the same scholar's use of *antiqua exemplaria* in France increased the text of Nonius Marcellus by a third;[42] Cuspinianus supplied Aldus

with missing parts of Valerius Maximus that he had found in a manuscript in Vienna;[43] the codex that Francesco Negri unearthed in a remote part of what is now Romania did the same for the text of Julius Firmicus Maternus; a manuscript from Britain made an improved edition of Prudentius possible.[44] Nearer to home, Aldus himself spent time searching for manuscripts in Lombardy in 1506–7, two years for most of which the press was inactive.

In some respects, then, the text of some of the Aldine editions marked an improvement over previous ones as a result of manuscript discoveries. But overall, it was a hit-or-miss affair, depending on the quality of the manuscripts used by his fellow editors and the quality of the editors themselves. Avanzi made improvements to the vulgate text of Catullus, in correcting errors in previous editions with the use of two manuscripts, but his text of that poet was still far removed from that in modern editions. Even a manuscript of high quality, such as that of Pliny's *Letters* that was brought to Aldus from France, was poorly and unsystematically drawn on.[45] As for his choice of editors, one wonders why Aldus did not employ the services of Raffaele Regio for the 1514 edition of Quintilian. Regio was public lecturer in Latin in Venice at the time and he had earlier published an imposing work on textual problems in the author.[46] Instead, Aldus seems to have taken an edition published a few years earlier and handed it over to Andrea Navagero and Giovanni Battista Ramusio to serve as their base text. Despite these criticisms, however, the text of most of his Latin editions would have compared favorably with that of contemporary ones, and it would be harsh and unfair to judge them by the editing principles of the nineteenth century.

If we can admit the shortcomings of some of Aldus' editions, what is to be made of him as a scholar? He had an excellent education at Rome and Ferrara, two outstanding centers of learning, under the tutelage of well-respected scholars and teachers, and there is no reason to think that he did not widen his intellectual

horizons in Venice through his association with Giorgio Valla and others.

Aldus never published separately a scholarly work of his own, such as a collection of notes on the scale of Poliziano's *Miscellaneorum centuria prima* or Filippo Beroaldo's *Annotationes centum*, or a commentary on a particular author or work. The most extensive piece of scholarship is his *Adnotationes in Horatium*, included as an appendix to the edition of Horace published in 1509. Aldus discusses over twenty passages of the poet's work, making textual corrections on the basis, among other things, of meter (on which he is clearly an expert), the prosody of Greek words used by Horace, and manuscript evidence. The notes are presented in a scholarly manner, and to support his points Aldus draws on a wide range of authors and works, including the *Suda*, the grammarians and metricians of antiquity, and such evidence as the commentaries of Porphyrio and pseudo-Acro. Most of his suggestions are correct, but they do not improve the text of Horace in a significant way.

It is primarily in the prefaces to his editions that Aldus displays his learning, whether it is in airing scholarly questions that interested him or providing useful information for his readers. In the Ovid of December 1502, he argues that *Heroides* 17, 19, and 21 (the letters of Helen, Hero, and Cydippe, respectively) were the work of the poet Sabinus, whom Ovid refers to at *Amores* 2.18. The authenticity of the letters of Pliny to the emperor Trajan in Book 10 is well defended at length in the edition of Pliny's *Letters* of 1508. Conversely, he argues against Ciceronian authorship of the *Rhetorica ad Herennium* in the preface to the edition of Cicero's rhetorical works. Even when he is not arguing a point, the information he imparts to his addressee is often of a learned nature, as in the preface to Ovid's *Metamorphoses*, where he identifies several Greek writers of *Metamorphoses*, adducing Plutarch, Poliziano, and Aristotle. His explanation in the volume of writers on agriculture

(Preface 25) of how the sundial works is impressive, and the detailed map of Gaul that he included in the edition of Julius Caesar's *Commentaries* is no mean feat of scholarship.

Another aspect of Aldus' aspirations in the area of scholarship was his desire to set up an academy. In this he was probably influenced by his experience in Rome in his student days, where he would have known of the academy led by Pomponio Leto and other similar informal associations, such as the group of scholars, including his teacher Domizio Calderini, who were in the entourage of Cardinal Bessarion. The Neapolitan academy under Giovanni Pontano would also have been known to him.

This project, whose main focus was on Greek rather than Latin studies, surfaces on several occasions throughout his printing career, from hints in the preface to Aristotle's *Physics* (1497) of its being established in Carpi in facilities provided by Alberto Pio, to a request to Pope Leo X in the preface to Plato in September 1513 that such an academy be set up in Rome. His high hopes for such an academy, which included on more than one occasion a possible location in Germany,[47] were never fulfilled, and some form of it seems to have functioned in some capacity for only a few years, primarily between 1502 and 1504. The Aldine edition of Sophocles of 1502 was the first to give the publishing information as "In Venice in the Academy of Aldus of Rome" in its colophon, and we find reference to the Academia and the Neacademia in other editions of these years, either in the colophons or in the prefaces.[48] Its constitution, which has survived, suggests that it did not become much more than an occasional forum for learned discussion, conducted in Greek, of literary and other classical topics.[49]

His scholarly projects were not confined in 1513 to his continuing struggle to establish an academy. In his preface to Pindar of that year, he writes of a plan to publish the ancient and medieval commentaries on Pindar and several other Greek writers and to complement these with an index of important topics within

them;[50] in the preface to Caesar's *Commentaries*, he seems to be envisaging an illustrated encyclopedia that would cover many aspects of life in the ancient world. These ambitious plans came to naught, however; Aldus died just two years later, in February 1515.

Aldus' mission in life was less to display his own erudition than to serve the scholarly needs of his contemporaries, whether they were young students, educated readers, learned academics, or distinguished authors. To this end Aldus accomplished much; his contribution to the promotion of classical languages and literature was a considerable one, and it was recognized as such by his contemporaries:

> In the recent death of Aldus Manutius we have suffered a grievous wound and a greater affliction than any one could imagine. This has befallen not only me, who have been deprived of enjoying the pleasant company of a close and dear friend and of engaging in the activities that we had in common, but also and clearly all men of learning and all devotees of the liberal arts.[51]

I am most grateful to my colleague Randall McLeod for providing me with information on the prefaces on several points and for comments on the Introduction, and to Charles Fantazzi for his views on some difficult Latin passages. Nigel Wilson kindly allowed me access to the manuscript of his edition of the prefaces to the Greek works (volume 70 in the I Tatti Renaissance Library), and this was of considerable help. Robert Maxwell of Brigham Young University generously gave of his time to check some readings in Aldine editions held by the Harold B. Lee Library. As in the past, I am greatly indebted to James Hankins for making improvements to my manuscript in preparing it for the press.

NOTES

1. See Appendix VII, below. Full references to works cited briefly in the notes may be found in the Abbreviations.

2. This he tells us in the preface to Statius (ANT 11). Since Domizio Calderini moved to Rome in 1466 or 1467, it seems more likely that 1452 (rather than 1449 or 1450) was Aldus' year of birth.

3. In the preface to his Latin grammar of 1493, Aldus tells us that he held that position "for more than six years," although it is generally thought that he was in Carpi from 1480 to 1489 (*DBI* 69 [2007]: 237). It is possible, therefore, that for some of those nine or so years he held some other position, perhaps serving in some capacity the brother of Caterina, Giovanni Pico della Mirandola, whom he probably met in Ferrara and with whom he spent some months in 1482.

4. See 11 below. Similar sentiments are expressed in the preface to the second volume of the Christian poets (see 33 below).

5. The number depends on how composite volumes are counted. Lowry (218) counts 112 editions, based on the listings in Renouard, where the composite volumes, such as the Catullus-Propertius-Tibullus, count as one. I have seen the number being reported as high as 134.

6. *Greek Classics,* Preface 6 (p. 27).

7. On his death in 1472 Cardinal Bessarion had bequeathed his library to Venice, but for the most part it lay unused and uncataloged. It seems doubtful that this was an attraction for Aldus, as he never seems to have mentioned it.

8. Lowry, 78.

9. The preface to Constantine Lascaris' grammar refers to the "great wars which now afflict the whole of Italy" (*Greek Classics,* Preface 1). The danger that war and invasions pose to manuscripts surfaces elsewhere, as in the preface to Euripides ten years later: "Have we not seen in our own time in Italy very large libraries of good books dispersed within a few years, do we not see them closed because of some disaster and consigned

to moths and book-worms?" (*Greek Classics,* 115). See also the preface to Pliny's *Letters* (ANT 17, §2).

10. However, the first appearance of Torresano's name in a colophon alongside that of Aldus does not occur until the edition of Pliny in 1508.

11. A convenient list of Aldine publications in Greek, Latin, and Italian from 1494 to 1500 can be found in Lowry, 112–13.

12. See N. Barker, "The Italic Script," *Aldus Manutius and the Development of Greek Script and Type* (New York: Fordham University Press, 1992).

13. See Barker, 105–6, who points out that there exist a small number of manuscripts of similar size that contain literary texts, but these texts are late medieval.

14. See especially the prefaces to Catullus, Cicero's *Letters to Friends,* and Lucan (the last two both appearing in April 1502). For one reader's a preciation of the handiness of the new format, see the letter of Sigismund Thurzó (Appendix III).

15. Aldus applied to the Venetian senate in March 1502 for a *privilegium* to protect his italic font, but even though this was obtained, it was ineffectual against the presses of Lyons. He resorted to his *Warning to the Typographers of Lyons* (see Appendix IV).

16. Although one gets the clear impression that Aldus was the man-in-charge in the running of the press and in the choice of what to print, the preface to the Vergil of 1505 (ANT 17) shows that he did not always get things all his own way. There he admits to including, against his will, the book composed by Maffeo Vegio to extend the *Aeneid,* claiming that he had to give in to certain persons.

17. A third edition of Vergil appeared in 1514. A new edition of Lucretius (originally printed by Aldus in 1500) was issued in 1515.

18. The volumes of Sophocles and Euripides were published in the pocket-sized format.

19. More in keeping with the nature of the initial publications in Greek in the last six years of the century are the *Vocabularium* of Pollux and Stephanus' *De urbibus,* both published in 1502.

20. On these techniques, see Martin Lowry, "The Manutius Publicity Campaign," in *Renaissance Culture*, 31–46. The next few paragraphs draw in part on this essay.

21. For the expense and difficulties that printers faced, see Lowry, chapter 1.

22. Reproduced in facsimile in Orlandi as plates IX–XVIII.

23. See Lowry, "The Manutius Publicity Campaign," 34–37.

24. In the case of Latin authors, the descriptions were short, usually consisting of the author's name alone. Latin works seem to have sold themselves. One assumes that in addition to other means of distribution these lists were sent out with customers' orders in the hope of eliciting more purchases.

25. The catalogs are reproduced in Orlandi, tavv. IX–XVIII.

26. The word *studiosi* has been rendered differently in the following translations of the prefaces, depending on context and the nature of the work.

27. *Greek Classics*, Preface 2. A similar appeal can be found in the colophon of the Greek grammar of Constantine Lascaris (*Greek Classics*, Preface 1 C).

28. Giovanni Taberio, who held a chair at Brescia, is the dedicatee of the edition of Stephanus of Byzantium (1502), and Aldus sees this as a way of thanking Taberio for having previously ordered Greek books for his pupils (*Greek Classics*, 91). Other recipients of similar rank are Giovanni Calpurnio (*Greek Classics*, Preface 22) and Demetrius Chalcondyles (*Greek Classics*, Preface 23).

29. See p. 3, below.

30. He is also the addressee of the preface to the edition of Xenophon of 1503 (*Greek Classics*, Preface 25).

31. Pio was honored primarily in philosophical works such as the five volumes of Aristotle (1495–98). Giovanni Francesco Pico is the addressee in the grammar of Urbano da Belluno (1498), Lucrezia Borgia in the edition of the poems of Tito and Ercole Strozzi (1513), Pope Leo X in the edition of Plato (1513). The *Erotemata* of Chrysoloras (1512) is dedicated to Cesare d'Aragona, the son of Federico I of Naples.

32. Erasmus, *Adagia* 2.1.1 (*CWE* 33:13–17). The quotation that follows is taken from Phillips, 179.

33. Erasmus and Aldus worked closely together in the production of the edition, as described by Erasmus in his expansion of the essay on this proverb in the 1526 edition.

34. Seminal works for an evaluation of how Aldus and his colleagues utilized their manuscript sources are Martin Sicherl, *Handschriftliche Vorlagen des Editio Princeps des Aristoteles* (Mainz, 1976), and (by the same author) "Die *Editio Princeps Aldina* des Euripides und ihre Vorlagen," *Rheinisches Museum* 118 (1975): 205–25; *Griechische Erstausgabe des Aldus Manutius: Druckvorlagen, Stellenwert, kultureller Hintergrund* (Paderborn: Schöningh, 1997). See also Lowry, 234–42.

35. See Wilson (1977): 153, where he refers to manuscripts (of Theophrastus and Aristotle) in the collection that Aldus would have used if he had had access to it.

36. As acknowledged in Aldus' preface to the volume (see *Greek Classics*, 261). See Wilson (1992), 152–53; Geanakoplos, 154–55. E. J. Kenney, *The Classical Text: Aspects of Editing in the Age of the Printed Book* (Berkeley: University of California Press, 1974), 18, has a less favorable view of Musurus' edition of Hesychius.

37. Errors in the Aldine text of Aristotle's *De historia animalium* were soon pointed out by Urceo Codro, who taught at the university in Bologna. See Wilson (1992), 128.

38. Giocondo certainly provided Aldus with information about man script readings for the text of Pliny, but it is not clear whether he was physically present when the edition was being produced.

39. See ANT 14, §§3 and 7.

40. The Aldine edition is the sole source of *De prodigiis*. There was an earlier edition of the complete *Mathesis*, printed in Venice in 1497, but it was the Aldine edition that acquired the status of *editio princeps*, its text being the basis for later editions; see the Teubner edition of the work by W. Kroll and F. Skutsch, xxviii–xxxiii. The Prudentius in the first volume of the collection of Christian poets had a similar status.

41. In the Lucretius of 1500, Vergil of 1505, Quintilian of 1514, and Lucretius of 1515.

42. The information about Fra Giocondo's use of allegedly ancient manuscripts of Nonius Marcellus in France is given in the table of contents of the 1513 edition of Perotti's *Cornucopiae*, which included other items.

43. However, the missing parts are to be found in earlier editions; see ANT 12, n. 100.

44. For Aldus it almost seemed that the remoteness of a manuscript's location suggested superiority: *remotiores, non deteriores*.

45. See Kenney, *The Classical Text*, 18.

46. See ANT 26, n. 334. Regio was into his seventies, however, when the edition of Quintilian was being prepared, and his age may have been a deterrent.

47. See HUM 8, n. 82.

48. References to the academy are not confined to Greek works. We find *Academia* in the colophon of Ovid's *Fasti, Tristia*, etc. of 1502, and there are references to the Academy in the prefaces of Statius and Valerius Maximus (both of 1502). The term *Neacademia* is to be found in the colophon of a May 1504 edition of a speech by Scipio Carteromachus (a member of the academy) in praise of Greek literature, as well as in editions of Xenophon (1503) and Gregory of Nazianzus (June 1504) and in the *Warning To the Typographers of Lyons* (1503, Appendix IV).

49. This is what is suggested by the surviving copy of the statutes of the academy, in which criteria for membership are also pointed out. See *Greek Classics*, Appendix V. On the academy, see M. J. C. Lowry, "The 'New Academy' of Aldus Manutius: A Renaissance Dream," *Bulletin of the John Rylands Library of Manchester* 58 (1975–76): 378–420; Wilson (1992), 127–33; Stefano Pagliaroli, "L'Accademia Aldina," *Incontri triestini di filologia classica* 9 (2009–10): 175–87.

50. *Greek Classics*, 221.

51. From the beginning of the eulogy of Egnazio in the edition of Lactantius (Appendix VII).

PREFACES

: I :

Aldus Manutius Romanus Guido Pheretrio Urbini duci s. p. d.

1 Operae pretium mihi videtur, Guide Pheretri, dux illustrissime, ut quaecunque volumina formis excudenda curamus praefatione aliqua veluti clypeo quodam munita exeant in manus hominum, et quo sit illis plus auctoritatis viris vel doctrina vel dignitate vel utroque perinsignibus dedicentur. Quod minime arroganter id a me fieri existimetur velim, quandoquidem alienos libros nostra cura impressos illi vel illi dedicare idcirco mihi licere arbitror quod eos maximo quaesitos studio tanquam ab inferis ad superos revocemus.

2 Nam, si potuere quidam latas ab aliis leges sub suo nomine promulgare, exolescente metu antiquiorum, quemadmodum olim de duodecim[1] tabulis factum constat, 'quarum cum contemni antiquitas coepisset, eadem illa quae iis legibus cavebantur in alia legum latorum nomina transierunt,' cur ipse non queam in alicuius clarissimi ac summi viri nomine eos edere libros, qui, cum tot

EDITIONS OF ANCIENT LATIN AUTHORS

: I :

Julius Firmicus, Astronomica; *Manilius,* Astronomica

(October 17, 1499)

Aldus Manutius of Rome to Guido da Montefeltro, duke of Urbino, warmest greetings.[1]

Guido da Montefeltro, most illustrious duke, I think it is well worthwhile for all the volumes that we undertake to print to reach the hands of the public with the protection of a preface that acts, as it were, as a shield, and for them to be dedicated to men who are highly distinguished by their learning or rank (or by both of these) so that these books may carry more weight with our readers. I would not wish me to be thought in any way presumptuous in doing this; for I think it is permissible for me to dedicate to this individual or that one the works of other persons that we have undertaken to print, inasmuch as we have taken great pains to search them out and are restoring them to life, bringing them back, so to speak, from the netherworld into the light of day. 1

I say this because, when some ancient laws evoked less fear, certain individuals were allowed to promulgate under their own name these same laws that had been brought in earlier by others. It is well known that this happened in the past with respect to the Twelve Tables. "When disrespect for their antiquity was growing, the very actions that these laws guarded against were the subject of laws that were given the names of those who proposed them later."[2] Why then should I not be able to publish these books under the name of some famous and exalted man when after lying hidden for so many centuries, mutilated and covered in filth, they 2

secula squalidi et laceri iacuerint, summis meis laboribus reviviscunt? Id igitur meo iure facere mihi videor.

3 Quapropter Iulium Maternum sub tuo foelici nomine aere nostro excusum publicare voluimus tibique dono mittere, Guide, princeps doctissime, rati fore tibi gratissimum quod integer et absolutus abusque Getis in Italiam redeat suosque revisat et patriam: nam qui vagabatur prius valde quam depravatus erat ac mutilus et fere dimidius.

4 Sed quoniam contendunt quidam a Christiano viro haudquaquam legendum Firmicum quod fatis agi humana omnia et necessario evenire affirmet, ipsius verba recitare placuit quibus docet posse ununquenque stellarum resistere potestatibus, si sit prudentia. Sic enim dicit:

> Invocemus suppliciter deos, et religiose promissa numinibus vota reddamus, ut confirmati animi nostri divinitate ex aliqua parte stellarum violentis decretorum potestatibus resistamus. Hoc debere nos facere vir divinae sapientiae Socrates docuit. Nam, cum quidam ei de moribus suis cupiditatibusque dixisset quas ille simili ratione collegerat, 'Sunt' inquit 'ut dicis, agnosco, confiteor'; et, vir prudentissimus, latentia corporis vitia facili confessione detexit. 'Sed haec' inquit 'omnia a me prudentia ac virtutum auctoritate superata sunt, et quicquid vitii ex prava concretione corpus habuerat animi bene sibi conscia divinitas temperavit.' Hinc intelligi datur, stellarum quidem esse quod patimur et quod nos incentivis

come to life again through my strenuous labors? I think I am within my rights to do so.

3 For these reasons, Guido, most learned prince, we wished to publish under your propitious name Julius Maternus, printed in our bronze type, and to send it to you as a gift. We thought you would find it most pleasing that Maternus returns to Italy all the way from the land of the Getae, complete and unimpaired, and looks again upon his kinsmen and his native land.[3] For the edition that has been in wide circulation before this one is dreadfully corrupt and fragmentary as well as lacking almost half of the work.[4]

4 However, some persons contend that Firmicus should in no way be read by a Christian because he avers that all human actions are driven by fate and happen by necessity. I have decided therefore to quote his actual words in which he explains that every single person can resist the powers of the stars through wisdom. For this is what Firmicus says:

> Let us call upon the gods in supplication, and let us scrupulously fulfill our vows to the gods so that, strengthened by the divinity of our souls, we may resist to some extent the violent powers of the stars' decrees. The teaching of Socrates, a man of divine wisdom, was that we ought to do this. For when some individual had spoken to him about his immoral behavior and his desires, vices which that fellow himself had succumbed to in a similar way, Socrates said, "They are as you say, I acknowledge it, I confess it." That wisest of men laid bare the hidden weaknesses of the body by this freely given confession. "But," he said, "I have overcome all these through wisdom and the power of virtue, and whatever faults the body had from its corrupt composition have been mastered by the divinity of the soul, conscious of its power." From this we can infer that our emotions and the driving

quibusdam stimulat ignibus, divinitatis vero esse animi quod repugnamus.

Sed haec et alia in Materno tu ipse longe melius. Vale, principum aetatis nostrae decus.

Venetiis, decimo sexto calendas Novembres M.ID.

: II :

Aldus Manutius Romanus Alberto Pio
Carporum principi s. p. d.

1 Titum Lucretium Carum mea cura nuper expressum publicare sub tuo nomine tibique iam consummato philosopho philosophum suae sectae doctissimum dare muneri statui, Alberte, princeps eruditissime. Nam qui ante impressus habetur in manibus adeo est mendosus ac mutilatus ut paucis in locis queat intelligi; noster vero sic emendatus et integer prodit in vulgum ut perpauca castigatione indigeant.

2 Qua in re habenda est plurima gratia Hieronymo Avancio Veronensi, viro Latinae linguae ac liberalium disciplinarum non mediocriter perito, quod multos annos Lucretio corrigendo in pristinamque restituendo integritatem accuratissime elaborarit tandemque eo ipso Tito adiutore correxerit, quod in eo non hemistichia solum atque integri versus, sed multa etiam carmina saepe repetita more Homerico inveniantur. Cum igitur Avancius noster

passions that goad us on depend on the stars, while our resistance to these comes from the divinity of the soul.[5]

But it is much better to read these and other things in Maternus for yourself. Farewell, most glorious of the princes of our age.

Venice, October 17, 1499.

: II :

Lucretius

(December 1500)

Aldus Manutius of Rome to Alberto Pio,[6] *prince of Carpi, warmest greetings.*

I have decided to publish under your name, Alberto, most learned prince, this edition of Titus Lucretius Carus, the printing of which I recently undertook, and to bestow as a gift the most learned philosopher of his school on you, who are already a philosopher of the highest order. For the earlier printed texts of Lucretius that are in circulation are so full of errors and so disfigured by the loss of verses that our author can be understood in very few passages. This text of ours that is now available to the public is so free of mistakes and lacunae that very few passages require correction. 1

In this respect we are deeply grateful to Girolamo Avanzi of Verona,[7] a man with extraordinary mastery of the Latin language and the liberal arts, for having worked so laboriously and carefully for many years in correcting Lucretius and restoring him to his original purity, and for having emended Lucretius with the help of the author himself. For in Lucretius are to be found not only half-lines or complete verses but even many longer passages that are often repeated elsewhere, in Homeric fashion. Accordingly, since 2

Lucretium memoria teneat ut digitos unguesque suos, perfacile hemistichium hemistichio et carmen carmine emendavit; idemque factum est eorum auxilio versuum qui sparsim apud authores Latinae linguae adducti habentur.

3 Tu itaque debes, Alberte humanissime, librum hunc benigna fronte in doctissimam academiam tuam admittere, tum quia ipse dignus sua ipsius authoritate et gratia—non quod vera scripserit et credenda nobis; nam ab Academicis etiam et Peripateticis, nedum a theologis nostris multum dissentit—sed quia Epicureae sectae dogmata eleganter et docte mandavit carminibus, imitatus Empedoclem, qui primus apud Graecos praecepta sapientiae versibus tradidit, cuius scripta vel iniuria temporum vel barbarorum incursionibus a quibus saepe et Graeciam spoliatam et Italiam constat deperierunt. Vix pauca quaedam ab Aristotele in Meteoris et alibi citata visuntur, quanquam et apud Stobaeum, qui eclogarum ex antiquissimis magnum volumen confecit, multa et Empedoclis et aliorum quorundam quorum scripta iamdiu interierunt, aliquando volente Deo expressa publicabimus. Tum etiam perhumaniter a te suscipiendus est Lucretius, quod ab Avancio tibi deditissimo summa cura emaculatus est, tum praeterea quia, tibi ab Aldo tuo nuncupatus, dono ad te mittitur. Vale.

our dear Avanzi knows the poems of Lucretius as well as his fingers and nails,[8] he has emended hemistichs and verses with the greatest of ease by using other hemistichs and verses of the poet. He achieved the same results with the help of those verses that are cited in various places in other Latin writers.

And so, Alberto, the most civilized of men, you ought to admit 3
with pleasure this poet into your most learned academy,[9] partly because he deserves the prestige and esteem in which he is held—not that all of his work is true and to be believed by us, as he is in deep disagreement even with the Platonists and the Aristotelians, let alone our own theologians—but partly because with elegance and learning he rendered the beliefs of the Epicureans in poetic form. He imitated Empedocles, who was the first of the Greeks to set down in verse the precepts of philosophy.[10] However, the writings of Empedocles have been lost, either through the ravages of time or because of the invasions of the barbarians, who, as is well known, often pillaged both Greece and Italy. We know barely a few fragments of Empedocles that are cited by Aristotle in his *Meteora* and elsewhere, although there are also many fragments of Empedocles and some other authors whose works have long been lost can also be found in Stobaeus, who put together a massive work containing short extracts from the ancient authors.[11] At some time, God willing, we shall publish these in print.[12] Another reason for your accepting Lucretius in a most generous spirit is that he has been purged of his errors by the great diligence of Avanzi, a man who is deeply devoted to you. Moreover, Aldus is dedicating the poet to you and giving him to you as a gift. Farewell.

: III :

A

Aldus Romanus Danieli Clario Parmensi bonas literas Ragusii profitenti s.

1 Vide an ita sit quod aiunt, mi Clari, malos et daemonas et homines rebus bonis semper esse contrarios, quod, ex quo statui Christianos poetas cura nostra impressos publicare ut loco fabularum et librorum gentilium infirma puerorum aetas illis imbueretur, ut vera pro veris et pro falsis falsa cognosceret, atque ita adolescentuli non in pravos et in infideles, quales hodie plurimi, sed in probos atque orthodoxos viros evaderent, quia 'adeo a teneris assuescere multum est,' tot illico oborta sunt impedimenta, malorum invidia et domesticorum *καὶ ταῖς τῶν καταράτων καὶ δραπετευόντων δούλων ἐπιβουλαῖς*, ut pene opprimerer. Tandem, Iesu Christo Deo optimo maximo adiuvante—nam, si ipse pro nobis, quis contra nos?—, Prudentius, primus ex Christianis poetis qui in manus nostras pervenerunt, ab usque Britannis accitus, cum iam mille et centum annis et plus eo delituisset, exit in publicum typis nostris excusus, ut prosit Christianis suis.

: III :

Prudentius, Prosper, John of Damascus, Christian Poets,[13] Volume I

(January 1501)

A

Aldus of Rome to Daniele Clario[14] *of Parma, public lecturer in classical literature at Ragusa, greetings.*

Is it not true what people say, my dear Clario, that evil spirits and 1
wicked human beings always stand in the way of progress? For from the time that I decided to undertake to print and publish the Christian poets, so many obstacles immediately arose through the hostility of scoundrels and members of my household, and the plotting of workers who were no better than damnable runaway slaves[15] that I was almost completely overwhelmed.[16] And yet my aim was to introduce young children of impressionable age to these poets instead of to the myths and works of pagans and to lead them to recognize what is really true and what is really false so that, in their adolescent years, they would not turn out to be morally corrupt and unfaithful to their religion, as very many are at the present time, but rather upright men and strict adherents of the Christian faith—"so important is habituation in one's tender years!"[17] Finally, with the help of Jesus Christ, Lord God Almighty—for if he is on our side, who can be against us?—Prudentius, the first of the Christian poets who have come into our possession, has been brought all the way from Britain and has now been published by our printing house, after having lain hidden for eleven hundred years and more, so that this author may be of benefit to his fellow Christians.[18]

2 Idque sub tuo nomine, Clari suavissime, ut in ista urbe Ragusio, inclyta et plena nobilitatis, sereno vultu quo optimus quisque ac doctissimus istic solet excipiatur. Utetur primum te hospite, ut per te, qui vitae integritate ac bonarum literarum quas publice profiteris doctrina apud istos optimos virtutisque amantissimos cives multum et authoritate et gratia vales, ab omnibus cognoscatur.

3 Illud fortasse miraberis, *Dittochaeum* inter Prudentii opera connumeratum necnon Prosperi epigrammata digna lectu quod una cum Prudentio imprimenda curarim me censuisse; sed magis mirabere, cum et *Dittochaeum* perlegeris et epigrammata, cur ab omnibus fere doctis aetatis nostrae barbara indignaque lectu habita fuerint condemnataque indicta causa. Nemo enim ex doctis ea opera, ut opinor, legit, nec quivi adhuc invenire qui nisi primum versum legerit; in quibus et ipse annumerabar. Quaedam tamen correctiora desiderabis; quae nos ut in antiquissimo invenimus exemplari, quod unum erat duntaxat, dimisimus.

4 Iuvencum praeterea, Sedulium, Aratorem, quos tamdiu typi nostri parturiunt ob circiter octo millia Gregorii Nazanzeni carminum et Nonnum, qui Euangelium κατὰ Ἰωάννην heroico carmine elegantissime scripsit, et id genus caetera, quae Graece addidimus cum Latina interpretatione, perbrevi parient, confestimque nata ad te advolabunt. Vale.

We publish this under your name, Clario, the most agreeable of men, so that Ragusa, that renowned and most distinguished city of yours, may welcome it as gladly as it welcomes all the finest and most learned of men. It will profit from your being its host initially in that all will get to know it through you; for you enjoy great standing and affection in the eyes of these noble and most virtuous fellow citizens of yours, thanks to the blameless way in which you live and the learning you display in your public position as teacher of classical literature. 2

You will perhaps be surprised that the *Dittochaeum* has been included among the works of Prudentius and also that I thought that the epigrams of Prosper[19] were worth reading, inasmuch as I have undertaken to print them along with Prudentius. But you will be more surprised, when you read through the *Dittochaeum* and the epigrams, why almost all learned men of our age have regarded them as crude and unworthy of being read and have condemned them without a hearing. For no learned man now reads these works, so I believe, and up till now I have been unable to find anyone who has read past the first line, and I include myself in that company. Be that as it may, you will feel that some material needs correction. What we have released to you is what we found in a very old manuscript, the only source we had. 3

Our printing house has had Iuvencus, Sedulius and Arator[20] in our plans for a very long time, the delay being caused by the almost eight thousand lines of Gregory of Nazianzus[21] and Nonnus' elegant version of the Gospel of John in dactylic hexameters[22] and other things of this nature, which we have added in Greek with Latin translation. We will produce these authors very soon, and the moment they appear they will fly to you at full speed. Farewell. 4

B

De metris, quibus hoc in libro Prudentius usus est, ad Danielem Clarium Parmensem virum doctissimum

Metra quoque quibus Prudentius usus est breviter enarrata sub tuo nomine exire in manus studiosorum placuit, Clari doctissime, quod et numerosus sis et vere Clarius. Ea vero sunt.

C

Aldus lectori s.

Si forte nescieris, studiose lector, quonam modo quae Graece imprimenda curavimus cum interpretatione Latina ordinanda sint ut pagina paginae respondeat et versus versui, utpote qui videas separatos quinterniones Graecos ab iis qui Latinam ipsorum continent tralationem, sic accipe: posse te pro arbitrio tuo Latinum Graeco insertare et ex duobus quinternionibus unum et ex uno duos facere, si prius tamen adverteris ut Latina pagina semper Graecae opponatur. Et quia binae eae quae in singulorum quinternionum medio sitae sunt paginae abundabant, quoniam nullas habebant oppositas Graecas quae Latinas[2] ostenderent, operae pretium duximus aliquid Graece lectu dignum cum Latino e regione in ipsis, ne perirent, imprimendum curare. Quod si evenerit ut ibi esse non potuerit quod Graece imprimebatur, quaerendum reliquum in sequentium quinternionum medio. Cur vero curarimus ut Latinum a Graeco separari queat non te fugiat; a nobis ob id factum ut et doctis, qui nullo egent adiumento legendis Graecis, et Graecarum literarum rudibus, qui, nisi Latinum e regione in Graecis operibus viderint, a Graecorum librorum lectione deterrentur, satisfaceremus. Vale.

B[23]

To Daniele Clario of Parma, a most learned man, on the meters used by Prudentius in this book.

I decided to put the meters used by Prudentius, with a brief explanation, into the hands of students under your name as well, most learned Clario, because you very clearly have metrical expertise.[24] Here they are.

C[25]

Aldus to the reader, greetings.

Perhaps you do not know, studious reader, how what we have printed in Greek[26] should be arranged with the Latin translation in such a way that facing page and verses match each other; for you see that the Greek quires are separate from those containing the Latin translation. Here is what you can do. You can insert as you wish the Latin into the Greek and combine the two quires into one (and enlarge one into the size of two) if you first take care that the Latin page always faces one in Greek. And because there were two surplus pages in the middle of each quire (for there was no Greek on one page facing one that would display a Latin translation), we thought it worthwhile to print there some Greek that is worthy of reading with the Latin opposite so that these pages would not be wasted. But if it turns out that not all of the Greek could be printed on that page, you have to look for the rest in the pages at the middle of the following quires. It will be obvious to you why we arranged it in such a way that the Latin can be separated from the Greek. We did it for this reason so that we could satisfy on the one hand our learned readers who need no help in reading Greek and, on the other, those who are neophytes in Greek and would be deterred from reading books in that language unless they saw a Latin version opposite works written in Greek. Farewell.

: IV :

A

Aldus studiosis omnibus s.

1 P. Vergilii Maronis *Bucolica Georgica Aeneida* quam emendata et qua forma damus videtis. Caetera quae poeta exercendi sui gratia composuit et obscoena quae eidem adscribuntur non censuimus digna enchiridio.

Est animus dare posthac iisdem formulis optimos quosque authores. Valete.

B

In grammatoglyptae laudem.

Qui Graiis dedit Aldus, en Latinis
dat nunc grammata scalpta Daedaleis
Francisci manibus Bononiensis.

C

Aldus studiosis s.

2 Si quisquam est qui accusandi casus in is per ei diphthongum miratur excusos typis nostris, id a nobis consulto factum ne sit nescius, tum quia facere ad eruditionem videbatur, tum etiam ut imitaremur antiquos, qui dandi etiam et auferendi casus in is, nedum accusandi, per ei diphthongum scripsisse leguntur, ut vieis,

: IV :

Vergil[27]

(April 1501)

A

Aldus to all students, greetings.

You see with what an unblemished text and in what form we give you the *Eclogues,* the *Georgics* and the *Aeneid* of Publius Vergilius Maro. We did not think that all the other poems that he composed to practice his skills and the obscene poems that are ascribed to him were worthy of this pocket-book size format.[28] 1

It is our intention to publish from now on all the best authors in the same format. Farewell.

B[29]

In praise of the die cutter.

Look! Aldus, who gave you letters for Greek works
now gives you letters for Latin ones,[30]
both cut by the Daedalean[31] hands of Francesco of Bologna.[32]

C[33]

Aldus to students, greetings.

If there is anyone who is surprised that accusative cases ending in *is* are printed in our type with the diphthong *ei,* let him be aware that we have done this deliberately, not only because this practice seemed to be in line with what we teach, but also so that we might imitate the ancients. For we read that they wrote the case endings 2

officieis, captiveis, pro viis, officiis, captivis; sed hi nunc penitus exoleverunt. Accusativos autem eorum tantum nominum, de quibus Priscianus meminit, ad recti patriique casus differentiam per ei scribere operae pretium ducimus, praesertim in poetis Plauto, Lucretio, Catullo, Vergilio et antiquis caeteris: nam in aliis nondum ausim propter criticos. Praeterea, quia dictiones Graecas accentu Graeco pronuntiandas grammatici iubent, idcirco Simóis, Corýdon, Amaryllída, Eurystéa, Dáreta, Ádonis, Aethéra, Didó, Mantûs et id genus multa accentu Graeco imprimenda curavimus. Qua re Aristotéles etiam, Penelópe, Pentecosté et similia accentu Graeco pronuntianda existimem, alibi ostendemus.

3 Nunc autem, quia tonis caeterisque accentibus usi sumus interdum differentiae et eruditionis gratia, libuit quaedam subiungere non inutilia bonas litteras discere cupientibus. Ea vero sunt: [. . .]. Haec placuit subiungere, tum quia multum profutura existimamus iis, qui optime scire Latinam linguam desiderant, tum etiam ut rudium acueremus ingenia. Valete.

D

4 In primo *Aeneidos* libro, 'Lavinaque venit': scribe 'Lavinia venit.' Sic enim in antiquissimo codice Romae in bibliotheca Palatina scriptum est.

Libro sexto, 'Quin protinus omnem perlegerent oculis': scribe 'Quin protinus omnia,' quia sic legitur in antiquis codicibus.

of the dative and the ablative, let alone the accusative, with the diphthong *ei*. Examples are *vieis, officieis* and *captiveis* for *viis, officiis* and *captivis,* but these forms have completely fallen out of use. We think it is useful to write only the accusatives of those nouns mentioned by Priscian[34] with *ei* in order to differentiate them from the nominative and genitive cases, especially for the poets Plautus, Lucretius, Catullus, Vergil and all the other ancient authors. I would not yet dare to do this for other writers because of the critics. Moreover, because the philologists bid us pronounce Greek words with Greek accentuation, we have undertaken to print with the Greek accent names like Simóis, Corýdon, Amaryllída, Euryestéa, Dáreta, Ádonis, Aethéra, Didó, Mantûs and many others of this sort. Why I think Aristotéles, Penelópe, Pentecosté and similar words should be pronounced with the Greek accentuation we shall demonstrate on another occasion.

Because we have employed the acute and other accents some- 3
times to indicate differences and for instructional purposes, I am pleased to add some useful aids for those wishing to learn good letters. These are:[35] [. . .] We decided to add these, not only because we think they will be of considerable help to those who wish to have the best possible knowledge of the Latin language, but also to sharpen the minds of beginners.

D[36]

In the first book of the *Aeneid,* for *Lavinaque venit* write *Lavinia* 4
venit; for this is what is written in the very ancient manuscript in Rome in the Palatine library.

In book six for *Quin protinus omnem perlegerent oculis* write *Quin protinus omnia;* for this is what is read in the ancient manuscripts.

Libro septimo, 'Furit intus aquae vis': scribe 'Furit intus aquai, / fumidus atque alte spumis exuberat amnis.'

Libro octavo, 'Quod fieri ferro liquidove potestur electro': scribe 'potest electro.'

In eodem, 'Sceptra Palatini sedemque petivit Euandri': scribe 'Sedemque petit Euandri.'

: V :

Aldus Romanus Marino Sannuto, patritio Veneto, Leonardi filio, s.

Cum celeberrimos quosque poetas brevissima forma excusos publicare statuerim, impressis nuper Vergilianis operibus mox Horatium Flaccum aggressi sumus, ut, sicut post Maronem cultu et doctrina facile secundus est, ita secundus exeat in manus hominum, factus cura nostra enchiridium. Eum igitur ad te dono mittimus, Marine Sannute, vir omnium humanissime, ut libris quorum plenam tibi esse bibliothecam vidimus et Flaccus brevissima hac forma excusus addatur quo te sua parvitate ad se legendum, cum vel a muneribus publicis vel a Venetarum rerum componenda historia cessare potes, invitet. Sed in Veronensi quaestura, in qua nunc Veneti senatus suffragiis electus es, satis ocii ad haec cultiora studia evolvenda futurum tibi existimamus. Vale.

In book seven for *Furit intus aquae vis* write *Furit intus aquai, / fumidus atque alte spumis exuberat amnis.*

In book eight for *quod fieri ferro liquidove potestur electro* write *potest electro.*

In the same book for *Sceptra Palatini sedemque petivit Evandri* write *Sedemque petit Evandri*

: V :

Horace

(May 1501)

Aldus of Rome to Marino Sanuto,[37] *patrician of Venice, son of Leonardo.*

When I decided to publish in a very small format all the most famous poets, we first printed a short while ago the works of Vergil, and we then quickly turned to Horace. For just as he easily holds second place after Vergil in stylistic elegance and learning, so he would then be the second poet to come into the hands of readers in my pocket-book format. We send him as a gift, therefore, to you, Marino Sanuto, the most cultured of all men, so that Horace, printed in this small format of ours, may be added to the many books, as we have seen, that fill your library, and invite you by its smallness to read him when you can take a rest from performing your public duties or from writing your history of Venice. But we think that you will have sufficient leisure to read through these more refined works now that you hold the office in Verona to which the senate of Venice has elected you. Farewell.

: VI :

Aldus Scipioni Carteromacho suo s.

Iunii Iuvenalis et A. Persii satyras, ut commodius teneri manibus et edisci nedum legi ab omnibus queant, minima forma excusas publicamus, atque eo tempore quo omne vitium magis stat in praecipiti quam stabat cum conderentur. Non enim dubito ne non 'cognoscat mores vita legatque suos.'

Eas ad te mittimus, Scipio suavissime, ut tibi iterum familiares sua brevitate fiant, ut olim fuerant, cum te Romae adolescens continebas, quando eas non minus tenebas memoria quam digitos unguesque tuos. Vale.

: VII :

Aldus Manutius Romanus Marino Sannuto
patritio Veneto Leonardi filio s.

1 Valerium Catullum Veronensem his diebus cura nostra impressum eo libentius ad te legendum mittimus, Marine Sannute humanissime, quoniam in urbe ista doctorum virorum parente et altrice ingeniorum Verona, unde oriundus Catullus, quaesturam agis. Scimus enim munus nostrum tibi gratissimum fore, tum ipso

: VI :

Juvenal, Persius

(August 1501)

Aldus to his dear friend Carteromachus, greetings.[38]

The satires of Juvenal and Persius that we are publishing are printed in a very small format so that everyone can more conveniently hold them in their hands, and not just read them, but study them thoroughly—this at a time when every vice is more rampant[39] than when these satires were originally composed. For I have no doubt that "those living now will read and recognize their own behavior."[40]

We send them to you, my most charming Scipione, so that their smallness may allow them to become familiar to you again as they were when you lived in Rome in your youth. For you knew them as well as your fingers and nails.[41] Farewell.

: VII :

Catullus, Tibullus, Propertius

(January 1502)

Aldus Manutius of Rome to Marino Sanuto,
a Venetian of patrician birth and son of Leonardo, greetings.[42]

Marino Sanuto, most cultured of men, we are sending for your reading pleasure this edition of Valerius Catullus of Verona that we have just printed in the past few days, and we do so all the more gladly because you are now magistrate in that city which has produced learned men and nourished brilliant talent[43] and from where Catullus hailed. For we know that you will take very great 1

munere (quid enim gratius Catulliano lepore?), tum quia, quoties post occupationes publicas relaxare animum voles, percommode et haberi in manibus et evolvi arctatus cura nostra Catullus poterit.

2 Delectabit te praeterea quod longe alius quam qui erat videbitur ob multas emendationes et versus tum additos tum in pristinum locum restitutos; in qua re adiutus sum maxime ab Hieronymo Avantio Veronensi, homine doctissimo et summo ingenio tibique deditissimo. Qua re vel eo gratiorem tibi Catullum putamus futurum, quoniam Avantius tuus Veronensis, vel noster potius, illi corrigendo et in pristinum candorem restituendo, et olim per se diu et multo labore, et una mecum inter imprimendum accuratissime incubuimus.

3 Quae tamen asterisco videbis notata, ea in fine operis aliter atque aliter legi excudenda curavimus, ut possit studiosissimus quisque quod melius visum fuerit eligere pro arbitrio suo. Idem et in Tibullo et Propertio fecimus, quos ad tria millia voluminum et plus eo hac minima forma excusos in manus tuas et caeterorum commode assidueque una cum Catullo et ire et redire speramus. Vale.

pleasure in our gift, not just because of the nature of the gift itself (what can me more delightful than Catullus' wit and charm?) but also because whenever you wish to relax after seeing to your public responsibilities, it will be extremely convenient for you to be able to hold in your hand and turn the pages of this edition of Catullus that we have produced in a small format.

It will give you even more pleasure that, as you will see, it is 2
quite different from earlier editions[44] because of the many emendations and verses that have been added or restored to their original state. In this undertaking I was especially helped by Girolamo Avanzi of Verona, a most learned and brilliant man,[45] and one who is very devoted to you. Because of this we think that our Catullus will give you all the more pleasure because your Avanzi of Verona (or rather our Avanzi) expended much energy on correcting the text and restoring it to its pristine splendor, doing so for a long time on his own in the past and with great labor, and then together he and I applied ourselves with extreme diligence to the same end while the book was being printed.[46]

Those passages that you see marked with an asterisk we have 3
undertaken to print at the end of the work with alternative readings so that all the most conscientious of our readers can exercise their judgment in choosing whatever seems the better.[47] We have done the same in the case of both Tibullus and Propertius, of which we have printed about three thousand copies or more[48] in this very small format of ours. We hope therefore that you and everyone else will find them convenient to use and will continually pick them up, along with Catullus, to read time and time again. Farewell.

: VIII :

Aldus Manutius Romanus Sigismundo Thurzo Pannonio Albensi praeposito ac viro regio a secretis s. p. d.

1 Acer et ad palmae per se cursurus honores,
si tamen horteris, fortius ibit equus.

Vide quantum valet hortatus, quod et equos et id genus ἄλογα reddit alacriora, nedum homines. Nam, etsi ipse eram paratissimus ut omnia M. Tullii parva forma excusa ad commodiorem usum studiosorum publicarentur, tamen, lecta tua eleganti epistola, qua me et tuo et Georgii Varadiensis episcopi nomine ad ea ipsa Ciceronis opera imprimenda hortaris, ut, cum et propriis et regiis negotiis occupatissimi non queatis domi in bibliothecis vacare politioribus studiis, habeatis hosce libellos a nobis quos commode foris legatis, vobis morem gerere cupientes M. Tullii epistolas familiares damus, mox et quae ad Atticum, et deinceps reliqua, tum aliorum omnia digna lectu. Curabimus enim ut vel portatiles bibliothecas et Latine et Graece studiosis, Iesu favente, suppeditemus.

2 Hae vero *Familiares epistolae* ut correctissimae e thermis nostris exirent magnopere elaboravimus, quod legens statim tu ipse cognosces. Illud non praetereundum putavi, omnia M. Tullii opera

: VIII :

Cicero, Letters to Friends

(April 1502)

Aldus Manutius of Rome to Sigismund Thurzó of Hungary, provost of Transylvania and personal secretary to the king,[49] *warmest greetings.*

The steed that is eager and of its own accord ready to run for the prize 1
Will run even more vigorously if you encourage it.[50]

Consider the enormous power of encouragement; it gives more energy to horses and such beings that lack speech, let alone to humans. I myself was all set to publish all the works of Cicero in small format for the greater convenience of students. Then, however, I read your eloquent letter,[51] in which you, on your own account and that of György, bishop of Varád,[52] urged me to print these very works of Cicero. Thereby you would have these books of ours to read with convenience when you were away from home. For heavily engaged as you are in your own and royal affairs you cannot find the leisure time to devote to the more refined arts at home in libraries. Wishing to oblige you, we now give you Cicero's *Letters to his Friends;* soon we shall also publish the letters to Atticus[53] and then his remaining works. After that will come all the works of other writers that deserve to be read. For we shall see to it that, with Jesus' support, we supply devotees of learning with portable libraries, so to speak, in both Latin and Greek.

We have toiled extremely hard to ensure that these *Letters to his* 2
Friends would leave our Baths[54] in the most correct form, as you will immediately recognize the moment you read them. I think that it must be said that, although all the works of Cicero are marvelously beneficial if they are read continually and carefully,

conferre[3] mirum in modum, si legantur assidue, sed epistolas maxime: nam et copiosum et elegantem et, quod facio plurimi, perfacilem in scribendo studiosum sui efficiunt. Qua re saepe mecum mirari soleo de industria quosdam in dicendo duros; qui quam recte sentiant, Ciceronis scripta ostendunt. Sed, inquies, sunt quibus non placet Cicero. At Fabius: 'Ille se profecisse sciat, cui Cicero valde placebit.'

Sed γλαῦκα εἰς Ἀθήνας, qui ad te haec. Vale cum nostro Varadiensi, meque amate.

: IX :

Aldus Romanus Marco Antonio Mauroceno Veneto et equiti clarissimo s. p. d.

1 Omnes libros qui industria nostra excusi exeunt in manus hominum aliqua epistola, quae sit tanquam eorum argumentum, amicis iisque doctissimis nuncupare statuimus. Quare Anneum Lucanum hisce characteribus nostris in tuo nomine publicamus, eques inclyte, tum quia tuum mihi Lucanum et antiquum et correctum ut eo exemplari uterer et benigne et humaniter commodasti; tum etiam quod, cum Lucanus bella terra marique a Romanis inter se gesta sic scripserit ut oratoribus magis quam poetis adnumerandus videatur, et tu exercitibus Serenissimae Urbis una cum imperatoribus summa laude olim praefueris oratorque doctrina et eloquentia singulari a senatu tuo sapientissimo ad summos Christianorum

this is especially true of his letters. For the writings of anyone who studies them closely will display richness, eloquence and, what I value most highly, fluency. Because of this I am often amazed that some persons deliberately cultivate harshness in the way that they speak—the writings of Cicero show whether they are right in holding this view! But, you will say, there are some who dislike Cicero. Quintilian, however, writes: "He who takes great delight in Cicero will know that he has made great progress."[55]

Saying this to you is like sending "an owl to Athens."[56] Farewell to you and our friend in Varád, and hold me dear to your heart.

: IX :

Lucan

(April 1502)

Aldus of Rome to Marcantonio Morosini of Venice and a most illustrious knight,[57] warmest greetings.

We decided that every book that is printed by our hard work and comes into the hands of the public should be dedicated to friends, and learned ones at that, by means of a letter that would plead its case, so to speak. Accordingly we are publishing Lucan in this font of ours in your name, distinguished knight. I do so both because of your kindness and generosity in lending me your ancient and corrected copy of Lucan to use as my exemplar[58] and because we thought that this work especially suits your qualities. For Lucan wrote of the wars fought on land and sea between Romans in such a way that he seems more worthy of being thought of as an orator than a poet,[59] while you have not only been dispatched by your senate in its great wisdom as ambassador to the highest of Christian princes because of your outstanding learning and eloquence, 1

missus fueris, haec tibi maxime convenire existimavimus. Adde quod Lucanum propter eius orationes sublimes et concitatas esse tibi scimus valde familiarem.

2 Munusculum vero hoc nostrum gratum tibi fore putamus, et quia tu es humanissimus, et quia ipse liber dignus, cum propter plurima, tum etiam quia commodius in manibus sua parvitate haberi poterit. Vale.

: X :

Aldus Manutius Romanus Danieli Clario Parmensi, in urbe Rhacusa bonas literas publice profitenti, s. p. d.

1 Christianos poetas, iam annum in thermis nostris excusos, tandem, mi Clari, emittimus tibique viro Christianissimo et morum magistro nuncupamus; qui ne cito, ut ego statueram et tu optabas, publicarentur tot mihi impedimenta fuerunt ut ipse mecum saepe sim admiratus duxerimque κακοδαιμόνων id fieri opera, ne, si in locum gentilium lascivorumque poetarum hi nostri Christiani poetae in scholis ubi teneri puerorum animi instituuntur succederent, facile in bonos plerique omnes evaderent, quoniam 'quo semel est imbuta, recens servabit odorem testa diu,' atque 'adeo a teneris assuescere multum est.'

but you also performed with the greatest distinction when you once shared command of the armies of the most serene city of Venice. Moreover, we know that his sublime and stirring speeches make Lucan a most congenial companion to you.

We think that this modest gift of ours will give you pleasure on two accounts. On the one hand you are the most cultured of men; on the other the book itself is a suitable offering, since, among its many other fine qualities, it is more convenient to hold because of its small size. Farewell. 2

: X :

Sedulius, Iuvencus, Arator,[60] Christian Poets, Volume 2

(June 1502)[61]

Aldus Manutius of Rome to Daniele Clario of Parma, appointed by the city of Ragusa to lecture in classical literature, warmest greetings.

My dear Clario,[62] we are finally sending you the Christian poets that we printed in our Baths[63] last year and are dedicating the volume to you, who are a most devout Christian and an instructor of good morals. So many things prevented their being published as quickly as I had planned and as you were hoping that I was often quite taken aback and believed that this was the work of evil spirits, who thought that if these Christian poets of ours took the place of pagan and indecent poets in schools where children of tender years are taught, almost all of these pupils would without difficulty turn out to be fine young men, for "long will a crock retain the taste of what in it when fresh was placed,"[64] and "so important is habituation in the tender years"[65] — and this is what these evil spirits wanted to prevent! 1

2 Sed Iesu Christo Deo optimo maximo adiuvante vicimus. Nam sanctissimos libros, qui circiter mille annos latuere, publicavimus ut amentur leganturque in scholis fiatque non ut antehac, cum fabulae quibus tenera puerorum aetas imbuitur pro historia habebantur—quae est potissima, ut puto, causa quod quam plurimi e doctis et vitiosi sunt et infideles—, sed contra pro falsis falsa habeantur et vera pro veris.

3 Et si usquam hisce libris proficient studiosi, id erit maxime in ista urbe Rhacusa, tum civium probitate quam a parentibus longa serie tanquam haereditatem accipiunt, tum te magistro. Deus, quam bene convenit optimum virum eumque doctissimum in optima urbe et bonarum literarum perstudiosa esse praeceptorem! Quamobrem et tibi et Rhacusae gratulor plurimum idemque oro eveniat in caeteris Christianae religionis civitatibus.

4 Quod tamen facillime spero futurum si a teneris annis hosce Christianos poetas pueri doceantur imbuanturque divinis. Nam cum ad gentiles iam bene instituti legendos se conferent, bona quaecunque invenerint legendis illis, ut e spinis rosas et id genus flores, accipient; mala vero et quae moribus obsunt prudentes, tanquam scopulum, evitabunt.

Vale, mi Daniel, cum Daniele Restio nostro, homine integerrimo necnon tam moribus quam literis ornatissimo; meque amate, ut facitis.

Venetiis mense Iunio M.D.II.

But we have prevailed, with the help of Jesus Christ, God Almighty. For we have published these holy works which have lain hidden from view for about a thousand years[66] so that they may be cherished and read in schools and so that what has happened before may not happen again, when the myths to which young children were incessantly exposed were thought by them to be true.[67] For this is the foremost reason, in my opinion, that many highly educated men turn out to be sinful and unfaithful to their religion. Now, on the contrary, falsehoods and truths will be recognized for what they are. 2

If students anywhere will profit from these books, it will especially be in that city of yours of Ragusa, not only because of its citizens' high morals, which they have inherited from a long line of ancestors, but also because you are their teacher. Goodness! How appropriate it is for the noblest of men, and a most learned one at that, to be an instructor in the noblest of cities and one that is deeply committed to good letters! My heartiest congratulations to you and Ragusa, and I pray that the situation may be the same in all other Christian cities. 3

I think this will be most easily accomplished if children are given instruction on these Christian poets in their early years and have their minds filled with sacred material. For when they have been well instructed and turn to reading pagan authors they will cull from them whatever good things they find while reading them, like picking roses and similar flowers from thorn bushes. As for bad things and material that subvert their morals they will have the good sense to avoid them like reefs in the sea. 4

Best wishes to you, my dear Daniele, and also to our friend Daniele Resti,[68] a man of most upright character and one whose learning matches his moral standards, and may you both continue to love me as you do.

Venice, June 1502.

: XI :

A

Aldus Manutius Ioanni Pontano s. d.

1 Superioribus diebus venit ad me Soardinus Soardus Bergomas, vir bonarum literarum studiosus ac 'integer vitae scelerisque purus' et tui amantissimus, tulitque divinum illud opus tuum de signis coelestibus cui Urania, quod τὰ κατ᾽ οὐρανόν tractet, a te inditum nomen; item *Meteororum* libros, et *Hortos Hesperidum* heroico carmine, dialogum praeterea quendam prosa oratione. In quibus omnibus contendis meo quidem iudicio cum antiquis autoribus. Quamobrem statim, mi Pontane, coepi, ut soleo doctissimos quosque, amare te vehementer. Ante quidem magnum te virum esse a multis audiveram, sed, ut de Isaeo scribitur, maior inventus es et carmine et prosa oratione. Quod nemini adhuc non modo nostrorum, sed ne Graecorum quidem video contigisse ut idem in utroque scribendi genere feliciter elaboraret.

2 Quare, cum Papinii libros haberem in manibus, statui eos typis nostris excusos sub tuo nomine publicare, ut quo possem modo benevolentiam erga te meam tibi ostenderem, simulque ut pollicerer tibi omnia a te composita, si ea ad me dederis, curaturum me

: XI :

Statius

(August 1502)

A

Aldus Manutius to Giovanni Pontano,[69] *greetings.*

A few days ago Suardino Suardi of Bergamo,[70] a man devoted to good letters, one who is "unsullied of life and untouched by wickedness"[71] and who loves you dearly, came to me bringing that divine work of yours on the heavenly constellations, called *Urania* by you since it deals with heavenly things.[72] He also brought me your books of *Meteora* and *The Gardens of the Hesperides,*[73] in dactylic hexameters, and in addition a dialogue in prose. It is my opinion that in all of these you rival the authors of antiquity. And so I immediately felt deep affection for you, my dear Pontano, the feelings that I often have for all learned men. To be sure, I had earlier heard from many persons that you were a great man, but, as is written about Isaeus,[74] you exceeded your reputation when I read your works, both verse and prose. My perception is that among our own countrymen and even among the Greeks it has never happened up till now that one person could achieve such perfection in both genres of writing. 1

Because of this, seeing that I had in my hands the books of Statius, I decided to publish this edition of them, printed in our type, under your name so that I might show you as best as I could how much goodwill I have toward you. Another purpose was to give you a promise at the same time that I will undertake to print with the utmost care all the works that you have written, if you 2

quam diligentissime imprimenda, ut videant gaudeantque studiosi omnes habere nos hac aetate quem opponere possimus antiquitati. Vale.

B

Aldus Romanus Marco Musuro Cretensi s. d.

3 Quoniam operae pretium duximus scire studiosos orthographiam Graecarum dictionum omnium, quotquot in Papinii operibus inveniuntur, quibusque in casibus eis poetae nostri, servatis etiam Graecis accentibus, uti consueverunt, dictiones ipsas secundum ordinem alphabeti, non parvo labore collectas, et Latine et Graece imprimendas curavimus, atque sub tuo nomine, Musure eruditissime, publicamus, quod tanti laboris particeps mecum fueris, cum forte in Academia nostra esses, profectus ab Alberto nostro, Carporum principe et gloria huiusce aetatis philosophorum, quem subsicivis temporibus cum a theologorum librorum multa lectione vacaret Graecas literas accurate docebas. Non est enim moris nostri fraudare quenquam sua laude; immo decrevimus omneis, quicunque mihi vel opera vel inveniendis novis libris vel commodandis raris et emendatis codicibus vel quocunque modo adiumento fuerint, notos facere studiosis, ut et illis debeant, si mihi debent.

4 Atque utinam plurimos id genus haberemus reipublicae literariae benefactores! Quanquam plurimos speramus futuros non in Italia solum, sed et in Germania et Galliis atque apud 'toto orbe divisos Britannos.' In quibus habemus Grocinum sacerdotem et Thomam Linacrum, viros undecunque doctissimos, qui olim Florentiae sub Demetrio Chalcondyle, viro clarissimo et Graecae fa-

will give them to me, so that all students may see and rejoice that we have someone of this generation whom we can place alongside those of antiquity. Farewell.

B[75]

Aldus Romanus to Marcus Musurus of Crete,[76] greetings.

We thought it worthwhile for students to know the orthography 3
of all the Greek words that are found in Statius' works and in what cases our poets were accustomed to use them, preserving even the Greek accents. We have therefore undertaken to print these very words in alphabetical order in both Latin and Greek, words that we have collected at the cost of no little labor. We publish them here under your name, most learned Musurus, since you shared with me this arduous task. (For you happened to be in our Academy, having left our dear Alberto, prince of Carpi and the most glorious of the philosophers of this generation, whom you were teaching Greek literature with great thoroughness on the odd occasions when he had free time from his extensive reading of theological works.) For it is not in my character to cheat anyone of the praise that he deserves. Indeed we have decided that all who have helped me by offering their labor or by finding new books or lending rare manuscripts of high quality or in any way at all should be made known to students, so that their debt to me is also a debt owed to my helpers.

I only wish that we had a great number of such benefactors of 4
the republic of letters. And yet we hope to have very many of these soon, not only in Italy, but also in Germany and all parts of France and among "the Britons, though cut off from the whole world."[77] (For from Britain we have the cleric William Grocyn[78] and Thomas Linacre,[79] both learned in every area; sometime ago they devoted themselves in Florence to the study of Greek literature under Demetrius Chalcondyles,[80] a man of great renown and the

cundiae instauratore magnoque decore, Graecis literis incubuerunt. Quapropter ex Germania Valerii Maximi quaedam quae in Italia non habentur, ex Gallia vero duodecim Asconii Pediani elegantiarum libros percupidi expectamus, quos extare esseque M. Fabii Quintiliani ac inde bonam partem elegantiarum suarum accepisse Laurentium Vallam, vel puer Romae, cum audirem Domitium, intellegebam.

5 Gaudeant igitur bonarum literarum studiosi. Nam, Deo optimo maximo annuente, assiduisque laboribus nostris, atque Academicorum nostrorum auxilio et caeterorum bonorum doctorumque hominum qui bonas literas bonasque artes propagari nostra aetate desiderant, omnia suppeditabimus quibus in summos viros queant evadere. Vale.

C

Aldus lectori s.

6 Superiore aestate, cum Valerius Maximus, Papinius, Ovidius typis nostris excuderentur, quia ipse cum aliis plurimis tum lite quadam impeditus emendandis illis vacare non poteram, dedi aliis eorum corrigendi provinciam. Quare, cum iam impressum Statium quo potui studio recognoscerem — opprimor enim paene reipublicae literariae negociis —, quaedam, ut infra videbis, lector, adnotavi.

renewer of Greek eloquence, as well as being its most glorious practitioner.) And so we are eagerly awaiting from Germany some parts of Valerius Maximus[81] which are not to be found in Italy, while from France we eagerly await twelve books on the *Principles of Style* of Asconius Pedianus.[82] Even when still a boy in Rome, studying under Domizio,[83] I understood that they were in existence and that they were in the possession of Quintilian and that Lorenzo Valla[84] had drawn a good part of his *Principles of Style* from them.

Let all students of good letters rejoice then; for by the will of 5
God Almighty and our unstinting labors and the help of our Academicians[85] and all other noble and learned men who long for the propagation of classical literature and the liberal arts in our age we shall supply everything that will enable them to turn out to be the finest of men.

C[86]

Aldus to the reader.

Last summer when Valerius Maximus, Statius and Ovid were be- 6
ing published by our press, I assigned the responsibility of correcting them to others, as I was prevented by a certain lawsuit as well as by many other things from having the time to remove errors. And so, when I was reviewing the already printed Statius with as much application as I could muster (for I am almost suffocated by the weight of the business demands of the republic of letters), I noted down some comments, dear reader, as you will see below.[87]

: XII :

A

Aldus Romanus Ioanni Ludbrancio Polono iurisperito ac Posnaniensi episcopo regnique Poloniae a consiliis s. p. d.

1 Dicta ac facta memoratu digna quae ab illustribus et Latinis et Graecis electa authoribus breviter quidem sed eleganter delegit Valerius tuo felici nomine hisce excusa typis emittere ex Academia nostra constituimus, praesul optimeque et humanissime. Nam quid convenientius quam optima et utilissima sub optimi viri nomine et eius qui prodesse semper studeat publicare? Valerii enim hasce eclogas exemplis et documentis suis sic ego esse utiles censeo, ut putem die noctuque legendas, quod nesciam an quisquam ex Latinis libris conferre tantum queat hominibus. Atque ideo ut commodius haberi in manibus possint a nobis enchiridium factum est, ut brevitati operis parvitas voluminis responderet.

2 Te vero et probum esse et commodum, cum docti omnes uno ore tam Patavii quam Venetiis praedicant, tum ipse multis animadverti modis, et praecipue cum, in hemicyclo Patavii in cubiculo tuo sedens, cum et ego essem una et Raphael Regius noster, homo fide plenus et doctrina, et pauci admodum alii, pollicitus es tua quamvis magna impensa ad Dacas usque mittere inveniendi librorum gratia, quod ibi antiquorum librorum plena turris esse

: XII :

Valerius Maximus
(October 1502)

A

Aldus of Rome to Jan Lubański, of Poland, a jurist, bishop of Poznań and an advisor to the Polish throne,[88] *warmest greetings.*

It is under your felicitous name, most kind and noble prelate, that we have decided to publish from our Academy in this type of ours the memorable sayings and deeds that Valerius culled from famous Greek and Latin authors and expressed with such conciseness and elegance. For what is more appropriate than to publish under the name of the finest of men and one who always strives to be of help to others what is in itself the finest and most useful? I say this because I believe that the examples and teachings in these extracts of Valerius are so useful that they should be read day and night, in my opinion, since I am inclined to think that no Latin author can contribute as much as he to human conduct. And so that these examples can be more conveniently used, we have printed it in our pocket-book format, the smallness of the volume thereby matching the shortness of the work. 1

Not only do all learned men, both in Padua and Venice, declare with one voice that you are upright and obliging, but I myself have observed this in many ways. This was especially so when you were sitting on a semicircular couch[89] in your bedroom in Padua in the company of our friend Raffaele Regio, a most honest and learned man,[90] and a few others in addition to me, and you promised to send someone as far as Romania to find manuscripts, and to do so at your own expense no matter how great it might be. For there is said to be a tower[91] there full of ancient manuscripts. You added 2

dicatur; amplius addidisti teipsum eo, si opus fuerit, profecturum. Utinam tui simillimos plurimos haberemus antistites! Optime enim ageretur in humanis. Tu nanque es temporibus nostris probitate 'tertius Cato,' tu consilio Nestor, de quo Agamemnon apud Homerum:

> Αἲ γάρ, Ζεῦ τε πάτερ καὶ Ἀθηναίη καὶ Ἄπολλον!
> τοιοῦτοι δέκα μοι συμφράδμονες εἶεν Ἀχαιῶν·
> τῷ κε τάχ' ἠμύσειε πόλις Πριάμοιο ἄνακτος,
> χερσὶν ὑφ' ἡμετέρῃσιν ἁλοῦσά τε περθομένη τε.

3 Tu etiam pietate Aeneas, de quo poeta noster, Homerica haec imitatus, sic ait:

> Si duo praeterea tales Idaea tulisset
> terra viros, ultro Inachias venisset ad urbes
> Dardanus et versis lugeret Graecia fatis.
> Quidquid apud durae cessatum est moenia Troiae,
> Hectoris Aeneaeque manu victoria Graium
> haesit, et in decimum vestigia rettulit annum.
> Ambo animis, ambo insignes praestantibus armis;
> hic pietate prior.

4 Cupio igitur te tot ornatum virtutibus ad communem hominum utilitatem, et studiosorum praecipue, inter Christianos summum videre; quod faxit Deus. Interea munus hoc nostrum hilari qua soles fronte accipias velim. Vale.

Venetiis Octobri mense M.D.II.

that you yourself would set out for there if it was necessary. If only we had many bishops just like you! For then all would be well for the human state, since in our times your uprightness makes you "a third Cato,"[92] in counsel you are a veritable Nestor,[93] of whom Agamemnon says the following in Homer:

> Father Zeus and Athene and Apollo,
> would that among the Achaeans I had ten such counselors.
> Thereby the city of lord Priam would quickly fall to us,
> captured and pillaged by our hands.[94]

You are also an Aeneas in your sense of duty,[95] about whom our 3
own poet, imitating these words of Homer, says this:

> If the land of Troy had brought forth two such men,
> the Trojans would have come of their own accord to the cities of Greece
> and it would be Greece in mourning, in a reversal of fate.
> Whenever fighting broke off before the walls of unyielding Troy,
> the victory of the Greeks was stalled by the hand of Hector and Aeneas,
> and moved back until the tenth year.
> Both were distinguished by outstanding courage, and fighting,
> Aeneas however, was the superior in his sense of duty.[96]

I wish therefore to see you attain the highest standing among 4
Christians, for you possess so many virtues that serve the common good of mankind, especially of students and scholars. May God bring this to pass. Meanwhile I would like you to accept this gift of ours with your usual happy countenance. Farewell.

Venice, October 1502.

B

Aldus Romanus Cuspiniano Germano s.

5 Etsi privatim tibi gratias egimus quod quatuor et viginti exempla quae omnibus in Italia Valerii Maximi exemplaribus tam impressis quam manu conscriptis deerant ad me perhumaniter miseris, tamen ut et publice idem facerem meas esse partes existimavi, ut tibi una mecum studiosissimus quisque deberet; et eo magis, quod tu sponte tua, audito tantum excudi Valerium in aedibus nostris, mihi significaveris vidisse te in praeclara urbe Vienna, cum publice studia humanitatis inibi profitereris, Valerium antiquissimum, in cuius principio quaedam nunquam ante a te visa haberentur, titulosque omnium scripseris, ut, si ea mihi non essent, facerem te certiorem, quandoquidem ad me illico ea esses daturus. Quod et factum est.

6 Deerant enim in fine *De neglecta religione* exempla quatuor, *De simulata religione* totum caput, necnon et *De auspiciis totum*, praeter exemplum *De Deiotaro rege*, quod perperam in aliis omnibus Valerii exemplaribus quae ipse viderim principium erat *De ominibus*, cum *De auspiciis* ultimum esse deberet, *De ominibus* autem principium esse illud: 'Ominum etiam observatio aliquo contactu religionis innexa est,' et caetera. Nam, ante quam ad exempla veniat, praefatiunculam aliquam ubique fere Valerius solet praemittere.

7 Id vero, mi Cuspiniane, fuit mihi longe gratius quam si auri multum gemmarumque misisses muneri. Illud impenditur, consumitur, disperit; hoc, etsi omnibus impertitur, tamen aeque apud impertientem ac impertitum divino excusorio munere manet

B[97]

Aldus of Rome to Cuspinianus of Germany,[98] *greetings.*

5 Although we have thanked you privately for having sent me with such great generosity twenty-four examples that were missing in all copies of Valerius Maximus in Italy, either in printed editions or in manuscripts, I nevertheless thought that it was incumbent upon me to do the same in a public way, so that all students and scholars should share in my indebtedness to you. This is all the more justified because immediately you heard that Valerius was being printed in our press you volunteered the information to me that you had seen a very old manuscript of Valerius in that illustrious city of Vienna when you held a public chair in Latin there, and that the beginning of this manuscript contained some items never seen by you before. You wrote out the titles of all of these so that I might inform you if I did not have these since in that case you would immediately send them to me. And this was what was done.[99]

6 The missing material comprised the following: four examples at the end of the section of *On the rejection of religion*; a whole chapter of *On feigned religion*; a whole chapter of *On auspices*. In addition an example of *On King Deiotarus* was wrongly placed at the beginning of the section *On omens* in all copies of Valerius that I myself have seen, although it ought to be the last example of *On auspices*. *On omens* actually begins with "Also the observation of omens has close connection with religion," etc. For before giving examples Valerius almost always provides a short preface.[100]

7 My dear Cuspinianus, I have taken far greater pleasure in this kindness of yours than if you had given me the gift of much gold and many jewels. These are expended, used up and lost; this gift of yours, although it is distributed to everyone, nevertheless remains intact forever through the divine gift of printing, and this is

aeternum. Hoc et viventes et posteri perpetuo habebunt utrique nostrum plurimam gratiam. Huiusmodi dentur mihi reipublicae literariae benefactores! Quanquam habemus et alios plurimos, ex quibus unus ab extremo nuper orbe daturum se mihi Donatum integrum in *Aeneidem* totumque Servium et Probi grammatici antiquissimos libros et alia quaedam quae non habentur pollicitus est.

Vive autem tu diu vel hoc solo beneficio, Cuspiniane; vivant et caeteri tales, et rumpantur siqui sunt βιβλιοτάφοι et invidi.

Venetiis calendis Aprilis M.D.III.

: XIII :

Aldus Manutius Romanus Marino Sannuto patritio Veneto, Leonardi filio, Ordinum Sapienti s.

1 Multos iam libros in aedibus nostris excusos tibi superioribus annis nuncupavimus, Sannute suavissime, tum quod plurimum studiosis omnibus semper faveris tutatusque fueris provinciam nostram, tum etiam quia, etsi eras assidue reipublicae maximis rebus occupatissimus, magnopere tamen delectari te politioribus literis cognoverimus. Nam eo tempore te vel sexvirum sontibus et maleficis puniendis vel in gravissimi cum Turcarum rege belli principio Ordinum Sapientem in collegio patrum vel in urbe Verona, parente assidua ingeniorum doctissimorumque hominum, quaestorem integerrimum et diligentissimum vidimus.

true equally for the giver and the receiver. Those now living and those who follow will be deeply grateful to both of us. May I enjoy the help of such benefactors as you who serve the republic of letters. And yet we have many others including one from the edge of the world[101] who promised that he would give me a complete copy of Donatus' commentary on the *Aeneid*[102] and the whole of Servius[103] and a very old copy of the works of Probus the philologist[104] as well as some other items that we do not have.[105]

May this kindness alone give you a long life, Cuspinianus; long live too all other men like you! And may the enemies and buriers of books[106] be damned!

Venice, April 1, 1503.

: XIII :

Ovid, Metamorphoses

(October 1502)

Aldus Manutius of Rome to Marino Sanuto,[107] *a Venetian patrician, son of Leonardo,* Savio agli Ordini, *greetings.*

In the past few years past we have dedicated many of the books printed in our press to you, Sanuto, most charming of men,[108] not only because you have always given extensive support to all scholars and have protected our professional activities,[109] but also because we know that, although you were always extremely busy with important affairs of state, you took great pleasure in more refined letters. For in that period we saw you either as one of the board of six men for punishing wrongdoers and criminals or as *Savio agli Ordini* in the college of senators at the beginning of that most troublesome war with the king of the Turks[110] or as a most upright and conscientious magistrate in Verona, a city that continually produces highly talented and learned men.[111] 1

2 Unde tanta cum civium omnium gratia et benevolentia decessisti ut adhuc Marini Sannuti nomen in ore habeant reverenter, teque summopere et ament et colant. 'Dii immortales! homini homo quid praestat? stulto intellegens quid interest?' Hic est fructus, haec bene acti magistratus appetenda gloria: ut, cum functus officio fueris, te omnes uno ore tollant in coelum laudibus, tui simillimum sibi dari magistratum vehementer desyderent, petant, comprecentur.

3 Sperabam equidem cum Academicis nostris viris utriusque linguae perstudiosis ut tecum inde reverso esse die noctuque possemus atque de re literaria communicare, sed vix Venetias rediisti cum iterum tua magistratus agendi peritia Ordinum Sapiens in patrum collegio creatus es. Quapropter, cum transmutationes ingeniosissimi poetae nuper imprimendas curarimus, eas sub Sannuti nomine emittere ex Academia nostra placuit, ut in magnifica illa tua bibliotheca, ubi supra quingenta electorum librorum habes volumina, una cum caeteris reponantur, utarisque domi lucubrationibus nostris dicatis tuo nomini, ubi tua iucunda praesentia nobis in Academia nostra uti non licet.

4 Idque eo etiam feci libentius quod maximo mihi adiumento fueris, ut privilegium pro republica literaria ex hoc amplissimi sapientissimique senatus consulto mihi omnium pene consensu decerneretur quod infra in laborum nostrorum tutelam imprimendum iussimus simulque ut cognoscerent omnes quanti a senatu hoc gravissimo virtutes et bonae literae aestimentur, Romanos illos

You left that city with such gratitude and goodwill of all the citizens that they still speak the name of Marino Sanuto with reverence and show their great love of and respect for you. "O ye immortal gods! In what way is one man better than another? In what way does the intelligent man differ from the fool?"[112] This is the reward, this is the glory for good performance of a magistrate's duties that should be sought after, namely, that, when you have completed your term of office, everyone praises you to the heavens with one voice and deeply longs for, seeks out and prays that a magistrate most like you will be given them. 2

I used to hope along with our fellow members of the Academy,[113] learned in both languages as they are, that on your return from Verona we could have your company day and night and discuss literature. But you had scarcely returned to Venice when your skillful performance of your magisterial duties led to your appointment again as *Savio agli Ordini* in the college of senators. As a result of this, when we recently undertook to print the *Metamorphoses* of a most talented poet, we decided to release it from our Academy under the name of Sanuto so that it may take its place among the more than five hundred copies of choice works that are in that magnificent library of yours and that you may enjoy at home the results of our laborious toils that are dedicated to your name, seeing that we may not enjoy your delightful presence in our Academy. 3

I have done this all the more gladly because you have been of immense help to me in that by a decree of the most venerable and wise senate, passed almost unanimously, I was granted the privilege of having exclusive rights for the republic of letters.[114] We have ordered the *privilegium* to be printed below so as to protect our labors and so that at the same time all may recognize how highly excellence and good letters are valued by this most august senate. In doing so its members have emulated the Romans, those 4

rerum dominos aemulando, qui virtute praeditos omneis iuvandos, fovendos, extollendos certatim curabant.

5 Accipies igitur laeto vultu vel hasce portatili forma *μεταμορφώσεις* Ovidii, quandoquidem gratissimas tibi futuras certo scio, cum doctrina et candore poetae, tum ut Marcum Sannutum, patruelem tuum et senatorem clarissimum doctissimumque imitere, qui praeter caeteras quibus quam maxime praeditus est virtutes huius nostri poetae libros omneis quam familiarissimos habet ac pene callet ut digitos unguesque suos; atque ideo ego tam sum illius quam meus.

6 Adde quod is liber est multarum rerum cognitione et Latinis et Graecis pernecessarius; quamobrem a Maximo Planude e Latino in Graecum ad suorum utilitatem accurate tralatus est, quoniam, etsi apud Graecos *μεταμορφώσεων* libros multi scripserunt — ex quibus, ut taceam reliquos, Callisthenis et Theodori in libro *περὶ παραλλήλων* his verbis Plutarchus meminit: Τῆς δὲ ὡρισμένης προθεσμίας παρελθούσης, χρύσεος ὁρᾶται, ὡς Καλλισθένης ἐν δευτέρῳ Μεταμορφώσεων; et in eodem: Περὶ Μύῤῥας Κινύρου θυγατρός· ἡ δὲ κατὰ πρόνοιαν Ἀφροδίτης εἰς ὁμώνυμον δένδρον μεταμορφώθη, καθὰ Θεόδωρος ἐν ταῖς Μεταμορφώσεσι — nullus tamen eorum transmutationum liber extat iam multis seculis.

7 Quare, cum habere nostras eos oporteat, illud Angeli Politiani, viri utriusque linguae peritissimi, vel hic apte adduci potest: *οἵγε νέοι τὴν γραῦν ἀντιπελαργέομεν*; ciconias enim in senectute a filiis invicem enutriri aiunt. Quod cum alii tum Aristoteles in nono *De historia animalium* ait his verbis: Περὶ μὲν τῶν πελαργῶν, ὅτι ἀντεκτρέφονται, θρυλλεῖται παρὰ πολλοῖς. Φασὶ δέ τινες καὶ τοὺς μέροπας ταὐτὸ τοῦτο ποιεῖν, καὶ ἀντεκ-

masters of the world, who vied with each other in helping, cherishing and exalting all who showed great ability.

You will be happy then to accept these *Metamorphoses* of Ovid, 5
even in this pocket-book format, since I am certain that they will be most pleasing to you, not only because of the learning and lucidity of the poet but also so that you may imitate Marco Sanuto, your cousin and most distinguished and learned senator.[115] Besides all the other virtues with which he is generously endowed, he is extremely familiar with all the works of our poet and knows them almost as well as his own fingers and nails;[116] for that reason I am as much his friend as I am my own.

In addition the investigation of many topics in this work makes 6
it indispensable for those working in both Latin and Greek. That is why it has been carefully translated by Maximus Planudes[117] from Latin into Greek to serve the needs of his countrymen, since none of the many Greek authors who wrote books of *Metamorphoses* has been available for many centuries. To say nothing of the rest, these authors include Callisthenes and Theodorus, who are mentioned by Plutarch in the work *Parallel Lives*[118]: "When this limited time had passed, it [the altar] is seen to be golden, as Callisthenes says in the second book of his *Metamorphoses*," and in the same work: "About Myrrha the daughter of Cinyras: by the foresight of Aphrodite she was transformed into the tree that bears her name, according to Theodorus in his *Metamorphoses*."

Therefore since it is right for the Greeks to have our *Metamor-* 7
phoses, what was said by Angelo Poliziano, a man of great learning in both languages,[119] can be aptly adduced here: "We who are young now, like storks, cherish our old mother in turn."[120] For it is said that aged storks are nurtured by their young. In addition to the testimony of other authors, Aristotle in his ninth book *On the History of Animals* writes this,[121] elegantly translated, as always by Theodore: "It is common knowledge that storks look after their old parents, but some claim that bee eaters do the same and the

τρέφεσθαι ὑπὸ τῶν ἐκγόνων οὐ μόνον γηράσκοντας, ἀλλὰ καὶ εὐθύς· ὅταν οἷοί τ' ὦσι, τὸν δὲ πατέρα καὶ τὴν μητέρα μένειν ἔνδον; hoc est, ut Theodorus elegantissime, ut omnia, transfert: 'Ciconias genitorum senectutem invicem educare invulgatum est, sed sunt qui meropes idem facere confirment vicemque reddi, ut parentes non modo senescentes, verum etiam statim, cum iam datur facultas, alantur opera liberorum; nec matrem aut patrem exire, sed in cubili manentes pasci labore eorum quos ipsi genuerunt, enutrierunt, educarunt.' Sic igitur et Graecis evenit ut, cum μεταμορφώσεις Ovidius ab illis didicerit, ipsi ab eo invicem edoceantur. Itaque vel ob id hos libros et tibi et caeteris gratissimos fore non dubitamus. Vale.

: XIV :

A

Aldus Romanus Marino Sannuto Leonardi filio, Ordinum Sapienti, s.

1 Vide quanta in te sit suavitas, mi Marine; equidem tecum esse, tecum vivere semper velim. Quod quia non licet maximis utriusque nostrum occupationibus, meis quidem in republica literaria, tuis vero in inclyta hac republica Veneta, in qua ne hora quidem vacare potes a muneribus publicis (nam Verona rediens, ubi summa cum laude summaque civium omnium benevolentia quaestorem egisti, statim magistratus creatus es). Quia igitur tecum esse

role is reversed in such a way that the parents are nurtured by their children, not only when they are old, but even immediately that the young are able to do so. The mother and father do not go out, but remain in their nest and are fed by the labor of those whom they themselves have produced, reared, and brought up." It turns out then that although Ovid learned about metamorphoses from the Greeks, the Greeks themselves are informed in turn by him. And so for this reason, we do not doubt that these books will give you and others much pleasure. Farewell.

: XIV :

Ovid, Heroides, Amores, Ars amandi, Remedia amoris, etc.

(December 1502)

A

Aldus of Rome to Marino Sanuto,[122] *son of Leonardo,* Savio agli Ordini, *greetings.*

1 What a most charming man you are, my dear Marino! I wish I could always be in your company, always live with you. However, the great demands of both our careers do not allow this. Mine is in the republic of letters, yours in this renowned republic of Venice, where you do not have even an hour's break from your public duties (for on your return from Verona, where you fulfilled the responsibilities of your position with the highest distinction and won the complete goodwill of all citizens, you were immediately elected to office).[123] And so, since I cannot be with you, I assuage

non licet, solor desyderium tui huiuscemodi ad te epistoliis, ut una cum hisce enchiridiis sim tecum, sim tibi in manibus. Vale.

B

Aldus Romanus

2 Sabinus poeta Ovidii temporibus scripsit epistolas quibus Ulysses Penelopae, Hippolytus Phoedrae, Aeneas Didoni, Demophon Phillidi, Iason Hypsipylae, Phaon Sapphoni respondent, sed non extant. Nam tres hae quae habentur mihi non modo non videntur Sabini, sed ne excellentis quidem cuiusquam poetae.

3 Immo centum et quatuor versus insertos in epistola Paridis ad Helenam ab eo versu 'Nec tamen est mirum' usque ad illum 'Credis et hoc nobis' censeo non esse Ovidii. Sunt enim duri nec digni divino Nasonis ingenio; tum, si Ovidii illi essent, non idem in eadem epistola repetisset his versibus: 'Cum Venus et Iuno Pallasque in vallibus Idae / corpora iudicio supposuere meo.' Erant praeterea et alii duo statim post illum versum 'Sed Nymphis etiam curaque amorque fui' quos ego subtraxi, tum quia nullum omnino habent sensum, tum etiam quia sine illis cohaeret materia. Hi vero sunt: 'Quas super Oenonem faciem mutarer in orbem, / nec Priamo est ad te dignior ulla nurus.'

4 Ovidius ipse de Sabino haec in libro secundo elegiarum:

Quam cito de toto rediit celer orbe Sabinus
  scriptaque diversis rettulit illa locis
Candida Penelope signum cognovit Ulyssis;
  legit ab Hippolyto scripta noverca suo.

this longing of mine for you with letters to you of this kind,[124] so that I can share your company with these handy-sized editions and you can hold me, as it were, in your hands.[125] Farewell.

B[126]

Aldus of Rome

In Ovid's time the poet Sabinus[127] wrote letters in which Ulysses 2
replies to Penelope, Hippolytus to Phaedra, Aeneas to Dido, Demophon[128] to Phyllis, Jason to Hypsipyle and Phaon to Sappho, but these have not survived. For I think that the three that we do have,[129] so far from being composed by Sabinus, are not even by a poet of any merit at all.

What is more I do not think that one hundred and four verses 3
in the letter of Paris to Helen, running from *nec tamen est mirum* down to *credis et hoc nobis*[130] are by Ovid. For they are harsh and unworthy of the divine talent of Ovid. In addition, if they were the work of Ovid he would not have referred to the same incident in the same letter with these verses: *Cum Venus et Iuno Pallasque in vallibus Idae / corpora iudicio supposuere meo* ("When Venus and Juno and Pallas subjected their bodies to my judgment in the valleys of Mount Ida").[131] Moreover I have removed two other lines that immediately follow the verse *Sed Nymphis etiam curaque amorque fui.*[132] These are *Quas super Oenonem faciem mutarer in orbe, / nec Priamo est ad te dignior ulla murus.*

Ovid himself says the following about Sabinus in book two of 4
his elegies:[133]

How quickly has swift-moving Sabinus returned from his travels over all the world
and brought back what he has written in different places.
Shining Penelope recognized the seal of Ulysses;
his stepmother read what her beloved Hippolytus wrote.

Iam pius Aeneas miserae rescripsit Elisae;
quodque legat Phillis, si modo vivit, habet.
Tristis ad Hypsipylen ab Iasone littera venit;
dat votam Phoebo Lesbis amica lyram.

5 Idem de Ponto libro tertio in invidos:

Et qui Penelop‹a›e rescribere iussit Ulyssem
errantem saevo per duo lustra mari,
quique suam Troezena imperfectumque dierum
deseruit celeri morte Sabinus opus.

C

Aldus studiosis s.

6 Diximus superius Sabini epistolas de quibus in amoribus Ovidius meminit non extare, tum quae Sabino inscribuntur non modo videri mihi non fuisse Sabini, sed nec egregii cuiusquam poetae. Idem et hic confirmamus, nisi quod super his consideranti mihi accuratius epistolae Helenes Paridi, Herus Leandro, Cydippes Acontio Sabino adscribendae videntur, cum nusquam constet Ovidium in *Heroidibus* responsorias scripsisse epistolas, sed contra in amoribus Sabinum illas scripsisse testetur inquiens, 'Quam cito de toto rediit meus orbe Sabinus' et caetera. Quibus versibus, si treis eas epistolas Helenes, Herus, Cydippes non Sabinus, sed ipse composuisset, ne suo labore privaretur certe meminisset. Quod quia non facit, Sabini potius eas esse contenderim. Quanquam in epistola ad Acontium, quod sequitur post illum versum 'Quos vereor paucos, ne velit esse mihi' non videtur esse Sabini, sed alterius cuiuspiam incelebris poetae.

Now dutiful Aeneas has replied to the lovelorn Dido,
and Phyllis has something to read if only she lives.
A sad letter comes to Hypsipyle from Jason,
and the lover of Lesbos hands over her lyre dedicated to Phoebus.

He also writes of Sabinus in a poem in book three of *Letters from* 5
the Black Sea, directed at those who malign Ovid:[134]

And Sabinus who bade Ulysses, wandering for ten years
over the cruel sea, to reply to Penelope,
and whose premature death
left his *Troezen*[135] and his *Days* incomplete.

C[136]

Aldus to his students, greetings.

We said above that the letters of Sabinus which Ovid refers to in 6
the *Amores* have not survived, and that those which are attributed to Sabinus did not seem to me to be by Sabinus or by any poet of accomplishment. We make the same assertion here too, except that on more careful consideration I think that the letters of Helen to Paris, of Hero to Leander and of Cydippe to Acontius should be attributed to Sabinus, since nowhere is there clear evidence that Ovid composed letters of response in his *Heroides,* while Ovid attests that Sabinus wrote such letters, saying "How quickly has my dear Sabinus returned from his travels all over the world" etc.[137] If Ovid, and not Sabinus, had composed these three letters of Helen, Hero and Cydippe, he would certainly have mentioned this so as not to lose the credit for his toil. Because he does not do this, I would argue that they are more likely to be the work of Sabinus. However, in the letter to Acontius I do not think that what follows the verse "I fear she may wish my years to be few"[138] is by Sabinus, but by some other undistinguished poet.

7 Illud non duxi silentio praetereundum, in epistola Phillidis ad Demophontem duos hosce adinventos esse versiculos:

Sum prece turicremis devenerata focis.
Saepe videns ventos coelo pelagoque faventeis,

additosque sic:

Saepe deos supplex, ut tu, scelerate, valeres,
sum prece turicremis devenerata focis.
Saepe videns ventos coelo pelagoque faventeis
ipsa mihi dixi: si valet, ipse venit.

Qui etiam sunt pernecessarii. Nam sine ipsis nulla haberi constructio potest; quod facile est volenti cognoscere. Valete.

: XV :

Aldus Romanus Marino Sannuto Leonardi filio, patritio Veneto ac Ordinum Sapienti s.

1 En tibi ingeniosissimi poetae reliquum, 'o et praesidium et dulce decus meum,' Sannute humanissime. Sunt autem *Fastorum* libri sex. Nam caeteri iniuria temporum ad nos non pervenerunt, id est alii sex; nam duodecim scripsit, ut testatur ipse hisce versibus:

I did not think that we should pass over in silence the fact that the following two verses in the letter of Phyllis to Demophoon are later additions: 7

I prayed, honoring them with holy incense.
Often, seeing that the winds were favorable for weather and for sea.[139]

These have been inserted in the following way:

Often begging the gods as suppliant, that you, scoundrel, should be well,
I prayed, honoring them with holy incense.
Often, seeing that the winds were favorable for weather and for sea,
I said to myself: "If he is well, he is on his way."

The verses are quite necessary,[140] for without them no sense can be made of the syntax, as can be readily seen by anyone who wishes to look at them.

: XV :

Ovid, Fasti, Tristia, Ex Ponto

(February 1503)

Aldus of Rome to Marino Sanuto,[141] *son of Leonardo, a Venetian of patrician birth, and* Savio agli Ordini, *greetings.*

Here for you, Sanuto, "my guardian and my sweet source of glory"[142] and the most civilized of men, is the remainder of that most talented of poets. There are only six books of *Fasti;* for the rest of them, the other six, have not come down to us, having suffered the ravages of time. Ovid wrote twelve in all as he himself attests in these verses: 1

sex ego fastorum scripsi totidemque libellos,
cumque suo finem mense libellus habet.

Sed eo scio delectaberis plurimum, in sexto *Fastorum* libro sex additos versus, qui in caeteris omnibus ante impressis non habentur, et sunt hi:

ipsa volubilitas subiectum sustinet orbem,
quique premat partes angulus omnis abest;
cumque sit in media rerum regione locata
et tangat nullum plusve minusve latus,
ni convexa foret, parti vicinior esset,
nec medium terrae mundus haberet onus.

2 Qui sequuntur statim post hos versus:

Terra pilae similis, nullo fulcimine nixa,
aere suspenso tam grave pendet onus.

Quos versus—ut fatear per quem profecerim—dedit mihi imprimendos Franciscus Roscius Veronensis, vir utraque lingua eruditus ac diligens indagator antiquorum voluminum; seque ab antiquissimo codice accepisse retulit.

3 Insunt praeterea huic volumini de *Tristibus* libri v, quos sic appellavit, quod tristitiam et moerorem suum continerent; item *De Ponto* libri quatuor, a loco unde eos ad amicos dedit. Tu vero, Marine, inter maximas in republica occupationes tuas vel hos leges. Vale.

I have written six books of *Fasti* and as many again,
and each book has its own month to itself.[143]

But I know that you will take special pleasure in the addition of six verses in the sixth book of the *Fasti*, verses that are not to be found in all other previously printed editions. They are as following:

The earth's very power of rotation sustains the world beneath it[144]
and there is not any angle that presses upon any part,
and since it is placed in the middle of the universe
and touches no part in any degree,
if it were not convex, it would be nearer to some part than another
and the universe would not have the earth as its central weight.[145]

This passage immediately follows these verses: 2

The earth is like a ball, propped up by no support,
its great weight hanging in suspended air.[146]

These verses, so that I may confess to whom I owe this improvement, were given me to be printed by Francesco Rosetti[147] of Verona, a man who is learned in both languages and who unremittingly searches after ancient manuscripts. He has told me that he got them from an extremely old codex.

This volume also contains five books of Ovid's *Tristia*, as he 3
calls them, because they expressed his sadness and sorrow, and also four books, *From the Black Sea*,[148] the place from where he sent them to his friends. You can read these too, Marino, even though you have very important obligations to the republic. Farewell.

: XVI :

A

Aldus Manutius Aegidio Viterbensi, divinorum verborum oratori excellenti, ordinis eremitarum, s. p. d.

1 Origenis homilias in pentateuchum et librum iudicum a divo Hieronymo Latinitate donatas informatasque nuper cura nostra ut sub tuo nomine publicarem, Aegidi, pater pervenerande, habui quidem plurimas causas, sed duas praecipuas. Quarum altera est ut virum illum in omni disciplinarum genere singularem, tum divinarum rerum et magistrum summum et oratorem, tu, qui aetate nostra es eloquio et doctrina quam ornatissimus, populis commendares et, quo potes modo, protegeres et tuereris; altera quoniam, si ipse viveret, sub nullo magis patrono exire vellet in manus hominum quam sub Aegidio, qui apud omnes gratia et autoritate plurimum valet.

2 Equidem, mi Aegidi, doctissimi illius hominis vicem summopere doleo, quod idem omnium et optimus et pessimus scriptor et habitus olim fuerit et nunc habeatur. Scis enim illud de Origene uno ore dici fere ab omnibus: ubi bene, nemo melius; ubi male, nemo peius. Sed ea de re nequid ego scriberem fecit tractatus quidam Ioannis Pici Mirandulae, miro hominis ingenio miraque doctrina, qui in *Apologia* sua quaestionem hanc copiosissimeque et doctissime disputavit. Illud tamen libuit addidisse, Origenem suos

: XVI :

Origen,[149] Homilies

(after April 4, 1503)

A

Aldus Manutius to Giles of Viterbo,[150] *excellent preacher of the Divine Word, a member of the Augustinian order, warmest greetings.*

Most reverend father Giles, when I recently undertook to put into 1
print Origen's homilies on the Pentateuch and the book of Judges as translated into Latin by St Jerome, of the many reasons I had to publish them under your name there were two in particular. One was that, since you are the most distinguished man of our age in eloquence and erudition and Origen was not only outstanding in every discipline but also a supreme teacher of theology and an excellent preacher, you would commend him to all people and protect and guard him to the best of your ability. The second reason was that if he himself were alive he would choose no better patron under whom he might come into readers' hands than Giles of Viterbo who enjoys considerable and universal popularity and influence.

For my own part, my dear Giles, I grieve most deeply at the 2
fate of that most learned of men, that, as in the past, he is still now in the present thought to be both the best and the worst of writers. For you know that almost all agree in this about Origen: when he writes well, no one is better, when he writes badly, there is no one worse. But a tract of Giovanni Pico della Mirandola, a man of marvelous talent and erudition, allows me to say nothing of this matter. For he discussed this question at great length and with much learning in his *Apologia*.[151] Nevertheless he chose to add this, that Origen complained in a letter to some friends in

libros ab inimicis corruptos in epistola ad quosdam amicos in Alexandria conquestum in hunc sensum:

3 Haudquaquam miror adulterari et corrumpi nostra ab inimicis, cum et in Apostoli epistola idem evenerit. Conscripserunt enim quidam sub Pauli nomine falsam epistolam, quo Thessalonicenses conturbarent atque seducerent quasi instaret dies Domini; atque propterea in secunda epistola ad Thessalonicenses ait apostolus, 'Rogamus autem vos, fratres, per adventum Domini nostri Iesu Christi nostraeque in ipsum congregationis, ne ab eo quod sentitis cito amoveamini, neve quispiam vos aut spiritu aut verbo aut epistola aliqua tanquam ad vos a nobis missa deterreat, quasi instet dies Domini; nemo vos ullo modo seducat.'

4 Eodem modo et nobis videmus accidere, quandoquidem haereticus quidam, cum disputationi nostrae plurimi interfuissent, ab iis qui descripserant codicem scriptis acceptis, addidit, dempsit, permutavit, ut voluit, atque ita corrupta circunfert ostentatque sub meo nomine. Quibus indignati, qui in Palaestina sunt fratres miserunt ad me Athenas cui archetypum ipsum ad se darem, quod nunquam antea relectum a me recensitumve fuerat, sed ita neglectum et abiectum iacebat ut vix inveniri potuerit; tandem inventum misimus. Et Deus est mihi testis, eum qui scripta mea adulteraverat inventum interrogatumque a me quamobrem id fecisset 'Quoniam expolire magis atque exornare purgareque disputationem ipsam volui' respondisse. Videte, quonam illam purgaverit modo, ita certe, quemadmodum Marcion Euangelia et qui postea illius successor fuit, Apelles. Nam, sicut illi

Alexandria that his works had been corrupted by enemies. This was what he wrote:[152]

> I am in no way surprised that our works are defiled and cor- 3
> rupted by enemies since the same happened in the case of the Apostle's letter. Some persons composed a spurious letter under the name of Paul to upset the Thessalonians and deceive them into believing that the day of the Lord was at hand. Because of this the Apostle says in the second letter to the Thessalonians, "Concerning the coming of our Lord Jesus Christ and our assembling to meet him we beg you, brethren, not to be quickly shaken in mind, nor let anyone frighten you either by spirit or by word or by a letter purporting to be from us to the effect that the day of the Lord has come. Let no one deceive you in any way."[153]
>
> We see the same thing happening to us. Some heretic or 4
> other (for a very large number had attended our debate) took our writings from those who had copied out the manuscript and then added, removed and changed at will material in them. And in this corrupt state he carries them about and displays them under my name. My brothers in Palestine, angry about this, sent an emissary to me in Athens, to whom I was to give the original document for them. I had never reread this or reviewed it; it lay about somewhere, discarded and so neglected that it could scarcely be found. Finally we discovered it and sent it off. And, God is my witness, when I found the man who had corrupted my writings and asked him why he had done so, he replied, "Since I wanted to embellish and purify the debate." Just look at how he has purified it! Certainly he has done so, in the way Marcion and his successor Apelles clarified the Gospels.[154] For just as these men subverted the truth of the Scriptures, so that fellow re-

scripturarum veritatem subverterunt, sic iste, ut nos criminaretur, sublatis veris, falsa inseruit.

5 Haec in Origenis epistola legi scribit Picus; deinde subiungit in hanc sententiam, 'Si scripta Origenis eo vivente depravare audebant haeretici, nonne post eius mortem hoc idem audentius illos fecisse existimandum? Queritur autem et alibi de haeretico quodam, qui in Epheso falsa permulta sub nomine suo ostentans circunferebat. Extat et alia eius epistola in qua suos libros adulteratos et corruptos ab haereticis summopere dolet.' Haec Mirandula, et alia abunde multa in quaestione de salute Origenis.

6 Sed adulterata fuerint necne scripta illius aliorum sit iudicium qui ista subtilius quaerunt, et tuum maxime, Aegidi disertissime, qui sacra volumina coepisti a teneris 'nocturna versare manu, versare diurna.' Nos autem optimis quibusque illius legendis, et quae barbatus Hieronymus approbavit, quales sunt hae sane quam utiles admirandaeque homiliae, admodum certe proficiemus. An vero salvus sit Origenes, non est meum diiudicare. In hoc equidem et id genus caeteris accedo orthodoxis et sanctae ecclesiae. Sed ἐς θάλασσαν ὕδωρ qui haec ad te divinarum rerum optimum doctissimumque censorem.

7 Qua re haec tibi et caeteris sacrae theologiae peritissimis tractanda disputandaque relinquimus; sed si te unum illud etiam atque etiam rogaverimus ut hunc ipsum Origenis homiliarum librum apud te semper habueris ἐς μνημόσυνον amoris summi erga te mei.[4] Quod libentius facturum te existimamus, cum Platonis tui divina volumina in tuam gratiam Graecis characteribus nostris brevi, ut speramus, simus publicaturi. Vale, decus nostrum.

Venetiis pridie nonas Aprilis M.D.III.

moved the truth from my writings and added what was false in order to incriminate us.

This is what Pico says was read in Origen's letter. Then he adds 5
the following to these words of Origen: "If heretics dared to distort Origen's writings when he was alive, surely we must think they did this same thing more brazenly after his death. He complains elsewhere[155] about some heretic in Ephesus who was carrying around and displaying very many spurious items under Origen's name. There is also another letter in existence[156] in which he expresses his deep displeasure that his books have been defiled and corrupted by heretics." So says Mirandola, in addition to many other things about the salvation of Origen.

Let others who go into such matters with more discernment be 6
the judges of whether or not his writings have been defiled, especially you, most eloquent Giles; who from your tender years "day and night turned the pages"[157] of the holy books. For our part we shall certainly strive to ensure that all the best of his works can be read and those that the bearded Jerome approved of, such as these useful and marvelous homilies. As for the question of Origen's salvation, it is not my place to judge. In this and all other matters of this kind I yield to orthodox theologians and the holy church. But I am pouring water into the sea in saying this to you who are such a fine and most learned judge of divine matters.

Therefore we leave these topics for you and all other experts in 7
theology to handle and debate. But we ask of you most urgently this one favor, that you always keep close to you this very book of Origen's homilies as a reminder of my deep love for you. We think you will be all the more glad to do so since we are soon about to oblige you by publishing in our Greek font the divine works of your beloved Plato.[158] Farewell, you who are our source of distinction.

Venice, April 4, 1503.

B

Recognito hoc Origenis opere quaedam tum addendo tum demendo tum immutando ita correximus. Sed nota, lector carissime, primum numerum conclusum utrinque punctis significare chartas, secundum vero chartarum columnas, tertium autem columnarum versus.

: XVII :

A

Aldus studiosis s.

P. Vergilii Maronis *Bucolica Georgica Aeneida* accuratissime recognita curavimus secundo informanda parvis characteribus nostris, ut commodi vobis quamvis longae viae comites forent. Addidimus etiam opuscula, tam quae in iuventute poëta composuit, quam quae illis inserta habentur. Et quanquam obscoena non censebamus digna enchiridio, tamen, multis assiduo convitio efflagitantibus, addenda ea lege iussimus ut pro uniuscuiusque arbitrio separari possent. Quam autem ea opuscula incorrecta atque depravata vagarentur, facillime, si cum nostris collata a vobis fuerint, cognoscetis. Valete.

B[159]

I have checked through this work of Origen and have made some corrections, by adding, removing or altering some things. But please note, dearest reader, that the first number, which has points on each side of it, indicates pages, the second number designates the columns, while the third refers to the lines of the columns.

: XVII :

Vergil

(December 1505)

A

Aldus to devotees of good letters, greetings.

After checking with the utmost care the text of the *Eclogues, Georgics* and *Aeneid* of Publius Vergilius Maro we have undertaken to print them a second time in our small font so that they may conveniently accompany you no matter how long a journey you may undertake.[160] We have also added his short works, both those that he composed in his youth and those that are included with them.[161] We did not think that the obscene poems[162] were worthy of our pocket-sized volume but since many persons have demanded them with constant clamor we ordered them to be added to the volume on condition that they could be detached separately if anyone so wished. You will readily see in what a corrupt and depraved state these short works have been circulating widely when you compare such copies with ours. Farewell.

B

Aldus studiosis s.

Sperabam daturum vobis *Culicem, Aetnam, Cirin, Diras,* Vergilii *Lusus,* correctiores, habitis alicunde emendatis exemplis; quod quia non licuit, quales circunferebantur dedimus. Vegii praeterea libellum divinis *Aeneidos* libris inviti adiunximus; sed obsequendum fuit quibusdam. Valete.

: XVIII :

Aldus Pius Manutius Romanus Aloisio Mocenico equiti et senatori Veneto s. p. d.

1 Solebam superioribus annis, Aloisi, vir clarissime, cum aut T. Livii decades quae non extare creduntur aut Sallustii aut Trogi historias aut quemvis alium ex antiquis autoribus inventum esse audiebam, nugas dicere ac fabulas; sed ex quo tu e Gallia, ubi pro senatu tuo integerrime accuratissimeque legatum agens magnam tibi laudem et gloriam peperisti, cum plurimis quae inesse optimo oratori oportet, tum eloquentia illa tua singulari qua tibi ante et divitias et gratiam in hac republica excellentissima comparaveras, has Plinii epistolas in Italiam reportasti, in membrana scriptas atque adeo diversis a nostris characteribus ut nisi quis diu assueverit non queat legere, coepi sperare mirum in modum fore aetate nostra ut plurimi ex bonis autoribus quos non extare credimus inveniantur.

B[163]

Aldus to devotees of good letters, greetings.

I had been hoping to provide you with a much improved text of the *Culex,* the *Aetna,* the *Dirae* and the *Lusus* of Vergil after obtaining better manuscripts from some source or other. Since I was unable to do this we have given these works in the form that they have been circulating.[164] In addition we have added, against our will, Vegio's book[165] to the divine books of the *Aeneid;* we had to follow the wishes of certain individuals. Farewell.

: XVIII :

Pliny the Younger, Letters[166]

(November 1508)

Aldus Pius Manutius of Rome to Alvise Mocenigo, knight and senator of Venice,[167] warmest greetings.

In the past few years, Alvise, most distinguished sir, whenever I 1
heard of the discovery of either the decades of Livy that are thought to be lost, or of the histories of Sallust or of Trogus[168] or of any other ancient author, my usual reaction was to say "stuff and nonsense." But then from France, where you were serving most honorably and conscientiously as your government's representative, displaying all the many qualities that a fine ambassador should have, in addition to that singular eloquence which had earlier won you riches and esteem in this most excellent of republics, you brought back to Italy these letters of Pliny, which are written on parchment and in a script so different from ours that one cannot read it without a great deal of practice.[169] This led me to have wonderful hopes that our age would witness the discovery

Est enim volumen ipsum non solum correctissimum, sed etiam ita antiquum ut putem scriptum Plinii temporibus.

2 Quamobrem si, ut videtur, a Plinii aetate ad haec usque tempora hoc epistolarum volumen servatum est, fit ut facile credam et T. Livium et alios quos tum vetustate tum hominum negligentia tum vi aliqua incursioneve exterarum gentium periisse credimus, alicubi, tanquam in impio conclusos carcere, squalidos delitere, speremque exituros in lucem; idque temporibus nostris ac mea, si diu vixero, praecipue opera, Christo Iesu annuente, δοτῆρος ἐάων. Nunc autem, quod possumus, hasce Secundi epistolas damus quam correctissimas; in quibus etiam multae sunt quae antehac non habebantur.

3 Sed tibi in primis habenda est plurima gratia, inclyte Aloisi, qui exemplar ipsum epistolarum reportasti in Italiam mihique dedisti ut excusum publicarem; deinde Iucundo Veronensi, viro singulari ingenio ac bonarum literarum studiosissimo, quod et easdem Secundi epistolas ab eo ipso exemplari a se descriptas in Gallia diligenter, ut facit omnia, et sex alia volumina epistolarum, partim manu scripta partim impressa quidem, sed cum antiquis collata exemplaribus, ad me ipse sua sponte, quae ipsius est erga studiosos omneis benevolentia, adportaverit, idque biennio ante quam tu ipsum mihi exemplar publicandum tradidisses. Exeunt igitur hae Plinii epistolae in manus literatorum, et tua et Iucundi nostri in illos benevolentia, emendatissimae.

4 Sed quoniam epistolas decimi libri quae scribuntur ad Traianum imperatorem sunt qui non esse Plinii putant, tum quia stylo

of very many fine authors whom we believe to have perished. For the manuscript is not only very free of errors, but is also so old that I think it was written in Pliny's lifetime

And so if, as seems to be the case, this manuscript of letters has 2
survived from Pliny's time right down to the present, I can readily believe that Livy and others who we think have been lost because of their antiquity or human negligence or as a result of the violent invasions of foreign tribes are lying hidden somewhere, covered in filth, shut up in some foul prison, as it were; and so I can hope that they will be brought to light, especially in our times and, if I live long enough, through my efforts (Jesus Christ, "the giver of all good things,"[170] being willing!). But as for now, we publish these letters of Pliny the Younger, to the best of our ability, in the most correct form possible. They also include many letters that were previously not known.[171]

But I must give my most profuse thanks to you above all, my 3
renowned Alvise, who brought the actual manuscript of the letters to Italy and gave it to me to publish in print, and then to Giocondo of Verona, a man of outstanding talent and a most learned scholar of classical literature.[172] For while in France he copied out, with the care that he shows in all matters, the same letters of Pliny from this very manuscript, and, such is his goodwill to all scholars, brought them to me on his own initiative, as well as six other volumes of letters, some hand written,[173] some in printed form (these latter, however, having been collated against ancient manuscripts). And all this took place two years before you handed over to me the actual manuscript for publication. And so these letters of Pliny now come into the hands of educated readers with a text quite free of errors, thanks to the kind consideration that you and our friend Giocondo have for scholars.

There are some who believe that the letters of book ten, which 4
are addressed to the emperor Trajan, are not the work of Pliny, because they seem different in style and elegance from the others

et elegantia diversae ab aliis videntur, tum etiam quia praeter doctorum consuetudinem 'domine' dicat Plinius ad Traianum scribens, operae pretium fuerit et illas a Secundo scriptas fuisse ostendere.

5 Non imus inficias scripsisse Plinium alias epistolas, ut ipse ait, paulo accuratius, sed et has ad Traianum, siquis diligenter inspiciat, et doctas esse et eleganteis fatebitur nec a stylo Plinii alienas, id quod cum ex omnibus id genus epistolis licet cognoscere, tum ex ea manifestius quae de Dione quodam scribitur, qui suorum reliquias in religioso loco posuerat. Recitat enim ibi quae in caussa utrinque dicta fuerant se iudice, quemadmodum in aliis quibusdam facit epistolis, cum de caussis quas ipse egerat ad amicos scribit. 'Domine' autem principibus dicere temporibus Plinii iam receptum fuisse, illud etiam Martialis in epistola libri octavi ad Domitianum ostendit: 'Omnes quidem libelli mei, Domine . . .'; item illud: 'Edictum domini deique nostri.'

6 Esse autem Plinii epistolas ad Traianum multis rationibus probari potest, sed his potissimum: primum, quia in antiquissimo exemplari una cum aliis, ut nos imprimendas curavimus, sub Plinii Secundi nomine scriptae sunt; deinde, quia Plinii illud de Christianis ad Traianum et rescriptum Traiani super ea re habetur in una ex eisdem epistolis ad Traianum, cuius rei Tertullianus, Eusebius, Paulus Orosius meminere.

7 Praeterea in iisdem epistolis multa habentur quae luce clarius ostendunt ab eodem manasse et has ad Traianum et illas familiareis, ut illud de Voconio Romano in secundo libro ad Priscum: 'Convertere ad nostros, nec hos multos, sed meae verecundiae sufficit unus aut alter, ac potius unus; is erit Voconius Romanus.' Et paulo post subiungit, 'Hunc ego, cum simul studeremus, arcte

and because, contrary to practice as scholars believe, Pliny uses the term *dominus* when writing to Trajan. It will be worthwhile therefore to show that these letters too were written by Pliny.

We do not deny that Pliny wrote other letters in a somewhat 5
more careful style, as he himself says,[174] but whoever examines closely these letters to Trajan will admit that they too are learned, elegant, and not at all out of keeping with Pliny's style. We can recognize this from all the letters of this kind, but more clearly so from the letter that is written about a certain Dion, who had buried the remains of his family in forbidden ground. For Pliny reports there what had been said on both sides in the case in which he was judge.[175] This is what he does in some other letters when he writes to friends about the cases which he himself had conducted. As for *domine,* that it was an accepted mode of addressing the emperors in the time of Pliny is shown by its use in Martial too, in the letter to Domitian that introduces book eight: "All my books, *Domine* . . ." and "the edict of our god and *Dominus.*"[176]

There are many considerations which prove that these letters to 6
Trajan are the work of Pliny, but especially the following. First, in the ancient manuscript they have been copied out under the name of Pliny the Younger, like the others, and we have seen to it that they are printed accordingly. Secondly, Pliny's famous letter to Trajan about the Christians and Trajan's rescript on this matter are among these same letters to Trajan, and this is mentioned by Tertullian, Eusebius, and Paulus Orosius.[177]

Moreover, from many features in the content of these same let- 7
ters it is clearer than daylight that the letters to Trajan and those of a personal nature are by the same author. Take, for example, what he says about Voconius Romanus to Priscus in book two:[178] "Consider my friends, quite small in number [. . .][179] but one or two suffice me in my modesty; and I prefer to have only one: he is Voconius Romanus." And a little later he adds: "When we were studying together I loved him as a dear and close friend. He was

familiariterque dilexi. Ille meus in urbe, ille in secessu contubernalis; cum hoc seria, cum hoc iocos miscui. Quid enim aut illo fidelius amico aut sodale iucundius?'

8 In eadem epistola laudat Voconium quod patrem habuerit in equestri gradu clarum, clariorem vitricum; laudat et a doctrina, a moribus; meminit et matris eius. Haec eadem in quarta epistola libri decimi ad Traianum de Voconio scribit his verbis: 'Indulgentia tua, imperator optime, quam plenissimam experior, hortatur me ut audeam tibi etiam pro amicis obligari; inter quos sibi vel praecipuum locum vendicat Voconius Romanus, ab ineunte aetate condiscipulus et contubernalis meus.' Et paulo inferius ait, 'Pro moribus Romani mei, quos et liberalia studia exornant et eximia pietas, quae hanc ipsam matris liberalitatem et statim patris haereditatem et adoptionem a vitrico meruit. Auget haec et natalium et paternarum facultatum splendor.'

9 Praeterea in secundo libro in epistolis ad Arrianum de Mario Prisco sic scribit: 'Marius Priscus accusantibus Afris quibus proconsul praefuit, amissa defensione, iudices petiit. Ego et Cornelius Tacitus, adesse provincialibus iussi, existimavimus fidei nostrae convenire notum senatui facere excessisse Priscum immanitate et saevitia crimina quibus dari iudices possent, cum ob innocenteis condemnandos, interficiendos etiam, pecunias accepisset.' Eiusdem Marii Prisci meminit in tertia epistola libri decimi ad Traianum his verbis: 'Qua ex caussa, cum patronum me provinciales optassent contra Marium Priscum, et petii veniam huius muneris et impetravi.'

my companion in the city, and in the countryside. With him I shared happy times as well as sober ones. No one is a more loyal friend and pleasing companion than he."

In the same letter he praises Voconius for having a distinguished father of equestrian rank, and an even more distinguished stepfather. He also praises Voconius for his learning and his character, and in addition mentions his mother. When writing to Trajan, Pliny says the same about Voconius in the fourth letter of book ten in the following words:[180] "Noble emperor, your generosity, which I enjoy to the fullest, encourages me to dare to be obliged to you on behalf of my friends as well. Among these Voconius Romanus, who has been a fellow student and companion of mine from our early years, claims particular pride of place for himself." And a little later he says: ". . . for the character of my dear Romanus, enhanced as it is by his liberal studies and outstanding sense of duty which deservedly brought him this generosity of his mother, an immediate inheritance from his father and adoption by his stepfather. These qualities are heightened by the splendor of his birth and his ancestral wealth." 8

In the second book in the letters to Arrianus[181] he says this about Marius Priscus:[182] "When the Africans whose governor he was brought charges against Marius Priscus and his defense had been unsuccessful[183] he asked for the case to go before judges for assessment. Cornelius Tacitus and I were ordered to represent the provincials and thought that we were honor bound to inform the senate that Priscus had surpassed in cruelty and savagery the crimes for which a commission could be appointed, since he had accepted money in return for finding innocent people guilty and even for having them executed." He mentions the same Marius Priscus in the third letter of book ten to Trajan, writing as follows:[184] "For this reason, when the provincials had wanted me to represent them against Marius Priscus, I asked to be excused from this task and my request was granted." 9

10 Suetonio quoque Tranquillo cum ex aliis quibusdam ad illum literis amicum summum fuisse Plinium facile est cognoscere, tum ex his: 'Libera tandem hendecasyllaborum meorum fidem, qui scripta tua communibus amicis spoponderunt.' Deinde sic claudit epistolam: 'Patere me videre titulum tuum, patere audire, describi, legi, venire volumina Tranquilli mei. Aequum est nos in amore tam mutuo eandem percipere ex te voluptatem quam tu perfrueris ex nobis.' De eodem ad Traianum libro decimo sic scribit: 'Suetonium Tranquillum, probissimum, honestissimum, eruditissimum virum, et mores eius secutus et studia, iam pridem, domine, in contubernium adsumpsi, tantoque magis diligere coepi, quanto hunc propius inspexi. Huic ius trium liberorum necessarium faciunt duae caussae: nam et iudicia amicorum promeretur et parum felix matrimonium expertus est, impetrandumque a bonitate tua per nos habet quod illi fortunae malignitas denegavit.' Adde quod omnibus fere literis quibus Plinio respondet Traianus inest familiarissima illa appellatio: 'Secunde carissime.'

11 His igitur aliisque rationibus colligi potest has ipsas epistolas de quibus agimus Secundum scripsisse. Sed hae sint satis vel obstinatioribus et qui, quod dicitur, nodum in scirpo quaerunt.

12 Operae pretium etiam visum est addere huic operi Plinii panegyricum de laudibus Traiani, primum quia quaecunque ipsius habere potui convenientissimum existimavi in uno volumine simul edere, deinde quia adeo illum elegantem, doctum, acutum, utilem iudico ut in eo seipsum superasse Plinius videatur. Legendus ille quidem assidue omnibus, tum sententiarum gravitate, tum rerum copia, tum ad bene beateque vivendum sanctissimis optimisque

That Pliny was the closest of friends with Suetonius Tranquillus is readily established from the following words as well as from some other letters addressed to him:[185] "Fulfill the pledge of my hendecasyllabics, which promised your writings to our common friends." Then he closes the letter in this way: "Allow me to see your name being listed, allow me to hear that the works of my dear Tranquillus are being copied, are being read, and are on sale. From the deep love that we share for each other it is only fair that you should give me the same pleasure that I give you."[186] Pliny writes the following about the same Tranquillus to Trajan in book ten: "My lord, some time ago I took on as a member of my staff Suetonius Tranquillus, a man of probity, honesty and learning, after studying his character and his pursuits. The more closely I have examined him, the more my affection for him grows. Two reasons make it essential that he be granted the privileges of being the father of three children: he has earned the esteem of his friends and his marriage has not been fruitful; through us you, in your goodness, can grant him what the niggardliness of fortune has denied him."[187] An additional point is that in almost all the letters in which Trajan responds to Pliny, he uses that intimate form of address, "my dearest Secundus." 10

For these and other reasons we can conclude that these letters under discussion were written by Pliny. But let this be enough for those who stubbornly do not give up their views, and who, as the saying goes, "are looking for a knot in a bulrush."[188] 11

It seemed worthwhile to add to these letters Pliny's panegyric on the achievements of Trajan, first, because I thought it would be very convenient to publish together in one volume everything I had of this author's work, secondly, in my opinion, the panegyric is so eloquent, learned, perceptive and useful that in it Pliny seems to have surpassed himself. This deserves to be read time and again by everyone for the gravity of its sentiments, the range of subject matter, and the virtuous and noble precepts it offers for a good 12

praeceptis, sed praecipue magnis viris et principibus iisque omnibus qui aliis praesunt et quibus *λαοί τ' ἐπιτετράφαται καὶ τόσσα μέμηλε*. Talem enim fuisse Traianum scribit ut quaecunque habere oporteat optimum principem, *ᾧ ἔδωκε Κρόνου παῖς ἀγκυλομήτεω / Σκῆπτρόν τ' ἠδὲ θέμιστας, ἵνα σφίσι βασιλεύῃ*, Traianus habuerit. Quamobrem non immerito creandis imperatoribus dicitur, 'Sis felicior Augusto et melior Traiano.'

13 Qui quidem ipso Cyro Xenophontis eo maior, quod ille non ad historiae fidem scriptus, sed ad effigiem iusti imperii, ut refert Marcus Tullius in epistola ad Quintum fratrem; hic autem re vera talis fuit qualem fuisse legimus. Quare, ut Africanus ille Xenophontis libros non sine caussa de manibus ponere non solebat, quia nullum esset praetermissum in his officium diligentis et moderati imperii, sic nos hunc Secundi nostri panegyricum de manibus ponere non debemus, ut optimi viri, fortissimi imperatoris, iustissimi principis exemplo tales et ipsi efficiamur.

14 Addidimus praeterea duos libros, alterum eiusdem Plinii de iis qui vel in armis vel in administranda republica clari extiterunt, alterum Suetonii Tranquilli de claris grammaticis et rhetoribus. Nec me latet a quibusdam hos libros utrosque Tranquillo potius adscribi, idque divi Hieronymi autoritate, qui in eo libro quem et ipse scripsit de viris illustribus, Tranquillum se imitaturum dixit his verbis: 'Hortaris, Dexter, ut, Tranquillum sequens, ecclesiasticos scriptores in ordine digeram, et quod ille in enumerandis gentilium literarum viris fecit illustribus, id ego in nostris faciam.' Haec divus Hieronymus.

15 Sed illi hac eadem Hieronymi autoritate redarguuntur. Non enim testatur Hieronymus Tranquillum scripsisse de viris in re

and happy life. But it should especially be read by important men and princes and all those who are in positions of authority over others and who "nurture their subjects and are concerned with such matters."[189] For Pliny writes how Trajan actually had all the qualities that should be possessed by the noblest of princes, "to whom the son of crooked Cronos granted the scepter and the authority of laws to govern his people."[190] This is why when emperors are appointed it is said to them for good reason, "May you be luckier than Augustus and more virtuous than Trajan."[191]

This panegyric is much more important than Xenophon's 13
Cyrus.[192] For Xenophon's work was not written as an accurate historical record, but as a picture of how power should be wielded justly, as Cicero says in his letter to his brother Quintus;[193] the content of Pliny's panegyric reflects what was actually true. And so, just as the famous Africanus[194] would rarely, and not without cause, put aside the books of Xenophon because they covered every aspect of how to administer power with care and restraint, so we ought not to lay aside this panegyric of our own Pliny; for through the example of the noblest of men, the bravest of generals and the most just of emperors, we too can acquire his qualities.

In addition we have included two more books, one by the same 14
Pliny on the subject of those who attained fame in warfare or in government,[195] the other by Suetonius Tranquillus on famous philologists and orators.[196] I am quite aware that some persons ascribe both works to Tranquillus, and that they do so on the authority of St Jerome; for in the book which Jerome himself wrote on the subject of famous men he said that he would imitate Tranquillus, saying, "You urge me, Dexter, to follow Tranquillus, and rank ecclesiastical writers, and to do with our authors what he did in going through the illustrious authors of pagan literature."[197] This is what St Jerome says.

But those who ascribe both works to Suetonius are refuted by 15
this same authority of St Jerome. For Jerome does not attest that

militari atque in republica administranda claris, quemadmodum in hoc Secundi libro licet videre, sed de iis tantum qui in literis fuere illustres, quos ipse gentilium literarum illustreis dicit. Id vero fecit Tranquillus in eo libro qui *De claris grammaticis et rhetoribus* inscribitur; quem secutus divus Hieronymus Dextri rogatu de iis scripsit qui in literis sacris fuere illustres. Esse autem Plinii Secundi eum librum in quo viri clari in armis et in republica administranda enumerantur tutatur titulus, qui in omnibus id genus libris qui manu scripti habentur sub Plinii nomine, non Suetonii aut Cornelii Taciti aut cuiusvis alius legitur.

16 Hos vero libellos de viris illustribus, ut correctiores exirent in manus literatorum, Ioannes Baptista Egnatius, vir in utraque lingua eruditissimus et polyhistor maximus, mecum accurate quidem sed cursim, quod parum daretur ocii, recognovit; addito etiam Iulii Obsequentis libro de prodigiis, quem mihi Iucundus meus iucundissimus dono dedit, ut una cum aliis in hoc volumine imprimendum curarem. Idque fecimus sub tuo nomine, Aloisi Mocenice, gravissimi senatus Veneti decus, ut, quia non solum Secundi epistolas ad nos sedulus e Gallia reportasti, sed publicandas etiam mihi dedisti, tibi praecipue debeant, te plurimum ament studiosi omnes de hoc munere. Vale.

Venetiis mense Novembri MDVIII.

Suetonius wrote on famous men in warfare and politics, as we can see is the case with this work of Pliny's, but only on those who were distinguished in literature (Jerome says distinguished in pagan literature). Suetonius did this in that work entitled *On famous philologists and orators*. At the request of Dexter, St Jerome followed Suetonius, writing about distinguished writers in sacred writings. The view that the book which surveys those who won fame in warfare and in politics is by Pliny the Younger is supported by the heading of the work as found in all manuscripts containing it. For the work goes under the name of Pliny, not Suetonius or Cornelius Tacitus or anyone else.

To ensure that these short works on famous men would come 16
into the hands of educated men with a more correct text, Giambattista Egnazio,[198] a man most learned in both languages and a great polymath, reviewed them with me carefully, but quickly, because of the shortage of time he had at his disposal. I have also added the work of Julius Obsequens on prodigies, which my most amiable[199] Giocondo gave me as a gift, so that I would have it printed along with the other items in this volume.[200] This we have done under your name, Alvise Mocenigo, adornment of the most august Venetian senate. Not only were you so conscientious as to bring back to us Pliny's letters from France, you also give them to me to be published. For this gift of yours all scholars will be particularly indebted to you and will think of you with great affection.

Venice, November 1508.

: XIX :

Aldus Pius Manutius Romanus Iafredo Carolo iurisconsulto ac regii senatus in urbe Mediolano moderatori s. p. d.

1 Agitur iam triennium, inclyte Carole, ex quo me in amicorum tuorum numerum accepisti, idque Mediolani, ubi sic me vidisti libenter ut saepe etiam, quae tua est humanitas, convivam tuum esse volueris, cum multi una coenarent familiares, iidemque Academici et doctissimi viri, qui ad te, ut olim doctissimi quique ad Mecoenatem, frequentes concurrunt ac confugiunt.

2 Ex quo item, cum paucis post diebus Cremona Asulam proficiscerer per Mantuanum agrum, et milites Mantuani principis, nescio quos capturi illius inimicos qui eo die transituri illac equis dicebantur, me per errorem cepissent,[5] Cannetique, quod ab Mantua XX millia passuum abesse aiunt, in carcere detinerent, tu, qui forte tunc eras Mantuae, legatum agens regium, statim re cognita, liberaturus me adiisti principem, eaque re facile impetrata, ipsemet, omni equitatu tuo comitante necnon et aliis quibusdam ex Mantuanis nobilibus, ad id ipsum oppidum profectus es ac me accersitum liberasti, pecunia ad assem, vestibus, equis et caeteris quaecunque surripuerant, redditis.

3 Ubi illud mirum, ut praetor loci illius, qui prima nocte qua me adducendum ad se iusserat viris prope centum armatis

: XIX :

Horace

(after March 30, 1509)

Aldus Pius Manutius of Rome to Geoffroy Carles,[201] *jurisconsult and president of the royal senate in the city of Milan, warmest greetings.*

My distinguished Carles, three years have now passed since you welcomed me into your group of friends. What was more, this was in Milan,[202] where you were so pleased to see me that in your great generosity you often wished me to be your special dinner companion, although many associates were dining at the same time, as well as Academicians and very learned men, who all hasten in great numbers to seek refuge in you, as in times past all the most learned men turned to Maecenas.[203] 1

Three years have passed too from that time when I set out a few days later from Cremona, making for Asola through Mantuan territory, and soldiers in the service of the marquis of Mantua[204] took me prisoner. They were intending to seize some enemies of the marquis who were said to be going to pass through that way on the same day on horseback. In error they captured me instead and imprisoned me in Canneto sull' Oglio which is said to be twenty miles from Mantua. It chanced that you were in Mantua, in your role of the king's ambassador.[205] The moment you heard what had happened you approached the marquis to have me freed, and when your request was readily granted you yourself set out for that very town, accompanied by all your cavalry and some other noblemen from Mantua. You had me summoned and then set free. Everything that they had stolen from me was returned to me, including my money (to the penny!), clothes and horses. 2

Then this strange thing happened. As we were dining (for I too was at the table in such a fine gathering, sitting closest to you, as 3

circundatum, ab hora quinta ad decimam usque Iulio mense in teterrimo carcere inclusum tenuerat, coenantibus nobis—discumbebam enim et ipse in tanto coetu, contra te secundus, iussu tuo—non solum astaret, sed etiam, ut Nasidienus olim apud Horatium coenante Mecoenate, architriclinium ageret, tum veniam peteret quod me non tractasset humaniter. Adde quod ipse princeps literas ad me Asulam quam humanissimas dedit, offerens, quantum aut molestiae aut incommodi per errorem passus fueram, nesciente se, tantundem vel iucunditatis vel commodi aliquando se repositurum.

4 Non immemor igitur, Iafrede Carole, tanti beneficii in me tui, saepe cogitavi quanam in re gratum me tibi esse ostenderem. Tandem, Horatii Flacci cultum poema daturus studiosis excusum cura nostra, illud sub tuo nomine statui emittere, ut, quemadmodum Horatius ipse Mecoenati, benefactori suo ac doctissimo et liberalissimo principi, hoc opus a se compositum dedicavit, ego itidem id ipsum a me recognitum diligenter et emendatum dedicem tibi, servatori meo et cum aliis plurimis tum doctrina et liberalitate Mecoenati aetatis nostrae. Cui fortasse verius ego quam Mecoenati Horatius dixerim, 'O et praesidium et dulce decus meum.' Nam longe maius esse beneficium reor hominem e carcere liberare quam donare divitiis. Saepe igitur iuvat dicere. 'O et praesidium et dulce decus meum!'

5 Idem autem opus etsi abhinc septennium curavimus imprimendum, nunc tamen id iterum damus, sed multo emendatius meliusque. Nam et rationem undeviginti metrorum generum, quibus Horatius in hoc opere usus est, sic inserui suis locis ut se sponte

you had bidden), the town magistrate who had ordered me to be brought before him on the first night with almost a hundred armed men around me and had kept me shut up in the foulest of cells from the fifth hour to the twelfth hour (and that too in the month of July!), not only stood by us in attendance, but even assumed the role of master of ceremonies, like Nasidienus in times past when Maecenas was dining at Horace's home.[206] He then begged forgiveness for having treated me in such an inhumane manner. Moreover, the marquis himself sent the kindest of letters to me at Asola, in which he offered to compensate me for the distress and harm that I had suffered in error, unknown to him, with matching favors and generosity in the future.

Not unmindful of your great kindness to me, Geoffroy Carles, 4
I often thought in what way I might show my gratitude to you. Finally, when I was about to deliver to devotees of learning the refined poetry of Horace that we had undertaken to print, I decided to release it under your name. In this way, just as Horace himself dedicated this work of his to Maecenas, his benefactor and a preeminent citizen in the state, as well as being most learned and generous, so I also will dedicate this collection of poetry, as reviewed and corrected by me,[207] to my savior and to one who is a Maecenas of our times, not only in learning and generosity but also in many other respects. Perhaps I may say to my Maecenas with more justification than Horace did to his, "O you who are my guardian and my sweet source of glory!"[208] I say this for I think it is a far greater kindness to release a man from prison than to endow him with riches. And so I often take delight in saying, "O you who are my guardian and my sweet source of glory."

We printed this work seven years ago, but now we are publish- 5
ing it again, in a much improved and better form. For the system of the nineteen kinds of meter used by Horace in this work has been inserted by me at the appropriate place so that these are readily at hand, even for those who do not wish them, and I have

offerant vel nolentibus, et distinctiones subdistinctionesque ut quisque locus exigebat apposui, quae, cum bene collocatae sunt, commentariorum vice funguntur. Notavi praeterea quaedam inter corrigendum, quae rati profutura hic subiunximus. Vale, 'praesidium et dulce decus meum.'

Venetiis tertio calendas Apriles M.D.IX.

: XX :

Aldus Pius Manutius Bartholomaeo Liviano Venetarum copiarum gubernatori Romanaeque militiae instauratori s. p. d.

1 C. Crispi Sallustii *De coniuratione Catilinae* et *De bello Iugurthino* duo antiquissima exemplaria e Lutetia Parisiorum Ioannes Lascaris, qui superioribus annis egit apud Venetos legatum regium, et Iocundus Veronensis, viri bonarum literarum studiosissimi, in Italiam attulerunt mihique, quae utriusque est liberalitas, excudenda dederunt.

2 Quae quam sint correcta et emendata statim in principio *De coniuratione Catilinae* licet cognoscere. Nam, quod fere in aliis legitur, 'Nam imperium facile his artibus retinetur quibus in initio partum est; verum, ubi pro labore desidia, pro continentia et aequitate libido atque superbia invasere, fortuna simul commutatur cum moribus; ita imperium semper ab optimo quoque ad minus bonum transfertur,' in his sic habetur: 'Ita imperium semper ad optimum quenque a minus bono transfertur,' quae vera est lectio. Est enim sensus 'Imperium in initio virtute ab optimis partum,

added headings and subheadings as each passage demanded; these function as commentaries when they are helpfully positioned. In addition, while correcting the volume I noted some things and we have added them in this edition since we thought they would be of value.[209] Farewell, "my guardian and sweet source of my glory."

Venice, March 30, 1509.

: XX :

Sallust

(April 1509)

Aldus Pius Manutius to Bartolomeo d'Alviano,[210] *commander of the Venetian forces, and the reviver of the military skills of Rome, warmest greetings.*

1 Janus Lascaris,[211] who for the past few years has been the ambassador of the French king to Venice, and Giocondo of Verona,[212] a man devoted to good letters, brought from Paris two very old manuscripts of Sallust's *The Catilinarian Conspiracy* and *The Jugurthine War,* and such is the generosity of both of them that they gave them to me to put into print.

2 One can see immediately how free of errors and unblemished they are by looking at the beginning of *The Catilinarian Conspiracy.* For the reading in almost all other ones[213] is as follows:[214] *nam imperium facile his artibus retinetur quibus in initio partum est; verum, ubi pro labore desidia, pro continentia et aequitate libido atque superbia invasere, fortuna simul commutatur cum moribus; ita imperium semper ab optimo quoque ad minus bonum transfertur.* In these manuscripts, however, we read *ita imperium semper ad optimum quenque a minus bono transfertur,* and this is the correct reading. The sense is "power is initially acquired by the best men by reason of their virtue, and

eadem virtute facile retinetur; pravis autem rectoribus factis, immutatur fortuna cum moribus, et imperium rursus ad optimos redit.'

3 Hos libros, Liviane, tibi dicavimus, tum quia te ducibus iis quorum his libris gesta traduntur fortitudine et rei militaris scientia iam adaequasti, tum etiam, quod paucis admodum datur, et legis facta et facis legenda; deinde quia saepe me hortatus es ut encheiridii forma libros quibus clarorum virorum gesta continentur excudendos curarem, quo belli eos tecum commodius habere posses. Accipe igitur nunc quae Sallustii ad nostram aetatem historiae pervenere sintque apud te longa monimenta mutuae benevolentiae nostrae.

Venetiis mense Aprili M.D.IX.

: XXI :

Aldus Manutius Romanus Philippo Cyulano Morae Pannonio a secretis regis ac oratori apud Venetos et compatri observantissimo s. p. d.

1 Multa mihi grata contingunt in hac mea provincia plena laborum, inclyte Cyulane, sed illud gratissimum, quod magni etiam viri ac principes, quicunque amantes sunt bonarum literarum, et nos de tantis assiduisque laboribus nostris amant plurimum, quemadmodum et tu facis; es enim et literarum et nostri amantissimus, quod

is easily retained by the same quality; when the rulers become depraved, however, fortune changes with their character and power returns to the best men."

We have dedicated these works to you, d'Alviano, first of all because you have already matched in bravery and in your military skills those leaders whose achievements are recorded in these books and because not only do you read about exploits but, something that is granted to very few, your own exploits are worthy of being read. The second reason is that you have often urged me to publish books recounting the achievements of famous men in the pocket-book format so that you could more conveniently have such works with you when you are in the field. Accept now therefore the histories of Sallust that have come down to our age, and may they be a long reminder of our mutual goodwill. 3

Venice, April 1509.

: XXI :

Cicero, Letters to Atticus, Brutus and His brother Quintus

(June 1513)

Aldus Manutius of Rome to Filippo Csulai Móré of Hungary,[215]
secretary to the king and his ambassador to Venice,
and the most obliging of friends, warmest greetings.

In this extremely demanding vocation of mine I find many things that gratify me, my renowned Csulai, but the most gratifying is that all who love good letters, and these include even great men and princes, show me the deepest affection for my considerable and continuous labors. And this is true of you too; for because of your outstanding erudition you are devoted to literature as well as 1

sis apprime doctus necnon ingens decus non modo Cyulanae familiae, quae cum maioribus tuis clara est et insignis tum te, praeposito Agriensi ac a secretis regis et oratore gravissimo et integerrimo iam quartum apud Venetos, et tribus fratribus tuis, Ladislao, Georgio, Nicolao, ductoribus fortissimis, qui saepe magnam Turcarum manum pro fide Christiana et patria strenue pugnantes summa cum laude profligaverunt, verum etiam ipsius patriae tuae, Pannoniae. Nam, praeter doctrinam et eloquentiam quibus es praeditus, summa in te est modestia, mira probitas, tum acutum ingenium acri adiunctum iudicio, id quod futurum in te censuit Beroaldus, quem audivisti adolescens, idque Bononiae, cum tibi suos in *Thusculanas* M. Tullii *quaestiones* commentarios nuncupavit.

2 Quoniam igitur multis ornaris virtutibus, et nos, quae tua est humanitas, valde amas, ut cognoscas Aldum tuum non esse ingratum, sed contra, amanteis sui amare vehementer, sic tibi id videbatur ostensurus si M. Tullii ad Atticum, ad Brutum, ad Quintum fratrem epistolas encheiridii forma nuper excusas cura nostra sub tuo nomine emitteret in manus studiosorum.

3 Quod eo etiam fecit libentius, quia valde delectari te dictione et eloquentia Tulliana prae te fers, nec laudandos ducis qui, eorum authorum qui citra mille et ducentos trecentosve annos fuerunt stylo delectati, contemnunt Ciceronem et quicunque Ciceronis est simillimus, ac si, spreto et fastidito triticeo pane, glande vescantur. Doctos ais esse illos quidem et legendos, sed stylum eorum non

to me. You are the great adornment of your Csulai family, which has won fame and distinction not only through its ancestors but also through you yourself and your three brothers, Ladislav, Georg and Nicolas. You are provost of the church in Transylvania, secretary to the king and a most august ambassador of the highest principles (now in your fourth year of service in Venice); your brothers are the bravest of commanders and have fought energetically for their country and the Christian faith, often having routed with magnificent skill large forces of the Turks. But you bring distinction to your native land of Hungary as well. For in addition to your erudition and your eloquence, you show great self-restraint, you are an admirable model of probity and you have a sharp intellect to which is joined keenness of judgment. Beroaldo[216] saw this potential in you when you were a student of his as a youth—and in Bologna at that[217]—when he dedicated his commentary on Cicero's *Tusculan Disputations* to you.

Since you have so many fine qualities and show your great love for me (such is your kindness), your friend Aldus wants you to know that he is not an ungrateful person, but, on the contrary, one who returns the love of others with deeply felt affection. And so he thought he would show his love for you if it was under your name that he put into the hands of students and scholars the letters of Cicero to Atticus, to Brutus and his brother Quintus, which we have recently undertaken to print in pocket-book size. 2

Aldus takes all the more pleasure in having done this because you make clear your great delight in Cicero's style and eloquence and you do not think that praise is merited by those who take pleasure in the style of those authors who lived twelve or thirteen hundred years ago and despise Cicero and all who resemble him closely[218]—it is as if they spurn and turn up their noses at baked bread and prefer a diet of acorns![219] You say that those authors are learned and certainly worth reading, but you think that their styles 3

modo non imitandum, sed fugiendum pro viribus censes. Et recte, meo quidem iudicio.

4 Idem memini olim dicere Paulum quendam Pannonium, optimo iudicio adolescentem ac condiscipulum meum — dabamus enim operam Baptistae, Guarini filio, in urbe Ferraria —; idem item Sigismundum Turzum, hospitem olim meum Venetiis, humanissimum sane ac doctissimum hominem et admodum quam studiosum Ciceronis, qui paucis post annis praepositus Albensis, deinde Varadiensis episcopus creatus est, cuius immaturo et repentino interitu, ut debeo, doleo (debeo autem plurimum) tanto viro amicoque meo summo orbatus. Videntur mihi Pannonii omnes — multis enim familiarissime usus sum, quod 'nescio quod me vobis temperat astrum' — ingenii iudiciique bonitate delectari maxime Ciceronis operibus, et tu, mi Philippe, praeter caeteros.

5 Quamobrem accipe nunc XX haec tui Ciceronis epistolarum volumina, ex quibus sexdecim scripsit ad Titum Pomponium Atticum, quicum a pueritia — fuerunt enim condiscipuli — coniunctissime semper et amantissime vixit, ac multo etiam familiarius quam cum Quinto fratre, ut iudicari possit plus in amicitia valere similitudinem morum quam affinitatem. Sic autem vehementer amabant inter se ut alter alterius absentiam aegerrime ferret lacrymaretque qui remanebat, siquo forte alter procul a patria proficisceretur. Id quod cum alibi tum libro XV ea epistola, cuius initium: 'Antium veni VI calendarum,' testatur ipse Cicero his verbis: 'Te, ut a me discesseris, lacrymasse, moleste ferebam. Quod si me praesente fecisses, consilium totius itineris fortasse mutassem. Sed illud praeclare, quod te consolata est spes brevi tempore congrediendi; quae quidem expectatio me maxime sustentat.'

should be avoided at all costs, far less imitated. And you are quite right in my opinion.

I remember hearing the same thing from a certain Paul, a Hungarian, a youth of the finest judgment and a fellow student of mine (we were both studying under Battista, the son of Guarino, in Ferrara)[220] and also from Sigismund Thurzó, a guest of mine in Venice at one time, who was a very civilized and learned man, as well as being a devoted follower of Cicero. A few years later he was provost of the church in Transylvania and then was created bishop of Varád.[221] I grieve, as I ought (for I owe him a great deal), at his premature and sudden death, having lost such a great man and dearest friend. I think that all Hungarians (I have been on very friendly terms with many of them, since "some star or other brings us together"[222]) have fine intellect and judgment that make them take the greatest delight in the works of Cicero; and this is true, my dear Filippo, of you more than all the others. 4

Receive now, therefore, these twenty books of your beloved Cicero. Sixteen of them he wrote to Titus Pomponius Atticus, ever a very close and loving friend of his from boyhood (for they were students together) and indeed much closer to him than he was to his brother Quintus. You can judge from this that for friendship similarity of character is more important than blood relationship. They were so close to each other that one would be extremely upset by the other's absence and if by chance one traveled far from home he who was left behind would weep. Cicero himself testifies to this on many occasions, including the letter in book fifteen that begins "I came to Antium on the sixth day before the Calends" where he says, "I was upset that you wept after leaving me. If you had done so in my presence, I would have given up my plans for the whole journey perhaps. But it is splendid that the hope of our seeing each other within a short time has consoled you, and I am greatly sustained by the same expectation."[223] 5

6 Unum ad M. Brutum, quem semper fecit maximi propter illius summam doctrinam, integritatem, animi magnitudinem, atque ita amavit ut in quadam ad illum epistola sic scripserit: 'Nec vero ulla res erit unquam in qua ego non vel vitae periculo ea dicam eaque faciam quae te velle quaeque ad te pertinere arbitror.' Hoc loco illa digna Bruto verba non praeterierim quae ipse in ea gravi epistola ad M. Tullium, cuius initium: 'Particulam literarum tuarum,' sic ait: 'Sed mihi prius omnia dii deaeque omnes eripuerint quam illud iudicium, quo non modo haeredi eius quem occidi non concesserim quod in illo non tuli, sed ne patri quidem meo, si reviviscat, ut patiente me plus legibus ac senatu possit.'

7 Tria ad Quintum Ciceronem fratrem; quibus in epistolis de omni fere illorum temporum tumultu et miseria fit mentio, quibus temporibus simillima mihi videntur nostra haec miserrima et infelicissima tempora, cum aliis plurimis, tum crudelitate, caede, rapinis, depopulationibus agrorum, direptione urbium, crebra varietate fortunae, quorum malorum et fuerunt semper et sunt et erunt causa pernitiosa bella, et ut Ciceronis nostri in epistola quadam ad M. Brutum utar verbis, *ταῦτα ὁ τλήμων ἐργάζεται πόλεμος*. Incidimus enim in ea tempora ut et nos illud vere queamus dicere:

> Vicinae ruptis inter se legibus urbes
> arma ferunt, saevit toto Mars impius orbe.

Ex iis ipsis epistolis colligere facile possumus quae in commentariis suis *De bello Gallico* et *civili* scripsit C. Caesar esse quam verissima.

There is one book addressed to Marcus Brutus, whom he always deeply admired because of his consummate learning, his faultless character and nobility of mind. He was so fond of him that in a letter to him he wrote the following: "There will never be any situation in which, even at the risk of my life, I will not say and do what I think you wish and what is of concern to you."[224] At this point I should not pass over those words, worthy indeed of Brutus, which he himself wrote in that important letter to Cicero that begins, "A small part of your letter." These are his words: "All the gods and goddesses will snatch everything away from me before I stand idly by and accept in the heir of the man whom I killed what I did not tolerate in him, let alone my own father, if he were brought back to life, namely to be more powerful than the law and senate."[225] 6

There are three books to his brother Quintus, and in these books reference is made to almost all the tumult and misery of those years, which the terrible and disastrous times we now live in closely resemble, in their cruelty, slaughter, plunder, devastation of estates, sacking of cities, frequent changes of fortune and many other things. The cause of these evils is, as it always has been and always will be, ruinous war. To use our own Cicero's words in a letter to Brutus: ταῦτα ὁ τλήμων ἐργάζεται πόλεμος ("all this is the work of wretched war").[226] For we happen to live in such times that we can truly say: 7

Neighboring cities break the pacts that bind them
and bear arms against each other. Throughout the whole world
the unholy god of war is on the rampage.[227]

We can readily infer from these very letters that what Julius Caesar wrote in his *Gallic War* and his *Civil War* could not be more true.[228]

8 Qua de re, quae in vita Pomponii Attici scripsit Cornelius Nepos, qui floruit illis temporibus fuitque in familiarissimis Attici, non ab re visum est subiungere. Ait enim:

> Quanquam eum praecipue dilexit Cicero, ut ne frater quidem ei Quintus carior fuerit aut familiarior. Ei rei sunt indicio, praeter eos libros in quibus de eo facit mentionem, qui in vulgus sunt editi, sexdecim volumina epistolarum ab consulatu eius usque ad extremum tempus ad Atticum missarum; quae qui legat non multum desyderat historiam contextam eorum temporum. Sic enim omnia de studiis principum, vitiis ducum, aemulationibus reipublicae perscripta sunt ut nihil in his non appareat, et facile existimari possit prudentiam quodam modo esse divinationem. Non enim Cicero ea solum quae vivo se acciderunt futura praedixit, sed etiam quae nunc usu veniunt cecinit ut vates.

Haec Nepos. Quae tu, Cyulane, legendis assidue hisce epistolarum voluminibus—invitabit enim te encheiridii forma—vera esse agnosces. Nam, etsi familiarissimae tibi sunt hae M. Tullii epistolae, fient hac parvitate voluminis magis etiam familiares.

9 Recognoscuntur nunc accuratissime caetera quaecunque extant opera Ciceronis, quae tribus voluminibus edituri sumus in vulgus excusa typis nostris, ut uno volumine comprehendantur libri morales et philosophici, altero rhetorici, tertio orationes, sic, ut spero, emendati ut pauca in illis desyderentur. Quo facto non dubito quin studiosi aetatis nostrae, si quibus inest tanta perversitas ut minime eis Cicero placeat, redeant ad sanitatem ac sani potius evadant mutato consilio habeantque semper in manibus Ciceronis divina volumina.

On this point it does not seem inapposite to add what Cornelius Nepos, who lived at this time, wrote in his life of Pomponius Atticus, whose close friend he was. For he says: 8

> And yet Cicero was deeply attached to Atticus, not even his brother Quintus being dearer or closer to him. Apart from the works in which Cicero mentions him and which have already been published, proof of this lies in the sixteen books of letters sent to Atticus, dating from his consulship up to his death. Whoever reads these does not miss much of the complete history of those times. For he covers comprehensively the policies of the leading men, the faults of the commanders, and the rivalries of the republic in such a way that everything is clear and one could think that his good sense was in some way prophetic. For Cicero foretold not only what happened while he was still alive but even, like a seer, prophesied what is now coming to pass.[229]

So says Nepos. You will recognize the truth of his words, Csulai, by frequent reading of these books of letters (for the pocket-book format will encourage you to do so). For even though these letters of Cicero are very familiar to you, the small size of the volume will make them even more so.

All the other extant works of Cicero are being prepared at the present moment with the utmost care and we will publish them in three volumes in our type. The first will bring together his works on moral philosophy, the second his rhetorical writings, the third his speeches. It is my hope that they will be so free of errors that hardly any deficiencies will be seen.[230] When this is done I have no doubt that those students of our times who are perverse enough to find no pleasure in reading Cicero will come to their senses and, having changed their opinion, will turn out to be of sound mind and always have the divine works of Cicero in their hands. 9

10 Quoniam autem in iis ipsis epistolis multa Graece dicta habentur, ea nos Latina fecimus ac subiunximus, idque primum propter Graecarum literarum rudes, deinde ut de iis quae varie leguntur meminerimus quaedamque obiter non inutilia dicamus.

Haec nos cursim quidem, sed diligenter interpretati sumus, adiutore viro doctissimo et compatre meo carissimo Marco Musuro, qui tanto mihi castigandis libris adiumento assidue est ut, 'si duo praeterea taleis Argiva tulisset terra viros' ἐμοὶ συμφράδμονας, sperarem brevi optimos quosque libros utriusque linguae daturum studiosis emendatissimos.

Vale, mi Cyulane, et gentis tuae et patriae ingens decus.

Venetiis V calendas Iulias MDXIII.

: XXII :

Aldus lectori s.

1 Non possum non vehementer irasci audaculis ac temerariis quibusdam, etiam antiquis, qui deminuendis et mutilandis alienis libris delectati, totam in eo studio curam operamque posuerunt, id quod, si fecissent ut sibi inde eligerent quae magis probarent quaeque facilius memoriae mandare et tenere tenacius possent, non inprobarem eorum consilium, sed ob eam causam id fecisse videntur ut relictis ac spretis tanquam verbosis et nugacibus propriis

Since there are many Greek words in these letters, we have 10
added Latin translations of them. First of all, this is for the benefit of those who know little or no Greek, but it also allows us to mention variant readings and to give other useful information in passing.[231]

We have translated these in some haste but carefully, with the help of my dear Marcus Musurus. a most learned man, friend and colleague.[232] He has been such a constant help to me in correcting my books that, "if the land of the Argives had produced two other such men" as my collaborators,[233] I would hope to produce for students in a very short time all the best books in each language with a text quite free of errors.

Farewell, my dear Csulai, the great adornment of your family and native land.

Venice, June 27, 1513.

: XXII :

Festus, On the Meaning of Archaic Words[234]

(*November 1513*)

Aldus to the reader, greetings.[235]

I cannot help being extremely angry at certain shameless and bra- 1
zen individuals, some of them actually living in ancient times, who took such pleasure in abbreviating and mutilating the works of others that they devoted all their energy and efforts to this pursuit. If they had done this with the purpose of picking out for themselves material from there that they thought was more laudable and that they could more readily memorize and more retentively remember, I would not find fault with their plan. However, their motive seems to have been to abandon and spurn the true

authoribus, ipsi laudarentur, ipsi legerentur obliteratoque illorum nomine suum substituerent. Sic Trogi Pompeii Iustinus, sic T. Livii Lucius Florus, sic Sexti Pompeii nescioquis Paulus abbreviator factus est, qui utinam antequam tam iniquum facinus aggrederentur ipsi vel mutilati vel discerpti occidissent. Esset enim in manibus Trogus, integri et Livius et Pompeius haberentur, quamquam Trogum brevi me spero daturum in medium. Extat enim est penes amicum quendam meum frugi hominem et fide plenum nec despero et Livium quoque et caeteros bonos vel mea vel aliorum cura aliquando inventum iri. Faveat Deus coeptis nostris.

2 Cur autem Paulus is cuius modo memini Sextum Pompeiium mutilaverit cognosces ex eius epistola quam curavi imprimendam, non quod digna lectu videretur (est enim indocta sane ac barbara) sed ut, qualiscumque ea est, pleniore testimonio foret ab arroganti homine doctissimas Pompeii lucubrationes indigne ac inique diminutas et laceratas fuisse. Vale.

: XXIII :

A

Aldus lectori s.

1 Etsi potes, studiose lector, per te ipse legendo cognoscere curnam C. Caesar rerum ab se gestarum confecerit commentarios, tum et

authors as being verbose and useless so that they themselves might be praised, so that it was their work that was being read and so that they might obliterate the names of the authors and put their own names in their place. So Justin became the abbreviator of Pompeius Trogus,[236] Lucius Florus of Titus Livius,[237] some Paul or other of Sextus Pompeius. I wish they themselves had been mutilated and torn to pieces before they undertook such a wicked task! For in that case we would have Trogus in our possession, and we would have the complete works of Livy and Festus. And yet I hope that I will shortly make Trogus available to the public. For a friend of mine who is honest and most trustworthy has a copy of him,[238] and I do not despair of Livy and other good authors being found at some time through my efforts or those of others. May God look kindly upon our attempts.

You will recognize why that Paul whom I have just mentioned 2
mutilated Festus from his letter that I have had printed,[239] not because I thought it worthy of being read (it reveals ignorance and stylistic crudity!) but so that you will have fuller evidence from it, such as it is, that the erudite studies of Festus have been shamefully and wickedly abbreviated and torn to pieces by an arrogant fellow. Farewell.

: XXIII :

Julius Caesar[240]

(December 1513)

A

Aldus to the reader, greetings.

By simply reading these works, learned reader, you can find out for 1
yourself not only why Julius Caesar wrote historical accounts[241] of

quos et quot confecerit, tamen non inutile futurum existimavi, si hic id promptius tibi fieret mea cura.

2 Res gestae ab C. Caesare in Gallia novem annis quibus in ea cum imperio fuit octo libris scriptae sunt, primo et reliquis usque ad octavum ab ipso Caesare tanta elegantia tantoque dicendi ornatu ut, licet et hi et tres primi de bello civili adversus Pompeium 'editi sint ne scientia tantarum rerum gestarum scriptoribus deesset, tamen praerepta potius quam praebita illis sit scribendi facultas,' octavo autem ab A. Hircio, qui et de bello Alexandrino et Africano commentarios videtur scripsisse, id quod ex ipsius praefatione in octavum librum de bello Gallico colligi potest. Ibi enim sic ait:

> Caesaris nostri *Commentarios rerum gestarum Galliae* non comparandos superioribus atque insequentibus eius scriptis contexui, novissimeque imperfecta ab rebus gestis Alexandriae confeci usque ad exitum, non quidem civilis dissensionis, cuius finem nullum videmus, sed vitae Caesaris.

3 Haec ille. Ex quibus videmur posse inferre, si confecit Hircius gesta Caesaris usque ad illius vitae exitum, ergo reliqui commentarii, praeter decem supradictos Caesaris, esse illius videntur[6] nec extare quidem quae scripsit omnia, quandoquidem usque ad exitum vitae Caesaris scripsisse se ait. *Commentarios* tamen *de bello Hispaniensi* non modo non esse Hircii dixerim, sed ne eruditi quidem cuiusquam; sunt enim admodum quam inconditi ac barbari.

his achievements but also how many of these accounts there were and what their subject matter was. Despite this, I thought that it would be useful if I took the trouble here to deal quickly with these questions.

Julius Caesar's accomplishments in Gaul in the nine years in 2
which he had a command there were written in eight books. The first seven were written by Caesar himself with such elegance and style that, although these and the first three books on the civil war against Pompey "were published to ensure that other writers would have knowledge of his great achievements, he deprived them of, rather than provided them with, the opportunity to write histories on these topics."[242] The eighth book was written by Aulus Hirtius, who seems also to have written the histories on the Alexandrian and the African wars,[243] as can be gathered from his own preface to book eight of *The Gallic War*. For this is what he says there.

> I have inserted our Caesar's incomparable *Commentaries on the Gallic War* between his earlier and later writings and most recently I have completed what was missing from the Alexandrian campaign right through to the end, not of the civil war admittedly, of which there is no end in sight, but of Caesar's life.[244]

These are his words, and from them I think we can infer that if 3
Hirtius covered all of Caesar's accomplishments right up to the end of his life, the remaining histories, apart from the ten books named above that were written by Caesar, were done by Hirtius and that not all of what he wrote has survived, since he says that his writings went right up to the end of Caesar's life. I would say however, that the author of *Commentaries on the Spanish War* is not only not Hirtius but not even anyone very learned; for they are quite roughly and crudely done.

4 De iis ipsis Caesaris *Commentariis* quid scripserit M. Tullius in libro de claris oratoribus operae pretium visum est subiungere. Cuius haec sunt verba:

> *Commentarios* scripsit valde quidem probandos. Nudi sunt, recti et venusti, omni ornatu orationis tanquam veste detracta. Sed dum voluit alios habere parata[7] unde sumerent qui vellent scribere historiam, ineptis gratum fortasse fecit, qui illa volunt calamistris inurere, sanos quidem homines a scribendo deterruit.

Haec Cicero.

5 Illud insuper addiderim, bonam partem eorum quae his commentariis scripta sunt haberi etiam in epistolis M. Tullii ad Atticum, in quibus, cum quid novi gestum erat a Caesare, statim Atticum Quintumve Ciceronem fratrem aut M. Brutum certiorem faciebat. Id quod maximo testimonio est verissima esse quaecunque his commentariis scripta habentur. Vale.

Venetiis mense Novembri MDXIII.

B

Aldus studiosis s.

6 Superiorem totius Galliae picturam divisae in treis parteis, Belgicam scilicet, Celticam, Aquitaniam, ut statim in principio primi libri *Commentariorum de bello Gallico* docet Caesar, sic nos curavimus faciendam ut facile quis singulas queat parteis cognoscere.

Nam Celtae, qui et Galli appellantur quique medii sunt inter Belgas et Aquitanos, concluduntur Sequana Matrona fluminibus, punctis ab Matrona ad Rhenum usque perductis, tum Rheno,

As for the *Commentaries* of Caesar themselves I think that it is worthwhile to add here what Cicero wrote in his work on famous orators. These are his words: 4

> His *Commentaries* are quite admirable. They are like nude figures, straight and attractive, stripped of all adornment of style, like models that have lost their finery. He wanted to provide others who wished to write history with the material that they could draw on, but in doing so he has done a favor only to the incompetent who wish to use their curling irons on his material. Men of good sense, however, have been deterred from writing.[245]

So says Cicero.

I would add the following. Much of what is written in these accounts is also attested in Cicero's letters to Atticus, in which the orator immediately informs Atticus or his brother Quintus or Marcus Brutus of any new accomplishment of Caesar. This provides the strongest evidence for believing that everything contained in these *Commentaries* is extremely accurate. Farewell. 5

Venice, November 1513.

B[246]

Aldus to students, greetings.

At the very beginning of the first book of his *Commentaries on the Gallic War* Caesar informs us that the whole of Gaul was divided into three parts, namely Belgica, Celtica and Aquitania.[247] Accordingly, we have undertaken to provide above a map of Gaul in such a way that anyone can readily recognize each part. 6

For the Celts, who are also called Gauls and live between the Belgians and the Aquitanians, are bounded by the rivers Seine and Marne, by a line of dots drawn from the Marne as far as the Rhine, then by the Rhine and by the same line when extended up

iisdemque punctis usque ad lacum unde oritur, item lacu Lemano ac Rhodano Lugdunum usque, rursus Lugdunensium Arvenorumque finibus, tum Garumna fluvio quam longus est.

7 Belgae, qui spectant in septentriones, dividuntur ab Germanis Rheno, ab Celtis, sive Gallis, iis ipsis punctis ab Rheno ad Matronam, tum Matrona et Sequana.

Aquitani discluduntur ab Gallis Garumna flumine, iisdemque Lugdunensium et Arvernorum finibus, attinguntque Pyrenaeos monteis; ab provincia, Tholosae et Narbonae finibus. Reliqua quae superest pictura continet Germaniam, Provinciam, Rhodanum ab Lugduno ad mare, Tholosam, Narbonam, Alpeis et caetera quae inibi notata licet videre.

8 Illud praeterea notandum: ubi in inferiore parte Rheni sunt characteres numerorum, 1 scilicet sub Menapiis, 2 contra Ubios, ibi vel circa fuisse ponteis, de quibus meminit Caesar in commentariis; ubi 3 inter Lingones et Virodunum, ibi fuisse Alexiam; ubi 4 ad mare Mediterraneum, non longe illinc esse Massiliam, quae fere ex tribus oppidi partibus mari alluitur; ubi 5 prope Lemovices, ibi Uxellodunum; ubi 6 sub dictione Ligeris, ibi fuisse Avaricum; ubi 7 sub dictione Sequani, ibi scribendum esse Arar fluvium. Quae per incuriam praetermissa sunt.

9 Totam autem picturam, ut esset cognitu facilior, variis coloribus distinguendam iussimus: Aquitaniam scilicet purpureo, qui Graece *πορφυροῦς* dicitur; Celticam fulvo seu luteo croceove, qui Graece *χρυσοειδής*; Belgicam rubro rufove, qui *ἐρυθρός*; Germaniam flavo, qui *ξανθός*; eam autem partem quae est a finibus Tholosatium Mediolanum usque viridi, qui *ποώδης*; maria caeruleo sive caesio, quem Graeci *γλαυκόν* et *κυάνεον* appellant.

to the lake which is its source, and also by Lake Geneva and the Rhone as far as Lyons, then again by the territory of the people of Lyons and Auvergne, then by the extremely long river Garonne.

The people of Belgica live in the north and are separated from the Germans by the Rhine, from the Celts (or Gauls) by that same line of dots joining the Rhine and the Marne, as well as by the Marne and the Seine. 7

The Aquitanians are separated from the Celts by the Garonne, and by those territories of Lyons and the people of Auvergne already mentioned; their domain stretches as far as the Pyrenees. The territories of Toulouse and Narbonne mark the boundary that separates Aquitania from the province of Gaul. The rest of the map contains Germania, Transalpine Gaul, the river Rhone from Lyons to the sea, Toulouse, Narbonne, the Alps and everything else that one can see identified there.

It should be further noted that the numbers in the lower part of the Rhine, 1 under the Menapii and 2 opposite the Ubii, mark the position or the approximate position of the bridges that Caesar mentions in his *Commentaries*. The number 3, between the Lingones and Virodunum, marks the position of Alexia. Marseilles, three parts of which are washed by the Mediterranean, is situated not far from the number 4, which is written close to that sea. Number 5, near Lemovices, marks Uxellodonum; number 6, under the word Ligeris, indicates the site of Avaricum; at 7, under the word Sequani, there should be written the river Arar. All these were overlooked through carelessness. 8

We had the whole map done in different colors for easier comprehension:[248] Aquitania in purple (πορφυροῦς in Greek); Celtica in a tawny or brownish-golden color (χρυσοειδής in Greek); Belgica in red or rust (ἐρυθρός in Greek); Germany in yellow (ξανθός in Greek); the part stretching from the territory of Toulouse to Milan in green (ποώδης in Greek); the seas in blue or bluish gray (γλαυκός and κυάνεος in Greek). 9

10 Hos colores an recte appellarimus viderint doctiores. Scimus enim colorum appellationes perincertas esse, tum certasse olim super ea re obnixe priscos grammaticos et certare nunc maxime, cum multae sint uniuscuiusque coloris species, nunc intensi, nunc remissi, nunc temperati; atque id quoque varie. Nam purpureas violas dicimus, purpureas rosas, purpureum narcissum, lilium, mare, purpuream auroram, purpuratos reges; item fulvum aurum, fulvos leones, galeros, fulvam aquilam, arenam, fulvum iaspidem; sic flaventes comas, flavam aquam, flavum pulverem, flavas quoque olivarum frondes. Quod propterea contigit, quia plures res sunt quam nomina; quod et Aristoteles testatur his verbis: Τὰ *μὲν γὰρ ὀνόματα πεπέρασται καὶ τὸ τῶν λόγων πλῆθος, τὰ δὲ πράγματα τὸν ἀριθμὸν ἄπειρά ἐστιν· ἀναγκαῖον οὖν πλείω τὸν αὐτὸν λόγον καὶ τοὔνομα τὸ ἓν σημαίνειν.*

11 Sed et colorum appellationes et herbarum et animalium, tam quae in aquis quam quae in terris degunt, tum instrumentorum, quibus artifices, quibus rustici, quibus nautae utuntur, necnon et vestium atque aliorum plurium id genus, vel pictura aliquando dabuntur mea cura, si instituta, ut spero, perfecero. Faveat Deus.

12 Item, quia in pictura praecedenti quaedam locorum nomina vix legi possunt, in quibusdam Oedipo coniectore opus est—eius culpa qui incidit literas absente nobis—, curavimus omnia quae in ea pictura habentur nomina hic imprimenda, ut his, cum libuerit, queat quis quae in pictura sunt corrigere. Ac ut facilius inveniantur, in sex parteis ea distinximus [. . .].

Valete, et miseremini tantorum laborum, ac orate multis precibus ut quantum cupimus—cupimus autem plurimum et quantum

Let others more learned than I decide whether we have given 10
the correct terms for these colors; for we know that color terms are very uncertain, that the ancient philologists argued strenuously on this topic and that philologists do so nowadays, especially since there are many variations in each color—sometimes it is deep, sometimes pale, sometimes a shade in between these two and that aspect too is described in different ways. For we apply the term "purple" to violets, roses, the narcissus, the lily, the sea, the dawn, and we describe kings as "purpled." Similarly we use the term "tawny" to describe gold, lions, wigs,[249] an eagle, sand, jasper, and apply the color "golden" to hair, water, dust and the leaves of olive trees. The reason for this is that the number of things in existence is larger than the words we have, as Aristotle attests in these words: "For on the one hand the names and the great number of words are limited while, on the other, objects are countless in number. Therefore the same word and name has necessarily more than one meaning."[250]

But as for color terms and the names of plants and animals, 11
both those that live in water and those that live on land, and of the tools used by craftsmen, farm workers and sailors, as well as the names of clothes and many other things of this sort, it is my intention to provide illustrations of these, if, as I hope, I bring to completion at some time what I have begin work on.[251] May God look favorably upon me.

In addition, through the fault of the man who cut the letters in 12
our absence, certain place-names in the above map can scarcely be read (in some cases we need an Oedipus to guess what they are). We have therefore undertaken to print here all the names that are in this illustration so that anyone who wishes can use them to correct the errors therein. And so that they may more easily be found we have separated them into six parts:[252] [. . .].

Farewell and have sympathy for our great labors and utter many a prayer that we can serve you and posterity to the extent that we

fortasse vix unquam alius quisquam—prodesse et vobis queamus et posteris.

Venetiis mense Decembri M.D.XIII.

: XXIV :

A

Aldi Pii Manutii ad Andream Naugerium patritium Venetum, compatrem, in libros de arte rhetorica praefatio.

1 Omnes, Andrea Naugeri, qui se vel componendis novis operibus vel instaurandis corrigendisve antiquis tradunt ut non solum sibi sed et aliis prosint (quoniam, ut praeclare scriptum est a Platone, non nobis solum nati sumus, sed ortus nostri partem patria, partem parentes vendicant, partem amici), otium sibi sumant et quietem, ac a coetu hominum frequentiaque in solitudinem, tanquam in portum, se recipiant. Sacra enim studia literarum et Musae ipsae semper quidem otium amant et solitudinem, sed tunc praecipue cum quae scripturus es victura cupias 'atque linenda cedro et levi servanda cupresso.'

2 Quam quidem rem tu, mi Naugeri, persaepe et feliciter facis. Relicta enim urbe et frequentia hominum, rus te confers et in loca quietis et tranquillitatis plenissima, ut superioribus annis in laureta et oliveta Benaci, cum 'dirae ferro et compagibus arctis clausae

wish (for we wish to serve you as best we can and perhaps more than anyone else can).

Venice, December 1513.

: XXIV :

Cicero, Rhetorical Works

(March 1514)

A

Preface of Aldus Pius Manutius to books on the art of rhetoric, addressed to Andrea Navagero,[253] *a Venetian of patrician standing and a dear colleague.*

All who devote themselves, Andrea Navagero, either to composing original works or to restoring or correcting ancient ones for the benefit of others as well as of themselves (for, as Plato famously wrote,[254] we are born not just for ourselves, since our country claims one part of us for itself, our parents another, and our friends yet another) should seek out peace and quiet, and withdraw into solitude, into a harbor, so to speak, giving up social contact with the mass of humanity. For the sacred study of letters and the Muses themselves always love peace and solitude, but particularly so when we wish our writings to live forever and "to be smeared with cedar oil and preserved by the oil of the smooth cypress tree."[255] 1

You, my dear Navagero, do this very often and successfully. You abandon the city and the throng who live there and take yourself off to the countryside, to places that are completely peaceful and tranquil. You have done this in the past few years, going off to the laurel and olive groves of Benacus, when "the dreadful iron gates of 2

essent belli portae,' ubi et tu, vacuus curis et molestiis iis quaecunque impediunt praeclara studia literarum, 'tale facis carmen docta testudine, quale / Cynthius impositis temperat articulis.'

3 At mihi duo sunt, praeter sexcenta alia, quibus studia nostra assidua interpellatione impediuntur: crebrae scilicet literae virorum doctorum quae undique ad me mittuntur, quibus, si respondendum sit, dies totos ac noctes consumam scribendis epistolis; et ii qui ad nos veniunt, partim salutandi gratia, partim perscrutaturi siquid novi agatur, partim, quae longe maior est turba, negotii inopia; tunc enim 'Eamus,' aiunt, 'ad Aldum.' Veniunt igitur frequentes et sedent oscitabundi, 'non missura cutem nisi plena cruoris irudo.' Mitto qui veniunt recitaturi alii carmen, alii prosa oratione aliquid quod etiam excusum typis nostris publicari cupiant, idque rude et incastigatum plerunque, quod et eos offendat limae labor et mora; nec advertunt reprehendendum esse carmen, 'quod non / multa dies et multa litura coercuit, atque / perfectum decies non castigavit ad unguem.'

4 A quibus me coepi tandem permolestis interpellatoribus vindicare. Nam iis qui ad me scribunt vel nihil respondeo, cum quod scribitur non magni intersit, vel, si intersit, Laconice. Quam quidem rem, quoniam nulla id a me fit superbia, nullo contemptu, sed ut quicquid est otii consumam edendis bonis libris, rogo nequis gravius ferat, neve aliorsum atque ego facio accipiat. Eos autem qui vel salutandi vel quacunque alia causa ad nos veniunt, ne posthac molesti esse pergant neve importuni interpellent labores et

war, with its close-fitting bars, have been closed;"[256] and there, free of cares and the troublesome interruptions that impede the splendid pursuit of literature, "you compose verses on learned lyre, such as those that Apollo blends together when he puts his fingers to the strings."[257]

There are hundreds and hundreds of things that constantly in- 3
terrupt and impede our work, but there are two in particular: numerous letters from scholars that come to me from all parts of the world, to reply to which would mean spending whole days and nights writing letters; visitors who drop in on us, some to pay their respects, others to find out what new work we are engaged in, still others — and they are by far in the greatest number — because they have nothing else to do! For this is when they say, "Let's go and visit Aldus." And so they come in droves and take a seat, with mouths agape, "like leeches that will not let go until they are full of blood."[258] I say nothing of those who come to read their works to me, some in verse, others something in prose that they actually want to be printed in our type and published by us; not only that, this work is usually in a crude and uncorrected state because they find the labor and time involved in polishing it to be too much trouble. They do not accept that there must be flaws in a poem "that has been released without much time for thought or many changes, and one that has not been brought to complete perfection by ten revisions."[259]

I have finally begun to rescue myself from these very trouble- 4
some interruptions. For I do not reply at all to those who write to me when their letter contains nothing of significance, or, if it has some import, I do so with the utmost brevity. I do not behave like this out of arrogance or contempt, but so that I may spend what time I have in publishing fine books. And so I ask that no one be annoyed at me for this or take it differently from how it is meant. As for those who visit us to pay their respects or for some other reason, we have seen to it that they should be warned against con-

lucubrationes nostras, curavimus admonendos epigrammate, quod quasi aliquod edictum videre licet supra ianuam cubiculi nostri, his verbis:

5 Quisquis es, rogat te Aldus etiam atque etiam ut siquid est quod a se velis perpaucis agas, deinde actutum abeas — nisi tanquam Hercules, defesso Atlante, veneris suppositurus humeros. Semper enim erit quod et tu agas et quotquot huc attulerint pedes.

Id ipsum et hic propterea inseruimus ut magis magisque innotescat.

6 Sunt tamen multi et Graece et Latine docti, qui frequentando aedes nostras Herculem, mihi suppetias veniendo, sedulo agunt. Ex quibus tu, Naugeri excellentissime, hisce Marci Tullii de praeceptis oratoriis deque dicendi copia et studio eloquentiae libris, accuratissime cum antiquis exemplaribus conferendo, recognoscendis, vel Atlas requiescente me factus es; idemque nunc in illius orationibus et in divinis de philosophia libris assidue atque adeo feliciter facis ut brevi et correctissimi ab iisque qui passim habentur longe alii exire possint in manus studiosorum.

7 Taceo quam diligenter, quam ingeniose, quam docte cum alios prosa oratione ex bonis codicibus indefessus emendaveris libros et penes te habeas,[8] tum praecipue optimos quosque poetarum quos mihi, quae tua est humanitas, qui tuus amor erga bonas literas, daturum te, cum publicare eos excusos typis nostris voluero, benignissime polliceris. Immo saepe etiam instas, sic inquiens, 'Alde, quid facis? Cur non petis a me Vergilium, Horatium, Tibullum,

tinually bothering us from now on or from interrupting so annoyingly our labors and our studies. For above our bedroom door they can see an inscription, rather like a proclamation, that reads as follows:

> Whoever you are, Aldus insists on asking you to state whatever you want from him as briefly as possible, and then immediately to leave—unless, that is, you have come, like Hercules, when Atlas was exhausted, to shoulder the load.[260] For there will always be something that you and all the many others that have made their way here can do. 5

We have included these words here too so that the message will become more widely known.

Nevertheless, there are many scholars, learned in both Greek and Latin, who are eager to play the part of Hercules and help me when they frequent our establishment. These include you, my most excellent Navagero. In reviewing the text of these books on the principles of rhetoric and the rich style of speaking and the pursuit of eloquence, you collated them most carefully against ancient manuscripts, and so became even Atlas himself, while I rested. And at the present moment you are working so assiduously and successfully on Cicero's speeches and his divine books on philosophy[261] that it will not be long before scholars have them in their hands, with a text that is purged of errors and very different from those that are now in circulation everywhere. 6

I say nothing of the care, brilliance and erudition with which you have tirelessly corrected, on the basis of good manuscripts, other prose works that you have in your possession. And the same is true, though even more so, of all the best poets, whom you most generously promise to give to me when I wish to print them in our type and publish them—such is your kindness and love of good letters! Indeed you often even press me hard, saying, "Aldus, what's up with you? Why don't you ask me for Vergil, Horace, Tibullus, 7

Ovidium et alios quosdam? Vix credas quam sint penes me emendati ex antiquis codicibus.'

8 Quamobrem sic me tibi devinxisti ut te non secus amem quam me ipsum, tibique aeque ac mihi longissimam vitam exoptem. Nam, cum adeo iuvenis tantus et prosa et carmine evaseris ut te vel antiquis qui utroque in genere summa cum laude elaborarunt fere aequaveris, non dubito quin futurus sis maximum decus et gloria nostrorum temporum, et una cum Bembo nostro 'magnae spes altera Romae.'

9 Etsi non me fugit haec te, qui tuus est pudor, non libenter audire, tamen, quia scio me vera dicere et te abs te cognosci quam optime, 'atque illud γνῶθι σεαυτόν non ad arrogantiam minuendam solum esse dictum, verum etiam ut bona nostra norimus,' sic tibi de te loqui volui multorum exemplo et doctorum virorum.

10 Et ut taceam caeteros et Graecos et Latinos qui hoc ipsum factitarunt, Plinius iunior in panegyrico illo ingeniosissimo ac divino quem initurus consulatum Traiano imperatori dixit frequenti senatu summas illius laudes coram ipso dicere dignissimum accommodatissimumque esse existimavit, quod et verissimas esse illas certo sciret et principem suarum virtutum maxime conscium. Fuit enim Traianus non solum imperator, sed et homo omnium optimus; unde et nunc inter creandum imperatorem hoc illi primum imprecantur: 'Sis felicior Augusto et melior Traiano.'

11 Adde quod id est huiusmodi nostrarum vel epistolarum vel praefationum genus, ut sic licere nobis vel ea ratione videatur, quod, etsi uni privatim videmur scribere, publice tamen iisque

Ovid and some others? You would scarcely believe the purity of the text of these poets that I have in my possession on the basis of ancient manuscripts."

In this way you have bound us so closely together that I love you as I love myself and I wish that we both enjoy the longest of lives. For you have turned out to be such a talented young man in both prose and verse that you almost match even those men of antiquity who worked in both areas with the highest distinction. I do not doubt, therefore, that you will be a most glorious adornment of our times and, along with our own Bembo,[262] will be "a second hope for mighty Rome."[263] 8

I am well aware that your modesty makes you uncomfortable to hear such words, but I know that I am telling the truth and that you know yourself as well as anyone can "and that the point of the expression 'know thyself' was not only that we should be less arrogant but also that we should be aware of our good qualities,"[264] and this was why I wished to talk to you on your being an example for many learned men. 9

To say nothing of all the other Greek and Roman writers who did this very thing, Pliny the Younger thought that it was very appropriate and fitting to speak of Trajan's great achievements in the presence of the emperor himself, when he delivered that brilliant and divinely inspired panegyric before a packed senate as he was about to take up the consulship. Pliny knew for certain that these achievements were real and that the emperor was himself especially aware of his own virtues. Trajan was not only emperor but also the finest possible human being. This is why even now, when the emperor is being appointed, the first words addressed to him are "May you be more lucky than Augustus and more virtuous than Trajan."[265] 10

The nature of these epistles or prefaces of ours is such that it is permitted for us to speak in this way[266] since, although we seem to be writing privately to one person, we are actually writing to the 11

omnibus scribimus qui nostra haec amice legerint. Ob eam quoque causam licere nobis arbitramur ut ei ad quem scribimus non nihil quasi argumentum dicamus de iis libris in quibus huiusmodi vel epistolas vel praefationes praeponimus, non ut ipsum doceamus (arrogantis esset id quidem), sed ut et tueatur nostra et sit eorundem iudex, et qui nesciunt (semper enim prodesse volumus) id discant e nobis.

12 Quamobrem idem et hic faciendum censuimus et te, Naugeri doctissime, iudicem elegimus, cum propter alia, tum etiam quod omnia quae his libris de ratione dicendi tractantur 'sic teneas ut digitos unguesque tuos.' Debemus enim quae publicanda elucubramus iis recitare vel scribere qui possint, si bona sunt, laudare, sin mala, reprehendere, ut olim Quintilio poemata recitabantur, qui, cum aliquid non probaret 'Corrige, sodes, hoc,' aiebat, 'et hoc.'

13 Laudandus igitur Peripateticus ille Phormio prudenterque fecisse existimandus est, quod coram Annibale de officio imperatoris et de omni re militari disputaverit, non ut illum doceret (nunquam enim tantum insaniisset Phormio), sed ut Poenus vel delectaretur ea audiens quorum esset peritissimus (praesertim si copiose, ornate, docte a philosopho dicerentur) vel ut iudicaret potius an perite ea de re disputatum esset; rustice contra et inhumaniter fecisse Annibal (semper enim fuisse dicitur insuavis et difficilis), qui, cum Phormionem audisset, et caeteri qui interfuerant, vehementer delectati, quaesivissent quidnam ipse de illo philosopho iudicaret,

public at large and to all those who will read these works of ours in a friendly frame of mind. For this reason too we think that in these books with such letters or prefaces it is permitted for us to say something about the books themselves, making a case for them, as it were, to the addressee. The reason is not to instruct him (that would be quite arrogant) but to allow him to be an advocate for our work and be a judge of it; another reason is to give those who are ignorant of the subject (for we always wish to be of help) the opportunity to learn from us.

This is why we thought the same should be done here as well, 12
and we chose you, most learned Navagero, as judge, for many reasons, but especially because you know "as well as you know your fingers and nails."[267] all that is dealt with in these books about rhetoric. For when we contemplate publishing the product of our long hours of study, we ought to read it out or submit it in writing to those who can praise it if it is good and find fault with it if it is bad, just as once poems were read out to Quintilius, who, when he did not approve of something, would say, "Correct this, please—and this!"[268]

We should praise, therefore, the Peripatetic Phormio and judge 13
that he acted wisely when he argued about the duties of a commander and about the whole of warfare in the presence of Hannibal, not with the purpose of instructing him (for Phormio would never have been so mad), but so that the Carthaginian either would take pleasure in listening to those topics in which he was expert, particularly if the philosopher was expounding them with eloquence, style and erudition, or would pass judgment on whether the arguments on the topic had been presented knowledgeably.[269] However, Hannibal must be judged to have acted rather boorishly and cruelly (for he was always disagreeable and intransigent); after he had listened to Phormio and was asked by all the others present, who had taken great pleasure in what Phormio had said, what

responderit multos se deliros senes saepe vidisse, sed qui magis quam Phormio deliraret vidisse neminem.

14 Quod contumeliosum responsum tantopere probari a M. Tullio miror, atque eo magis quod non propterea delirare Phormionem visum esse ait quia inepte aut indocte de re militari praecepta narraverit, sed tantum quia Annibali, 'cuius nomen erat magna apud omnes gloria' . . . 'quique tot annos de imperio cum populo Romano omnium gentium victore certaverat' cum potius delirus vere fuisset Phormio, si apud rusticos et id genus alios qui non intelligerent de re militari disputavisset; quemadmodum si surdis quispiam suaviter canat aut narret fabulam, vel si coram caecis in numerum quis quam optime ludat aut manuum celeritate praestigiatoriam agat.

15 Tu autem, mi Naugeri, haec tibi dici a nobis facile patieris, quod simul et doctissimus sis et humanissimus, tum etiam quia, cum tibi sic dicuntur, omnibus dicuntur in quorum manus haec nostra pervenerint. Quamobrem leges tu quidem quae breviter de his libris quasi argumenta scribuntur; et leges non, ut Phormionem Annibal, contumeliose — barbarum id quidem — sed benigne, ut soles, me, cum ea legeris, dimissurus. Ea vero sunt haec.

16 In primo et secundo libro *Rhetoricorum ad C. Herennium,* et non nihil in tertio, de inventione, prima ac maxima parte rhetorices, tractatur. Primus exordium, narrationem, divisionem et pauca quaedam de confirmatione et confutatione continet. Secundus

he himself thought about the philosopher, he replied that he had often seen mad old men, but never one more mad than Phormio.[270]

I am surprised that this insulting reply won such approval from Cicero, and all the more so as he says that he did not think Phormio was mad because the principles of warfare that he expounded were foolish or stupid, but only because he expounded them to Hannibal, "whose name held great glory in the minds of all"[271] and "who had engaged in a power struggle for so many years with the Romans, who were conquerors of the whole world."[272] Rather, Phormio would have been truly mad if he had argued his case on warfare before an audience of peasants and others of this ilk who had no understanding of the subject. This is the same as someone singing sweetly or telling a story to the deaf or as someone using all his skill to play dice[273] against the blind or performing magical tricks by sleight of hand before a similar audience. 14

My dear Navagero, because of your erudition and courtesy you will not at all mind that what follows is addressed by me to you. For what I am saying to you I am also saying to all those who will have a copy of these efforts of ours. You are about to read the topics of these books, given in brief form, like summaries. And yet you will have no intention, after reading them, of dismissing me with an insult, as Hannibal did Phormio (that was a cruel thing to do), but will let me go with your usual kind-spiritedness. Here are the topics of the books. 15

The first and second books of the *Rhetorica ad Herennium*, and to some extent the third, handle the topic of devising the subject matter of a speech (*inventio*). This is the first and most important part of rhetoric. The first book deals with the introductory part of a speech (*exordium*), then with the statement of the facts of the case and of what is at issue (*narratio*), then how the subject matter should be arranged (*divisio*), and then, to a small degree, with proofs (*confirmatio*) and rebuttals (*confutatio*). The second book sets 16

reliquas inventionis partes, et quemadmodum ad omnem iudicialem causam inventionem rerum accommodari oporteret ostendit.

17 Tertius inveniendarum rerum quae pertinent ad causas deliberativas et demonstrativas, rationem absolvit; hinc quomodo quae invenimus disponamus atque in ordinem redigamus, et quibus rebus ad dicendum pronuntiatio, quibus item 'inventorum thesaurus atque omnium partium rhetorices custos, memoria' comparanda sit, docet. Quartus, reddita ratione quare praeter Graecorum consuetudinem suis author utatur exemplis, praecepta elocutionis, quae est ultima pars ex iis quinque quas in oratore esse oportet, non indiligenter tradit.

18 Primus autem liber inchoati tantum operis, exposito genere artis rhetoricae et officio et fine et materia et partibus, continet genera controversiarum et inventiones et constitutiones, deinde partes orationis et in eas omneis omnia praecepta. Et quoniam in eo caeteris de rebus distinctius dictum est, disperse autem de confirmatione et reprehensione, certi in secundo libro confirmandi et reprehendendi in singula causarum genera loci traduntur. Et quia quo pacto tractari conveniret argumentationes in primo libro accurate expositum est, in secundo tantum inventa unanquanque in rem exponuntur simpliciter sine ulla exornatione, ut ex secundo inventa ipsa, ex primo expolitio inventorum petatur.

19 Postremo, quoniam omne in causae genus argumentandi ratio tradita est, deque inventione satis dictum videtur, reliquas partes orationis quae oratori necessariae sunt se deinceps dicturum Cicero pollicetur; sed postea, mutato consilio, sic inchoatum opus

out the remaining parts of *inventio,* and demonstrates how the subject matter should be adjusted to suit the whole court case.

The third completes the method of devising material that relates to deliberative and epideictic speeches, then gives instruction on how we should arrange and order the material, how the delivery must be adapted in its expression to different situations and how memory, "the treasure house of what is supplied by *inventio,* and the guardian of all the parts of rhetoric,"[274] should be developed. After an account of why a teacher of rhetoric should use examples from his own work rather than follow the custom of Greek rhetoricians,[275] he gives in the fourth book a careful account of the principles of style, style being the last of the five elements that an orator should master.[276] 17

Book One of the incomplete work [*De inventione*], after the explanation of the nature of the art of rhetoric, its function, ends, subject matter and parts, deals with the kinds of controversies, the inventions, the definitions of what is at issue (*constitutiones*), then the parts of a speech and all the precepts that apply to all of these. And since in this book he talks about all things separately, while dealing with proofs and refutations at scattered points, in Book Two specific sections dealing with proofs and refutations for each kind of speech are given. And because he explained very carefully in the first book how one should handle argumentation, in the second book only the topics for every single matter are expounded in a simple manner without any elaboration. The result is that you will find the topics themselves in the second book, and the stylistic adornment of these in the first. 18

Finally, since the method of argumentation has been given for every kind of case and enough seems to have been said about invention, Cicero promises that he will then talk of the remaining parts of oratory that an orator needs to master. Later however, he changed his mind, and left the work in the unfinished state that we have it, because, as I suppose, he thought it unpolished and he 19

reliquit, puto, quia rude videbatur, sibique puero aut adolescentulo, ut ipse in primo libro *De oratore* testatur, exciderit. Atque ob eam causam rogatus a fratre, treis libros de omni ratione dicendi adeo doctos, ingeniosos, elegantes, copiosos composuit, ut qui in aliis libris semper omneis, in his se ipsum Cicero superaverit. Ipse etiam illos tanti faciebat, ut in epistola quadam ad Leptam haec scripserit:

> 20 *Oratorem* meum tantopere abs te probari vehementer gaudeo. Mihi quidem sic persuadeo me quicquid habuerim iudicii de dicendo in illum librum contulisse. Qui si est talis qualem tibi videri scribis, ego quoque aliquid sum; sin autem aliud, non recuso quin, quantum de illo libro, tantundem de iudicii mei fama detrahatur.

21 Hi igitur tres libri *De oratore* ea quae tribus diebus viri omnium eloquentissimi clarissimique de omni ratione dicendi vel disseruerant vel docuerant complectuntur. Quorum librorum argumenta, tum aliorum qui hoc ipso volumine continentur breviter narranda hoc ordine visa sunt.

22 In primo libro, 'ludorum Romanorum diebus, cum L. Crassus colligendi sui causa se in Thusculanum suum' cum adolescentibus C. Cotta et P. Sulpitio 'contulisset, venissetque eodem Q. Mutius Scaevola Augur, Crassi socer, et M. Antonius, homo et consiliorum in republica socius et summa cum Crasso familiaritate coniunctus.' . . . 'Primo die de temporibus illis deque universa republica, quam ob causam venerant, multum inter se usque ad extremum tempus diei collocuti dicuntur'; sed ea alibi sunt a M. Tullio mandata literis.

23 'Postero autem die, cum illi maiores natu satis quievissent atque in ambulationem ventum esset, et Scaevola, duobus spatiis tribusve factis,' quod infirmis esset pedibus, 'dixisset ut, imitantes

had let it slip from his grasp while in his boyhood or youth, as he attests in the first book of *De oratore*.[277] And for this reason, at the request of his brother, he composed a work in three books on the whole topic of rhetoric; these were so learned, brilliant, eloquent and wide ranging that Cicero, who surpassed all others in the rest of his works, in these surpassed himself. He himself even thought so well of them that in a letter to Lepta he wrote the following:[278]

> I am extremely pleased that you think so highly of my *De* 20
> *oratore*.[279] I am indeed of the firm opinion that I have brought together in this work whatever I know and think about rhetoric. If the work matches your assessment of it, I too have some value. But if it is otherwise, I accept that the reputation of my judgment will be diminished as much as the reputation of the work itself is diminished.

These three books of *De oratore* contain what the most eloquent 21
and distinguished of men discussed or expounded on the whole theory of rhetoric in three days. I have thought it helpful to describe briefly the topics of these books as well as of the other works contained in this volume in the order that follows.

Book One is set "on the days of the *Ludi Romani*,[280] when Lu- 22
cius Crassus had taken himself for recreation to his Tusculan villa" with the youths Caius Cotta and Publius Sulpicius. "Quintus Mucius Scaevola, the augur, and father-in-law of Crassus, had come there too. So also had Marcus Antonius, who was a partner in the political plans of Crassus and was a very close friend of his."[281] "On the first day they conversed at great length right till nighttime about those critical times and the whole question of the republic, the reason that they had come there."[282] But Cicero has written about this elsewhere.

"On the second day when the older men had had sufficient rest, 23
they had gone for a stroll. Scaevola had taken two or three turns and then," because he had problems with his feet, "had said that

Socratem illum, qui est in *Phaedro* Platonis, sub platano et ipsi quiescerent,' allatis pulvinis, 'omnes in iis sedibus quae erant sub platano dicuntur consedisse. Ibi, ut ex pristino sermone relaxarentur animi omnium,' cum Crassus sermonem quendam de studio dicendi intulisset, et quaedam ab Scaevola contra ea quae dixerat Crassus comiter dicta fuissent, ab Antonio et Crasso de rhetorices materia et de iis quae oratori necessaria sunt in toto primo libro ornate copioseque disseritur.

24 Cui satis longae disputationi adfuit quidem senex Scaevola; sed quoniam in Thusculanum suum ire constituerat, sermoni qui de arte dicendi instituebatur non interfuit. Cur autem illius persona ab reliquis libris dimota sit, docet ipse Cicero in quarto libro epistolarum ad Atticum his verbis:

> Quod in his oratoriis libris quos laudas personam desyderas Scaevolae, non eam temere dimovi, sed feci idem quod in πολιτείᾳ deus ille noster Plato. Cum in Peiraeum Socrates venisset ad Cephalum, locupletem et festivum senem, quoad primus sermo ille haberetur, adest in disputando senex; deinde, cum ipse quoque commodissime locutus esset, ad rem divinam dicit se velle discedere neque postea revertitur. Credo Platonem vix putasse satis consonum fore si hominem id aetatis in tam longo sermone diutius detinuisset. Multo ego satius hoc mihi cavendum putavi in Scaevola, qui et aetate et valetudine ea, qua esse meministi, et iis honoribus ut vix satis decorum videretur eum plureis dies esse in Crassi

they should imitate Socrates in Plato's *Phaedrus* and that they too should rest under a plane tree."[283] We are told that cushions were brought and that "they all sat down in the chairs that were under the tree. In this setting, so that all of them should relax after the conversation of the day before,"[284] the whole of the first book is taken up by an eloquent and expansive discussion of Antonius and Crassus on the constituent parts of rhetoric and on those qualifications that an orator should possess. This occurs after Crassus had started to talk about the art of speaking and Scaevola had voiced some disagreement with what Crassus had said, though he did so in an amicable fashion.

The elderly Scaevola was certainly present at this fairly long 24
discussion, but since he had decided to go to his Tusculan villa, he took no part at all in the subsequent conversation, whose subject was established as the art of speaking. Cicero himself tells us in Book Four of his letters to Atticus why this character was removed from the remaining books:[285]

> As for your missing the character of Scaevola in those books of *De Oratore* that you praise, I did not lightly dispense with him. I followed the precedent in the *Republic* of our beloved and divine Plato. When Socrates had come to the Piraeus to the house of Cephalus, a wealthy and congenial old man, Cephalus took part in the discussion until the first topic was getting under way. Then, although having spoken in a most agreeable way, he says that he wishes to attend a sacrifice and never returns.[286] I think that Plato believed it would hardly have been appropriate if he had retained a man of such years any longer in such a protracted discussion. I thought that this was all the more reason that I should avoid this same inappropriateness in the case of Scaevola. For his age and ill health, which you remember well, and his civic responsibilities were such that it scarcely seemed proper for him to

Thusculano. Et erat primi libri sermo non alienus ab Scaevolae studiis. Reliqui libri τεχνολογίαν habent, ut scis; huic ioculatoriae disputationi senem illum, ut noras, interesse sane nolui.

25 Die tertio, cum iam in Thusculanum Laelii soceri sui abiisset Scaevola, et Q. Catulus senex et C. Iulius Caesar fratres e Thusculanis suis in Crassi Thusculanum ad audiendum Antonium venissent, cuius esse partes ut eo die de arte dicendi loqueretur, ab Scaevola Iulius, cum ad fratrem veniret, audiverat. In secundo quidem libro, ante meridiem, ab Antonio de inventione, dispositione, memoria, tribus de quinque quasi membris eloquentiae, interpellantibus interdum aliis vel interrogando vel approbando vel etiam addendo vel utcunque aliter videretur, doctissime agitur.

26 Et quoniam 'suavis est et vehementer saepe utilis iocus et facetiae,' haec Iulio pars, quod in eo genere aliis excelleret, consensu omnium datur. Quamobrem ille coram consumatissimis ac divinis oratoribus Antonio et Crasso, tanquam in scena gestum spectante Roscio acturus, verecunde quidem, sed, cum iam defessus esset disputando Antonius, cum perpauca adhuc restarent, peropportune se interposuit munusque suum diligenter iucundeque peragit.

27 In tertio autem, 'inclinato iam in pomeridianum tempus die,' Crassus de elocutione et actione, reliquis rhetoricae partibus, quae ei ab Antonio ex constituto relictae fuerant, disertissime et copiosissime loquitur. In his libris non ieiunas rhetorum artes, sed

> spend more days on the Tusculan estate of Crassus. Moreover, the topic of the first book was closely related to Scaevola's own interests; the remaining books are more technical, as you know, and I did not at all wish that this elderly man as you knew him should participate in this lighthearted[287] discussion.

On the third day, after Scaevola had gone off to the Tusculan 25
estate of Laelius, his father-in-law, the elderly Quintus Catulus and his half brother, Gaius Julius Caesar,[288] came from their Tusculan properties to that of Crassus in order to hear Antonius. When Julius was on his way to his brother's, he had learned from Scaevola that Antonius' role was to speak on the art of eloquence on that day. And indeed, in the second book, in the morning Antonius deals in a most learned way with invention, arrangement, and memory—three of the five constituent parts of eloquence;[289] at times the others interrupted, or asked questions or expressed their approval or offered their own opinion when they disagreed on some point or other.

And "since humor and wit is pleasing and very often useful,"[290] 26
this topic was assigned by unanimous agreement to Julius, since he surpassed all others in this area. And so, in the presence of those consummate and superlative orators, Antonius and Crassus, he took over from the former (it was as if he were going to act on stage with Roscius[291] as a spectator!). Julius did so with modesty, but, since Antonius was then tired out by the discussion and very little remained to be covered, his intervention was also extremely convenient, and he performed his task in a careful and pleasant manner.[292]

In the third book, "when the time of day was now the after- 27
noon,"[293] Crassus talks at length and with great learning on style and delivery, the remaining parts of rhetoric, which by agreement Antonius had left for him untouched. In these books Cicero seems

locupletissimos Aristotelis libros secutus videtur Cicero, idque in Crassi maxime sermone, ut hinc quoque perspici possit hoc ab eo vere in *Oratore* dictum esse: 'se oratorem, si modo sit vel quicunque sit, non ex rhetorum officinis, sed ex Academiae spatiis extitisse.'

28 In libro de claris oratoribus, qui *Brutus* dicitur, deplorata summo cum dolore morte Hortensii, quicum Cicero semper coniunctissime et amantissime vixerat sociusque et consors gloriosi laboris fuerat, enumerat quicunque usque ad sua tempora Latini oratores clari extiterant, ante tamen Graecis qui excelluerant quasi in transcursu breviter enumeratis.

29 In libro qui *Orator* appellatur, cum a Cicerone M. Brutus per literas petivisset ut quod optimum esset genus dicendi sibi ostenderet, id ille diligentissime et copiosissime fecit. Et quamvis de elocutione tantum ab Bruto requisitus videretur, nonnulla tamen de inventione, dispositione, actione, ut plenius foret opus, adiecit.

30 In *Topicis* de communibus locis, unde argumenta ducuntur, breviter quidem inter navigandum, cum etiam libros Cicero non haberet, sed docte et dilucide agitur. Exempla tamen, quod ad Trebatium iurisconsultum scribatur, ex iure sumuntur.

In *Partitionibus* in omne causarum genus praecepta colliguntur.

31 In libro qui *De optimo oratorum genere* inscribitur, cum falsam Cicero eorum vellet opinionem ostendere qui eos solos Attice dicere contendebant qui tenui quodam et sicco scribendi genere uterentur, Aeschinis et Demosthenis inter se contrarias orationes convertit, ut, cum hi Attici omnium consensu haberentur neque

to have followed the rich material in the works of Aristotle and not some jejune handbooks on the arts of orators; and this is especially true in what Crassus says. So this shows too the truth of what he said in *Orator:* "Whatever talents I have as an orator have come, not from rhetoricians' workshops, but from the spacious grounds of the Academy."[294]

In the book on famous orators, entitled *Brutus,* Cicero begins by 28
lamenting with deep sorrow the death of Hortensius, to whom Cicero has been most close and most dear, and who was his colleague and fellow practitioner in this glorious profession. Then he goes through all the Latin orators who had won fame, right up to his own times, after first listing briefly, almost in passing, those Greeks who had excelled in oratory.

In the book entitled *Orator,* written in response to a request 29
from Marcus Brutus in a letter, to show him what was the best style of oratory, Cicero treated this topic in a very careful and expansive way. Although Brutus' request seemed to be limited to the topic of style, Cicero added some remarks on invention, arrangement and delivery to fill out the work.

Because Cicero wrote the *Topics* when he was at sea and did not 30
even have his books with him, his treatment of the common topics from which proofs are drawn is brief, but it is erudite and clear. However, the examples are taken from law, since the work is addressed to Trebatius, a jurisconsult.

In his *Partitiones* precepts for every kind of case are gathered together.

In the book entitled *On the Best Kind of Orator* Cicero wanted to 31
show that those who claimed that only those writing in a thin and dry style were practitioners of the Attic style were quite wrong. He revealed how clearly they were mistaken by translating the speeches of Aeschines and Demosthenes that they delivered against each other;[295] for although everyone agreed that these orators were

tenui solum genere, sed amplissimo etiam ac mediocri nonnunquam uterentur, manifestus illorum error deprehenderetur. Sed ipsae orationes ad nos non pervenerunt; id quod habetur praefatio est quaedam.

32 Sed quoniam sunt qui libros de arte rhetorica ad Herennium Ciceronis esse contendant, non ab re facere mihi videor si quod ipse ea de re sentiam hoc loco breviter disputavero.

33 Qui librorum *Ad Herennium* authorem esse Ciceronem volunt, duorum alterum fateantur necesse est, ut aut antequam quae inchoata atque rudia puero aut adolescentulo sibi excidisse ait, aut post, Cicero illos composuerit.

34 Ante non puto dicturos quia, si puer aut adolescentulus illa imperfecta, hoc est duos illos libros de inventione, composuit, quando hos ad Herennium componere potuit? Num puerulus? Quis hoc credat? At a viro etiam maturae aetatis ac patrefamilias et philosopho compositi illi videntur, id quod ex ipso authore facile est cognoscere, cum et haec dicit, 'Etsi negotiis familiaribus impediti vix satis otium studio suppeditare possumus, et id ipsum quod datur otii libentius in philosophia consumere consuevimus,' et haec, quae habentur in fine quarti libri:

35 Nam et simul libenter exercemur propter amicitiam, cuius initium cognatio fecit, caetera philosophiae ratio confirmavit; et nobis non diffidimus, propterea quod et aliquantulum processimus, et alia meliora sunt quae multo intensius

Atticists, Cicero showed that they used not only the simple style, but even the grand style as well as the middle style. (The actual translations of the two speeches have not come down to us; what we have is just a preface, as it were.)

Since some persons claim that Cicero is the author of the books on the art of rhetoric addressed to Herennius, I do not think it out of place if at this point I offer briefly in argument my own opinion on the matter.[296] 32

Those who wish Cicero to be the author of the books *Ad Herennium* must admit one of two possibilities: Cicero composed them either before or after the work [*De inventione*] which he says he let go of, in an incomplete and unpolished state, when he was boy or a youth.[297] 33

I do not think they will say "before." For if he composed those imperfect works, the two books on invention, when he was a boy or a youth, when could he have written the books addressed to Herennius? Surely not when he was a little boy! Who can believe this? But in fact these books to Herennius appear to have been composed by a man of mature years, who was head of a household and a philosopher, as one can readily see from the author himself when he says the following: "My family responsibilities prevent me from finding enough leisure time for study, and what leisure time I have found I usually have preferred to devote to philosophy."[298] Consider also what can be found at the end of book four: 34

> For we enjoy practicing our skills together because of our friendship; this sprang out of our being related by blood, and has been strengthened in other respects by the study of philosophy. We do not lack self-confidence; for we have made some progress and there are other better things in life that we strive for with much more intensity. Even if we have 35

petimus in vita. Et etiamsi non pervenimus in dicendo quo volumus, parva pars vitae perfectissimae desyderetur.

Impediri negotiis familiaribus et vix propterea esse otium ad studendum, et siquid superesset otii in philosophia consumere consuevisse, tum parvam vitae perfectissimae partem desyderari non puero, sed viro conveniunt et patrifamilias.

36 Adde quod, cum consuevisse dicit quod daretur otii in philosophia consumere, praetermisso studio eloquentiae, diu videtur philosophiae dedisse operam. Praeterea in iis ipsis libris de inventione fecisset aliquam eorum qui sunt ad Herennium mentionem, cur scilicet de arte rhetorica iterum scriberet, quemadmodum in libris oratoriis eorum meminit quae inchoata atque rudia sibi puero aut adolescentulo excidisse refert. Non ante igitur hos ad Herennium quam illos de inventione libros composuit.

37 Post autem si dixerint, parum diligenter videntur eam rem consyderasse, quia, si ita sit, sequeretur politiores et magis cultos esse hos *Ad Herennium* quam illi ipsi quos *De inventione* composuit, quod et doctior et plures natus annos eos elucubrasset. Sed longe est secus. Rudes quodammodo hi videbuntur, si iis quos *De inventione* composuit comparentur. Et quanquam sunt docti, tamen longissimo distant intervallo a divina illa M. Tullii eloquentia; immo, siquis accuratius consyderaverit, plurima in his *Ad Herennium* libris dure et ieiune dicta deprehendet.

not made the progress in public speaking that we wanted, that would be only a small part of the perfect life that we lack.[299]

The impediment of family responsibilities, the difficulty in finding time for study, and his practice of devoting what leisure time he does have to philosophy, the lack of only a small part of the perfect life—all these fit a grown man and one who is head of a household, not a mere boy.

An additional point is that when he says that he has been in 36
the habit of leaving the study of rhetoric aside and devoting what leisure he has to philosophy, he seems to have been giving philosophy his close attention for a long time. Moreover in these books on invention he would have made some mention of the *Rhetorica ad Herennium,* no doubt on why he was writing again on the art of rhetoric, just as he mentions in *De oratore* those books that he says he let go of in an incomplete and unpolished state when he was a boy or youth. The conclusion must be that he did not compose the *Rhetorica ad Herennium* before those books on invention.

But if those proponents of Ciceronian authorship say that he 37
composed the *Rhetorica* after the books *On Invention,* I do not think that that they have considered the situation with sufficient care. For, if this were the case, it would follow that the work addressed to Herennius would be more elegant and polished than those books that he composed *On Invention,* because he would have expended his energies on it when he was older and more learned. But the truth of the matter is quite different. The *Rhetorica* will seem somewhat crude when compared with the books on invention. And although it is a learned work, it is very far removed from the divine eloquence of Cicero. In fact, whoever looks more carefully will find in these books addressed to Herennius many examples of harshness and aridity in its style.

38 Adde quod in libris *De oratore*, ubi inchoatorum a se rhetoricorum meminit, et horum *Ad Herennium* meminisset, atque eo magis quod perfecta et absoluta sint omniaque artis rhetoricae praecepta contineant, ut ipse author ostendit his verbis, 'Et viam quam sequamur habemus, propterea quod in his libris nihil praeteritum est rhetoricae praeceptionis.'

39 Ergo *Ad Herennium* libri, si nec ante nec post quam illi *De inventione* a Cicerone compositi sunt, non sunt Ciceronis. Nam post divinos illos oratorios *Ad Herennium* libros compositos dicere amentia est.

40 Illud praeterea non praeterierim, existimandum esse Hieronymum et Priscianum et alios qui aut illa aetate aut post extiterunt huius rei investigandae minimum sategisse, sed alterum alterius indiligenter, ut solet accidere, errorem secutos.

41 Quis autem illorum author fuerit, 'grammatici certant et adhuc sub iudice lis est.' Sunt tamen qui authorem fuisse dicant M. Gallionem, propterea quod in libro quodam *Rhetoricorum ad Herennium* antiquissimo qui dicitur esse Romae in bibliotheca Palatina sic est titulus: 'M. Gallionis rhetoricorum ad C. Herennium liber primus,' ubi 'Gallionis' deletum esse aiunt, ita tamen ut legi possit, et supra Gallionis scriptum 'T' cum binis utrinque punctis, inde 'Ciceronis.' Quod si ita est, puto eum qui delevit (quod existimarit perperam scriptum Gallionis), deceptum cum praenomine M., scilicet quod idem in utroque est titulo, tum similitudine quadam Gallionis et Ciceronis, apposuisse pro Gallionis T. Ciceronis.

42 Quam quidem rem cum aut ipse videro aut ab alio audivero cui fidem habeam, tunc credam, curaboque Gallioni librum suum quo

Moreover, Cicero would have mentioned the *Rhetorica ad Heren-* 38
nium in *De oratore,* where he mentions the books on rhetoric that he left incomplete, all the more so because the *Rhetorica* is a complete and finished work, containing all the principles of the art of rhetoric, as the author of the *Rhetorica* shows in the following words: "And we know the way to follow since no principle of rhetoric has been left out."[300]

The conclusion then is that the *Rhetorica* could not have been 39
composed by Cicero either before or after *On Invention* and is therefore not by him. For it is sheer madness to say that the *Rhetorica* was composed after the marvelous and magnificent *De oratore.*[301]

I should not pass over this point either, that we must suppose 40
that Jerome and Priscian[302] and others who lived at that time or later, had not the slightest interest in investigating this question. As often happens, one carelessly repeated the errors of his predecessor.

As to the identity of the author of the *Rhetorica* "philologists vie 41
with each other and the dispute awaits resolution."[303] Some say that the author was Marcus Gallio because in a very ancient manuscript of the *Rhetorica ad Herennium,* said to be in Rome in the library of the Palatine Library,[304] the title reads "The first book of the *Rhetorica ad Gaium Herennium* by M. Gallio." It is said that "Gallio" has been erased, but can still be read as such, and that above the name is written "T"[305] with two points on each side of the letter, followed by "Cicero." If this is the case, I think that whoever made the erasure (thinking that "Gallio" was an error) was led astray by the first name M(arcus), the same in both names, and because of some similarity between the names of Gallio and Cicero, wrote in "T. Cicero" for "Gallio."[306]

I shall believe this only when I actually see it for myself or hear 42
it from someone I can trust, and I shall see to it then that Gallio will be reunited with that book of his from which he has been

tot secula vel iniuria temporum vel ignorantia scriptorum privatus est restituendum. Cuiuscunque tamen fuerit liber, ei fatendum est multum Ciceronis hos quos diximus de inventione libros ad ea quae scripserit praecepta contulisse.

43 Gallionem autem hunc eum crediderim ad quem Ovidius in quarto libro *De Ponto* consolatoriam scripsit epistolam ob mortem uxoris; cuius epistolae hoc est initium:

> Gallio, crimen erit vix excusabile nobis
> carmine te nomen non habuisse meo . . .

Doctum etiam illum fuisse his eiusdem epistolae ostenditur carminibus:

> Sed neque solari prudentem stultior ausim
> verbaque doctorum nota referre tibi.

44 Haec habui, mi Naugeri, quae super his dicerem pro tempore. Habeo enim assidue plus negotii quam fortasse alius quisquam vel occupatissimus. Adsit Deus qui me et his malis et gravissimis quibus premor molestiis eripiat, ac velit ut, dum amissis agris et ipse haec queror:

> En quo discordia civeis
> perduxit miseros! en queis consevimus agros!

aut haec:

> Vivi pervenimus, advena nostri,
> quod nunquam veriti sumus, ut possessor agelli
> diceret: 'Haec mea sunt, veteres migrate coloni,'

separated for so many centuries, either through the unjust ravages of time or the ignorance of scribes. Yet, whoever wrote it will have to admit that Cicero's books on invention contributed much to the precepts that he offered in his work.

I might believe that this Gallio is the person to whom Ovid 43
wrote a letter of consolation on the death of his wife in Book Four of his *Letters from the Black Sea.*[307] It begins:

> Gallio, it will be an inexcusable crime on my part
> that your name has not appeared in my poetry.

That Gallio was learned is shown by these verses of the same poem:

> But, foolish as I am, I would not dare to offer consolation to such a wise man as you
> and to bring to your attention scholars' words that are known to you.

My dear Navagero, this is all that my situation allows me to say 44
on these works. For I have always more to do than anyone else, even the busiest of men. May God be with me to snatch me from these evil and most terrible misfortunes that oppress me. When I have lost my estate and make this plaint,

> See to where civil strife had brought its wretched citizens.
> See for whom we have sown our fields[308]

or

> We have lived to see what we never feared would happen:
> an incomer saying, as the holder of our little farm,
> "This belongs to me; begone, you tenants of old!"[309]

tu quoque divinus poeta — es enim alter ab illo — consolans compatrem tuum mihi aut haec canas:

> Fortunate senex, etiam tua rura manebunt,
> et longo quoque servitio te exire licebit
> et cito praesenteis alibi cognoscere divos

aut tale aliquid. Quod cum fuero adeptus, saxo quod tot annos indefessus volvo in montis apicem tandem perducto et collocato, 'recubans sub tegmine fagi' et ipse queam dicere, 'Deus nobis haec otia fecit.'

Vale, ingens decus Musarum.

B

Aldus lectori s.

45 Illud hic subiungere libuit, considerandum diligentius utrum in epistola ad Leptam, cum scripsit Cicero '*Oratorem* meum tantopere a te probari vehementer gaudeo,' etc., id dixerit *De libris oratoriis* ad Quintum fratrem, an de eo libro quem ad Brutum scripsit, qui quaesiverat quodnam eloquentiae genus Cicero probaret maxime, et quale ei videretur illud cui nihil addi posset, quod summum et perfectissimum iudicaret; cui libro *Oratori* inditum est nomen. Idque quoniam in praefatione nostra ad Naugerium de tribus illis de oratore libris dixisse Ciceronem scripsimus, cum potius de eo ipso libro ad Brutum illud dixisse videatur.

may God will it that you, who are also a divine poet (for you are second after him),[310] may console me your dear friend with these verses or something similar:

Happy old man, your fields will still be yours
and you will be able to leave your long period of servitude
and find elsewhere gods to be there to help you.[311]

When I have achieved this, finally dragging up and placing on the mountain top the rock that I have unwearyingly been rolling for so many years,[312] "may I recline in the shade of a beech tree"[313] and be able to say, "The gods granted us this peaceful abode."[314]

Farewell to you, the great adornment of the Muses.

B[315]

Aldus to his reader.

I would like to make the following addition at this point. It must 45
be considered more carefully whether in the letter to Lepta Cicero's words "I am very happy that you think so highly of my *Orator,* etc." refer to the books on oratory addressed to his brother Quintus [*De oratore*] or to the work that he addressed to Brutus. The latter had asked him what style of eloquence Cicero most approved of and what did he think was the supreme and perfect style to which nothing could be added. This work was called *Orator.* In our preface to Navagero we wrote that Cicero was speaking of the three books on *De oratore,* but he seems to have been referring to the book addressed to Brutus.

: XXV :

A

Aldus lectori s.

1 Illud significandum censui, amice et studiose lector, ordinem librorum Columellae alium esse in hoc volumine quam in aliis, idque Iucundi nostri diligentia, qui primus eum librum qui tertius erat cuius principium est

> Cum de cultu agrorum abunde primo libro praecepisse videamur, non intempestiva erit arborum virgultorumque cura, quae vel maxima pars habetur rei rusticae

non adnumerandum libris Columellae ad Sylvinum deprehendit, tribus praecipue rationibus. Quarum prima est, quia hic idem est cum eo qui statim sequitur quique incipit:

> 'Hactenus arvorum cultus,' ut ait praestantissimus poeta. Nihil enim prohibet nos, Publi Sylvine, de iisdem rebus dicturos celeberrimi carminis auspicari principia. Sequitur arborum cura, quae pars rei rusticae vel maxima est.

2 Ecce uterque est de arboribus, sed is cuius principium est[9] 'Hactenus arvorum cura' et maior multo est et magis cultus.

: XXV :

Cato, Varro, Columella, Palladius, On Agriculture
(May 1514)

A

Aldus to the reader, greetings.

My dear and studious reader, I think I have to point out that the order of Columella's books is different in this volume than in other editions, and that this is owed to the diligence of our beloved Giocondo.[316] The third book begins as follows: 1

> Since I think I have given copious instructions on the cultivation of fields in the first book, it will be most appropriate to deal now with the care of trees and shrubs, which is even regarded as the most important part of farm work.

Giocondo was the first to realize that this book should not be counted as part of Columella's work that is addressed to Silvinus. He had three particular reasons, the first being that this begins in the same way as the immediately following book, which starts in this way:

> "So much for the cultivation of the fields,"[317] as our most outstanding poet says. For, since we are going to talk on the same topic, nothing should prevent us, Publius Silvinus, from starting with the opening of that most famous book. Arboriculture now follows, perhaps the most important part of farm work.[318]

Note that the subject of both is trees, but the one beginning "so much for the cultivation[319] of the fields" is much weightier and 2

Secunda, quia in eo ipso libro quem non adnumerandum diximus Columellae hisce de re rustica libris nusquam nominatur P. Sylvinus, ut fit in aliis omnibus. Tertia, quia, si ille liber iis qui sunt ad Sylvinum inseratur, accusandus foret author indiligentia, qui de arboribus pomiferis, de cythiso, de olivis et aliis quibusdam et in hoc et in eo, qui nunc quintus est, tanquam oblitus tractaverit.

3 Praeterea quia in principio eius libri qui incipit 'Quae fere consummabant, P. Sylvine, ruris exercendi colendique scientiam quaeque pecuariae negotiationis exigebat ratio, septem memoravimus libris,' non septem, sed octo foret dicendum. Tum aliis in locis numerus librorum qui apud authorem legitur esset falsus; quia si illum, ubi non est nomen Sylvini, addideris, in eo libro qui villicus inscribitur quemque undecimum esse librum ipse dicit his verbis: 'Et hoc undecimum praeceptum rusticationis,' foret scribendum duodecimum, sed perperam. Nam, cum alius alium librum semper citet, ut facile est quaerenti cognoscere, necesse est eum esse ordinem librorum qui hic habetur et ubi author septimum dicit, septimum, ubi nonum, nonum, ubi undecimum, undecimum esse oportere.

4 Ipsum autem librum in fine totius operis curavimus imprimendum, ut et illum quis, cum libuerit, possit legere. An autem Columellae sit an alterius, tum qua re potius Columellae esse videatur, videant alii; nobis enim non erat otium. Vale.

more polished. The second reason is that in the very book that we have said should not be included in Columella's work on farming there is no mention of Publius Silvinus, as there is in all the others. The third reason is that our author would need to be accused of carelessness if this book is inserted into those that are addressed to Silvinus. For out of forgetfulness apparently he would then have dealt with fruit trees, medic, olives and some other trees on two occasions, in this book as well as in the one that is now the fifth.

Moreover, in the beginning of the book that starts, "we have 3
mentioned in seven books all that for the most part encompassed the science of working and cultivating the land as well as all the demands of stock raising,"[320] we would have to say "eight" instead of "seven." What is more, the numbers of the books that are mentioned in other places by the author would be wrong. In that book which is entitled "The Farm Manager" Columella himself says that this is Book Eleven in these words, "And this eleventh precept of agriculture."[321] But if one includes in the work the book that lacks an address to Silvinus, we would have to write "twelfth." But this would be wrong. For if you look at how different authors cite different books, as you can easily do, the conclusion must be that the order of the books is the one in this edition, and where Columella refers to the seventh, ninth or eleventh book these numbers are correct.

We have undertaken to print the book in question at the end of 4
the whole work so that anyone can read it whenever he wishes. But as for whether the author is Columella or another person, or why it would seem to be by Columella rather than anyone else, let others decide. I do not have the time to engage in this. Farewell.

B

Aldus lectori s.

5 Iam pridem decrevi, quacunque in re possum, prodesse studiosis; quam ob rem perquam utile visum est futurum, si hic de diebus, et qui in viginti quatuor partes et qui in duodecim dividuntur, tum de horis quae sunt apud Palladium non nihil dicamus, atque eo magis, quod a perquam paucis aetatis nostrae hominibus intelligantur.

6 Dierum duo sunt genera: alii naturales, alii civiles. Naturales, quibus nunc passim utimur, constant quatuor et viginti partibus aequalibus ab occasu solis ad alterum occasum, quae horae appellantur et Graece *ἰσημεριναί*, Latine aequinoctiales dicuntur. Civiles autem ab ortu solis ad occasum constant duodecim partibus inaequalibus, quae Graece *καιρικαί*, Latine temporales seu, quod idem est, vulgares nominantur.

7 Atque hae duodecim partes hybernis solstitiis brevissimae sunt et tertia parte minores quam aequinoctiales, aestivis autem longissimae eademque tertia maiores quam illae et, quod sequens est, vincunt hybernas duabus quartis sive, quod idem est, dimidio. Id quod significare voluit Virgilius eo versu, 'Anne novum tardis sydus te mensibus addas,' id est Iunio et Iulio, quibus horae longissimae sunt. At, vere sole Arietem, autumno Libram ingrediente, pares sunt aequinoctialibus, eaedemque ab hyberno solstitio ad aestivum cum die crescente crescunt, ab aestivo autem ad hybernum cum eodem decrescente decrescunt.

B[322]

Aldus to the reader, greetings.

I have long been of the mind to assist students in whatever way I 5
can. And so I thought it would be extremely useful if we said something here about the days, both those that are divided into twenty-four parts and those that are divided into twelve, and also about the hours that are in Palladius.[323] And there is all the more reason for doing so, as very few men of our era understand them.

There are two kinds of days; some are called natural, others 6
civil. The natural days, which we now adopt everywhere, consist of twenty-four equal parts, called hours, that extend from one sunset to the next. The hours are called "standard" (ἰσημεριναί in Greek and *aequinoctiales* in Latin). However, the civil hours, which extend from daybreak to sunset, consist of twelve that vary in length, called καιρικαί in Greek and in Latin *temporales,* or, which is the same, *vulgares.*

These twelve parts are briefest at the winter solstice and are 7
shorter by a third than the standard hours, while they are longest at the summer solstice and greater, also by a third, than standard hours. And so it follows that these hours at the summer solstice exceed in length the hours at the winter solstice by two-fourths or, what is the same, by one half. This is what Vergil was referring to in the verse "or whether you add yourself as a new star to the slow-moving months,"[324] meaning June and July, when the civil hours are longest. But in spring when the sun enters Aries and in autumn when it enters Libra, they are the same length as the standard hours; then from the winter solstice to the summer solstice they increase in length as the days grow longer, while from the summer solstice to the winter solstice they diminish in length as the days grow shorter.

8 Et quoniam singuli dies civiles ac noctes totius anni horis duodecim continentur, sexta diei hora semper est meridies, et prima incipit oriente sole, duodecima eodem occidente finitur. Verbi gratia mense Martio, cum hae ipsae horae temporales fere pares sunt aequinoctialibus, prima hora diei civilis est eadem cum tertia decima diei naturalis, secunda eadem cum quarta decima, tertia cum quinta decima, quarta cum sexta decima, quinta cum decima septima, sexta cum decima octava, septima cum decima nona, octava cum vigesima, nona cum vigesima prima, decima cum vigesima secunda, undecima cum vigesima tertia, duodecima cum vigesima quarta. Illud igitur in sacris literis, 'A sexta autem hora usque ad nonam tenebrae factae sunt super universam terram,' intelligendum est a decima octava hora usque ad vigesimam primam diei naturalis, ut nunc horae aguntur. Nam apud veteres solaria in horas tam noctis quam diei temporales, non aequinoctiales dividebantur.

9 Mense autem Iunio, cum horae quam longissimae sunt, prima hora temporalis est eadem quae nona cum tertia parte decimae aequinoctialis; secunda, quod reliquum decimae cum duabus tertiis undecimae; tertia, quae duodecima cum tertia parte undecimae; atque ita singulae tres horae temporales continent quatuor aequinoctiales. Pari modo quarta est eadem quae tertia decima cum tertia parte quartae decimae; quinta, quod reliquum quartae decimae cum duabus tertiis quintae decimae; sexta, quod reliquum quintae decimae cum integra sexta decima, et est meridies. Item tres temporales septima, octava, nona sunt eaedem quae quatuor aequinoctiales, videlicet decima septima, decima octava, decima nona, vigesima. Item decima, undecima, duodecima, eaedem quae vigesima prima, vigesima secunda, vigesima tertia, vigesima quarta.

Since in the civil system each day and night consists of twelve 8
hours throughout the whole year, the sixth hour is always in the middle of the day, and the first begins at sunrise and the twelfth ends at sunset. By way of example, in the month of March when the civil hours are of almost the same length as the standard hours, the first hour of the civil day coincides with the thirteenth hour of the natural day, the second with the fourteenth, the third with the fifteenth, the fourth with the sixteenth, the fifth with the seventeenth, the sixth with the eighteenth, the seventh with the nineteenth, the eighth with the twentieth, the ninth with the twenty-first, the tenth with the twenty-second, the eleventh with the twenty-third, and the twelfth with the twenty-fourth. Accordingly, what we read in the Bible, "from the sixth hour right up to the ninth darkness covered the whole world,"[325] must be taken to mean from the eighteenth hour to the twenty-first of the natural day, as the hours are now counted. For in antiquity sundials were divided into the civil hours of both night and day, not the natural or standard hours.

In the month of June, when the hours are at their longest, the 9
first civil hour is equivalent to the ninth hour and a third of the tenth hour in the standard reckoning; the second is made up of the remaining parts of the tenth hour and two-thirds of the eleventh; the third is made up of the twelfth and a third of the eleventh. And so three civil hours are equivalent in length to four standard hours. Similarly, the fourth is equivalent to the thirteenth hour and a third of the fourteenth, the fifth is made up of the remaining part of the fourteenth hour and the whole of the fifteenth, the sixth is made up of the rest of the fifteenth and the whole of the sixteenth and is the middle of the day. Likewise the three civil hours, the seventh, eighth and ninth, are equivalent to four standard hours, namely the seventeenth to the twentieth. Also the tenth, eleventh and twelfth are the equivalent to the four standard hours, the twenty-first to the twenty-fourth.

10 Non ab re hic visum est subiungere epigramma Martialis ad Euphemum structorem Domitiani, ubi harum horarum temporalium meminit. Est autem hoc:

Prima salutantes atque altera detinet hora;
exercet raucos tertia causidicos;
in quintam varios exercet Roma labores;
sexta quies lassis; septima finis erit;
sufficit in nonam nitidis octava palaestris;
imperat extructos frangere nona toros;
hora libellorum decima est, Eupheme, meorum,
temperat ambrosias cum tua cura dapes
et bonus aetherio laxatur nectare Caesar
ingentique tenet pocula parca manu.
Tunc admitte iocos: gressu timet ire licenti
ad matutinum nostra Thalia Iovem.

* * *

11 Horae autem de quibus agit Palladius sunt quae diem ab ortu solis ad occasum dividunt in partes duodecim; quae umbris sic deprehenduntur. Fiat planicies quadrata ad regulam et libellam in loco aperto qui toto die illustretur a sole, spectetque uno latere septentrionem, alio meridiem, solem alio orientem, occidentem alio. Deinde in medio quadrati collocetur indagator umbrae, qui Graece γνώμων seu σκιαθήρας dicitur, observeturque prima dies cuiusvis mensis, verbi gratia Ianuarii, idque coelo sereno.

12 Tunc, tacto gnomone a solis radiis, umbra gnomonis prima hora diei erit longa pedes 29, secunda 19, tertia 15, quarta 12, quinta 10, sexta 9. Atque hac hora semper, ut dixi, est meridies; tunc enim sol altissimus facit umbras brevissimas. Deinde incipit declinare et descendere ad occasum, atque umbrae eadem qua

It did not seem inappropriate to add here the epigram of Martial addressed to Euphemus, Domitian's carver, where these civil hours are mentioned:[326] 10

> The first and second hours keep busy those making their morning calls; the third puts the husky-voiced lawyers to work; Rome is engaged in her various toils until the fifth; the sixth brings rest to the weary, rest that is ended by the seventh; the eighth suffices for the gleaming wrestlers; the ninth bids us crush our heaped up palliasses. The tenth is the hour for my poems, Euphemus, when you in your role prepare the ambrosian feasts and noble Caesar relaxes with his heavenly nectar and holds modest goblets in his mighty grasp. Then is the time to allow for play; our Muse fears to approach with extravagant stride the morning sky.

* * *

The hours which Palladius deals with are those that divide the day, from dawn to sunset, into twelve parts. These are marked out by shadows in the following way. Let there be a flat area perfectly square and level in an open site so that the sun will shine on it the whole day, and let the four sides face north, south, east and west. Then the shadow pointer, called *γνώμων* or *σκιαθήρας* in Greek, should be placed in the middle of the square, and observations be made on the first day of any month you wish—and of course the sky must be clear. 11

Take January for example. At this time of year, when the pointer is touched by the rays of the sun, the shadow of the pointer will be twenty-nine feet in length at the first hour of the day, nineteen at the second hour, fifteen at the third, twelve at the fourth, ten at the fifth, nine at the sixth, which hour, as I have said, is the middle of the day. For at this time the sun is highest in the sky and casts the shortest shadow. Then the sun begins to get lower and to descend toward the west and the shadows increase by 12

decreverant mensura augentur. Quo fit ut septima hora, quae est prima post meridiem, umbra gnomonis sit longa pedes 10 et respondeat quintae antemeridianae (nam horae ante sextam antemeridianae, post sextam pomeridianae appellantur); octava sit longa pedes 12 et respondeat quartae; nona, 15, quanta fuerat tertia; decima, 19, quot pedum erat secunda; undecima, 29, quot prima. Et quoniam in horarum spatio Ianuarius cum Decembri mense convenit, eaedem erunt umbrae singulis horis hoc mense quae et Ianuario.

13 Idem quoque faciendum est in caeteris mensibus, ut bini scilicet coinputentur, et Februarius in horarum mensura cum Novembri mense concordet, Martius cum Octobri, Aprilis cum Septembri, Maius cum Augusto, Iunius cum Iulio, quemadmodum in fine cuiusque mensis apud Palladium licet videre.

14 Illud apud eundem in fine postremi mensis his verbis: 'Decembrem Ianuario in horis causa dispar adiunxit, cum linea simili ille augeatur, hic decrescat,' intelligendum est et de umbris, quod tam ante meridiem quam post pares atque eaedem in singulis binis mensibus sint idque dispari causa, et de diebus, quos constat sex mensibus augeri et sex decrescere. Nam, etsi eadem quantitate sunt horae mense Ianuario qua et Decembri, eademque mense Februario qua et Novembri, et sic in reliquis paribus, quemadmodum author ostendit, tamen ex singulis paribus quantum augetur alter, tantum alter diminuitur. Ascendente enim sole a Capricorno ad Cancrum, ut supra diximus, dies semper augentur; decrescunt contra descendente illo a Cancro ad Capricornum.

the same amount as they had decreased. So at the seventh hour, the first after the middle of the day, the shadow of the pointer is ten feet long, corresponding to the length at the fifth hour of the morning (for the hours preceding the sixth are called prenoon or morning hours and those coming after it are called the afternoon hours). Accordingly the shadow at the eighth hour is twelve feet long, corresponding to the fourth. At the ninth it will be fifteen feet, the same as at the third; at the tenth it will be nineteen, the same as at the second; at the eleventh it will be twenty-nine feet, the same as at the first hour. And since January agrees with the month of December in the length of the hours, the length of the shadows will be the same at each hour in December as in January.

The same has to be done for all the other months so that there 13
are two months which correspond with each other. February agrees with November in the length of the hours, March with October, April with September, May with August and June with July, as can be seen at the end of each month in Palladius.

At the end of the final month Palladius says the following: "A 14
differing reason joins December and January with respect to the hours, for in one the hours increase in length and in the other they diminish, but at the same rate." We must take this to refer both to the shadows, because they are equal before the middle of the day as well as after it and are the same in each pair of months (and that for a differing reason), and to the length of the days, which we all know increases for six months and decreases for six. For although the hours in January and December are the same in length, and the same in February as in November, and so on in the remaining pairs, nevertheless in each pair the hours grow longer in one by the same amount that they grow smaller in the other. For when the sun rises from Capricorn and is making its way to Cancer, the days continuously get longer; while they grow shorter when the sun is dropping from Cancer to Capricorn.

15 Notandum praeterea, crescentibus diebus decrescere semper umbras gnomonis, contra decrescentibus illis has semper augescere. Et hinc est quod mense Ianuario, cum dies brevissimi sunt et augentur, prima hora diei umbra gnomonis est longa pedes XXIX, quae est longissima, Februario XXVII, Martio XXV, Aprili XXIIII, Maio XXIII, Iunio XXII. Mense autem Iulio, cum dies longissimi sunt et decrescunt, prima hora diei umbra gnomonis est longa pedes XXII, quae est brevissima, Augusto XXIII, Septembri XXIIII, Octobri XXV, Novembri XXVII, Decembri XXIX.

16 Id quod ut melius cognoscatur, subiunximus et eos menses quibus dies augentur umbris decrescentibus, et eos quibus dies decrescunt umbris crescentibus. Incepimus autem ab Ianuario et Iulio. Quorum altero dies sunt brevissimi et semper augentur usque ad solstitium aestivum, et umbrae longissimae, sed decrescunt quandiu dies augentur; altero dies sunt longissimi et semper decrescunt usque ad solstitium hybernum, et umbrae brevissimae, sed augentur quandiu dies decrescunt.

17 Et licet a solstitiis incipiendum fuisset, quae Decembri et Iunio fiunt, tuncque dies vel augeri vel decrescere incipiunt, tamen incrementa vel diminutiones dierum cum diminutionibus incrementisque umbrarum sic facilius dignoscuntur; qua quidem re cognita, et dispar illa causa cognoscetur, qua in horarum spatio Ianuarius Decembri, Februarius Novembri, Martius Octobri, Aprilis Sep-

Moreover, it must be noted that as the days grow longer the 15
shadow of the gnomon continues to diminish each month, and as they grow shorter it continues to increase. And this is why in January, when the days are shortest in length and beginning to increase, the shadow of the gnomon at the first hour of the day is twenty-nine feet in length (the longest it can be), in February twenty-seven, in March twenty-five feet, in April twenty-four, in May twenty-three and in June twenty-two. But in the month of July, when the days are at their longest but are beginning to diminish in length, the length of the gnomon's shadow at the first hour of the day is twenty-two feet (the shortest it can be), in August it is twenty-three feet in length, in September it is twenty-four, in October twenty-five, November twenty-seven, and December twenty-nine.

So that this may be more readily be grasped, we have added a 16
list of those months in which the days lengthen and the shadows decrease and of the months in which the days grow shorter and the shadows lengthen. We have begun with January and July. In the former of these the days are shortest in the year and then continuously increase up to the summer solstice, while the shadows are longest but grow shorter as the days lengthen. In the latter, the days are the longest in the year and then continuously diminish in length up to the winter solstice, while the shadows are the shortest and lengthen as the days grow shorter.

Although I could have begun with the solstices in December 17
and June when the days begin to lengthen or decrease, the increases and the shortenings of the days accompanied by the shortening and lengthening of the shadows respectively will be more easily grasped by the method I have chosen. If this is grasped, one will understand the differing reason whereby, with respect to the length of the hours, January is partnered with December, February with November, March with October, April with September, May

tembri, Maius Augusto, Iunius Iulio adiuncti, linea simili, ut ait Palladius, augentur vel decrescunt.

18 Sed sciendum primos quosque dies mensis descriptos tantum a Palladio, nec tantas fore umbras caeteris diebus cuiusque mensis, quantae fuere primis, siquis eas describeret, sed semper vel minores, cum dies crescunt, vel maiores illis decrescentibus. Quae si describerentur omnes, magnum efficerent volumen. Esset praeterea opus multis annis, si id fieret in Europa. Nam, cum oporteat singulos quosque dies totius anni ab ortu solis ad occasum tunc esse serenos, nec id contingat unquam in Europa, observandi forent dies sereni multorum annorum donec omnes describerentur. Quod quia laboriosum est et longi taedii plenum, nec Palladius fecit nec alius quisquam, nec forte erit unquam qui faciat.

Sed de his haec satis; tu vero, lector carissime, vale et me ama.

C

19 Errata, quae recognito volumine deprehendimus, sic corrige. Sed notandum: primum numerum significare chartas, secundum versus, atque eos tantum qui scripti sunt versus esse numerandos; item, ne bis idem repetatur, id solum adnotatum esse quod vel distinguendum vel legendum est aliter quam in libro habeatur hoc modo.

with August and June with July, inasmuch as they increase or diminish at the same rate, as Palladius says.

It must be kept in mind, however, that only the first day of each month is marked out by Palladius and that for all the other days of each month the shadows would not be of the same length as they were on the first day if one were to include them; they would continue to diminish in length when the days of a month are growing longer or increase in length when the days were growing shorter. If information for every day was given, the result would be a huge tome. Moreover it would take many years if this were done for Europe. For in every day of the whole year there would have to be a clear sky from sunrise to sunset and this would never be the case in Europe. And so one would need to take observations on clear days over many years, until the result for every day was achieved. Because such a task requires much labor and entails great and lengthy tedium, neither Palladius nor anyone else has done this and perhaps no one ever will. 18

But enough of this. Dearest reader, farewell and think well of me.

C[327]

Correct the errors that we have caught in revising this volume as follows. But you should note that the first number refers to the pages, the second to lines and that only those lines that contains text are to be numbered. Also, so as not to repeat the same thing, we have noted what is to be punctuated or read in a different way from how it appears in the text.[328] 19

: XXVI :

Aldus Pius Manutius Ioannem Baptistam Rhamusium compatrem salvere iubet.

1 Si quisquam est cui nuncupare debeamus libros excusos cura nostra, tu ille es, Rhamusi suavissime. Nam, praeter eruditionem et modestiam tuam (es enim et Latinis et Graecis literis et moribus ornatissimus), nunquam nos in hac dura provincia nostra cessas iuvare, quae mira in bonas literas benevolentia est tua, non solum assidue et diligenter inquirendis antiquis exemplaribus, sed etiam illis ipsis sedulo suppeditandis. Quemadmodum superioribus diebus in Quintiliano a te est factum, quem dum cursim recognosceret Naugerius noster (minimum enim otii inter recognoscendum habuit, festinantibus impressoribus, quibus 'nec mora unquam est nec requies'), assiduus illi adiutor haesisti et comes, tanquam alter Achates Aeneae, quippe qui ab illius latere nunquam discedas ob tuam in illius summas virtutes assiduam observantiam.

2 Iure igitur tibi Quintilianum dedicamus. Quod etiam ea causa facimus ut, quicunque bonas literas amant, te quoque de animo, de studio tuo in illas ament plurimum. Quam autem correctus atque longe alius ab iis qui habentur in manibus exeat ex aedibus nostris, facile cognoscet qui cum illis hunc nostrum diligenter conferat. Multa tamen relicta esse inemendata non negamus, quibus corrigendis 'Oedipo coniectore opus foret'; sed, ut spero, corrigentur et ipsa aliquando, correctiore aliquo exemplari invento.

: XXVI :

Quintilian
(August 1514)

Aldus Pius Manutius to his dear friend Giovanni Battista Ramusio,[329] *greetings.*

If there is anyone to whom we should dedicate the books that we print by our efforts, you are that person, Ramusio, most delightful of men. For in addition to your erudition and your propriety (for you have great mastery of Greek and Latin letters and are of impeccable character) you never cease to help us in this demanding task of ours, not only by continuously and diligently searching for new manuscripts but even by zealously supplying us with these very objects—such is your admirable and loving devotion to good letters! An example of your assistance is what you did in the past few days in the case of Quintilian. When our dear Navagero[330] was quickly rechecking the text (I say quickly for he had little spare time for his review, since the printers, who never brook "any delay or rest,"[331] were bustling around), you stuck by him as an energetic helper and companion, like a second Achates to Aeneas,[332] since you never leave his side because of your unflagging respect for all his fine qualities. 1

It is right therefore for us to dedicate Quintilian to you. We also do so for this reason, so that anyone who loves good letters can also show his deep love for you because of your own commitment and devotion to literature. Whoever compares with care this edition of ours with those that are in circulation will readily see how free of errors and far different from them is this one that is now leaving our printing house.[333] We do not deny that many faults remain, but to correct these "one would need an Oedipus for a textual critic."[334] But it is my hope that these too will someday 2

Annuat Deus ac sinat, ut et id et quae cupimus caetera ad utilitatem hominum, et qui nunc sunt et qui post aliis erunt in annis, possimus efficere. Vale.

: XXVII :

Aldus Pius Manutius Petrum Bembum compatrem, a secretis Leonis X pontificis maximi, salvere iubet.

1 Cogitanti mihi, Bembe doctissime, cui potissimum dicarem ea Virgilii opera quae cum alibi tum moriens sua ipse testatus est, inquiens 'Cecini pascua, rura, duces,' tu occurristi dignissimus eo munere, et quia emendatissima emittuntur (idque auxilio Naugerii nostri, quem tu amas plurimum, et te ipse observat ob similitudinem quae inter vos. Virgilio enim ambo simillimi: 'Ambo florentes aetatibus, Aones ambo, / et cantare pares et respondere parati,' et quia nihil immistum est alieni carminis quod divini vatis macularet maiestatem. Adde quod parvam hanc enchiridii formam a tua bibliotheca ac potius iucundissimi parentis tui Bernardi accepimus.

2 Hic ipse etiam paucis ante diebus quam haec scriberem, quosdam eadem forma libellos — quae est venerandi senis et iam unum

be removed, when a more unblemished manuscript is found. May God grant and allow this to come to pass; then we can accomplish this as well all the other things that we wish to do for the good of mankind, not only those now living but also those who will come later in another age.[335] Farewell.

: XXVII :

Vergil

(October 1514)

Aldus Pius Manutius to his dear and close friend, Pietro Bembo, secretary to Pope Leo X.

Most learned Bembo,[336] when I was considering to whom in particular I should dedicate these works of Vergil, works which he himself attested on many occasion were his, but also when he was dying, saying "I have sung of pastures, of fields and commanders,"[337] you came to mind as being most worthy of this tribute. One reason is that they are they being published with a text purged of many errors (and this was done with the help of our dear Navagero, whom you love most dearly and who himself regards you with respect because you are very like each other; for you both closely resemble what Vergil says: "Both in the prime of life, both Aonians,[338] / and both ready in a match to sing and respond"[339]). A second reason is that no one else's poetry is included that would defile the grandeur of our divine poet.[340] Another reason is that we adopted this small pocket-book format from your library or rather the library of your most agreeable father, Bernardo.[341] 1

A few days before I wrote these words Bernardo himself promptly lent me some books of similar format that I had asked 2

et octoginta annos nati mira benignitas—statim rogatus mihi commodo dedit, quod[10] procul ab eo sint omnia quae senem circumveniunt incommoda. Eadem enim manet liberalitas, idem ingenii vigor, eadem etiam memoria quae iuveni fuit; sic adhuc est laboris patiens ut de illo vere dixeris, 'Sed cruda deo viridisque senectus.' Omnia praeterea quae in sene Catone fuisse scripsit Cicero, in parente tuo facile inveniuntur. O felicem tali patre filium! et te filio patrem!

3 Sed illius laudes non est hic scribendi locus. Nunc redeo ad Virgilium, cuius Lusus, quos tu correctissimos habes, tunc edam, cum a te accepero—quod erit, ut spero, brevi—, additis et aliis quae una cum illis vagari solent et nostris quibusdam in Virgilium annotationibus. Vale.

: XXVIII :

Aldus Pius Albertum Pium Carporum principem ac Caesareum oratorem apud pontificem maximum salvere iubet.

1 Iampridem, Alberte, decus principum, decus huius aetatis eruditorum, constitui omnes de philosophia libros, quotquot ex aedibus nostris exirent in manus studiosorum, tibi dedicare, tum mea erga te singulari benevolentia, tum etiam quia id genus libris praeter caeteros delectaris.

him for — such is the wonderful kindness of this venerable old man, now eighty-one years old. Because of this may all the ailments that beset an old man keep a far distance from him. He has the same magnanimity, the same intellectual powers, the same memory that he had when he was a young man. He still has such physical endurance that one can truly say of him "a god's old age is fresh and green."[342] In addition all the qualities that Cicero said were in the old Cato are readily found in your father.[343] What a lucky son to have such a father! What a lucky father to have you as a son!

However, this is not the time to sing his praises. Now I return 3
to Vergil. His *Lusus*[344] that you have in your possession in a most correct form I shall publish when I receive them from you — which, I hope, will be soon.[345] To these I shall add some other items that usually circulate with them, as well as some notes of ours on Vergil. Farewell.

: XXVIII :

Lucretius

(January 1515)

Aldus Pius to Alberto Pio, prince of Carpi and imperial ambassador to the pope,[346] *warmest greetings.*

Alberto, most distinguished among princes, most distinguished 1
among the learned of this age, I long ago decided to dedicate to you all the books on philosophy that were to leave our press and reach the hands of devotees of learning. I did so not just because of my special affection for you but also because you take more pleasure in books of this kind than in any others.

2 Deus perdat perniciosa haec bella quae te perturbant, quae te tandiu avertunt a sacris studiis literarum nec sinunt ut quiete et, quod semper cupivisti atque optasti, fruaris otio ad eas artes quibus a puero deditus fuisti celebrandas. Iam aliquem fructum dedisses studiorum tuorum, utilem sane et nobis et posteris. Qua te privari re ita moleste fers ut nullam aliam ob causam credendum sit nuper te Romae tam gravi morbo laborasse ut de salute tua et timerent boni omnes et angerentur.

Di, prohibete minas; di, talem avertite casum
et placidi servate pios.

3 En igitur tibi Lucretius, et poeta et philosophus quidem maximus vel antiquorum iudicio, sed plenus mendaciorum. Nam multo aliter sentit de Deo, de creatione rerum quam Plato, quam caeteri Academici, quippe qui Epicuream sectam secutus est. Quamobrem sunt qui ne legendum quidem illum censent Christianis hominibus, qui verum Deum adorant, colunt, venerantur. Sed quoniam veritas, quanto magis inquiritur, tanto apparet illustrior et venerabilior — qualis est fides catholica, quam Iesus Christus Deus optimus maximus, dum in humanis ageret, praedicavit hominibus — Lucretius et qui Lucretio sunt simillimi legendi quidem mihi videntur, sed ut falsi et mendaces, ut certe sunt.

4 Haec autem attigimus, ut, siquis haec nostra legens nesciat deliramenta Lucretii, id discat e nobis, licet ad te unum scribere videamur. Id enim est harum epistolarum genus, ut, cum ad unum scribuntur, ad omnes in quorum manus pervenerint tanquam argumenta scribantur.

May God put an end to these destructive wars that upset you, that divert you for so long from the sacred study of letters and do not allow you to enjoy the quiet and, what you have always desired and prayed for, the leisure to engage in these disciplines to which you have been dedicated since boyhood. You would have by now provided fruit of your studies, fruit that would certainly have been useful both for us and for posterity. Since the lack of time to study vexes you greatly, we must believe that its cause is the grave illness that recently struck you down in Rome, one so serious that all good men were distressed and feared for your life. 2

Ye Gods, hold at bay these threats; ye gods, avert such a
misfortune;
be indulgent and save the righteous.[347]

Here then is your Lucretius, both poet and, in the judgment of the ancients, a very great philosopher, though he is full of lies. For in his views of God and of creation he is quite different from Plato or all the other members of the Academy, since he followed the teachings of Epicurus. Because of this some people believe that he should not even be read by Christians, who adore, worship and venerate the true God. But since truth shines all the more brightly and becomes all the more revered the more it is searched for — as is the case with our Christian faith, which Jesus Christ, Lord God Almighty, proclaimed to mankind while he lived among mortals — I think that Lucretius and those who are very similar to him should be read, but only as falsifiers and liars, as they assuredly are. 3

We have broached this matter so that if anyone reading these remarks of ours does not know of the mad ravings of Lucretius he will learn of this from us, even though we appear to be writing to you alone. For this is the nature of epistles such as this one: although they are addressed to one individual, they are really written for all who come into possession of the works, like arguments addressed to a jury. 4

5 Quod autem longe correctior emittitur nunc Lucretius ex aedibus nostris quam consueverit, habenda est potissimum gratia Andreae Naugerio nostro, qui eum, quanquam cursim propter ipsius occupationes et importunam impressorum nostrorum festinationem, tamen accurate recensuit.

6 Capita praeterea mutata fere sunt omnia ut vere quod singulis quibusque locis complectitur contineant. Et licet non inserenda suis ea locis curaverimus ne librum dividerent, cum non Lucretius illa, sed alius quispiam inseruerit, tamen, ad evitandum inquirendi laborem, et pagellam citant et versum quo referenda sunt.

7 Quod si per adversam valetudinem mihi licuisset qua menses iam aliquot acerbiore conflictatus sum, addita essent infra non pauca quae diligentiae nostrae fidem omnibus facerent et Lucretium ipsum pleniorem redderent. Utcunque sit, cavendum etiam fuerat ne plus iusto opus excresceret et magnitudo voluminis molestiam afferret. Caetera ita praestita esse a nobis opinor Naugerii nostri industria, quam non contemnendam adhibuit, ut Lucretius legi atque intelligi tandem possit. Vale.

5 Now Lucretius is being issued from our printing house in a much more correct form than has often been the case in the past and for this we must thank especially our dear Andrea Navagero,[348] who has gone over the text with great care even though he has done so very rapidly because of his own obligations and the impatient demands of our printers.

6 In addition almost all the headings have been changed so that they truly reflect what is covered in every single passage. These are not the work of Lucretius but of someone else, and we decided that they should not be inserted at the appropriate place in the poem; in this way the text would not be broken up into many parts. Nevertheless, to avoid the labor involved in searching through the work, the headings give the page and line of the passages to which they should be referred.[349]

7 If it had been possible despite the ill health with which I have been afflicted, ever more severely, for some months now,[350] much more material would have been added below to prove to everyone our diligence and to give Lucretius in a fuller form. However it may be, I had to take steps to prevent the work from growing beyond what was proper and the size of the volume from becoming bothersome. Everything else, I believe, has been accomplished by us through the industry of our friend Navagero; he has applied himself blamelessly to the task, the result being that Lucretius can finally be read with understanding. Farewell.[351]

: I :

A

Aldus Manucius Bassianas Romanus Alberto Pio principi Carpensi s. p. d.

1 *Institutiones grammaticas* (id enim est illis inditum nomen, quoniam usque ad oratoriam et poeticen instituunt adolescentulos) iam tot annos pressi crebrasque pati lituras coegi, quod et tu optime nosti, Alberte Pie, princeps inclyte, quem una cum Leonello, magnifico fratre tuo, sex annos et plus eo summa fide curaque docuimus, ut Horatio Flacco non solum paruerim, qui in poetica ne praecipitetur editio suadet nonumque prematur in annum, sed plus etiam ocii quam sit ab eo praeceptum illis dederim.

2 Dicet fortasse quispiam, hoc *Aeneidi Iliadive*, divinis operibus, fuisset satis. Sic ita sane, sed 'si licet magnis parva componere,' siquis ingeniolum nostrum Vergilii Homerive ingenio conferat, tantum mihi minimum quodque opus esse quanta aut Virgilio *Aeneis* aut Homero *Ilias* fuit facile profecto cognoscet. Quanquam interim

EDITIONS OF HUMANISTIC AUTHORS

: I :

Aldus Manutius, Instructional Principles of Latin Grammar[1]

(March 5, 1493)

A

Aldus Manutius of Bassiano and of Rome to Alberto Pio, prince of Carpi, warmest greetings

For many years now I have kept to myself my *Instructional Principles of Grammar* (for that is the name I have given them since they provide youths with instruction right up to the study of rhetoric and poetry) and forced many changes upon them, as you know very well, Alberto Pio, illustrious prince, whom I taught along with your splendid brother, Leonello, for more than six years with the utmost devotion and attention.[2] In this regard I have not only obeyed Horace, who advises in his *Ars Poetica* that works should not be published precipitately and should be kept concealed for nine years[3] but have even devoted more of my spare time to them than he recommended. 1

Perhaps someone will say that this would have been sufficient time for the *Aeneid* or the *Iliad,* divine works. True enough, but "if one can compare small things with large,"[4] whoever compares our modest talent with the genius of Vergil or Homer will easily recognize that all the smallest works of mine mean as much to me as the *Aeneid* and *Iliad* meant to Vergil and Homer. In the meantime I have put together with great diligence a Greek grammar and 2

et Graecas institutiones et exercitamenta grammatices atque utriusque linguae fragmenta et alia quaedam valde, ut spero, placitura studiose composui, quae in manus hominum brevi, favente Christo Iesu, quam emendatissima venient.

3 Sed hisce institutionibus componendis quantam curam et diligentiam adhibuerim doctorum sit iudicium qui illas accurate perlegerint. Omni certe studio, omni cura usi sumus; sic diligentissime scripsimus ut laborem nostrum speremus non inutilem multis futurum, immo quicunque usi eo fuerint plurimam etiam nobis gratiam habituros. Illud ab omnibus vehementer petimus ne nos prius damnent quam librum perlegerint. Iniquum est enim et ab omni humanitate alienum si incertum sit an deliquerit hominem condemnare.

4 Sed citra reprehensionem esse quod scripsimus omnino existimamus. Nam aut placuero aut minime. Si placuero, non sum reprehensione dignus, sed laudibus; etsi id omne quodcumque nobis est laudum Deo optimo maximo acceptum referimus a quo optimum quodque bonum et donum omne perfectum proficitur. Sin minus, quare sum accusandus si, me non mihi solum sed aliis quoque natum cognoscens, quod in me fuit posteritati ut prodessem elaboravi?

5 Tibi vero meas lucubrationes, Alberte princeps, et Leonello fratri, quibus prodesse semper cupio legendas mitto, caetera quoque nostra si placuisse ita cognoro, propediem missurus. Vale.

Me lege, Romanae qui vis primordia linguae
discere; perlecto me, cito doctus eris.

grammatical exercises and passages in both languages and some other items that I hope will meet with warm approval. These will be available to the public in a short time, I hope, Jesus Christ willing, and free as possible of all errors.[5]

But let scholars who will read through this grammar with much 3
care judge how much trouble I have taken and diligence I have shown in composing it. We have certainly applied all our energy and attentiveness to it, and have taken such great pains in writing it that we hope not only that our labor will prove to be of some use to many readers, but also, more than that, we hope that all who use it will also be deeply grateful to us. We make this impassioned request of everyone, that they do not condemn us before they have read the book. For it is unjust and alien to the goodness of human nature to condemn a man if it is uncertain whether he has done anything wrong.

But it is my firm belief that no criticism can be directed at what 4
we have written. For I will either please my reader or I will not. If I please him, then I deserve praise, not rebukes—although whatever praise is accorded me we credit to God Almighty, from whom flow all the best blessings and all perfect gifts. If I do not please my reader, why do I deserve censure if I have recognized that I have been born not only to serve myself but also to serve others and have toiled to the best of my ability to be of value to those who will come after us?

I send these fruits of my labors to you, prince Albert, for you to 5
read, and to your brother Leonello, to both of whom I always wish to be of help. If I learn that these have pleased you, I will send you soon all our other books too. Farewell.[6]

Read me if you wish to learn the elements of the language of Rome.
When you have read me through, you will very soon be master of it.

Non mihi per scopulos aut devia parvus[1] Iulus
ducitur, Aonias ebibiturus aquas.
Est via per placidos colles, per florea rura:
hac iter ad Musas perbreve carpe, puer.

B

6 Haec de figuris satis esse duxi erudiendis pueris; nam eas quas elocutionis esse et sermonis ferunt consulto praetermisi, tum ne multitudine praeceptorum confunderem ingenia ediscentium, tum quia de illis a multis est copiose accurateque perscriptum (qui, si sic omnia quae sunt erudiendis pueris necessaria complexi essent consuluissent labori meo). Non enim gloria commotus grammatices rudimenta composui; nam quae esse potest gloria in re tam tenui? Licet in tenui non tenuem gloriam consequi summi queant viri, ut potuit ille qui ait 'In tenui labor, at tenuis non gloria, si quem / numina leva sinunt auditque vocatus Apollo.'

7 Id tamen praestare non posse arbitror ingenium meum, quod sentio quam sit exiguum, et quoniam unde esse nunc quaestus possit studiosis viris non video. Nam temporibus nostris pleraeque omnes divitum manus chiragra si dandum est laborant, si accipiendum vero, longe secus; valent enim quam optime; nihil est illis expeditius, nihil celerius; ita sunt tenaces ut in eas dici vere possit Plautinum illud: 'Novi ego istos polypos; quicquid tetigerint tenent.' Fuit moris antiqui doctos viros iuvare opibus et ornare

Young Iulus is not led by me over steep crags or on remote
paths
in order to drink of Aonian waters.
Our path takes us over gentle hills and flowering meadows.
In this way your journey to the Muses will be quick, young
boy.

B[7]

I thought that enough had been said about stylistic matters as far as the instruction of young boys was concerned. For I deliberately passed over what are called types of style and figures of speech,[8] not only to avoid confusing the minds of pupils with a multitude of precepts but also because many have written lengthily and most carefully about them (if they had included all that is required for instructing young boys, they would have spared me my labor). I excluded these topics since it was no desire for glory that goaded me into putting together the rudiments of grammar. What glory can there be in such a slight topic? And yet the greatest of men can attain no slight renown from an enterprise of little importance, as did that famous man who says, "Slight is the field of toil, but not slight the glory, if adverse powers leave one free and Apollo hearkens unto prayer."[9] 6

I do not think I am talented enough to achieve this. For I am aware of how modest my abilities are and I do not see that there is any source of money for men of learning to make a living nowadays. In these times of ours almost all the hands of the wealthy are afflicted with arthritis if they have to give out money,[10] while if they have to take it in, it is quite a different story—they could not be healthier and no one is more agile or more nimble. They are so grasping that one can apply these words of Plautus to them, "I know these octopuses; they won't let go whatever they touch."[11] It was the custom of old to provide scholars with resources and to 7

pecunia; nunc vero, ut alia speciosa et egregia, ita hoc in primis exolevit, atque adeo nemo favet ingeniis ut vel doctissimo cuique, si pauper est, illud quod est a Martiale ad Aemilianum scriptum, dici vere queat; 'Semper eris pauper, si pauper es, Aemiliane: / dantur opes nulli nunc nisi divitibus.'

8 Non scripsi item spe quaestus, sed et coactus ut brevi commodeque discipulos erudirem, et pene plorans quod non in alta et digniore materia ingenium exercerem, et praesertim cum viderem plerosque obtuso etiam ingenio viros, quia dignam sibi materiam cui incumberent elegerunt, plurimi fieri ubique et maximis efferri laudibus; me vero et quicumque mihi est simillimus non modo non aestimari, sed irrideri potius et haberi ludibrio.

9 Has igitur grammaticas institutiones non sponte venimus ad scribendum. Sed quid facerem? Docendi mihi omnino erant adolescentuli, nec id poteram commode quemadmodum cupiebam efficere. Grammaticos enim libros qui essent instituendis pueris accommodati nondum quisquam meo quidem iudicio scripsit, quandoquidem hic est sane brevis et concisus, ille admodum diffusus et vanus, alius perineptus et durus. Et quanquam sunt qui et docte et accurate scripserunt, tamen (dicam enim quod sentio) nec satis illi quidem mihi faciebant. Quodsi, quemadmodum ex tanta grammaticorum copia nemo mihi adhuc quod placeret scripsit, ita neque ego scripsi quod sit aliis placiturum, id tamen fuero consecutus, quod mihimet ipse satisfeci qui quo maxime indigebam ad pueros breviter commodeque docendum mihi conquisivi. At si forte caeteris quoque satisfecero, laudetur Christus Iesus, qui mihi dedit quo et placere possem et prodesse hominibus.

10 Ecce tibi Latiae ieci firmissima linguae
fundamenta, puer; quod breve monstrat opus.

give them money.[12] But nowadays, like other good and noble things, this is a custom that has been abandoned more than any others, and the universal lack of support for brilliant minds means that what Martial wrote to Aemilianus can truly be said to all the most learned of men if they are poor, "If you are poor, Aemilianus, you will always be poor. Nowadays only the rich receive money."[13]

I have not written this grammar to make money but under the 8
compulsion of having to teach my pupils with speed and convenience. I almost wept that I could not exercise my talent on lofty and more worthy material, all the more so since I saw that many men of limited ability were valued most highly and praised to the skies because they chose to apply themselves to material that matched their lack of talent, while I and everyone like me, so far from even being appreciated, are actually mocked and laughed at.

We did not turn to writing this grammar out of choice. But 9
what was I to do? I had to teach my young pupils and I could not achieve this very easily in the way that I desired. For in my opinion no one has yet put together a grammar that is suited to instructing young boys; one is too short and compressed, another is too verbose and insubstantial, another is chock-full of errors and written in a stolid style. And although some have written in a learned and careful way, all the same (for I shall speak my mind) not even they satisfied me. But if none of the vast number of schoolmasters has yet written a grammar that pleases me, and if I have not written one either that will please others, I will have achieved this at any rate, that I will have the satisfaction of having acquired for myself what I most dearly needed for teaching schoolboys in a speedy and convenient manner. If I happen to satisfy others as well, may the praise go to Jesus Christ, who gave me the power to please and help my fellow man.

Look, young boy, I have laid down the strongest of founda- 10
tions of the Latin language, as this brief work shows. Now

Iam potes Aonidum sacros haurire liquores,
volvere et eloquii scripta diserta patris,
nunc studio assiduo, totis nunc viribus usus.
Ipsa tibi vires docta Minerva dabit.
Te iuvet insano nunc indulgere labori,
si labor Orpheae plectra movere lyrae
si labor ornatis complere est vocibus aures,
quae quo plus haustae plus tamen usque iuvant,
si labor ambrosia est aut dulci nectare pasci
nulla unquam satias unde venire solet.
Est iocus, est lusus libros versare diurna
nocturnaque manu. quare, age, volve libros.
Sic Maro doctiloquus, magnus sic fecit Homerus,
sic patriae dixit quem sua Roma patrem,
sic regem aeterna lacerat qui voce Philippum
plus olei impendit quam bibit ille meri,
sic Plato, Graecorum facile doctissimus, et sic
huius discipulus magnus Aristoteles,
Punicus et doctor, sacrum et qui nomen habebat;
sic quicumque virum docta per ora volat.
Tu quoque, si doctis potes impallescere chartis,
polliceor, tolles nomen in astra tuum.
Illud, nate, precor — melioris partis et ipse
sum pater, et sanctus quisque magister erit —
sis bonus atque pius, sanctos neu desere mores.
Heu fuge quae faciunt omnia, nate, malum!
Sit cordi et virtus atque altum nomen Iesu
usque tibi: sic te clarus in astra feres.

you can drink in the sacred waters of the Muses, and read the beautifully expressed writings of the father of eloquence,[14] applying constant energy and all your strength (learned Minerva herself will give you strength). May it give you delight to give free rein to frenzied toil, if it is toil to pluck the strings of Orpheus' lyre, if it is toil to fill the ears of others with eloquent words (for the more they are absorbed, the more they delight), if it is toil to feed on ambrosia or sweet nectar, of which one can never get enough. Rather, it is a joyous pastime to turn over the pages of books by day and night.[15] Come then, read through your books. This is what the learned and eloquent Vergil did, and the mighty Homer, and he whom Rome called the father of his country,[16] and he who savaged King Philip with words that will never die and who spent more on the midnight oil than the king did on wine,[17] and Plato, easily the most learned of the Greeks, and his pupil, the great Aristotle, and the Doctor from Carthage,[18] and he who had a sacred name,[19] and whoever wins fame on the lips of learned men. You too, if you can grow pale in studying learned works,[20] I promise, will raise your name to the stars. Child, this is what I pray for — both I myself, father of your better part, and whoever will be your virtuous teacher — may you be pure and devout and do not abandon holy ways. Ah! Shun all that makes you sinful, child. May virtue and the exalted name of Jesus ever be dear to your heart. In this way your fame will lift you to the stars.

: II :

Aldus Manutius adolescentibus studiosis s. p. d.

1 Si quod ait poeta verum est, 'Foelix qui potuit rerum cognoscere causas,' foelices nimirum ob tantam bonorum librorum copiam quanta nullo unquam tempore fuit eritis studiosi. Undique enim vobis adsunt instrumenta ad liberales disciplinas comparandas. Habetis iam a nobis plurima Graeca volumina, tam in dialectice quam in philosophia, ut, nisi vobis ipsi defueritis, facile in viros doctissimos possitis evadere causasque rerum cognoscere. Non desunt praeterea vobis excellentes magistri quales prisca aetas tulit qui vobis et docendo et scribendo plurimum prosint. In quibus est Laurentius Maiolus Genuensis, vir apprime doctus ac miro ingenio. Is enim Ferrariae publico conductus stipendio philosophiam summa cum laude profitetur, itaque est ornatus moribus ut omnibus ea in urbe sit carus, praecipueque divo Herculi Estensi, qui mirum in modum favet ingeniis.

2 Idemque, cum semper aliquid in liberalibus disciplinis et medicina, cum exercendi ingenii gratia, tum praecipue ut vos erudiat, accurate conscribat, haec mihi misit imprimenda, scitu quidem perdigna, sed, ut oportebat, elegantia minime exornata. Quamobrem recusavi ipse primum rogavique ut expoliret, cum id quam optime praestare posset (est enim et Graece et Latine sane quam doctus), hinc ad me mitteret. Sed cum instaret amice nunc coram, nunc litteris, ut vel sic imprimerentur, quod ea edere, ut discipulis

: II :

Lorenzo Maioli, Gleanings[21] in Dialectics

(July 1497)

Aldus Manutius to his young students, warmest greetings.

1 The poet said, "Fortunate is he who has been able to discover the causes of things."[22] If that is true, students, you will surely be fortunate; for you now enjoy a greater supply of fine books than ever existed in the past. You are surrounded by the tools that will enable you to master the liberal arts. Already from us you have a large number of Greek works, both in dialectics and in philosophy,[23] so that if you realize your full potential you will easily turn out to be the most learned of men and be able to know the causes of things. Moreover you have excellent instructors, the equals of an earlier age, whose teaching and writings can be of the greatest assistance to you. These include Lorenzo Maioli of Genoa,[24] a man of outstanding erudition and marvelous intellect. For Ferrara appointed him to a teaching position in philosophy, a subject which he teaches with great distinction, and his character is such that everyone in that city holds him dear, especially the divine Ercole d'Este,[25] who gives wonderful support to men of talent.

2 Since Maioli is always engaged in carefully writing something in the liberal arts and in medicine, not just for the exercising of his mind but also and especially for your instruction, he sent me this work to be printed. The contents certainly deserve to be known but they lacked the appropriate elegance of style. At first I refused him and asked him to give the work some polish, since he could do this as well as anyone (for he is certainly most learned in Greek and Latin) and then to send it to me. But he pressed me in an amicable way, both in person and by letter, that it should be printed even just as it is, as he was under the compulsion of pub-

et amicis efflagitantibus morem gereret, cogeretur, recepi tandem facturum me quod petebat, eoque studiosius quod ea vobis magnopere profutura non dubitabam.

3 Litteras vero eius quibus me rogavit infra idcirco apposui ut ex ipsis cur minus eleganter haec vobis edere properaverit cognoscatis. Vestrum est igitur tanti viri lucubrationes assidua manu evolvere donec vos quantum profeceritis non poeniteat. Valete.

: III :

Aldus Manutius Romanus Marino Sannuto Leonardi filio, patritio Veneto, s. p. d.

1 Urbem hanc Venetam saepenumero mecum mirari soleo, Marine Sannute, vir praestantissime, cum infinitis prope rebus quibus alter orbis magis quam urbs mihi esse videtur, tum praecipue propter summos viros ac summis ingeniis praeditos, peritissimosque non in administranda solum republica regendisque populis, qua in re sic sunt admirabiles ut omnibus rerum publicarum rectoribus, et qui sunt et qui fuerunt, sint sine ulla controversia anteponendi, sed etiam in dicendi facultate atque in quocunque genere doctrinarum, quorum quantus sit numerus non facile dixerim.

lishing it in order to comply with the demands of his pupils and friends. And so I finally undertook to do what he asked and I did so all the more eagerly because I had no doubts of its considerable benefit to you students.

Because of all this I have added below the letter in which he 3
made his request so that you may learn from it why he hurried to publish this work for you in a somewhat inelegant style.[26] It is up to you to study with painstaking care the learned findings of such a great man until you are satisfied with the progress you have made. Farewell.

: III :

Angelo Poliziano,[27] Complete Works

(July 1498)

Aldus Manutius of Rome to Marino Sanuto, son of Leonardo, patrician of Venice,[28] *warmest greetings.*

I often think of this city of Venice with astonishment, Marino 1
Sanuto, most excellent of men, partly because of the almost countless features that make me think that it is another world rather than another city, but also, and especially, because of the outstanding men, endowed with the sharpest intellects, that it produces. They are skilled not only in governing the state and ruling its subjects — in respect to which they are so much to be admired that without any argument they must be judged superior to all rulers of states, both past and present — but also in rhetoric and in every possible branch of learning. I could not readily say how many of such men there are!

2 His et tu, Marine, acri tuo ingenio singularique doctrina ac summa modestia merito annumeraris, qui, publicis assidue negociis deditus, nunquam tamen a scribendo et componendo cessas quod sit lectu dignissimum. Vidi ego superioribus diebus in tua librorum omnis generis refertissima bibliotheca, quos de magistratibus Venetis, de vitis principum, quicunque ab urbe condita ad haec usque tempora extiterunt, ingeniose eruditeque scripsisti libros, nec non quos de bello Gallico iam multos menses absolutos et Latina et vulgari lingua premis, ut a doctis pariter et indoctis legantur.

3 Et quanquam es doctissimus, semper tamen cum veterum tum neotericorum legis aliquid, memor Pliniani illius, 'nullum esse tam malum librum qui aliqua in parte prodesse non possit.' Ex quo itaque accepisti Angeli Politiani, summo viri ingenio et singulari doctrina, lucubrationes excudi formis in aedibus nostris, me ut editionem accelerem hortari non desinis, quod summi ingenii labores praestanti ipse ingenio legere concupiscas, addito tamen Graeco adagio σπεῦδε βραδέως. Quare tibi Politiani quaecunque habere potuimus opera, Marine suavissime, dicata muneri mittimus. Quae vero ea sint, in indice qui statim post epistolam legitur licet videre.

4 Quod siquid doctas auris tuas offendet tanquam parum elaboratum et cultum, scito non esse haec edita ab ipso, sed ab amicis, et praecipue ab Alexandro Sartio Bononiensi, literatis omnibus pergrato viro, qui amicissimi viri quaecunque habere potuit opera, multum ac diu et accurate quaesita, imprimenda curavit. Est igitur dignissimus venia Politianus noster, siquid in eius scriptis de-

Your keen intellect, outstanding erudition and unmatched propriety, Marino, justify your inclusion too among these men. For although you constantly devote yourself to your public responsibilities, you do not take a rest from writing and composing what is most worthy of being read. A few days ago I was in that library of yours, which is packed with books of every kind, and saw the books you wrote with much brilliance and learning on the magistrates of Venice,[29] and on the lives of all the leading men of the city from its founding up till these times,[30] as well as your books on the war with France,[31] which you completed many months ago and which you have had printed in both Latin and Italian so that both the learned and the uneducated may read them. 2

Although you are extremely learned, you are always reading some modern works besides those of antiquity; you are mindful of those words of Pliny, "that no book is so bad that it cannot be useful in some way."[32] And so from the time you heard that our printing house was bringing out the scholarly work of Angelo Poliziano, a man of superb intellect and outstanding erudition, you have continuously urged me to speed up the production of the edition because you, a man of great talent yourself, are eager to read the labors of the highest talent—though you have done so with the added advice of the Greek proverb "make haste slowly."[33] And so, Marino, most charming of men, we send you now as a gift, dedicated to you, all the works of Poliziano that we have been able to find. You can see what they are in the index which you can read immediately after this letter. 3

If anything offends your learned ears because it lacks finish and refinement, you must remember that these works have not been published by Poliziano himself but by his friends, and especially by Alessandro Sarti of Bologna,[34] a man held very dear by all men of literature. After a long and careful search he undertook to have printed all the works of his dearest friend that he could obtain. And so our great Poliziano deserves to be forgiven if any fault is 4

prehendetur vitii, quandoquidem 'emendaturus, si licuisset, erat,' immo si annos suos vixisset, et leges ex pandectis quae olim Pisanae fuerunt in pristinam, quod coeperat facere, lectionem restituisset, commentariosque in illas, quod praedicabat, non barbare, sed more Romano et doctissime confecisset. Coeperat etiam foeliciter et miro successu a barbaris philosophiam ipsam asserere. Pollicebatur quoque intra decennium liberalissimas artes omnis et viva voce et scriptis se luculentissime enarraturum. O immaturam et crudelem mortem quae maxime saevit in summa ingenia! O iacturam semper dolendam, quando multa vir ille scitu dignissima posteris reliquisset quae fortasse nunquam scientur!

5 Sed utinam et secundam centuriam *Miscellaneorum*, et *Epiphyllidas*, et in Tranquillum, in Terentium, in Statium, in Quintilianum ingeniosas et doctas annotationes, et alia quam plurima, ex quibus vel centum facere centurias potuisset, habuissemus! Prodiissent et illa in publicum profutura hominibus, quae, ut audio, quidam Florentiae occultant ut edant pro suis. Sed stulte quidem; nam id profecerint, ut, siquid ipsi unquam dignum scitu invenerint ediderintque, magis Politiani quam eorum esse ⟨.....⟩[2] docti omnes, qui suppressa quam plurima Politiani esse opera a quibusdam quos alienis pennis se valere nihil pudet, obnixe contendent. Vale.

detected in his writings since "he would have made corrections if the opportunity had been granted him."[35] Nay, more than that! If he had lived his allotted span,[36] he would have restored the text of the laws from the *Pandects,* formerly in Pisa,[37] to their original form, as he had begun to do, and he would have completed commentaries on them, his declared intent, and would have done so in no crude fashion but in the Roman way and with great learning.[38] He had even begun fruitfully and with wondrous success to free philosophy from the grasp of the barbarians.[39] He also promised that within ten years he would shed great light on all the liberal arts, both in his lectures and in his writings. How awful it is that a cruel and early death especially strikes down the greatest talents! O what a loss that we shall always grieve for, since that man would have bequeathed to posterity many things most worthy of knowing, material that perhaps will never be known.

If only we had the second century of *Miscellanea,*[40] his *Epiphyl-* 5
lides, his brilliant and learned commentaries on Suetonius, Terence, Statius and Quintilian,[41] and many other works that would fill up even a hundred centuries! Mankind would also have benefited from the publication of those works which, so I hear, some people keep concealed in Florence, intending to publish them as their own.[42] But this is certainly foolish. For the only thing that they will gain from this is that all scholars will think that anything of value found and published by these persons is not so much their work, but that of Poliziano; they will strenuously argue that countless works of Poliziano have been suppressed by some individuals who are not ashamed to win success by flying with someone else's wings. Farewell.

: IV :

A

Aldus Manutius Romanus lectori s.

1 Omne inventum, quantumvis ingeniosum et conducibile, adulterari longa die, ac potius malitia hominum qui, se sibi solis rati natos, student semper ex alienis incommodis sua ut comparent commoda, converti in malum constat; quemadmodum temporibus nostris accidisse videmus in miro hoc et quam laboriosissimo modo scribendorum librorum.

2 Nam quantum quisque commodi ex ea re futurum sperabat nemo est qui non perspiciat; quantum item inde incommodi, quanta bonorum librorum pernicies, quanta ruina et iam sit et futura, nisi Deus prohibeat, videatur non queo dicere. Primum enim in quorum artificum manus pervenerint sacra literarum monumenta videmus; deinde qua literatura praediti quidam libros omnis enarrare, commentari, corrigere audeant scimus. Quamobrem periculum non mediocre est ne beneficium hoc imprimendi libros a Deo immortali hominibus datum ipsi, cum liceat vel infantissimo cuique pro animi sui libidine temere in quem vult librum grassari, in maximum maleficium convertamus et sanctarum literarum perniciem.

3 Sed de hoc alias. Non enim brevi epistola opus esset, si singillatim et cumulate tractare id velim. Illud nolo silentio praeteriri me,

: IV :

Niccolò Perotti, Cornucopiae

(July 1499)

A

Aldus Manutius of Rome to his reader, greetings.

It is generally agreed that every invention, no matter how ingenious and useful, is tainted by the passage of time and indeed becomes a curse less through time than through the wickedness of those human beings who are completely self-centered and are always eager to procure advantages for themselves at the expense of others. In our own times we have seen that this has befallen our marvelous, though most exhausting way of printing books. 1

Everyone can perceive how much profit each of such men was hoping to acquire from the printing press. I cannot say how much harm this invention seems to have caused, how much destruction and ruination of good books has arisen and will arise from it unless God prevents it. First of all, we see the kind of artisans into whose hands the sacred monuments of literature have fallen; secondly, we know how certain men with little education dare to explain, comment on and emend every book. Therefore there is no little danger that we ourselves may transform this blessing of how to print books, granted to us by immortal God, into the greatest of banes and bring about the destruction of noble letters; for all the most inarticulate of men can recklessly put their hands to any book at all as their desires lead them. 2

But more of this on another occasion. For it would need a very long letter if I wished to treat this topic comprehensively, point by point. I do not wish to leave it unsaid, that to the best of my abil- 3

quod in me erit — pedibus manibusque, ut aiunt — facturum ut laboranti rei literariae consulatur.

4 Quemadmodum hoc in libro fecimus, in quo plurima vulnera ope et labore nostro sanata sunt, licet multa sint praetermissa consulto, quod non esset satis ocii ad curandum. Quis enim in tanta operarum, ac potius inimicorum (nam tot inimici, quot operae) vel festinatione vel ignorantia vel malitia aliquid mediocri etiam dignum laude queat efficere? Si diem unum aut biduum triduumve ad summum mecum viveres, studiose lector, mirum diceres si quid a nobis bene factum est fieri potuisse. Sed si quo volo tandem hoc saxum volvero, si potuero aliquando parere quod iandiu et multos annos parturio, spero, volente Iesu, Deo optimo maximo, unde optimum quodque donum et omne bonum perfectum proficiscitur, effecturum quod cupio ac studiosis omnibus hac nostra perlaboriosa provincia satis abundeque facturum.

5 Habes nunc, lector amice, diligenter ac miro ordine typis nostris excusum Perotti Sypontini pontificis cornucopiae, in quo si quid vel a nobis vel ab ipso authore erratum fuerit, ignoscendum est nobis, ob eas ipsas quas supra diximus rationes, authori, quia non ipse, sed Pyrrhus fratris filius hunc librum ediderit. Morte enim praeventus recognoscere non potuit suas has perdoctas et laboriosas lucubrationes. Quare et ipse de suis Latinae linguae commentariis iure dicere moriens potuisset, 'Emendaturus, si licuisset, eram.'

6 Improbe igitur faciunt quidam in alieno libro ingeniosi, cum in mortuos de nobis bene meritos invehuntur. Quin potius, cum ali-

ity—with hand and feet,[43] as the saying goes—I will strive to look after the good health of the republic of letters in its distress.

That is what we have done in the case of this book, in which many defects have been removed through my aid and labor, although many have been deliberately passed over, since I did not have sufficient time to attend to them. For when one's workers (or rather, one's enemies, since one has as many enemies as one has workers) are consumed by haste, or are acting in ignorance or with malice, who can accomplish anything worthy of even moderate praise? If you were to live with me for one day or two days or three at the most, my learned reader, you would say it must have been a miracle that it was possible for us to do whatever we did well. But if I roll this stone of mine to where I wish,[44] if I can finally give birth to what I have been carrying, as it were, for many years now, I hope (Jesus, God Almighty, willing, from whom all perfect gifts and blessings flow) that I will fulfill my desire to do sufficient and more for all devotees of learning in this chosen profession of mine that is so demanding of my energy. 4

You now have in your possession, my dear reader, the *Cornucopiae* of Perotti, archbishop of Siponto,[45] which we have printed in our type with great care and with admirable organization of the material. If we or the author himself have made any errors, you must forgive not only us (for the very reasons we have just given) but also the author, because it was not he, but his nephew Pirro,[46] who published this book. For Perotti's premature death prevented him from reviewing these learned and painstaking deliberations of his. This is why, when he was dying, with justification he himself could have said about his commentary on the Latin language, "I would have corrected the errors, if it had been allowed me."[47] 5

And so some clever men are quite shameless in their treatment of someone else's book, when they revile the dead who have served us well. When they discover that an author has nodded at some point (human nature being what it is), they should not take pride 6

quo in loco dormitasse authorem, quae humana est natura, inveniunt, non praedicando gloriari, non scriptis publicare, sed taciti ac si ipsi opus composuissent emendare deberent, atque ita gratiam referre benefactori, qui quam maxime potuit utilis fuit studuitque prodesse posteritati. Vale.

B

7 Quo facilius noster hic inveniendorum vocabulorum index intelligatur, scito, carissime lector, primum numerum conclusum punctis semipaginam significare, secundum vero numerum, punctis item conclusum, semipaginae versum, et sic tertium, si quis fuerit, eiusdem semipaginae versum ostendere, donec ad *et* coniunctionem pervenias: nam primus numerus post *et* coniunctionem semipaginam ostendit, secundus vero semipaginae versum, et sic tertius et quartus semipaginae versus demonstrant, si qui fuerint. Exempli gratia, *examen* sic est in indice: 'Examen .36.21.25. et .281.34.' hoc est: semipagina trigesima sexta, versu vigesimo primo, versu vigesimo quinto, et semipagina ducentesima octogesima prima, versu 34; et sic in caeteris.

C

Ad lectorem.

8 Recognito diligenter toto volumine, carissime lector, errores qui alicuius momenti visi sunt collegi, ut facile tu tibi librum tuum emendare possis; caeteros, si qui relicti sunt, consulto praetermisi, ratus perfaciles cognitu vel mediocriter eruditis. Nec omnes impressorum incuria aut festinatione factos putes; nam multi exemplarium culpa evenerunt; quanquam, si studiose nostrum hunc librum cum caeteris conferas, in mille locis et amplius emendatum invenies.

in proclaiming it abroad or in publishing it in their writings, but rather they should correct an error silently just as if they themselves had composed the work. In this way they give thanks to their benefactor who was as useful as he possibly could be and strove to benefit posterity. Farewell.

B[48]

Dearest reader, so that you may more readily understand our index for finding words, be informed that the first number, marked off by periods, refers to a page,[49] while the second number, also marked off by periods, refers to a line of the page, and the third number, if there is one, indicates the line of the same page. When you encounter the conjunction *et*, the first number to follow it indicates a page, the second a line in the page, as do the third or fourth numbers, if there are any. By way of an example the entry for *examen* in the index is "*Examen* .31.21.25 et .282.34," that is, page 31, lines 21 and 25 and page 282, line 34. Likewise for all other entries. 7

C

To the reader.

Dearest reader, after carefully going through the whole volume, I have gathered together those errors that I thought were of some importance; you can then readily correct your own copy for yourself. I deliberately passed over all the other remaining ones, since I thought that they could be easily recognized by readers of even modest education. Do not think that all of these were the result of the carelessness or haste of the compositors. Many occurred because of the fault of the master copy. However, if you compare with keen attentiveness this book with all others in circulation,[50] you will find in it a thousand and more corrections. 8

: V :

Aldus Manutius Romanus literarii ludi magistris s. p. d.

1 *Rudimenta grammatices Latinae linguae* a nobis olim composita optime factum existimavi si ad vos iuventutis moderatores et morum magistros legenda committerem, non quia putarem indigere vos ineptiis nostris (quanquam dicere solebat Plinius 'nullum esse librum tam malum, qui non aliqua parte prodesset'), sed potius ut, siquid erratum fuerit (homines enim sumus), amice castigaretis, tum ut quod fieri a vobis velim erudiendis instituendisque pueris, quandoquidem id illis valde profuturum arbitrabar, vos rogarem.

2 Primum, ut memineritis oportere vos eorum quos accepistis instituendos sic satagere ut simul et docti fiant et sanctis imbuantur moribus, quia 'Quo semel est imbuta, recens servabit odorem / Testa diu' atque 'adeo a teneris assuescere multum est.' Nec solum rectores magistrosque vos esse adolescentium, sed et parentes putetis; scitis enim illud 'Qui praeceptorem sancti voluere parentis / Esse loco.'

3 Equidem bonos malosve vos esse tantum referre existimo ut ausim dicere bonorum malorumque omnium quae ubique terrarum fiunt vos esse potissimam causam. Nam iurisconsulti, philosophi, rectores urbium, principes item ducesque ac reges, necnon monachi, sacerdotes, episcopi, cardinales ipsique summi pontifices, et denique quicunque vel solas literarum notas tenent, sub

: V :

Aldus Manutius, Rudiments of Latin Grammar

(February–June 1501)

Aldus Manutius of Rome to grammar school teachers, warmest greetings.

I thought I had done something quite splendid by giving you to read my *Rudiments of Latin Grammar,* composed some time ago,[51] for you are in charge of our young students and give them moral instruction. It was not because I thought that you were in need of my trifling efforts (although Pliny was in the habit of saying that "no book was so bad that it did not have some good in it somewhere"[52]), but rather so that you might correct in an amicable manner any errors of mine (for we are human) and also so that I might request of you what I would like you to do in teaching and instructing young boys, since I thought that this would be of great profit to them. 1

First, you must remember that your prime concern should be that those whom you have taken on to instruct will turn out well educated and at the same time have high moral principles instilled in them, because "Long will a pot retain the taste / of what in it when fresh was placed"[53] and "so important it is to habituate them from an early age."[54] Do not think of yourselves just as tutors or teachers of young boys but also as parents; for you know the sentiment, "They wished the instructor to have the role of a revered parent."[55] 2

For my part I think it matters a great deal whether you are of good or bad character, so much so that I dare to say that you are the prime cause of all the good and bad things that are done in the world. Lawyers, philosophers, rulers of cities, princes, dukes and kings as well as monks, priests, bishops, cardinals and even popes (and in fact whoever who can do little more than read) — all these 3

disciplina olim vestra fuere parvuli, a vobis instituti sunt, virtus vestra vitiumve eorum profuit aut nocuit moribus. Tantum valet longa consuetudo ut, si cum sancto diu vixeris, sanctus futurus sis, si cum perverso, pervertaris: siquidem, ut inquit Fabius, 'Leonides Alexandri paedagogus quibusdam eum vitiis imbuit quae robustum quoque et maximum regem ab illa institutione puerili sunt prosecuta.' Quamobrem quantum boni et sancti praeceptores civitatibus prosint non facile dixerim; quantum item obsint pravi et vitiosi non queo dicere.

4 Quare non possum non multum mirari nullam fere puerorum patribus et rectoribus urbium in eligendis praeceptorum moribus esse curam. Non animadvertunt quantum inde boni malive infundatur in civitates. Nam, quales sunt qui instituunt, tales et qui instituuntur, velint nolint, evadent longa die. 'Longa dies homini docuit parere leones, / longa dies molli saxa peredit aqua.' Videte igitur vos, qui et longo tempore et assidue teneros et simplices adolescentulorum animos instituitis, quantum et prodesse potestis et obesse hominibus. Quod si quisquam est sic oblitus sui ipsius ut agnos suae commissos fidei ceu lupus devoret, heu quanta illum poena apud manes vel brevi expectat! Nam, qui ita pernitiosi sunt ut non solum obsint quod illi ipsi corrumpuntur, sed etiam quod corrumpunt plusque exemplo quam peccato nocent, immatura morte, ne tantum obesse queant, ne mundum corrumpant, rapiuntur.

5 Itaque enitendum pro viribus ut et sanctos mores et bonas literas simul edoceantur adolescentuli, quando alterum sine altero

were small boys under you as their teacher, they were instructed by you, your virtues or your vices nourished or harmed their character. Lengthy association with someone is so influential that if you live for a long time with a saint you will become a saint, if you live with a roué you yourself will become one. As Quintilian said, "Leonidas, the tutor of Alexander, instilled in him certain vices in his boyhood education that remained with him even when he was a mature and mighty king."[56] And so it would be hard for me to put into words how much good and upright teachers benefit our cities; how much harm done by depraved and dissolute teachers is beyond words.

This is why I cannot help being amazed that parents and rulers of cities show hardly any concern about teachers' morals when they choose them. They are unaware of how much good or harm teachers contribute to their cities. For, whether they wish it or not, those who are being taught will turn out over a long time to be like those who teach them. "A long time has taught lions to obey humans, a long time has eaten away rocks with gentle water."[57] Over a long time and with unceasing efforts you instruct the tender and ingenuous minds of youths; consider therefore how much good or harm you can do to your fellow human beings. But if anyone so forgets his position as to devour, like a wolf, the lambs that have been entrusted to his care, alas, what a speedy and severe penalty awaits him in the afterworld. For those who are so depraved that they do harm not just through their own corrupt state but also through their corruption of others and the damage they inflict (their example being more harmful than even their own sins) — those persons are snatched off by premature death so that they cannot do too much harm or corrupt the world too pervasively. 4

And so we must strive with all our strength to see to it that our young are taught virtuous behavior at the same time as they are being taught good letters, since in no way can one of these be done 5

facere nullo modo licet; at si in altero peccandum foret, potior mihi ratio vivendi honeste quam vel optime discendi videretur. Malo enim eos nullas scire literas ornatos moribus quam omnia scire male moratos, malisque simillimos esse daemonibus, qui, multa scientes — nam id ideo illis inditum est a Graecis nomen — sunt quam pessimi.

6 Alterum quod vos meminisse velim est, nequid nisi doctissimorum authorum ediscere cogatis adolescentulos. Immo ne grammaticas quidem regulas, nisi compendia quaedam brevissima quae teneri facile memoria queant, laudo eos ediscere; sed tantum ut illas assidue accurateque legant, nominaque et verba declinare optime sciant. Nam, dum lucubrationes nostras vel carmine vel prosa oratione, etiam de arte, commendare memoriae eos cogimus, erramus, ut mihi quidem videtur, multis modis.

7 Primum quod, quae summo labore edidicerunt, dediscunt paucis diebus; quod ego et puer olim et iuvenis, compositis etiam a me regulis, sum saepe expertus. Nam, cum generum regulas praeteritorumve summa cura mandassem memoriae, perbrevi obliviscebar; idem caeteris quoque evenire existimo. Praeterea difficultate tum materiae tum stili eo desperationis veniunt ut et scholas et literas fugiant, et studia quae amare nondum possunt maxime oderint. Tum eo ipso tempore quo nostra ediscunt facilius meliusque vel Ciceronis aliquid vel Vergilii aliorumve illustrium possent ediscere, olim et decori et commodo illis non mediocri futurum. Equidem puero mihi, cum Alexandri carmen ineptum de arte

without the other. But if one were to fall short in one area, I think that how to live an honorable life is more important than even how to acquire learning in the best possible way. For I prefer upright youths who know nothing of literature to immoral persons who know everything and are very like evil spirits, who know much — for that is why they are given the name they have in Greek[58] — but are as wicked as can be.

There is another point I would like you to remember, that you should compel your young pupils to learn by heart only what is in the most learned of authors. What is more, I am not even in favor of their learning by heart grammatical rules, apart from some very brief abridged ones that can be easily remembered — and only then to the extent that they read them constantly and carefully and have excellent knowledge of how to decline nouns and verbs. For in compelling them to commit to memory the results of our labors either in verse or prose, or even to memorize the *Ars*,[59] we are mistaken, in my opinion, in many ways. 6

First, they unlearn in a few days what they have struggled with the greatest labor to learn by heart. This was often my experience as a boy and young man, even of rules that I myself had composed. Although I exerted the greatest effort in committing to memory rules of gender and past tenses, I very soon forgot them. I think this same thing happens to everyone else as well. Moreover, because of the difficulty of both the material and its presentation pupils become so disheartened that they shun school and letters and have extreme loathing for pursuits that they are not yet able to enjoy. Another point is that in the time it takes them to learn by heart what we have devised it would be easier and more profitable for them if they could learn by heart something of Cicero or Vergil or of other famous writers that will at some time in the future be very useful to them and elicit admiration. For my part I am quite grieved that I was not allowed to do this when I 7

grammatica memoriae mandabam, non ita contigisse plurimum doleo.

8 Addite quod, cum incultos et barbaros discimus, tales et ipsi evadimus. Solemus enim iis quos imitamur plerunque esse deteriores. Quapropter 'optimos et statim et semper legendos,' putat Quintilianus, 'atque eorum candidissimum quenque et maxime expolitum.' Tum de Cicerone sic inquit: 'Cicero, ut mihi quidem videtur, et iocundus incipientibus quoque et apertus est satis, nec prodesse tantum, sed etiam amari potest. Tum, quemadmodum Plinius praecipit, ut quisque erit Ciceroni simillimus.' Sed de genere hoc longa haberi posset oratio. Haec vero attigimus nostro erga studiosos summo amore; quare vos etiam atque etiam rogo ut boni quicquid diximus consulatis. Valete.

Venetiis mense Iunio MDI.[3]

: VI :

Aldus Romanus Alberto Pio Carpensium principi s. p. d.

1 Adeo verum est, Alberte doctissime, quod aiunt, plurimum incendi homines ad studia maiorum exemplo, ut, cum quis extiterit ex aliqua familia clarus vel doctrina vel armis, omnes fere ex ea nati illius gloriam maxime aemulentur; atque hinc puto Romanos olim rerum dominos maiorum suorum statuas, et eorum illustrium, ordine domi positas summa cura habuisse quo iuvenes

was a young boy and was trying to learn by heart the artless poem of Alexander on the art of grammar.[60]

Moreover when we learn crude and barbarous material we our- 8
selves turn out that way since for the most part we are usually inferior to those whom we imitate. This is why Quintilian thinks "that the best authors should be read constantly and from the moment we start learning the language, and of these we should read all those who write in the most lucid and polished way."[61] Then he says of Cicero, "In my opinion, Cicero appeals to beginners and he writes in a clear style; not only can he help them but he can engender affection in them for him. Then as Pliny advises, each will be as similar to Cicero as possible."[62] But I could deliver a lengthy speech on this topic. However, we have touched on it from our deep devotion to our students. And so I earnestly beg of you to take in good part all that I have said. Farewell.

Venice, June 1501.[63]

: VI :

Gianfrancesco Pico,[64] On Imagination
(April 1501)

Aldus of Rome to Alberto Pio, prince of Carpi,[65] *warmest greetings.*

Most learned Alberto, it is quite true that, as is said, men are 1
greatly fired up to choose their pursuits by the examples of their forefathers. For when a member of a family wins fame in learning or in warfare, almost all of those born into this family strive mightily to emulate his glory. This is why I think that the Romans, once masters of the world, were scrupulous in placing statues of their ancestors (and illustrious ones at that) in their homes in chronological order so that young men might be inspired by the

illorum gloria ad aliquid praeclare agendum incenderentur, ut et ipsi digni quibus statuae erigerentur evaderent; ipsas quoque respublicas claris viris statuas identidem erexisse. 'Quod temporibus nostris, ut alia praeclara, ita et hoc in primis exolevit.' Nam qui suorum statuas domi habeat nemo est; publice autem sic raro fieri solet ut nos vix semel, idque Venetiis ubi aliqua priscae illius antiquitatis vestigia remanent, viderimus.

2 Incendimur profecto plurimum ad virtutes et studia exemplo et gloria nostrorum; et, ne longe exempla petantur, te ad sapientiae studium, quo iam excellis, et avus excitat Albertus, qui non minus literis quam armis claruit, et avunculus Ioannes Picus, homo undecunque doctissimus. Hoc eodem sic excitatur ad bonas literas Ioannes Franciscus Mirandulanus princeps, amitinus tuus, ut iam tot opera quot patruus composuerit, quae fere omnia impressa visuntur. Idem nunc in psalmos commentaria quae patruus morte praeventus emendare non potuit accurate recognoscit: mirum opus et doctrinae plenum.

3 Eius ipsius *De imaginatione* librum cum superioribus diebus imprimendum curassem, placuit ad te, cui omnia debeo, dono mittere, quod scirem fore tibi gratissimum, tum ipso opere, tum etiam quod a Ioanne Francisco Pico amitino tuo sit editus, atque Aldi tui typis diligenter excusus. Vale.

glory of these men to achieve great fame in some endeavor and might themselves turn out to be worthy of having statues erected for them. Even states continued for a long time to erect statues of famous men. "In our times this custom, like many other excellent ones, has become quite obsolete."[66] For there is no one nowadays who has statues of his family in his home, and it is such a rare practice of cities that we have scarcely seen one such statue—and that is true even for Venice, where some vestiges of ancient customs remain.

We are certainly greatly fired up to aim for excellence and noble 2
achievements by the example and glory of our own family members. To take an example close to home, your grandfather Alberto,[67] who was as distinguished in the world of letters as on the battlefield, spurs you on to study philosophy, a discipline in which you now excel, as does also your uncle Giovanni Pico,[68] a man most learned on every subject. Your cousin, Gianfrancesco, prince of Mirandola, has been so inspired by this same person to engage in the study of good letters that he has already composed as many works as his uncle and almost all of these can be seen in print. He is also now engaged in going carefully over the commentaries on the Psalms that his uncle was prevented from correcting by his death—a marvelous work and full of erudition.[69]

When a few days ago I had seen to the printing of this very 3
man's book *On Imagination* I decided to send it as a gift to you, to whom I owe everything. I thought you would derive much pleasure from it, not only because of the nature of the work itself but also because it is a publication of your cousin Gianfrancesco and has been carefully set in the type of your dear friend Aldus. Farewell.

: VII :

Aldus Manutius Romanus Iacobo Sanazaro patritio Neapolitano et equiti clarissimo s. p. d.

1 Georgius Interianus Genuensis, homo frugi, venit iam annum Venetias; quo cum primum adplicuit, etsi me de facie non cognosceret nec ulla inter nos familiaritas intercederet, me tamen officiose adiit, tum quia ipse benignus est et sane quam humanus, tum etiam quia Daniel Clarius Parmensis, vir utraque lingua doctus et qui in urbe Rhacusa publice summa cum laude profitetur bonas literas, ei ut me suo nomine salutaret iniunxerat, mihique statim sic factus est familiaris ac si vixisset mecum. Est enim homo, ut nosti, facetus ac integer vitae et doctorum hominum studiosissimus. Tum visus est mihi Homeri Ulysses alter; nam et ipse *μάλα πολλὰ πλάγχθη . . . πολλῶν δ' ἀνθρώπων ἴδεν ἄστεα καὶ νόον ἔγνω, / πολλὰ δ' ὅγ' ἐν πόντῳ πάθεν ἄλγεα ὃν κατὰ θυμόν*. Non miror igitur si et tu plurimum eo homine delectaris, et Pontanus, vir doctissimus ac aetate nostra Vergilius alter, et Politianus, olim multi homo studii ac summo ingenio, qui etiam in *Miscellaneis* suis de eo ipso Georgio meminit, delectatus est.

2 Is vulgari lingua libellum de eorum Sarmatarum vita et moribus composuit, qui a Strabone et Plinio et Stephano Zygi appellantur, qui ultra Tanain fluvium et Maeotin paludem habitant orientem versus eumque ad me misit imprimendum hac lege ut ubicunque

: VII :

Giorgio Interiano,[70] The Land and Customs of the Zygians called Circassians[71]

(October 1502)

Aldus Manutius of Rome to Iacopo Sannazaro,[72] *patrician of Naples and most distinguished knight, warmest greetings.*

Giorgio Interiano of Genoa, a man of upstanding character, has 1
been in Venice for a year now. Even though he did not know me personally and we had had no dealings with each other, he approached me the moment he arrived and did so in a very respectful manner, not only because of his kind and courteous nature but also because Daniele Clario[73] of Parma, a man learned in both Greek and Latin and a most distinguished teacher of classical literature appointed by the city of Ragusa, had enjoined him to pay his respects to me on his account. Immediately we became friends. It was as if we had spent our lives together. For, as you know, he is witty, virtuous and extremely well-versed in the works of scholars. I also thought of him as Homer's second Ulysses. For he too had "traveled far and wide [. . .] seeing the cities and learning the ways of many men, enduring much suffering in his heart on the open sea."[74] I am not surprised, then, that you take great delight in this man as does Pontano,[75] a most learned man and a second Vergil in the present time, and as, in the past, did Poliziano, a man of great accomplishment and of the highest intellect. The latter even mentioned this very Giorgio in his *Miscellanea*.[76]

He has composed a book in the vernacular on the life and the 2
customs of the Sarmatians, who are called Zygians by Strabo, Pliny and Stephanus,[77] and who live in the east beyond the river Don and the sea of Azov.[78] He sent it to me to be printed on this condition, that I should make corrections wherever necessary.

opus esset emendarem. Sed ego immutavi tantum quod in orthographia peccare videbatur; caetera, ut maior fides historiae haberetur, dimisi ut ipse composuit.

3 Ipsum autem libellum, quoniam gratissimum tibi fore existimamus, tum ipsa historia tum summo ipsius Georgii in te amore ad te mittimus, simul ut hac ad te epistola peterem ut quae et Latina et vulgari lingua docte et eleganter composuisti ad me perquam diligenter castigata dares, ut excusa typis nostris edantur in manus studiosorum quam emendatissima et digna Sanazaro. Nam quae impressa habentur valde sunt depravata ab impressoribus.

4 Vale, vir doctissime suavissimeque; et me fac diligas, quemadmodum facere te accepi a Marco Musuro Cretensi, iuvene et Latine et Graece oppido quam erudito atque utriusque nostrum amantissimo.

Venetiis XX Octobris DII.

: VIII :

A

Aldus Ioanni Collaurio Caesaris ab epistolis s.

1 Frequens est apud Graecos proverbium, Collauri officiosissime: *χεὶρ χεῖρα νίπτει καὶ δάκτυλος δάκτυλον*, quod est Latine 'Manus manum lavat et digitus digitum.' Quoniam tu plurimum favisti nobis apud Maximilianum Caesarem pro Academia con-

However, I changed only what seemed to be errors in orthography. All the rest I published just as he composed it, so that there would be greater confidence in the truth of his account.

The book itself we are sending to you as we think that because 3
of its content and Giorgio's deep love of you it will give you the greatest pleasure. At the same time I thought I would use this letter to ask you to give me your learned and elegant writings in both Latin and Italian, after carefully correcting them. In that way they will be printed in our type and given into the hands of scholars in as perfect a form as possible and one worthy of Sannazaro. I say this for the copies that are available now have been terribly corrupted by the printers.[79]

Farewell, most learned and most charming of men, and assure 4
me that your love for me is as I heard of it from Marcus Musurus of Crete,[80] a young man who is very erudite in both Latin and Greek and is devoted to both of us.

Venice, October 20, 1502.

: VIII :

Giovanni Pontano,[81] Urania, Meteora, The Gardens of the Hesperides, etc.

(May–August 1505)

A

Aldus to Johann Kollauer,[82] *secretary to the emperor.*

The Greeks have a popular proverb, my dear Kollauer, you who 1
are the most obliging of men: *χεὶρ χεῖρα νίπτει καὶ δάκτυλος δάκτυλον*, "hand washes hand and finger washes finger."[83] You have shown to Emperor Maximilian very great support for us on

stituenda, cum Ioannes Fruticenus, eruditus iuvenis, istic meo nomine accurate rem literariam procuraret, et, qui tuus est amor in literatos viros et doctrinas, assidue faves, meas esse partes duxi ut, quo possem modo, gratum mihi extitisse officium tuum cognosceres. Nam etsi nihil est adhuc factum, tamen quod et tu et Matthaeus Longius, viri doctissimi ac integerrimi Caesaris a secretis, ad me scripsistis, tum vero Caesar ipse benignissimis literis significavit, futurum tua opera, tuo studio facile spero, praesertimque cum rex natus ad commune bonum id maxime cupiat, ut, quemadmodum est armorum, ita et bonarum literarum sit decus et gloria.

2 Qua re Ioviani Pontani poëmata, quae et meo et doctorum omnium iudicio cum antiquis certant, sub tuo nomine publicamus tibique muneri mittimus. Delectabit te, scio, non mediocriter Urania, cum et ortus et occasus syderum leges solisque ac lunae prognostica et pleraque alia lectu dignissima; delectabunt Meteora, cum nubium, ventorum, pluviarum, grandinum, maris procellarum, terrae motuum atque id genus plurium causas leges; delectabunt *Horti Hesperidum* citriorum et citrorum cultu pervario, praeterea Macronis et Lepidinae rusticae dulcesque confabulationes, et caetera omnia Pontani nostri docta, culta, elegantia, varia, copiosa et plena ingenio. Vale.

the question of establishing an Academy when Ioannes Fruticenus, a learned young man,[84] was giving careful attention there to a literary matter on my behalf, and persist in giving that support (such is your devotion to men of literature and scholarship). Therefore I thought that it was incumbent upon me to make you aware as best I could of how grateful I am for your services. For although nothing on this front has happened yet, nevertheless from what you and Matthaus Lang,[85] both of you in the secretariat of the emperor and both of you men of learning and the utmost integrity, wrote to me and from what the emperor himself expressed in a most generous letter, I have high hopes (especially when the king, born to serve the common good, particularly desires it) that thanks to your efforts and zeal he will be the glory and adornment of good letters as well as of warfare.

Accordingly we are publishing under your name and sending 2
you as a gift the poems of Giovanni Pontano. In the judgment of all learned men as well as in mine these match in quality the work of the classical poets. I know that you will take no little pleasure in the *Urania* when you read of the rising and setting of the stars, the weather signs provided by the sun and moon, and many other topics that deserve to be read. You will take pleasure in the *Meteora* when you read the causes of clouds, winds, rain, hail, storms at sea, earthquakes and many other things of this kind. You will take pleasure in *The Gardens of the Hesperides,* with the great variety of methods in how to cultivate citrons and citron trees. You will in addition take pleasure in the sweet rustic dialogues of Macron and Lepidina,[86] and all the other works of our dear Pontano, which display erudition, polish, elegance, a wide range of topics, much detail and pervasive talent. Farewell.

B

Aldus lectori s.

3 Non ab re visum fuit si quae Pontanus ipse in principio libri meteororum manu sua scripta paucis ante diebus quam e vita discederet ad me misit imprimenda hoc loco curarem. Ea vero sunt: 'Liber hic *Meteororum* fuerat ante *Uraniae* libros scriptus; verum, prius quam ederetur, furto fuit ob livorem subreptum. Itaque, absoluta *Urania,* autor illum refecit et tanquam instauravit, additque *Uraniae* libris.'

C

Aldus Suardino Suardo Bergomati s.

4 Summa benevolentia in te mea ob dulceis mores tuos et vitae integritatem, suavissime Suardine, fecit ut Pontani nostri hendecasyllabos cura nostra excusos sub tuo nomine emittendos curarem in manus studiosorum; tum etiam quia, cum Venetiis esses, hendecasyllabos ad te treis et triginta supra centum quos de te composuerat misit, ut una cum *Urania* et caeteris poëmatis suis mihi imprimendos dares.

5 Atque utinam tunc id facere licuisset, cum et tu aderas et ipse vivebat praesertimque cum quam maxime id cupere videretur, et quasi praesagiret id quod evenit, ut ante e vita discederet quam characteribus nostris nostro studio suos lusus excusos videret; satis enim et nostro et illius desyderio fecissemus. Vidisset quantum curae, studii, laboris doctissimis suis ac divinis poëmatis informandis adhibitum a nobis fuisset; vidisset lucubrationes suas, suos

B[87]

Aldus to his reader.

I did not think it out of place if I undertook to print here what Pontano himself wrote in his own hand at the beginning of the book *Meteora* and sent to me a few days before he died. These are his words: "I had written this book of *Meteora* before the books of *Urania*. However, before it could be published, it was stolen from me out of spite. And so, after completing his *Urania*, the author did a new version of the *Meteora*, giving it a second life, so to speak, and added it to the books of his *Urania*." 3

C[88]

Aldus to Suardino Suardi[89] *of Bergamo.*

The deep affection for you that your pleasant disposition and unsullied way of life have stirred in me has prompted me to undertake the printing of the hendecasyllabic poems[90] of our dear Pontano and to deliver them into the hands of devotees of literature under your name, Suardino, the most agreeable of men. Another reason is that it was to you, when you were in Venice, that he sent one hundred and thirty-three hendecasyllabics which he had composed for you.[91] You were to give these to me to be printed along with his *Urania* and all the other poems. 4

I only wish it had been permitted for me to do so then when you were here and Pontano himself was alive, especially so because he seemed to desire this with all his heart[92] and because it was as if he foresaw what actually happened, that he would die before he set eyes on his short poems, printed by our efforts in our font. For if that had happened, we would have satisfied our desires as well as his. He would have seen with what care, effort and toil we had put into type his most learned and divine poems. He would have 5

lusus, sua pignora amari, amplecti, venerari a studiosis iisdemque doctissimis. Quam quidem rem non accidisse et tunc tuli moleste et nunc maxime doleo.

6 Adde quod, primo exemplari intercepto, alterum sua ipsius manu perscriptum te absente ad me misit, orans obsecransque etiam atque etiam ut accelerarem editionem. Sed vide infortunium. Simo ille philosophus cui ad me librum dederat in febrem gravissimam in itinere incidit paucisque post diebus Patavii moritur iisdemque diebus et Pontanum ipsum decessisse renuntiatum est. Illud etiam mirabere, anno fere post ex quo is obiit mortem exemplar ipsum mihi fuisse redditum.

7 Haec autem ad te propterea publice scripsimus, ut nos quod in hunc usque diem istaec opera edere distulerimus et apud te, cuius censuram facio plurimi, et caeteros vel istorum poëmatum cupidissimos vel Pontani amantissimos hac epistola expurgaremus. Vale.

: IX :

Aldus Adriano cardinali s.

Adeo me delectavit *Venatio* tua, pontificii senatus decus Adriane, ut dignissimam iudicarim quae excusa typis nostris prodiret in publicum, tum elegantia dicendique ornatu, tum admonitionis in calce pie simul prudenterque positae utilitate. Ego te antea uti

seen that the results of his own labors, as well his short poems, his offspring, so to speak, were loved, embraced and honored by both students and men of great learning. I was sorry then that this did not happen and even now I feel it most grievously.

Moreover, when the first manuscript went missing, he wrote 6
out another one in his own hand and sent it to me in your absence, begging and beseeching me again and again to speed up the production of the edition. But just consider the ill luck. The philosopher Simone[93] to whom he had given the book was struck down by a severe fever on his journey and died a few days later in Padua, and during these same days the news came that Pontano himself had died.[94] You will be amazed at this too, that almost a year after he died, his actual manuscript was delivered to me.

We have aired all this to you in this public fashion so that by 7
this letter we can justify both to you, whose opinion I value most highly, and to all others who are most eager to read these poems or are devoted friends of Pontano why we have postponed until now the publication of these works. Farewell.

: IX :

Adriano Castellesi,[95] On Hunting, dedicated to Cardinal Ascanio Sforza[96]

(September 1505)

Aldus to Cardinal Adriano Castellesi, greetings.

Your poem *On Hunting* gave me so much pleasure, Adriano, you who are a glorious adornment of the Curia, that I thought it most worthy of being printed in our type and published by us, both because of its elegance and noble style and the usefulness of the advice that is given with devoutness and wisdom at the end.[97] I

ecclesiae antistitem optimum ob religionem venerabar, nunc etiam admiror ob doctrinae ac morum suavitatem. Mirum in modum igitur debeo Pherno nostro, qui ad me cultissimas hasce lucubrationes tuas muneri misit. Quia vero parentem filia desyderare impendio videbatur, remitto eam ad te qua potui ornatam veste. Tu tuam recognosces, in eaque Aldi tui erga te animum. Vale.

: X :

Aldus studiosis s.

1 Quia nihil aliud cupio quam prodesse vobis, studiosi, cum venisset in manus meas Erasmi Roterodami, hominis undecunque doctissimi, hoc adagiorum opus eruditum, varium, plenum bonae frugis, et quod possit vel cum ipsa antiquitate certare, intermissis antiquis autoribus quos paraveram excudendos, illud curavimus imprimendum, rati profuturum vobis et multitudine ipsa adagiorum quae ex plurimis autoribus tam Latinis quam Graecis studiose collegit summis certe laboribus, summis vigiliis, et multis locis apud utriusque linguae autores obiter vel correctis acute vel expositis erudite.

2 Docet praeterea quot modis ex hisce adagiis capere utilitatem liceat, puta quemadmodum ad varios usus accommodari possint.

revered you previously as the finest of prelates of the church for your wonderful piety; now I admire you also for the agreeableness of your erudition and character.[98] To a marvelous degree, therefore, I am in debt to our friend Ferno,[99] who sent me this extremely polished result of your labors as a gift. However, because I thought it missed you as deeply as a daughter misses her parent, I am sending it back to you, adorned in the finest garment that I could provide. You will recognize it as yours, and in it the warm feelings of your friend Aldus for you. Farewell.

: X :

Erasmus of Rotterdam,[100] Adages[101]

(September 1508)

Aldus to devotees of learning, greetings.

I wish only to be of assistance to you, my scholarly readers, and so 1 when I obtained this learned, wide-ranging and most informative collection of adages put together by Erasmus of Rotterdam, a man of erudition in every discipline, I put aside for the time being the classical authors that I had prepared for publication, and undertook to print this instead.[102] For it is a work that can stand comparison with the products of antiquity. I thought you would profit from it, not only because of the huge number of adages that he has collected so conscientiously — and indeed with much toil and assiduity — from very many authors, both Greek and Latin, but also because of the many passages in the authors of both languages that he has brilliantly corrected in passing or explained with such learning.

Moreover he shows in how many ways these adages can be of 2 profit to us; how, for example, they can be used in many different situations. This work also contains about ten thousand verses

Adde quod circiter decem millia versuum ex Homero, Euripide et caeteris Graecis eodem metro in hoc opere fideliter et docte tralata habentur, praeter plurima ex Platone, Demosthene et id genus aliis. An autem verus sim, *ἰδοὺ Ῥόδος, ἰδοὺ καὶ τὸ πήδημα.* Nam, quod dicitur, *αὐτὸς αὐτὸν αὐλεῖ.*

: XI :

A

Aldus Manutius Romanus divae Lucretiae Borgiae duci Ferrariae s. p. d.

1 Cum essem Ferrariae superiore anno, diva Lucretia, adierunt me Guidus et Laurentius Strozae, nobilissimi iuvenes, rogaruntque ut quae Titus pater et Hercules frater poemata incastigata morte praeventi reliquissent accurate recognoscerem, deinde typis nostris imprimenda curarem.

2 Quorum alterum, etsi eram occupatissimus, nec ita affectus ut suavioribus Musis delectarer, culpa horum temporum, quibus, si unquam alias, nunc maxime 'vicinae ruptis inter se legibus urbes / arma ferunt, saevit toto Mars impius orbe,' tamen recepi me facturum, atque eo libentius, quod et Hercules unice me diligebat (audivit enim me puer) et nunc tota domus Stroza diligit; alterum vero non posse praestare respondi, cum aliis plurimis, tum quia

from Homer, Euripides and all the other Greek poets, verses that he has translated into Latin in the same meter, doing so with accuracy and great learning; there are also many passages from Plato, Demosthenes and other prose writers. As for the truth of what I say, "Here is Rhodes, here is my leap."[103] For as the saying goes, "He is his own flute player."[104]

: XI :

Tito and Ercole Strozzi,[105] Poems

(January 1513)

A

Aldus Manutius of Rome to the divine Lucrezia Borgia,[106] *duchess of Ferrara, warmest greetings.*

1 When I was in Ferrara last year, divine Lucrezia, Guido and Lorenzo Strozzi, the most noble of young men, approached me to ask me if I would read through carefully the poems that Tito, their father, and Ercole, their brother, had left uncorrected because of their deaths, and then to undertake to publish them in our font.

2 I was extremely busy and did not have the inclination to take pleasure in the sweeter Muses—the fault of these times, in which more than at any other period "neighboring cities break the pacts that bind them and wage war upon each other; unholy war rages over all the world."[107] All the same, I agreed to fall in with their first request, and I did so all the more gladly because Ercole was especially fond of me (for he was my pupil in his boyhood) and also because I now enjoy the affection of the whole Strozzi family. However, I replied that I could not fulfill their second request for very many reasons, not the least of which was that I did not think

nondum videretur commodum antiquis me includere curis. Cum vero illi nihilo minus instarent ut et id darem veteri amicitiae quae mihi cum eo ipso Hercule summa intercessit, curaturum me dixi ut hac in re quoque ipsis morem gererem.

3 Id quod est a me factum diligenter, postpositis interim antiquis authoribus qui corrigebantur exituri et ipsi ex aedibus nostris emendatissimi in manus studiosorum. Recognovi igitur omnia paucis diebus. Non enim diu, ut oportebat, in eam curam me incumbere permiserunt summae occupationes meae, nec inter imprimendum quidem id muneris adire diligentius Venetiis potui; sum enim semper occupatissimus.

4 Quoniam autem in utriusque poematis illustrissimi principes familiae Estensium tolluntur in coelum laudibus — Hercules etiam tui mentionem quam saepissime non sine tua summa laude facit, quin *Gigantomachia,* quam extremis temporibus suis inchoavit tantum, tibi dedicata est —, sub tuo nomine exire hos libros voluimus in manus hominum. Adde etiam quod pro summis quibus praedita es virtutibus dignissima es quam laudent, honorent, venerentur omnes, atque ipse in primis, cum propter alia, tum quia Academiam cui constituendae iam multos annos studeo tuis opibus, tuo solius sumptu facturam te, sinant tempora, ultro mihi receperis. Ais enim nihil te magis cupere quam et placere semper Deo immortali et iuvare mortaleis, tam qui nunc sunt quam nascituros omnibus seculis, relinquereque aliquid, cum e vita excesseris, quo non sine summa laude vixisse testeris. O praeclaram vocem dignamque Lucretia Borgia! Verissima certe illa est sententia, Δεινὸς

it was yet suitable for me to include these poems among the authors of antiquity in whom I was engaged in publishing. However, they kept pressing me to make a concession to the old and deep friendship that I had enjoyed with Ercole himself, and I said that I would undertake to fall in with their wishes in this other matter too.

I have done this with great diligence, putting aside for the 3
meantime the classical authors who were undergoing corrections and were actually just about to leave our printing house and come into the possession of students with a text free of blemishes. I reviewed the whole corpus of their poetry in a few days, since my extremely pressing obligations did not allow me to devote to this task the long time that I should have spent. Nor could I fulfill my responsibilities any more diligently in Venice when the work was being printed. For I am always extremely busy.

Since the most illustrious princes of the d'Este family are 4
praised to the heavens in the poems of both — Ercole very often refers also to you and does so in the most glowing terms, and indeed his *Gigantomachy*, which he had only just begun at the very end of his life,[108] was dedicated to you — we wished these works to reach our readers under your name. Moreover, you are most worthy of the praise, honor and veneration that all bestow on you for your outstanding virtues. Your admirers include me especially for several reasons, but particularly because of your own accord you gave me an undertaking that you would bring into being with your resources and at your own expense, should times allow it, the Academy that I have been eager to establish for many years now. For you say that your greatest desire is to please Immortal God and to help all mortals, both those who live now and those who will be born in all the ages to come, and to leave something behind when you have died that will attest to your having lived the most praiseworthy of lives. What a glorious sentiment and one that is worthy of Lucrezia Borgia. Certainly those well-known lines are

χαρακτὴρ κἀπίσημος ἐν βροτοῖς / ἐσθλῶν γενέσθαι, κἀπὶ μεῖζον ἔρχεται / τῆς εὐγενείας τοὔνομα τοῖσιν ἀξίοις.

5 Quid dicam de tua in Deum divosque omneis pietate? quid item de liberalitate in pauperes, de bonitate in tuos, de iustitia in omneis? Mirum est enim quantam pauperibus, qui mendicare erubescunt, clam per pios ministros pecuniam eroges, quot subvenias miseris, quanta praeterea gravitate et prudentia negociis rebusque publicis—cogitur enim apud te senatus—et intersis et praesis et, quod est iustitiae proprium, suum cuique tribuendum cures, tum probos ornandos, sceleratos puniendos et velis et imperes. Quibus in rebus miratur senatus ipse, mirantur cives tui acerrimum iudicium, acumen summum ingenii tui. Denique, quidquid loqueris, quidquid agis, nulla ex parte reprehendi potest. Sed tuis de laudibus pauca haec pro tempore attigimus, praesertim cum in his ipsis libris ubique fere ipsi Titus et Hercules summis te, quibus dignissima es, extollant laudibus.

6 Nunc redeo ad ipsos poetas patrem et filium. Quorum alter, etsi senex admodum obiit mortem, non tamen sua poemata, publicis privatisque negociis assidue impeditus, emendare unquam potuit; quapropter *Borseam,* cuius decem libros scripsit nec absolvit—continet autem, cum alia plurima digna lectu, tum praecipue Borsii ducis laudes et praeclara gesta, unde *Borsea* poemati inditum nomen—Herculi filio, ut una cum caeteris suis poematis quam diligentissime recognosceret, moriens iussit. Alter, quod iuvenis non multo post mortem parentis occidit, ne sua quidem nedum

very true: "It is a marvelous and remarkable stamp among mortals to be born of noble stock and yet the designation of nobility is enhanced in those who are worthy of it."[109]

What can I say of your devotion to God and all the saints, of 5
your generosity toward the poor, of your kindness to your fellow citizens, of your just treatment of everyone? It is marvelous how much, through loyal attendants, you secretly disburse money to the poor (in whom begging brings shame) and how many sad wretches you help; marvelous too is the statesmanship and wisdom you display when you participate in and supervise public matters (for the senate convenes before you) and when you see to it that each man gets his due (a particular feature of justice) and when your wish and command is that the upright be honored and the wicked punished. In these actions the senate itself and your fellow citizens marvel at the shrewdness of your judgment and the supreme sharpness of your intellect. In short no fault at all can be found in whatever you do or say. It suits the occasion for us to have said a few words about your achievements, especially so since almost everywhere in these very books Tito and Ercole extol you with the highest praise, of which you are most worthy.

Now I return to the poets themselves, father and son. Although 6
the former was a very old man when he died, he was never able to revise his poems, being constantly prevented from doing so by his public and private responsibilities. This is why when he was dying he ordered his son Ercole to review with the utmost diligence his *Borsias*, which he left unfinished, having completed ten books, as well as all his other poetry. (The *Borsias* contains very much that is worth reading, and this is particularly true of the achievements and outstanding exploits of Duke Borso;[110] this is the reason that Tito gave the name *Borsias* to the poem.) Because Ercole was killed when he was still a young man, not long after the death of his father, he had not revised even his own poetry, to say nothing of his

patris poemata emendavit. Quare, si ei liceret aliquid quo se tueretur in fronte libri praeponere, credendum est huiuscemodi carmen iubere praeponi:

7 Cum canerem divos horrentiaque arma Cyclopum,
cumque recenserem carmina culta patris
(iusserat id moriens) iam non indigna canentis
dissecuere truces stamina nostra deae.
Et vos crudeles nunquam crudelius ausae,
eheu crudeles terque quaterque manus!
Ergo haec non ipsi edidimus. Pia cura meorum
nostra patrisque simul qualiacunque dedit.
'Quidquid in his igitur vitii rude carmen habebit,
emendaturus, si licuisset, eram.'

Sed iam libros hosce lege, atque Aldi tui memineris. Iesus Deus optimus maximus res tuas fortunet.

B

Herculis Strozae epitaphium per Aldum Romanum.

8 Hospes, licet alio hinc propere eundum tibi,
rogo hoc legas carmen: scio miserebere,
humanitas quae est tua. Poetae hic sunt sita
ossa Herculis Strozae, poeta qui satus
patre est Tito. Quod si cupis cognoscere
qualis poeta uterque, queis honoribus
quantisque praeditus fuerit in patria,
quamque inclytis Stroza orta gens maioribus,

father's. And so if it were permitted for him to write something in his defense at the beginning of the book, one must believe that he would have had the following verses printed as a preface:

> When I was singing of gods and the dreadful arms of the Cyclopes,[111] and when, as he had bade me when he was dying, I was reviewing the polished verses of my father, whose poetry had great merit, the savage goddesses[112] cut the thread of my life, as did you, cruel hands, who never committed a more cruel crime—alas, hands that were thrice and four times cruel.[113] This is why we ourselves did not publish them. My family out of duty has supplied my poetry, such as it is, alongside my father's. "If it had been permitted me, I would have corrected whatever faults our unpolished verses have."[114] 7

But now read these books, and remember your friend Aldus. May the Lord Jesus, God Almighty, make your affairs prosper.

B[115]

Epitaph for Ercole Strozzi by Aldus of Rome.

Stranger,[116] although you need hasten from here to somewhere 8
else, I ask you to read these verses. I know you will show pity, such is your kindness. Here lie the bones of Ercole Strozzi, a poet, whose father was Tito, also a poet. If you wish to discover what kind of poet each was, with what great honors each was endowed in his native city and how the Strozzi family was descended from illustrious ancestors, it would take too long to tell you. You can

longum foret narrare: id e libris potes
cognoscere, hospes, quos pater, quos filius
(nam excusi habentur) fecit excultis modis.

9 Cantavit Anthiam atque Phulloroen pater,
quosque tulit heroas familia Estensium,
invisaque arma matribus; Lucretiae
hic Borgiae laudes, decus quae heroidum
quot sunt, fuere, quotque erunt. Hic et deos
canebat et gigantas et bella horrida
ac multa alia, cum rapitur. Heu fata impia!

10 Egisset integram vel aetatem alteram,
non sua minus gauderet hoc Ferraria
quam aut Mantua Marone aut Catullo nobilis
Verona Venusiumve ‹H›oratio suo.
Heu ter quater crudelia, heu fata impia.

Monimentum et ipse exegit aere perennius
atque altius pyramidibus regum, Iovis
quod ira nunquam diruet tempusve edax
aut aquilo impotens malive ignes: virum
nam sibi dicatum oppetere Pierides vetant.

11 Sed, mulierum quae est gloria et honos, Barbara
Taurella coniunx quam pientissima, viro et,
una ut quiesceret ipsa, donec corporum
erit excitatio, sibi hoc viva posuit.

Hoc te volebam scire; iamque abi et vale.

find this out, stranger, from the books that father and son composed in polished meters, for they are now to hand in print.

The father sang of Anthias and Phylloroe,[117] of the heroes that 9
the d'Este family bore, and of wars that mothers hate. Ercole sang the praises of Lucrezia Borgia, the most glorious of all the heroines "that are now living, of all that lived in the past and of all that will live in the future."[118] He also sang of the gods and giants, of dreadful wars and many other topics when he was snatched from us. Alas, what an evil fate!

If he had lived a full life or been given a second one, his city of 10
Ferrara would have no less pleasure in him than Mantua has in Vergil or noble Verona in Catullus or Venosa in Horace. Alas, for a fate thrice and four times cruel, alas for a fate unspeakably evil.

He also built a monument that would last longer that bronze[119] and was higher than the pyramids of kings, a monument that the wrath of Jupiter, corroding time, raging winds or evil fires will never destroy. For the Muses forbid the death of a man devoted to them.

In keeping with the glory and honor in which women are held, 11
his most devoted wife, Barbara Torelli,[120] erected this tomb for her husband and herself, while still alive, so that she might rest in peace beside him until their bodies are resurrected.[121]

I wished you to know this. Now go and fare you well.

: XII :

Aldus Pius Manutius Accio Syncero Sannazaro s. p. d.

1 Vide, mi Acci, quantum in hac mea laboriosa provincia mihi assumam. Cum quis mittit aliquid muneri ei cuius est munus, videtur temeritatis atque arrogantiae crimine accusandus; nostra enim, non aliena debemus dono mittere, praesertim ipsorum dominis. Ipse autem, id faciens, videor mihi meo iure quodammodo vendicare. Nam licet tu olim *Arcadiam* et prosa et Thuscis numeris docte et eleganter composueris, et sit illa, ut est, tua, tamen nescio quo modo sic edita facta est etiam mea. Quod igitur in hoc libro meum est, tibi et dono et dedico.

2 Atque utinam hoc idem in Urania Pontani nostri licuisset, quam ille bis ad me misit ut imprimendam enchiridii forma curarem, sed paucis ante diebus quam cura nostra ederetur excessit e vita. Qui, puto, si doctissimum poema illud suum volare per ora hominum feliciter et gratum omnibus vidisset, ut nunc volat, visus sibi fuisset superare omnium fortunas.

3 Sed redeo ad *Arcadiam* tuam. Cum dubitarem illam una cum Petrarchae poematis iniussu tuo edere, ne te, cui gratum facere semper velim, offenderem, Hieronymus Borgius, homo tui amantissimus et fide plenus (est enim, ut nosti, et literis et moribus ornatissimus), dixit mihi super ea re dedisse ad te literas et respondisse te id maxime cupere, quia, si nequeas tuis alis, at alienis

: XII :

Jacopo Sannazaro,[122] Arcadia

(September 1514)

Aldus Pius Manutius to Accius Syncerus Sannazarus, warmest greetings.

Just look, my dear Accius, how presumptuous I am in this demanding profession of mine. When a person sends a gift to someone to whom the gift actually belongs, it seems right that he should be accused of temerity and arrogance; for we ought not to give as a gift something that belongs to someone else, especially when the recipient is its owner. However, I myself think that in doing this now I am in some way justified in claiming that the gift belongs to me. For although you composed some time ago the learned and eloquent *Arcadia,* written in both prose and Tuscan verse, and it belongs to you, as it truly does, nevertheless somehow when it has been published in this way, it has become my property too. And so what is mine in this book I give and dedicate to you. 1

Would that it had been permitted me to do the same in the case of Pontano's *Urania.* He sent this work twice for me to print in pocket-book format, but he died just a few days before it was to be published by us. If he had seen how that most learned poem won universal acclaim and approval, as it still does, I believe he would have thought that he surpassed everyone in good fortune. 2

But to return to your *Arcadia.* When I was in doubt as whether I should include with it poems of Petrarch without having your permission (for I did not wish to offend you, and always want to do what will please you), Girolamo Borgia,[123] a man who is devoted to you and most trustworthy (for he is, as you know, highly distinguished in letters and is of the most upright character) told me that he had written to you on this matter and that you had replied, expressing strong support of my plan, because if you can- 3

voles. Quod responsum modestiae plenum est et verecundiae, mi Syncere, ut tua sunt omnia; nam Petrarcham ipsum Thuscis numeris iam adaequasti, Latinis autem tantum superas ut, siquis illud dixerit, vere dixerit:

> Lenta salix quantum pallenti cedit olivae,
> puniceis humilis quantum saliunca rosetis,
> tantum ille heroo cedit tibi carmine vates.

Sed de his plura, ut spero, coram vel brevi. Nunc Arcadiam tuam agnosce, et me, ut soles, ama. Vale.

not fly on your wings, you can fly on those of others. This response has all the modesty and reverence that mark everything you do, my dear Syncerus. For you are the equal of Petrarch himself in Tuscan verse, and you so surpass him in Latin poetry that if anyone said the following words he would be speaking the truth:

As far as the pliant willow yields to the pale olive,
As far as the lowly nard yields to the crimson rose beds,
So far does that bard yield to you in epic verse.[124]

But more of this face to face, I hope, even soon. Now take up your *Arcadia* and love me as ever. Farewell.

APPENDICES

: I :

Laurentius Maiolus Genuensis Aldo suo s. p. d.

1 Testarer et iureiurando, si opus est, affirmarem magnos te diu labores pertulisse et magnos sumptus fecisse ut aliquando tibi ad imprimendas bonas artes instrumenta comparares, non spe lucri et avaricia, sed summa benevolentia ac potius pietate erga homines studiosos. Suppeditasti tandem tibi omnia necessaria ad utranque linguam. Sunt tibi organa tanta arte fabricata ut unus merito possis pulcherrimorum characterum formam posteris ut imitentur relinquere. Omnis enim artifices tam Romanis quam Graecis figuris litterarum facile vincis et alteris quidem tuo ingenio iam reviviscens Graecia, bonarum omnium artium dulcissima nutrix, quae sophistica garrulitate pene interierat, tua cura et diligentia pristinum imperium obtinebit. Alteris vero siqua nondum impressa fuerint hominibus Latinis profutura dabuntur et ea quae iam ab aliis sunt impressa fient meliora. Utrunque certe praestabitur tua arte, pro qua perpetuo tibi studiosi omnes debebunt et se debere (nisi prorsus sint ingrati) fatebuntur. Ego vero me tibi debere ingenue palam fateor. Sum enim abs te maxime adiutus; essem itaque nisi gratias agerem ingratissimus.

APPENDICES

: I :

Lorenzo Maioli, Letter to Aldus[1]

(Spring 1497)

Lorenzo Maioli of Genoa to his dear friend Aldus, warmest greetings.

I would attest and swear on oath, if need be, that you have endured long and arduous labor and incurred great expense in finally obtaining the equipment for printing works in the liberal arts. You have done so, not in the hope of making money or out of greed, but because you have the greatest goodwill for scholars and indeed are devoted to them. You have equipped yourself with everything needed for both languages. You have the tools that have been made with such skill that you alone deserve to leave a font of the most beautiful characters for posterity to imitate. For you easily surpass all craftsmen in both Roman and Greek letterforms.[2] The result of the latter is that, thanks to your genius, Greece, the sweetest nurse of all the good arts, which had almost perished because of sophistic prattling, is coming to life again and will attain its former primacy through your work and diligence. The result of the former is that all those works that have not yet been printed will be offered as a great benefit to men engaged in Latin, and those that have already been printed by others will be improved. Each of these results will without doubt be achieved by your craftsmanship, for which all scholars will be ever in your debt — a debt they will acknowledge, unless they are completely devoid of gratitude. I sincerely and openly admit that I am in your debt. For you have been of the greatest help to me and I would be the most ungrateful of men if I did not thank you. 1

2 Sed tibi in posterum magis debebo, si dederis operam ut quam primum tuo admirabili artificio quaedam nostra in dialectice et philosophia publicentur nec recusaveris etiam si minus tibi exornata videbuntur et minore dicendi diligentia elaborata quam ut digni sint tuis typis excudi nec duxeris esse turpe nudam ab eloquentia tradere sapientiam quod minime tibi in eloquentia satisfecero.

3 Non enim tanti est haec ratio ut tantopere commovearis et tibi omnium amicissimo tuam operam deneges cum idem ambos vere a calumnia liberet; ea enim in quibus praecipue veritas inquiritur minus sunt reprehendenda (ut in Rhetoricis Aristoteles scribit) si minore arte fuerint pronunciata, cum non tam luculentae orationis lepos inspiciendus quam incorrupta veritas attendenda sit. Non hercle tantum natura eloquentiam a sapientia sicut officio disiunctam ab altera alteram puto. Non sum tamen eius sententiae ut pulchrum existimem bonas artes barbarica elocutione maculare. Sed potius divini Platonis mihi sententia placet quod non sit fas purum impuro attingere. Attamen non tantum exornandae orationis ratio habenda est ut eos desinamus iuvare sententiis quibus etiam stilo deberemus prodesse.

4 Sed si nequeo in praesentia amicis scripta nostra efflagitantibus praestare eloquentiam, non propterea debeo meam sententiam denegare. Quanquam mecum ipse decrevissem quam primum essem aliquid nactus ocii exornare, ne igitur falsi hominis nomen subeam aut plurimis videar promittendo dissimulare et amicis quibus iandudum promiseram illusisse quibusque liberaliter daturus eram meliora, statui communi stilo et pene vulgari haec nostra olim

I shall be more indebted to you well into the future if you apply your energies and marvelous skills to publishing as soon as possible some writings of ours on dialectics and philosophy, and if you do not refuse to do so, even if you will think them too lacking in stylistic elegance and too carelessly expressed for them to be worthy of being printed in your type, and if you do not deem it disgraceful to publish a philosophical work that lacks the adornment of eloquence—just because I do not at all satisfy you in this regard. 2

This is not a good enough reason for you to be so annoyed and to refuse your services to one who holds you more dear than anyone else, since our common goal frees both of us from captious criticism. For works in which the primary goal is to search for the truth should be less faulted (as Aristotle says in his *Rhetorica*)[3] if they are written in a less elegant way, since we should direct our attention to the purity of their truth rather than look for the charm of a brilliant style. Not only do I think that eloquence and philosophy are different in nature, they differ from each other in their function. I am not of the opinion, however, that I think it a noble thing to defile the liberal arts by cloaking them in a barbarous style; rather, the view of the divine Plato pleases me, that it is not right to infect what is pure with what is impure.[4] But nevertheless we should not give such weight to elegant writing that we cease to help by our philosophical views those whom we ought to aid also in matters of style. 3

If I cannot at the moment provide eloquence to those friends of mine who are demanding my writings, I should not on that account deny them my thoughts. I had made up my mind to embellish these as soon as I had some leisure time, but I wanted to avoid getting the name of a liar and to prevent many from thinking that I do not keep my word and that I have deceived the friends to whom I had made this promise some time ago and to whom I was intending to give freely material of higher quality. And so I have 4

dictata nunc edere quibus me qui perlegerint magis rationes quam verba perquisivisse cognoscant. Quapropter scripsi ad te has litteras, rogans obsecransque ut ex nostris lucubrationibus has tantum nunc communes faceres et me apud Romanos viros quod non eleganter scripserim excusares illisque pollicereris tuis litteris posthac me nihil in lucem daturum nisi prius Romana lingua loqueretur. Scis quo iure potes in hoc mihi apud studiosos patrocinari. Vale.

: II :

Hieronymus Avancius Valerio Superchio Pisaurensi bonam fortunam.

1 Dii tibi dent quod bene amas, Valeri amicorum spectatissime. Etsi non ignoro te divinis medicinae praescriptis pene obrutum et publicis mathematices lectionibus quas frequentissimo auditorio profiteris districtum, pro tua tamen in me non vulgari amicitia paulisper percursurum spero Lucretium hunc meum, cuius ad communem studiosorum utilitatem pene infinita loca corrupta et mendosa corrigere studui aut saltem totidem incurata vulnera indicare.

2 Ubi diu cogitans an quod volebam assecutus sim, te unum medicum insignem delegi cui hanc remediorum meorum meditationem honestius aut tutius pensandam committerem. Quis enim me

decided to publish my past lectures now, written in an ordinary and almost everyday style. Those who read them will realize that the object of my detailed study was how problems should be resolved rather than how they were expressed. I have therefore written this letter to you, beseeching you to publish only this part of my studies for the moment, making excuses for my inelegant style with the Romans and promising them in your letter[5] that I will not bring out anything else after this until it speaks with a Roman tongue.[6] You know how justifiably your support for me carries weight with scholars. Farewell.

: II :

Girolamo Avanzi, Letter to Valerio Superchio

(March 1, 1499)

Girolamo Avanzi[7] to Valerio Superchio of Pesaro,[8] best wishes.

May the gods grant you your heart's desire, Valerio, truest of friends. I am well aware that you are almost swamped by the superhuman demands of medicine and that you are kept busy by the public lectures in mathematics that you deliver to a packed auditorium. However, I hope that your exceptionally close friendship with me will allow you to spend a short time running your eye over this Lucretius of mine in which, for the common benefit of men of learning, I have striven to correct almost countless corrupt and faulty passages or to point out at least as many wounds, so to speak, that I have not treated. 1

After thinking for a long time whether I had achieved my goal I chose you as the only distinguished physician to whom I might entrust a surer and more honest evaluation of my remedies. For who would think that I on my own would administer medication 2

solum extreme laboranti ac fere conclamato pharmaca deprompturum opinetur, nisi te uti opificem Aesculapium iudicem vindicemque constituerim? Quum potissimum te disciplinarum omnium cognitione eminentissimum saepius Patavinum gymnasium declaraverit, quumque me (ut palam est) mutuo ames, haud patieris, scio, vigilias nostras prodire nisi prius ungue, obelisco liturisque tuis tam multa expunxeris, confoderis, deleveris ut caetera emendata credi possint. Plus itaque, amantissime Valeri, veritati quam benivolentiae tribuas, a Valerio non ab amico teque mei studioso nostra expendantur velim.

3 Diu, fateor, laboravi quum viro insigni obsequens emendare adniterer Catullum, Priapeias, Ausonium, Plinii epistolas ac Papynii *Silvas*, quas omnes castigationes nunc impressas adolescens publicavi, caeterum offendi adeo mutilata manca et lacera Lucretiana carmina ut ante iucundos labores meos vix ulla pars sincera maneret. Occurrebant tot inversi versus, tot portentosae dictiones ut iam (nisi Valerius adsit) ad haec verborum monstra tollenda plures mecum Hercules desiderarim. Laetabor vel si ostenderis complures Lucretii versus non depravatos sed a me non intellectos. Omnino enim quod quaerebam assequar, ut scilicet Lucretium Latinorum poetarum scientissimum et quem maxima aemulatione in plerisque imitatus est praecellentissimus Maro, in pristinum candorem in suam lectionem restitutum conspiciam ut iam auspiciis meis Virbius dici possit.

4 Verum si tibi variis occupationibus impedito immensum importunumque negocium impono, velim has lucubrationes Vincentio Quirino, literarum decori eximio, ac Mecoenati nostro, dum animum a philosophorum dogmatibus occupatissimum relaxare

to a patient who was in extreme distress and was almost given up as dead unless I appointed you, a skilled Asclepius,[9] as judge and champion. Since the University of Padua has often declared you to be most outstanding in your knowledge of all disciplines, and since you return my love for you (as is quite clear), I know that you will not allow our labors to be published unless you have applied the nail,[10] the obelisk,[11] and eraser in expunging, excising and removing so much that all that remains can be thought to be free of errors. And so, my loving Valerio, assign more weight to truthfulness than to kindly feelings; I would wish our efforts to be evaluated by you as Valerius,[12] not as a friend and one who is devoted to me.

I admit that I labored long when, following the wishes of a distinguished man, I strove to correct Catullus, Priapean poems, Ausonius, the letters of Pliny and the *Silvae* of Statius.[13] All of these corrections, now in print, were published by me in my youth. But as for the poem of Lucretius, I found so many passages that were mutilated, deformed and mangled that scarcely any part was free of corruption before my enjoyable labors. There were so many verses out of order, so many frightful expressions that without a Valerio at hand I would need the help of many more than a single Hercules to excise these monstrous words. I shall even rejoice if you show that many verses of Lucretius are not corrupt but have been misunderstood by me. For in this way I shall achieve all that I aimed for, namely that I will see Lucretius, the most knowledgeable of Latin poets and one whom the incomparable Vergil imitated to a very great extent in many places, completely restored to his original purity for those who read him, so much so that he can now be called Virbius[14] under my auspices. 3

If I am placing too large or too troublesome a task upon you, weighed down as you are by your various responsibilities, I would like you to hand over these scholarly efforts of ours to Vincenzo Querini,[15] an outstanding adornment of letters and a Maecenas to us, for him to read and check when it pleases him to relax from his 4

libuerit legendas et castigandas commendes. Pili enim faciam quicquid alii maligne irridebunt aut invidenter vellicabunt si tecum hunc Academiae nostrae assertorem, approbatorem subscriptoremque nactus fuero.

5 Huic[1] certe, quod in luculentissima mathematices praelectione liquido demonstrasti, tam fausta undequaque sidera sortitus est ut nulli sit facilius literarum arcana perspicere ac virtutum omnium apicem attingere. Quare diis bene iuvantibus ad meritissima dignitatum amplissimarum fastigia pleno gradu hunc evasurum spero et vehementer opto, quum praeter singularem humanitatem, inauditam modestiam et incredibilem prudentiam miro disciplinarum amore atque acerrimo studio beatissimam memoriam et fere divinum ingenium excolat foveatque.

6 Quis praeterea Vincentii in literis iudicio non lubens acquiescat? Quando eundem acutissime disputantem tum nos alias admirati sumus, tum nuper multis honoratis verbis approbarit vir ex bonis omnibus incomparabilis, alterum huius aetatis praecipuum lumen, omnium studiorum studiosorumque patronus, omnium scientiarum princeps et pene intimus naturae secretarius interpresque fidissimus Dominicus Grimanus et multiiugarum doctrinarum praestantia et Christiani cardinis custodia colendus. Quare ut egregius vates ab eius consortibus ex intimis Orci penetralibus prorsus redimatur, mediusfidius, debet doctorum nemo honestissimorum optatis meis non obsequi.

7 Quum perpauca sint scitu vel reconditissima quae mortalium aliquis non probe teneat, vobiscum eruditos omnes qui opus hoc adsument rogatos velim singuli singulas emendationes nostras perlegant, examinent et pro arbitrio castigent. Amplius namque

preoccupation with the beliefs of philosophers. For if I obtain the approval and support of this champion of our Academy,[16] along with yours, I do not give a fig for all the malicious scoffing or envious carping of anyone else.

As you have clearly shown in your brilliant introductory lecture 5
on mathematics,[17] this man has certainly drawn by lot such favorable stars on all sides that for no one is it easier to perceive the mysteries of literature and to reach the apex of all virtues. Therefore I hope and fervently pray that with the good help of the gods he will advance at full speed to the most worthy pinnacles of the highest offices. For apart from his outstanding generosity, unparalleled propriety and incredible good sense he cultivates and nourishes his most blessed memory and almost divine talent with admirable love of and keenest devotion to learning.

Moreover, who would not gladly be in agreement with the 6
judgment of Vincenzo on literary matters? Not only have we marveled on occasions at his keen skill in disputation but recently he has won many complimentary words of approval from a man of incomparable superiority over all good men, another leading light of this age, a patron of all learning and scholars, a master in every discipline and one who is an almost intimate associate of nature and its faithful interpreter — Domenico Grimani,[18] who is to be respected for his mastery of many disciplines as well as for his being a guardian of the church as cardinal. Therefore, as God is my witness, no honorable scholar should fail to comply with my wish that this outstanding poet should be totally redeemed from the deepest recesses of hell by those who are his joint heirs.

Since there are very few things of even the most abstruse nature 7
that any mortal cannot well grasp, I would like to ask that every single scholar who takes up this edition to join with you in reading through, examining and correcting as they see fit every single emendation of ours. I will gain more satisfaction from anyone who

mihi quivis satisfaciet si quae male habentia Lucretii loca a me intacta assignaverit et quae a me perperam reformata recognoverit in legitimam lectionem reposuerit quam si scriptis qualibuscumque contentus vigiliis nostris applauserit. Non enim is sum qui me huius omnium depravatissimi vatis pene infinitas mendas dempsisse censeam. Quin, nisi quis ocyus, quod malim, nostra haec acriori lima animadverterit, polliceor fore, si quam a divina Hippocratis nostri lectione dieculam succidere valuero, ut harum emendationum eundem me at authorem et exactorem plane cognoscant.

8 Interim Lucretium, iucundissime Valeri, opera mea iam se commodius habentem ac, ut arbitror, convalescentem, ubi tu scientissimusque Quirinus suaseritis, emittemus, parum verentes iniquam[2] scrupulosae curiositatis conditorem faciles quasque potius labeculas quam infinitas ut ita dicam emaculationes animadversuram quum praesertim hanc editionem imprimendam curarit Aldus Manutius, homo latinis graecisque eruditus, earundem mirifice cultor et adeo instaurator ut non tam Pisistratus et Nicanor Seleucus aut M. Varro de his promeruerint. Athenis enim illi, Romae Varro vel unicam et quidem privatam bibliothecam congesserunt.

9 Aldi vero solertia innumerabiles Latinae Graecae ac Hebraeae linguae authores quam emendatissimi passim habentur habebunturque. Lucretium autem eo accuratius Aldus affectat quatenus eum illustri Alberto Pio Carporum Principi inscripturus sit qui non Minervae modo sed Apollinis etiam ingenuas artes ac studia universa quibus poema suum ubertim refersit Lucretius examussim teneat, nec mirum quidem quando in eius splendidissima domo porticus Lycium aut Academiam nequaquam desideret.

marks out any corrupt passages of Lucretius that I have left untouched or who restores to their rightful form anything that he recognizes has been wrongly changed by me than if he simply applauds our scholarly efforts, content with whatever I have written. For I am not the kind of person to think that I have removed the almost countless errors of this most corrupt of all poets. No, not at all; I would prefer someone to anticipate me and apply a keener file to these efforts of mine, but if not, I promise that, if I am strong enough to cut out even one short day from my reading of our divine Hippocrates, men[19] will clearly come to realize that I can also reject these emendations that I have proposed.

In the meantime, my most congenial Valerio, we will release 8
Lucretius (now in a better state thanks to us and, in my opinion, growing healthier) when you and the most learned Querini advise it. We will have no worries that a malicious collector of minute quibbles will point out all the edition's easily recognizable flaws rather than the infinite number of "unblemishings," so to speak,[20] that we have performed. A special reason for this is that Aldus Manutius has undertaken to print this edition. He is a man learned in both Greek and Latin, one who so admirably cultivates and indeed revives works in these languages that neither Pisistratus and Nicanor Seleucus nor Marcus Varro served them as much. For these men amassed unique and private libraries, the former two in Athens, the latter in Rome.

Thanks to the resourcefulness of Aldus innumerable copies of 9
error-free works of authors writing in Latin, Greek and Hebrew[21] are in circulation everywhere and will continue to be so. However Aldus is treating the Lucretius all the more carefully since he is going to dedicate the book to Alberto Pio,[22] illustrious prince of Carpi, a man who has perfect knowledge of the noble arts of Minerva and Apollo and of all the disciplines which Lucretius has so richly packed into his poem; and this is no surprise since in Pio's splendid home his gallery is not lacking anything from the Lyceum

Vestris igitur studiis, Aldo assidente, labores nostros bonis non ingratos fore speramus. Diu valeas.

Kalendis Martiis MID.

: III :

Excellenti ac erudito viro domino Aldo Romano amico meo carissimo.

Sigismundus Thurzo prepositus Albensis ac
Serenissimi Hungarorum et Bohemorum, etc
Regis secretarius Aldo suo salutem.

1 Devenerunt iis diebus certi libelli in formam enchiridii redacti in meas ac Reverendissimi Domini Georgii episcopi Varadiensis manus, quibus propter eorum commoditatem mirifice oblectati fuimus. Nam ex quo propter varias meas occupationes vix tantum nobis ocii conceditur ut in aedibus nostris poetis vel oratoribus vacare possimus, iis propter eorum tractabilitatem et inter ambulandum et ut sic dixerim inter aulicandum, nacta opportunitate, pro maximis utimur deliciis utque duos ex illis, puta Virgil et Oratii opera, inter ceteros id genus libellos magis castigatos et pulchrioribus caracteribus impressos ex aedibus Aldi Romani emissos conspexi, mox mihi in mentem venit tuam et hortari et orare humanitatem ut pro veteri nostra amicitia Marcum quoque Tullium tam in epistolis quam etiam in aliis libris in hac eadem forma legendum nobis traderes.

or the Academy. By your efforts and with Aldus at my side, we hope that our labors will not be displeasing to good men. May you long enjoy good health.

March 1, 1499.[23]

: III :

Sigismund Thurzó, Letter to Aldus Manutius[24]

(December 20, 1501)

To my very dear friend, the excellent and learned Master Aldus.

Sigismund Thurzó,[25] *provost of Transylvania and secretary to his most Serene Highness, king of Hungary and Bohemia, etc., to his dear friend Aldus, greetings.*

In the past few days there were delivered to me and to his Grace, 1
most reverend György, bishop of Varád, certain books which were of pocket-book size and which because of their convenience gave us marvelous pleasure. My varied duties do not allow me much leisure time to read our poets and orators at home, and so I can have the greatest delight in these books while taking a stroll or, may I say it, even in the midst of my responsibilities at court, if I get the chance, so handy are they to use. When I saw that two of these books, namely the works of Vergil and Horace, when compared to all other books of this kind,[26] had a much better text and were printed in a much more beautiful font and that they had been published by the printing house of Aldus of Rome, it soon occurred to me to urge and beg you in your generosity and by virtue of our longstanding friendship to give us also the works of Cicero, his letters as well as his other books, to read in this same format.

2 Si igitur, charissime Alde, cognoveris hunc quem veteris amicitiae nostrae causa tibi impono laborem tibi non esse aliquid dampni allaturum, velis Reverendissimi Domini Varadiensis et meo desiderio morem gerere, atque libros Tullii quos sine tuo beneficio legere non possumus legendos nobis tradere. In quo et nobis et studiosis omnibus rem facies valde gratam. Vale feliciter.

Ex Buda XX Decembris anno a nativitate Christi millesimo quinquagesimo primo.

: IV :

Aldi monitum in Lugdunenses typographos

Aldus Manutius Romanus lectori s.

1 Cum primum coepi suppeditare studiosis bonos libros, id solum negocii fore mihi existimabam ut optimi quique libri et Latini et Graeci exirent ex Neacademia nostra quam emendatissimi omnesque ad bona literas bonasque artes cura et ope nostra excitarentur. Verum longe aliter evenit: 'tantae molis erat Romanam condere linguam.' Nam praeter bella quae nescio quo infortunio eodem tempore coeperunt quo ego hanc duram accepi provinciam atque in hunc usque diem perseverant ita ut literae iam septennium cum armis quodammodo strenue pugnare videantur, quater iam in aedibus nostris ab operis et stipendiariis in me conspiratum est, duce malorum omnium matre Avaritia; quod Deo adiuvante sic fregi ut valde omnes poeniteat suae perfidiae.

If then, dearest Aldus, you determine that you will not incur a loss from this labor that I impose upon you in the name of our friendship, I hope you will be willing to provide what the most reverend bishop of Varád and I long for and give us to read the works of Cicero—we cannot read them without your kindness![27] In this you will do something for which we and all devotees of literature will be extremely grateful. Farewell and best wishes; 2

From Buda, December 20, in the year of our Lord 1501.

: IV :

Aldus Manutius, Warning To the Typographers of Lyons

(March 16, 1503)

Aldus Manutius of Rome to his reader, greetings.

When I first began to supply scholars with fine books, I thought that my only concern would be to have all the best books in both Latin and Greek leave our Neacademy in as correct a form as possible and to rouse everyone by our efforts and with our help to embrace good letters and the liberal arts. But it has turned out quite differently, "such a heavy task it was to establish the Roman tongue."[28] For by some misfortune wars broke out at the same time that I took on these demanding responsibilities and have persisted right up to the present day, so much so that literature seems to have been fighting a fierce battle against armies for seven years now. Apart from these wars I have also been the victim of four conspiracies of my laborers and workmen in my publishing house, led by Avarice, the mother of all evils. With God's help I have so crushed these men that all of them deeply repent of their treachery.[29] 1

2 Restabat ut in urbe Lugduno libros nostros et mendose excuderent et sub meo nomine publicarent in quibus nec artificis nomen nec locum ubinam impressi fuerint esse voluerunt quo incautos emptores fallerent ut, et characterum similitudine et enchiridii forma decepti, nostra cura Venetiis excusos putarent. Quamobrem, ne ea res studiosis damno, mihi vero et damno et dedecori foret, volui hac mea epistola omnes ne decipiantur admonere, infrascriptis videlicet signis.

3 Sunt iam impressi Lugduni (quod scierim) characteribus simillimis nostris, Vergilius, Horatius, Iuvenalis cum Persio, Martialis, Lucanus, Catullus cum Tibullo et Propertio, Terentius. In quibus omnibus nec est impressoris nomen nec locus in quo impressi nec tempus quo absoluti fuerint. In nostris vero omnibus sic est: 'Venetiis in aedibus Aldi Romani illo vel illo tempore.' Item nulla in illis visuntur insignia; in nostris est delphinus anchorae involutus, ut infra licet videre. Praeterea deterior in illis charta et nescio quid grave olens; characteres vero diligentius intuenti sapiunt, ut sic dixerim, gallicitatem quandam; grandiusculae item sunt perquam deformes. Adde quod vocalibus consonantes non connectuntur, sed separatae sunt; in nostris plerasque omnes invicem connexas manumque mentientes operae pretium est videre.

4 Ad haec hisce quae inibi visuntur incorrectionibus non esse meos facile est cognoscere. Nam in Vergilio Lugduni impresso in fine epistolii nostri ante *Bucolicorum* Tityrum perperam impressum est 'optimos quousque autores' pro 'optimos quosque'; et in fine librorum Aeneidos, in prima epistolae nostrae semipagina ad studiosos, extremo versu male impressum est 'maria omnie cirtum'

Another problem remained. Our books were being printed—faultily—in the city of Lyons and were being published under my name, since those responsible for them did not wish to display the name of the artisan who produced these books or the name of the place where they had been printed. Their aim was to trick unwary purchasers. Deceived by the similarity of the font and the pocket-book format, they would think that the books had been printed by us in Venice. So that scholars may not incur financial loss because of this, and so that I do not lose my high reputation as well as money, I wish to use this letter to warn everyone against this deceit, by indicating below the characteristics of these books. 2

To my knowledge the following have been printed in Lyons in a font very similar to ours: Vergil, Horace, Juvenal with Persius, Martial, Lucan, Catullus with Tibullus and Propertius, Terence.[30] None of these has the name of the printer, the place where they were printed or the date of completion, while all of our publications read as follows: "Venice, in the printing house of Aldus of Rome, at such and such a date." Neither are there any emblems to be seen in them; our editions display a dolphin entwined around an anchor, as can be seen below.[31] Moreover, the paper in their books is of an inferior quality and is somewhat malodorous, while the font, if one looks carefully at it, smacks of a certain "Frenchness," so to speak, and the capitals are quite ugly. An additional point is that the consonants are not connected to vowels but are separate from each other; in our books almost all the letters are connected and simulate handwriting, a worthwhile sight to behold. 3

Besides all this, one can easily recognize that these editions are not by me from the errors that can be seen there. For in the Vergil printed in Lyons, at the end of our short letter that appears before the "Tityrus" of the *Eclogues*, *optimos quousque autores* has been mistakenly printed instead of *optimos quosque*; at the end of the *Aeneid*, on the first page of our letter to students,[32] *maria omnie cirtum* in 4

pro 'maria omnia circum'; ubi etiam nulli accentus observantur, cum ego eam epistolam propterea composuerim ut ostenderem quonam modo apud nostros utendum est accentiunculis.

5 In Horatio, in mea epistola, secundo versu sic est excusum 'imprissis Vergilianis operibus' pro 'impressis' et tertio sic: 'Flaccum aggrssi' pro 'aggressi.' Grandiusculae praeterea literae ante primam oden primo et secundo versu sunt impressorio atramento supra et infra quasi linea conclusae perturpiter.

6 In Iuvenale, in mea epistola, tertio versu est 'pubilcamus' pro 'publicamus'; et decimo versu 'Ungues quae suos' pro 'unguesque suos.' Item in prima semipagina: 'Semper et assiduo ruptae rectore' pro 'lectore.' In eadem 'si vacat et placidi rationem admittitis, eadem' pro 'edam.' Et paulo post 'Cum tenet uxorem' pro 'tener.' Item inibi 'Eigat aprum' pro 'figat.'

7 In Martiale, statim in principio primae semipaginae est impressum literis grandiusculis sic: 'AMPHITEATRUM' pro 'AMPHITHEATRUM.' Et in eadem: 'Quae tam se posita' pro 'seposita.' Item in libro secundo ad Severum deest Graecum *ἐσχατοκωλικόν*; et in Candidum ubique deest Graecum, id est *κοινὰ φίλων πάντα*, et in fine *κοινὰ φίλων*.

8 In Lucano nulla est epistola in principio; at in meo maxime. In fine Catulli eam quae in meo est epistolam praetermiserunt. Quae etiam possunt esse signa Lugdunine an Venetiis mea cura impressi fuerint.

9 Terentium etsi ego nondum curavi imprimendum, tamen Lugduni una cum caeteris sine cuiusquam nomine impressus est. Quod ideo factum est ut emptores, meum esse et libri parvitate et characterum similitudine existimantes, deciperentur. Sciunt enim

the last line is a printing error for *maria omnia circum*. They also do not indicate any accents, even though I wrote that letter with the purpose of showing how accents should be used in our books.

In the Horace, in the second line of my letter, *imprissis Vergiliani-* 5
bus operibus is printed instead of *impressis*, and, in the third line, *Flaccum aggrssi* instead of *aggressi*. Moreover, the capital letters in the first and second lines that stand at the head of the first ode are framed at their top and bottom by lines of printer's ink in a most unsightly way.

In the Juvenal, in the third line of my letter, we read *pubilcamus* 6
instead of *publicamus*, and, in the tenth, *ungues quae suos* for *unguesque suos*. Also, on the first page we read *Semper et assiduo ruptae rectore* instead of *lectore*,[33] and in the same place *si vacat et placidi rationem admittitis, eadem* instead of *edam*. And a little after this we read *Cum tenet uxorem* instead of *tener*. We also find there *Eigat aprum* for *figat*.

In the Martial, at the very beginning of the first page there is 7
printed in capital letters *AMPHITEATRUM* instead of *AMPHITHEATRUM*. And in the same place *Quae tam se posita* instead of *seposita*.[34] Also in the second book, in the poem to Severus the Greek ἐσχατοκωλικόν is missing,[35] and in the poem to Candidus the Greek is missing everywhere: κοινὰ φίλων πάντα and, at the end, κοινὰ φίλων.[36]

In the Lucan there is no letter at the beginning, although there 8
is certainly one in my edition.[37] The letter that stood at the end of my Catullus has been overlooked.[38] These too can be indications as to whether these editions have been printed in Lyons or in Venice under my supervision.

I have not yet undertaken to publish Terence,[39] yet a Terence 9
has been printed at Lyons along with all the others without giving the name of any printer. The purpose of this was to deceive buyers into thinking that the book was produced by me because of its small size and the similarity of the font. For these printers know

quem nos in pristinam correctionem, servatis etiam metris, restituendum curamus in summa esse expectatione; et propterea suum edere accelerarunt, sperantes ante eum venumdatum iri quam emittatur meus.

10 Sed quam ille emendatus exierit vel hinc cognosci potest quod statim in principio sic est impressum: 'EPITAPHIUM TEREMTII' pro 'TERENTII'; item 'Bellica praedia fui' pro 'praeda'; et 'Haec quunque leget' pro 'quicunque.' Praeterea in principio secundae chartae: 'Acta ludis Megalensibus M. Fulvio aedilibus et M. Glabrione Q. Minutio Valerio curulibus' pro 'M. Glabrione Qu. Minutio Valerio aedilibus curulibus.' Quod etiam putantes esse argumentum impresserunt 'ARGUMENTUM ANDRIAE.' Ante etiam 'Sororem falso' est 'TERENTII ARGUMENTUM,' cum argumenta omnia comoediarum Terentii non Terentius sed Sulpitius Apollinaris composuerit; sic enim in vetustissimis habetur codicibus: 'C. Sulpitii Apollinaris periocha.'

11 Metra etiam confusa sunt omnia. Versus enim primae scenae, quae tota trimetris constat, sic (tamquam chaos in elementa) separati ab invicem in suum locum sunt restituendi:

SI. Vos istaec intro auferte; abite. Sosia,
ades dum, paucis te volo. *SO.* Dictum puta.
Nempe, ut curentur recte haec. *SI.* Immo aliud. *SO.* quid est
quod tibi mea ars efficere hoc possit amplius? . . .

12 Item secunda scena, cuius tres primi versus sunt trimetri, quartus tetrameter, quintus dimeter et caeteri omnes quadrati, sic esse debet:

that an author on whom we are working to restore to his original correct form, with the meters also preserved, is most eagerly awaited by all. That is why they have speeded up the publication of their own edition, hoping that this would be on sale before mine was released.

But you can easily see in what state of correctness it has been 10
published from the following errors, printed right at the beginning: *EPITAPHIUM TEREMTII* for *TERENTII; Bellica praedia fui* for *praeda; Haec quunque leget* for *quicunque*. In addition, at the beginning of the second page we read: *Acta ludis Megalensibus M. Fulvio aedilibus et M. Glabrione Q. Minutio Valerio curulibus* for *M. Glabrione Qu. Minutio Valerio aedilibus curulibus*.[40] Thinking this was a plot summary, they printed *ARGUMENTUM ANDRIAE*. There is a heading *TERENTII ARGUMENTUM* [Plot summary of Terence] standing before the line beginning *Sororem falso*, although all the summaries of the comedies of Terence were composed by Sulpicius Apollinaris, not Terence. For this is what we find in the oldest manuscripts: *C. Sulpitii Apollinaris periocha* [Summary of Gaius Sulpicius Apollinaris].

The meters are also completely confused.[41] The verses of the 11
first scene, which consists wholly of trimeters, have to be disentangled from each other and restored to their proper position, like the elements that have to be extracted from chaos:

SI. Vos istaec intro auferte; abite. Sosia,
ades dum, paucis te volo. SO. Dictum puta.
Nempe, ut curentur recte haec. SI. Immo aliud. SO quid est
quod tibi mea ars efficere hoc possit amplius? . . .

In a similar fashion, in the second scene the first three verses 12
are trimeters, the fourth a tetrameter, the fifth a dimeter[42] and all the rest quadrati,[43] and the lines ought to be printed as follows:[44]

SI. Non dubium est quin uxorem nolit filius.
Ita Davum modo timere sensi, ubi nuptias
futuras esse audivit; sed ipse exit foras.
DA. Mirabar hoc si sic abiret et heri semper lenitas
verebar quorsum evaderet.
Qui postquam audivit non datum iri filio uxorem suo,
nunquam cuiquam nostrum verbum fecit neque id aegre tulit.
SI. At nunc faciet neque, ut opinor, sine tuo magno malo.
DA. Id voluit, nos sic opinantes duci falso gaudio,
sperantes iam amoto metu, interea oscitantes obprimi,
ne esset spatium cogitandi ad disturbandas nuptias.
Astute. *SI*. Carnifex quae loquitur? *DA*. Herus est, neque provideram . . .

13 Qua in re quantus sit mihi labor cogitent qui intellegunt. Certe plurimum die noctuque elaboramus.

Haec publicanda iussimus ut qui libellos enchiridii forma excusos empturus est ne decipiatur. Facile enim cognoscet Venetiisne in aedibus nostris fuerint an Lugduni. Vale.

Venetiis XVI Martii M.D. III.

: V :

Ioannes Iucundus Veronensis Iuliano Medici
s. p. d.

1 Si diligentius quis consideret, Iuliane illustrissime, quot is qui corrupta antiquorum scripta ut emendata in manus hominum exeant

SI. Non dubium est quin uxorem nolit filius.
Ita Davum modo timere sensi, ubi nuptias
futuras esse audivit; sed ipse exit foras.
DA. Mirabar hoc si sic abiret et heri semper lenitas
verebar quorsum evaderet.
Qui postquam audivit non datum iri filio uxorem suo,
nunquam cuiquam nostrum verbum fecit neque id aegre tulit.
SI. At nunc faciet neque, ut opinor, sine tuo magno malo.
DA. Id voluit, nos sic opinantes duci falso gaudio,
sperantes iam amoto metu, interea oscitantes obprimi,
ne esset spatium cogitandi ad disturbandas nuptias.
Astute. SI. Carnifex quae loquitur? DA. Herus est, neque provideram
. . .

Let those who understand these things consider how much labor is involved for me in this business of ours. To be sure, we toil extremely hard, day and night. 13

We ordered this to be published so that anyone intending to buy books printed in pocket-book format will not be deceived. Such a person will easily recognize whether books have been printed in Venice in our publishing house or in Lyons. Farewell.

Venice, March 16, 1503.

: V :

Giovanni Giocondo, Letter to Giuliano de' Medici

(April 1513)

Giovanni Giocondo of Verona[45] *to Giuliano de' Medici,*[46]
warmest greetings.

Most illustrious Giuliano, if anyone were to consider carefully how 1
many labors have to be endured by those whose concern it is that

curat labores exhauriat, quam vero nullius vel perexiguae admodum apud plurimos laudis particeps fiat, admiretur profecto cur sibi quisquam id oneris assumat, quo in perferendo, cum maxime enitendum sit, minimam tamen mercedem consequatur.

2 Quod enim in alieno elaboret neque suum aliquod ipse edat, id apud multos eiusmodi est ut omnem quem pro laboribus mereretur laudis fructum intercipiat. Qui mihi quidem, siqui sunt, iniqui esse videntur rerum aestimatores. Nihilo enim magis aequum eos sentire existimo quam si quis ei qui derelictum cuiuspiam ac sentibus occupatum agrum suo labore expurgarit colueritque nullam tamen inde enatarum frugum partem deberi arbitretur. Elaborat certe is in alieno solo, laborum tamen est quoddam iure praemium constitutum.

3 Ac mihi quidem longe videtur secus, atque eum qui munus hoc recte exequatur, seu rei ipsius difficultatem spectes seu quam inde literarum studiosi utilitatem consequantur consideres, in primis laudandum censeo atque (ut vere dicam quod sentio) non multo fortasse minus opus hoc existimo quam si ex te aliquid componas. Acrioris illud ingenii, exactioris hoc iudicii; latiore ibi campo evagari licet, angustissimis hic finibus coercemur; ibi, cum ingenii habenas effuderis, ferri quocunque volueris potes, hic ingenio ita moderandum est ut, cum maxime eo opus sit, circunscriptis tamen quibusdam terminis continendum sit.

4 Non unum quodlibet solum perlegendum, sed plurima conferenda exemplaria; ex varia lectione non quae tibi maxime placeat

the corrupt writings of antiquity reach the hands of the public in as correct a form as possible and how little or no praise they receive in the minds of most people, he would undoubtedly be amazed that anyone should take on this burdensome task. For it entails the greatest of effort in the endurance needed, but yields the least recompense.

That an editor expends his energy on someone else's work and 2
does not produce something of his own carries such weight with many persons that he fails to receive the full reward of praise that he deserves for his labors. In my opinion such men, whoever they may be, are quite unfair in their estimation of what is involved. I think that their view is as unjust as that of someone who does not think that any part of the harvest produced by land that he owns but has abandoned is owed to the man who has cleared it of its briars and cultivated it. Admittedly this fellow has been working another man's land, but equity demands the setting of some recompense for his labors.

I quite disagree with such persons, and I think that the man 3
who properly performs this task of editing is especially deserving of praise, whether you consider the difficulty of the activity itself or the advantages that devotees of literature derive from it. To say truly what I believe, I think that this task of editing is almost as significant as composing something of one's own. The latter requires a more vigorous natural talent; editing demands more precise discernment. In the latter one can range over a wider area; in editing we are constrained by very narrow boundaries. In the latter when you give free rein to your talent, you can be borne wherever you wish; in editing one must restrain one's talent in such a way that, even though there is a special need to exercise it, it must be confined within certain circumscribed limits.

Not just any one copy has to be read through; very many exem- 4
plars need to be compared. Of the different readings one must choose, not the one that especially pleases *you*, but the one that

eligenda, sed quae caeteris authoris ipsius scriptis magis accommodata esse videatur, ita ut illius tibi prope animus induendus sit; at vero ita parce, ubi quippiam corruptum sit, ex se aliquid addendum, ut, nisi certissimis indiciis ducaris (quae quandoque tamen occurrunt), corrupta potius lectio relinquenda sit. Quae omnia quanti laboris, quantae industriae sint quilibet qui id experiatur facillime iudicabit.

5 Utilitatem vero si consideres, multo hinc profecto maior reperietur; atque hoc tamen ita velim accipi uti a me dicitur neque enim tam ignarus rerum sum uti quemlibet librum emendare (cum multi praesertim sint quos corruptos esse expediat) utilius putem quam si possis tuum aliquid scribere neque, si talia quaedam qualia ea sunt quae emendes componere possis, hoc potius agendum. Sed hoc dico; cum permulta antiquorum sint scripta quibus ne sperandum quidem nobis sit ut aequales esse possimus cumque omnis nostra Latinae locutionis peritia inde emanet eaque corruptissima circunferantur, qui in eo vires intendit suas ut emendatiora legantur non solum id agit ut ipsa et intelligi melius et libentius legi, sed id etiam non minus, ut rectius quoque siquis quid scribere voluerit id agi possit.

6 Ac tanquam qui turbidum aliquem coeno fontem unde multi in omnes partes rivi deducantur perpurgat non id solum facit, ut fons ipse nitidior sit, sed et ut rivuli quoque ipsi qui lutulenti prius ac sordidi fluebant, puriore unda accepta, et aspectu gratiores et potu suaviores fiant. Sic is qui corrupta antiquorum scripta corrigit quasi fontem ipsum perpurgat nec id faciat modo, sed ut ea etiam

seems to be more in keeping with all the other writings of the author himself. It is almost as if you must assume his mindset. When there is some corruption, you should take material from the author to add to the text, but in a very sparing manner; unless you are guided by the surest of indications (as sometimes happens), it is better for a corrupt reading to be left. Anyone who has experience of editing will easily judge how much toil and labor are involved in all of this.

If you should consider the criterion of usefulness, much more 5
of this will be found to lie in editing. And yet I would wish this to be understood in the context in which I say this; for I am not so ignorant of how things are as to think that it is more useful to emend any book at all (especially when there are many books whose corrupt state is a boon to editors) than to be able to write something of your own; and if you can compose something of the quality of the works that you are emending, you should choose to do this over editing. But I say the following: since there are a vast number of works of antiquity which we cannot even hope to be able to rival, and since our whole knowledge of Latinity springs from them and these are circulating in the most corrupt state, the man who directs all his energy to this end, namely, that they be read with fewer errors, not only brings about a better understanding and a greater enjoyments of these very works but also, and no less importantly, makes it possible for whoever wishes to write something of his own to do so more correctly.

The man who clarifies a fountain which is turbid with mud and 6
which is the source of many streams that flow from it in every direction does not only make the fountain itself more sparkling, but also he also makes the streamlets themselves, previously muddy and filthy, more pleasing to look at and more refreshing to drink from, now that they have received purer waters from their source. Similarly, he who corrects the corrupt writings of antiquity is cleansing, as it were, the very source itself, but he would not be

quae a nobis edita ab fonte illo quasi quidam rivuli derivantur elegantiora esse possint. Non iniuria igitur, cum id omne hinc sit, hoc illi a nobis anteferri munus videtur.

7 Sed ne ego, dum id laudo in quo aetatis plurimum consumpsi, meipsum laudare videar, de hoc satis, ac nimis fortasse multa. Nam ut laudem nullam mereatur, eo fortasse magnificentius cuiquam videri possit; cum enim tam multi propositi labores sint, nulla laudis praemia, maximam tantum utilitatem studiosi hinc omnes adipiscantur, magni cuiusdam animi censendum est tot nullo proposito praemio labores subire ac propriam laudem communi utilitati condonare.

8 Sed ut ad te me tandem convertam, Iuliane illustrissime, C. Iulii Caesaris commentaria cura nostra emendata in manus eruditorum sub tuo nomine exeunt; quae quanto reliquis quae hactenus impressa circunferuntur castigatiora sint, cuicunque ea conferre libuerit cognitu erit facillimum. Ego quidem in eo multum elaboravi; conquisivi multa tota Gallia exemplaria, qua in provincia, quod multa eo semper ex Italia translata sunt atque ea minus praedae exposita ac bellis fuerunt, multo incorruptiora volumina cuiusque generis reperiuntur. Contuli omnia, diligenter excussi neque meo tantum iudicio contentus fui sed, cum multa undique collegissem, eruditos plures demum Venetiis convocavi eorumque ingeniis omnia subieci iudicanda; neque quicquam non perpensum. Ex quo effectum est ut pauca admodum restent quae in suum nitorem restituta non sint, sed et eas fortasse aliquis

achieving simply this. For in addition, our own publications (streamlets from that fountain, you might say) can have greater felicity of style. Since all this is the result of editing, it is with every justification that we place this activity above that other one.

But lest you think I am indulging in self-praise when I extol 7
that activity on which I have spent the greatest part of my life, I say no more, and perhaps I have said too much. For someone may think it all the more splendid perhaps to earn no praise, since, when there are so many labors facing an editor and there is no such reward, and the only result is that all scholars derive the greatest benefit from it, it must be thought indicative of a certain loftiness of spirit for someone to endure so many labors with no reward in sight and to sacrifice to the common good the praise that belongs to him.

To turn finally to you, most illustrious Giuliano, these com- 8
mentaries of Julius Caesar that we have corrected with much care are reaching the hands of scholars under your name. How much more free of errors these are than those which have been printed up till now and are in circulation will be extremely obvious to anyone who may have the inclination to compare them. I worked very hard on this task, I sought out many manuscripts in the whole of France. Because many copies were regularly taken there from Italy and they were less exposed to pillage and wars, much superior manuscripts of every kind can be found in that country. I collated all of them, and scrutinized them with great care. But I was not content to rely on my own judgment, and when I had gathered together many of these manuscripts from all sources, I brought together numerous scholars in Venice and put before them everything for their talents to pass judgment on. There was nothing that was not given careful assessment. The result was that very few passages are left that have not been restored to their original splendor. Eventually perhaps someone will wipe away

aliquando maculas deterget.[3] Nobis id satis sit egisse ut perpaucae omnino reliquae sint.

9 Hos autem labores meos multis de causis tibi potissimum dicandos duximus, primo quidem, quod tibi omnes omnium qui in literis versantur labores lucubrationesque quodam gentilitio iure deberi videntur. Ex ea enim familia es quae semper literatos mire fovit. Nam ut vetustiores praeteream qui et ipsi tamen hoc magnificentissime egerunt, Laurentius pater ita id enixe egit ut eius beneficentia ex foeda illa proximorum seculorem barbarie in eum in quo nunc sunt gradum tam Latinae quam Graecae literae provectae esse videantur. Frater vero ita semper literatos omnes amplexus est uti non inmerito spes ea enata videatur quae nunc iam in omnium animis insedit, eo ad summum pontificatus culmen evecto, non Christianam solum rempublicam felicem futuram, sed et bonas omnes literas, quae iniquis his temporibus prope exaruerant, tam feliciter proventuras ut omne praeteritorum annorum incommodum sarciatur. Qua in re tu quoque ita animatus cognosceris ut non adiuturus fratrem solum, non imitaturus patrem, sed et per te ipse totum hoc munus gesturus, et tanto omnes tuos superaturus sis quanto illi caeteris excelluerunt.

10 Ad hanc causam accedit quod Iuliano Julii commentaria, quod candidissimis animi tui moribus candidissimum hoc opus maxime conveniens videtur munus, quod ego non hoc solum, sed quicquid in me ingenii est, quicquid in literis possum tibi dedicare constitui ac iam dedico. Aetate quidem ea sum ut de me non multa tibi possim promittere, sed natura ipsa fortasse, ut plerunque assolet, extremo hoc tempore, subitum aliquod ingenii mei lumen effundet quod tuum totum erit, tibi serviet, tibi consecrabitur. Tu interea

these remaining blemishes. Let me be satisfied in having brought it about that very few of these now remain.

For many reasons we thought that these labors of mine should 9 be dedicated to you more than anyone else, but primarily because all the results of long laborious hours of study that are achieved by all who work in the field of literature seem to be indebted to you as a right earned by your lineage. For you belong to that family which has always given wonderful support to men of literature. To pass over more distant members, although they too did this in the most magnificent manner, your father Lorenzo[47] was so zealous in such activities that it is by his generosity that both Latin and Greek literature are thought to have progressed from the shameful barbarity of the last few centuries to their present level. Your brother[48] has always embraced all men of literature so warmly that with every justification the hope seems to have arisen and taken root in everyone's heart that, with his elevation to the supreme pontificate, not only will the republic of Christ now prosper but also all good letters, which had almost withered away in these unfavorable times, will flourish so abundantly that all the harm of the past years may be put right. Your own intentions in this regard will be recognized by all; you will not only help your brother and emulate your father but you by yourself will take on this whole responsibility and will surpass the members of your family by as much as they have surpassed all others.

An additional reason is that the commentaries of Julius seem a 10 most appropriate gift for a Giuliano, and this lucid history of Caesar befits the lucidity of your mind. And so I decided to dedicate to you (and now do so) not only this work but whatever talent I have and whatever I am capable of achieving in the republic of letters. I am of an age that I cannot promise you much, but, as often happens, perhaps at this last period of my life nature itself will release a sudden flash of my talent that will be completely yours, that will be in thrall to you, that will be consecrated to you. If you

haec si ita uti speramus accipies, quoddam quasi currenti calcar addetur, ad caetera quae in animo habemus perficienda.

: VI :

Iucundi Veronensis in libros De re rustica *ad Leonem X pontificem maximum praefatio.*

1 Rerum rusticarum studiis semper sum incredibiliter delectatus, Beatissime Pater, quod eae quae ex illis capiuntur voluptates proxime ad sapientis vitam videntur accedere. Habent enim rationem cum terra, quae nunquam recusat imperium nec unquam sine usura reddit quod accepit. Quam ob rem cupiens hanc vitam requiem aliquando oblectamentumque futuram senectutis, si ad eam unquam Iesu Dei Optimi Maximi munere pervenirem, cum alios libros de cultura agrorum, tum praecipue Catonis, Varronis, Columellae, Palladii sic semper studiose legi ut satiari delectatione non possem. Videbar enim illis legendis ruri esse villas habitare M. Curii, L. Quintii Cincinnati, felicem illam vitam degere. Quorum alter, cum de Samnitibus ac Sabinis triumphasset et de Pyrrho in agris consumpsit extremum tempus aetatis, ubi ad focum sedenti magnum auri pondus Samnites cum attulissent, spreto auro, magnificam illam vocem edidit non aurum habere praeclarum sibi videri, sed eis qui haberent aurum imperare. Alter dictator factus a villa in senatum accersitus est.

accept these offerings, as we hope you do, you will act like a spur to a horse already on the gallop,[49] and impel me to bring to completion all the other things that I have in mind to do.

: VI :

Giovanni Giocondo, Letter to Pope Leo X[50]

(May 15, 1514)

Giocondo of Verona's[51] *Preface to the* Books on Agriculture *to Pope Leo X.*[52]

Most Blessed Father, I have always taken unbelievable delight in agricultural pursuits because the pleasures that derive from them seem to approach most closely the life of a philosopher. For such activities concern themselves with the land, which never refuses a command and never returns without profit what it has once received. Therefore out of a wish that this kind of life would give me rest and delight in my old age if ever I should live that long by the gift of Jesus, God Almighty, I have always read books on agriculture, and especially those of Cato, Varro, Columella and Palladius, and have done so with such zeal that I could never get enough pleasure from them. For in reading them I seemed to be in the country, living in the villas and enjoying the blissful life of Marcus Curius[53] and Lucius Quinctius Cincinnatus.[54] When Curius had triumphed over the Samnites, the Sabines and Pyrrhus, he spent the last years of his life on his land; there the Samnites brought him a huge amount of gold as he was sitting at his hearth. He spurned the gold and uttered those magnificent words, that he did not think it was a mark of fame to possess gold, rather fame lay in ruling over those who possessed it.[55] It was from his country villa that Cincinnatus was summoned to the senate when he was appointed dictator. 1

2 Hos ipsos libros summa mea in illos benevolentia cum antiquis contuli exemplaribus accurateque emendavi, adhibito tamen iudicio amicorum et doctorum hominum. Tum Aldo nostro dedi ut suis typis excudendos curaret idque cum factum sit non indiligenter sanctitatis tuae felicissimo nomini eos nuncupavi, cum ob meam erga illam summam observantiam, tum etiam quia tu dignissimus omnium eo munere occurrebas. Nam libri in quibus de vitibus et pastoribus et patribus familiarum tractatur cui convenientius dicari possunt quam ei qui vitis est foecundissima, qui pastor optimus, qui pater omnium? *αὐτὸς ἔφη*, 'Ego sum vitis vera, vos palmites.' 'Ego pastor bonus, qui satago mearum ovium et cognosco oves meas et me illae contra.'

3 Tu vero, Beatissime Pater, accipias velim munus hoc, qualecumque est, a Iucundo servo tuo benigna fronte, ut, spero, facies; es enim persimilis dei cuius locum tenes in terris. Amat ille pium cor, amat puram mentem, amat simplicitatem offerentis, non munus.

Venetiis Idibus Maii MDXIIII.

: VII :

Optimo atque integerrimo antistiti Antonio Trivultio ac christianissimi Francorum regis oratori ad senatum Venetum praestantissimo, Ioannes Baptista Egnatius Venetus.

1 Grave nuper vulnus accepimus, antistes integerrime, atque ex Aldi Manutii morte maius opinione omnium incommodum. Neque

Because of my deep feelings of affection for these authors I collated these very books against ancient manuscripts and corrected them with care, drawing upon, however, the opinions of friends and scholars. Then I gave them to our dear Aldus for him to print in his type. When this was done with no little diligence I dedicated them to the most auspicious name of your Holiness, not only because of my utmost respect for you but also because you came to mind as the person most worthy of all to receive this gift. To whom is it more appropriate to dedicate books that deal with vines and shepherds and fathers who are heads of households than to the man who is the most fruitful vine, the finest shepherd, the father of all? Jesus himself said, "I am the vine, you are the branches,"[56] "I am the good shepherd and am devoted to my sheep, and I know my sheep and they know me."[57] 2

Most Blessed Father, I would like you to accept this gift, such as it is, from your servant Giocondo and look kindly upon it. This I hope you will do. For you are very like our Lord, whose position you occupy on earth. He loves a devout heart, he loves a pure mind, he loves when simple faith is given him, rather than a gift. 3

Venice, May 15, 1514.

: VII :

Giambattista Egnazio, Eulogy of Aldus Manutius[58]

(April 1515)

Giambattista Egnazio[59] of Venice to Antonio Trivulzio,[60] a most noble and upright prelate and excellent ambassador of the Most Christian King of France to the senate of Venice.

Most upright prelate, in the recent death of Aldus Manutius we have suffered a grievous wound and a greater affliction than any 1

vero uni hoc mihi tantum contigit, qui hominis amicissimi iucunda consuetudine et officiorum coniunctione charissimi privatus sum, sed universis plane literatis ac bonarum artium studiosis ut interitu singularis ac eximii viri non possimus non etiam atque etiam omnes commoveri. Auget vero molestiam hanc nostram quod in tanta doctorum virorum ac bonorum librorum penuria quanta hoc tempore plane dignoscitur, vir et egregie doctus et ad rem literariam suo periculo ac labore iuvandam natus alieno admodum tempore sublatus est ut plane et doctrinae suae et singularis industriae triste omnibus desyderium reliquerit.

2 Ad haec autem doloris acerbitas eo gravior quotidie recrudescit quod cum literatis omnibus ita vixit ut cum nullius unquam obtrectarit aut adversatus sit laudi, omnes incredibili pietate semper et amplexus sit et foverit ut nemo fere in omni Europa sit vel mediocriter eruditus qui non singulari aliquo Manutii beneficio sit affectus. Illi igitur et ego cum illis praecipue iure doleo, dolendumque magis omnibus censeo, quando vir ille defunctus vita sit cuius industriae parem nec nostra nec superior aetas habuit. Quod si memoriae proditum est vel mediocrium hominum morte vel etiam avicularum interitu civitates etiam magnas doluisse solennique pompa populum Romanum corvi funus celebrasse, quis non plane angatur animo cum amissum extinctumque illum virum intelligat qui rem literariam iam lapsam ac prope desperatam solus fere erexerit et restituerit?

3 Cuius erectae et restitutae laus tanto maior insigniorque aestimari debet quanto gravior literarum amissio futura erat quam imperii et finium diminutio. Illae enim cum semel amissae sunt, non modo non reviviscunt aut terrarum alibi florent, sed ita plane

one could imagine. This has befallen not only me, who have been deprived of enjoying the pleasant company of a close and dear friend and of engaging in the activities that we had in common, but also and clearly all men of learning and all devotees of the liberal arts. As a result we cannot help but be continually pained by the loss of an outstanding and exceptional man. At this time there is an obvious and considerable shortage of learned men and fine books; that a man of remarkable learning, one born to promote literature by his own toil and at his own risk, has been taken from us at such an inopportune time adds to this distress of ours. All of us clearly feel the sad loss of his erudition and his outstanding industriousness.

What is more, the bitterness of our grief swells up more keenly 2
every day since in his association with all men of literature he never disparaged or maligned the praise won by others and always embraced and supported them with incredible loyalty. In the whole of Europe hardly anyone with even a modest level of erudition has not experienced some special kindness from Manutius. It is right that they grieve and I especially along with them. I think that all should mourn the death of that man whose industriousness neither our age not any earlier age has matched. If it has been recorded for posterity that even great nations mourned the loss of men of just modest talent or even the death of little birds and that the Roman people marked the passing of a raven[61] with a solemn procession, who would not suffer obvious anguish at the realization of the loss and death of that man who almost alone raised up and restored literature when it was in a state of collapse and almost given up as lost?

The praise for having done so ought to be valued all the higher 3
and exalted all the more given that the loss of literature would have been much more damaging than the diminution of empire and territory. For once literary works are lost, not only can they not come to life again or flourish elsewhere, they perish so com-

intercidunt ut earum vestigia vix supersint. Imperium vero ac summa rerum ut apud unum populum gentemve intercidat, sic alibi laetius illustriusque exurgit ut ex unius populi nationisque lapsu maiestas illa et splendor imperii opumque magnitudo ad alium maior et clarior saepe transferatur.

4 Caeterum quando nec Aldo perpetua felicitas promissa fuerat nec nos in homine sperare id poteramus, dolori nostro terminum aliquem statuimus ne nostro incommodo ac detrimento dolere magis videamur. Vixit etenim ille quam diu licuit et vixit in summa omnium probitatis ac eruditionis opinione. Neque enim ulla tam barbara, tam remota gens hodie Europae finibus includitur cui non notissimum Aldi nomen ac celeberrimum fuerit.

5 Sed et plerosque non ignobiles viros vel hac sola causa Venetias venisse constat, ut unum hunc salutarent et viserent magnisque et muneribus donarent, et quos urbs tanta tamque admirabilis ad sui contemplationem non traxerat, unius viri fama perduxit, adhortati pro virili ut instituto restituendae Latinae ac Graecae linguae proposito insisteret. In cuius ille meditationem cum die noctesque[4] totus incumberet, gravi ac diuturno conflictatus morbo quem ex nimio labore ac vigiliis contraxerat, suo fortasse tempore nostroque certe alienissimo decessit. Neque enim ullum antea illi commodius hoc fuerat. Cum et longa illum experienta peritissimum fecisset et multa iam parasset quae si perpolire atque absolvere potuisset, non multum certe ad rei summam desyderares.

6 Ille igitur aliis alia, mihi Coeliii Lactantii Firmiani septem *Institutionum divinarum* libros et reliqua disertissimi Christianorum viri

pletely that they scarcely leave any trace. In contrast, one people or race may lose sovereignty and supreme power, but these attributes rise up again elsewhere more abundantly and more illustriously. The decline of one nation leads to the transfer to another of its majesty, splendor of empire and greatness of wealth, often at a higher and more renowned level.

But since everlasting good fortune had not been promised to 4
Aldus (and we could never hope for this for any human being), we set a limit to our grief lest we may seem to be grieving excessively because of our own personal sense of loss and discomfiture. He lived as long as it was permitted and during his life all considered him to be a man of the utmost probity and highest erudition. There is today no nation in the whole of Europe, no matter how uncultured or remote, to whom the name of Aldus has not been well known and highly celebrated.

It is well known that many men of no mean rank came to Ven- 5
ice for one reason only, to visit and pay their respects to this one man and to bestow great gifts upon him. Those who had not been induced by the greatness and wonder of this city to set their eyes upon it were drawn to it by the fame of this one man. They exhorted him urgently to press on with his aim of restoring the Greek and Latin languages. When he immersed himself day and night in achieving this end, he was afflicted with a serious and chronic illness that he had contracted as a result of excessive work and long hours of toil into the night. And so perhaps he died at his appointed time, though certainly one that was abhorrent to us. An earlier death would have been untimely, since it was lengthy experience that had honed his skills to the highest degree. He had already prepared many works for publication, and if he had been able to add polish to these and finish them, little would be needed to complete his mission.

He assigned different projects to different persons. To me he 6
had given for correction the seven books of *Divine Institutes* of

monimenta corrigenda tradiderat, ut ipse interim aut aliis commodius emendandis aut sublevandae valetudini vacare posset. Quo in opere quantum elaborarim quantumve industriae ac studii adhibuerim aliorum malumus esse iudicium. Illud affirmare possum, tanto hosce libros castigatiores esse caeteris Lactantii libris qui ad hanc diem impressi legantur quanto Aldus ipse in hoc genere laudis omnes alios facile praestitit.

7 Et ii quidem tibi iure nuncupari debuere, vel quod inter religionis nostrae proceres primum dignitatis locum tenes, vel quod clarissima in terra Italia familia natus es vel quod Christianissimi Regis ac potentissimi Legatus apud Venetum senatum incredibili civitatis gratia ac prudentiae opinione iam pridem fulges vel denique quod consilio, ingenio, authoritate, liberalitate parem fere habeas neminem.

8 Unum lectorem admonitum velim, Epitomen, quam curavimus addendam ex Hieronymi testimonio, non solum acephalon esse, quod ille et doctissimus et sanctissimus vir asserit, sed plane eius fragmentum quoddam. Quod tamen, qualecumque esset, ex tanto naufragio vel scalmum hunc servare studui. Quin etiam carmen *De resurrectione,* quod Lactantio adscriptum inveni, non modo ⟨non⟩ dignum eius viri eloquentia mihi visum est, sed ne cum *Phoenice* quidem quem cecinit comparandum, cum ad alia in syllaba etiam claudicet. Sed et notas illas in Lactantium nescio cuius fraterculi expunximus, tum quod multa ex illis imperite reprehendantur, tum etiam quod voluimus suum cuique iudicium integrum, cum praesertim illis temporibus hic floruerit quibus eorum multa nondum communi consensu damnata fuerant. Quae vir alioqui

Caelius Lactantius Firmianus and the rest of the works of that most eloquent of Christians. This was to allow him time to have more convenience to correct other writers or to have time to look after himself in his ill health. How much care we have expended in this task, how much diligence and learning I have applied to it, we prefer to leave to the judgment of others to decide. I can declare this, that in accuracy the superiority of these books over all other editions of Lactantius that have been printed up till now matches the superiority that Aldus easily held over all others in this laudatory profession.

It was right that these books had to be dedicated to you. You 7
hold the first place of rank among the leaders of our religion; you were born into a most famous family of Italy; you have long shone as ambassador to the senate of Venice of the most Christian and most powerful king, enjoying incredible goodwill in this city as well as a reputation for your wisdom; in counsel, intellect, influence and liberality you have scarcely an equal.

I would like the reader to be advised of one thing, that the 8
Epitome which we have undertaken to add on the basis of the testimony of Jerome[62] not only lacks its beginning, as that most holy and most learned man asserts, but is clearly just a fragment of the whole work. I was eager, however, to preserve this, such as it is, like a tholepin that has survived a shipwreck. As for the poem *On Resurrection* which I have found ascribed to Lactantius, not only did I not think that it matched the eloquence of that man, I did not even think it was comparable to his *Phoenix*, since in addition to other points it also limps by a syllable.[63] We have also removed those notes on Lactantius written by some monk or other;[64] they contain much ignorant criticism and we wished each reader to make his own judgment without influence, especially since Lactantius flourished in times when many points had not yet been condemned by common consent, points that a man of such eloquence

disertissimus nec pertinaciter affirmasset et admonitus facile emendasset.

Bene et feliciter vale.

: VIII :

Ad sacrosanctae Romanae ecclesiae cardinalem Ioannem Medicem
Raphaelis Regii Quaestio utrum
'Ars rhetorica ad Herenium' Ciceroni falso inscribatur.

1 Relegenti mihi nuper accuratius et duos Ciceronis *De inventione* rhetoricos et quattuor ad Herenium libros de eadem facultate conscriptos ut depravationibus sublatis castigatiores quam[5] mille et amplius exemplaria describerentur quaestio illa utrum *Ars Rhetorica ad Herenium* Ciceroni falso inscribatur ex operis utriusque stili comparatione pulcherrima tractatu est visa.

2 Cum enim Laurentius Valla perquam acri vir iudicio quodam in libello asserat opusculum illud vix Cicerone esse dignum et quidam citra omnem eorum quae contra dici possent refutationem Ciceronis esse negent, plerique vero adduci non possint ut illam a M. Tullii familia veluti subditiciam putent summovendam, rem tibi non ingratam, qui Ciceronis ipsius maxime es studiosus,

would not have persisted in asserting and would have easily corrected if advised.

We wish you well. Farewell.

: VIII :

Raffaele Regio,[65] The Authorship of the *Rhetorica ad Herennium*

(September 19, 1491)

To the cardinal of the Holy Roman Church, Giovanni de' Medici,[66]
Raffaele Regio's Inquiry into Whether the
"Ars Rhetorica ad Herennium" is falsely attributed to Cicero.[67]

I was recently reading again with great care the two books of Cicero's *De inventione* on rhetoric and the four books addressed to Herennius, written on the same topic. My purpose was to remove the corruptions in them and to have them copied out in a more correct form than is found in a thousand or more manuscripts. But then I thought that the question of whether the attribution of the *Ars rhetorica ad Herennium* to Cicero is false would be an excellent one to take up and examine on the basis of a comparison of the style in the two works. 1

Lorenzo Valla, a man of the keenest judgment, asserts in a tome of his that this work is scarcely worthy of Cicero,[68] and some individuals[69] deny that Cicero is the author (although they fall short of completely refuting all that could be said against their opinion). Despite this, many cannot be persuaded to accept that the work should be removed from membership of Cicero's household, so to speak, on the grounds of its being supposititious. Accordingly, I thought I would undertake a task that would please 2

existimavi me esse facturum si breviter ipsam descriptis utriusque opinionis rationibus explicuissem quaestionem.

3 Tametsi namque sublimi dignitate tua est minor, tenellae tamen adhuc aetati apta hoc mihi saltem praestabit ne singularis tuae in me humanitatis videar esse oblitus. Cum enim me nuper Florentiam contulissem ut vetustum illud Quintiliani exemplar quod in vestra biblioteca spectatur viderem, quanto studio quantaque liberalitate ut mihi perlegendum traderetur effecisti! Quare et eximia benignitate et aliis eminentissimis virtutibus tuis quarum clarissimo fulgore summus pontifex Innocentius octavus invitatus ac vere spiritu sancto repletus te in collegium illud sacrosanctum Romanae ecclesiae Cardinalium summa cum bonorum omnium laetitia cooptavit me tibi sic devinxisti ut non hanc modo quaestiunculam sed siquid est in me ingenii id totum me tibi debere putem. Sed iam ad explicandam quaestionem propositam revertamur.

4 Qui *Rhetoricam ad Herenium* Ciceronis opus esse aiunt tribus potissimum rationibus niti videntur, tum quod operis inscriptioni Ciceronis nomen est appositum, tum quod quidam non ignobiles auctores id esse Ciceronis opus aperte testari videntur Ciceronem in *Rhetoricis ad Herenium* allegantes, tum quod et filii Ciceronis et Terentiae uxoris in quodam opusculi illius exemplo mentio habetur.

5 Ac primum quidem argumentum facile refutatur cum id quod est controversum et in quaestione positum perinde atque si certum concessumque foret inconsiderate nimium imperiteque assumatur. Quid namque aliud quaeritur quam utrum *Rhetorica ad Herenium* Ciceroni falso per inscriptionem attribuatur? Neque enim appositis inscriptioni nominibus sed ex praeceptorum ac stili praesertim similitudine auctoribus opera adiudicari solent. Alioqui nunquam videretur quaerendum an aliquod opus alicui falso inscribatur. Sic enim unicuique facile foret suis scriptis ex

you, being a most devoted admirer of Cicero, if I described the positions held on both sides and briefly disentangled the problem.

3 Although this question is beneath your lofty eminence, nevertheless it is still suited to your tender years and will allow me to show that I have not forgotten your outstanding kindness toward me. For when I went to Florence recently to examine that ancient manuscript of Quintilian that is on view in your library, what zeal and generosity you showed in arranging that it be given to me to read through! Your outstanding kindness and other eminent virtues (the shining brilliance of which prompted Pope Innocent VIII, with the instigation and impetus of the Holy Spirit and to the great joy of all good men, to appoint you to the Holy College of the Cardinals of the Roman Church) have bound me so close to you that I owe to you not only this modest inquiry but all the talent that I possess. But let us return to the resolution of the question that we have put before us.

4 Those who say that the *Rhetorica ad Herennium* is a work of Cicero's seem to rely on three arguments in particular: first, Cicero's name is found in the title of the work; secondly, some writers of no mean repute seem to attest explicitly that Cicero is the author, referring as they do to "Cicero in his *Rhetorica ad Herennium*"; thirdly, there is mention of Cicero's son and of his wife Terentia in an example given in the work.

5 The first argument is easily refuted; for it would be a very rash and naive assumption to take what is under dispute and what is the point of the inquiry as certain and granted. Is not the whole topic of the inquiry the question of whether the title falsely ascribes the *Rhetorica ad Herennium* to Cicero? For works are ascribed to authors, not on the basis of names appearing in the title, but above all on similarities in the precepts and style. If this were not so, there would never seem to be any point in considering whether or not some work is falsely ascribed to someone, while if the criterion was the title, it would be easy for anyone at all to win prestige

praestantum virorum nominibus auctoritatem ac potius immortalitatem comparare.

6 At quidam scriptores, quorum est divus Hieronymus, id esse Ciceronis opus sentire videntur. Ante omnia tollatur e disputatione auctoritas nec mihi vitio detur si omnes eos qui *Rhetoricam ad Herenium* Ciceronis opus esse putant nominibus inscriptioni appositis deceptos et se et complures alios eam in opinionem coniecisse assevero, ut quod penitus a Ciceronis maiestate est alienum id Ciceroni putaverint inscribendum, neque scivisse in hoc opere diiudicando censoria illa virgula uti qua veteres grammatici non versus modo notabant sed libros etiam qui falso inscripti viderentur tanquam subditicios, ut inquit Fabius, sibi familia[6] summovere permittebant. Fabius quidem ipse Quintilianus Ciceronis librorum diligentissimus observator quem grammaticis omnibus aliisque scriptoribus non opposuerim modo sed facile anteposuerim nusquam illius opusculi facit mentionem, nequaquam praetermissurus si aut Ciceronis esse putasset aut certe suo tempore extitisset.

7 Verum quoddam illius opusculi exemplum et Ciceronis filii et Terentiae uxoris continet mentionem. Hoc quidem argumento Rhetorica ad Herenium non modo non probatur Ciceronis esse opus, sed contra non esse procul dubio mihi demonstrari videtur. Nam M. Tullius aut nunquam, quod paulo post verum esse colligam, aut certe dum adhuc puer esset, antequam aut uxorem duxisset aut filios sustulisset, *Rhetorica ad Herenium* scripsit. Neque enim mihi fieri verisimile potest ut eos matura iam aetate composuerit libros in quibus puerilia magis deprehenduntur errata quam in iis quos sibi ipse puero adhuc excidisse in prohoemio de oratore testatur. Non enim de Rhetoricis ad Herennium eo in loco Tullius

and indeed immortality for his own writings by using the names of outstanding men.

Some writers, however, including St Jerome,[70] seem to think that the work is by Cicero. But it is paramount that the criterion of any individual's prestige be removed from the argument, and let not me be criticized if I say that all who think that Cicero is the author of the *Rhetorica ad Herennium* have been led astray by the names that appear in the title and have themselves rushed to this belief as well as having driven many others to the same conclusion. As a result they think that a work which is quite incompatible with Cicero's grandeur ought to be attributed to him. In settling this question they did not know how to use the obelus with which the ancient philologists marked not only verses as suspect but also whole books that they thought were falsely attributed, thus allowing themselves, as Quintilian says,[71] to remove them from membership of an author's household on the grounds that they were supposititious. Indeed Quintilian himself, whom I would not just include among all philologists and other writers but readily rank ahead of them, and who pays heed most conscientiously to Cicero's writings, nowhere mentions this work, and he would have in no way overlooked it if he thought that Cicero was its author or if it actually existed in his time. 6

Ah, but this work includes an example that refers to Cicero's son and his wife Terentia![72] Far from proving that Cicero is the author, this argument seems to me to show, without a shadow of a doubt, the very opposite. For if Cicero ever actually wrote the *Rhetorica ad Herennium*, a hypothesis which I shall refute a little later, he must have written it when he was still a boy before he had married and had children. I cannot think it probable that he wrote these books when he was of a mature age, as puerile mistakes can be seen in them, more so than in those books which he himself attests in the introduction to *De oratore* he let slip from his grasp when he was still a boy.[73] Cicero is not talking about the *Rhetorica* 7

loquitur ut quidam omnia temeritate sua pervertentes opinantur, sed eam in qua Hermagoram fere est secutus, cuius duo tantum de inventione libri extant, damnare videtur. Quare exemplum illud de Ciceronis filio uxoreque compositum facile demonstrat *Rhetoricam ad Herenium* ab alio quam Cicerone fuisse conscriptam.

8 Ac si ea refutavimus quibus illud opusculum Ciceroni plerisque videtur inscribendum, iam quod ipsi sequamur aperiamus. Stilus ante omnia et compositione et sententiis sane quam puerilis nec ulli aliorum operum quae Cicero vel adolescens vel iuvenis vel senex composuit ulla ex parte similis ac minus quam ut Ciceronem ipsum deceat elegans prorsus alii quam M. Tullio opusculum illud adiudicare videtur.

9 Praeceptorum deinde ordo, ut de varietate sileamus, perversus ac iis quae a Cicerone ipso et Fabio Quintiliano aliisque accuratis rhetoribus traduntur contrarius aperte ostendit alium a Cicerone illius artis fuisse auctorem. Ut enim omittam quod ante de memoria atque pronunciatione quam de elocutione illis natura priore illo in opusculo praecepta traduntur, exordiendi certe narrandique rationes ante quam de constitutionibus praecipiatur descriptae longe a Ciceronis dispositione recedere videntur.

10 Nam, ut Cicero ipse in primo *De inventione* libro ait, non solum genus causae ante quam exordiamur considerandum est, sed constitutio quoque et quaestio et ratio et iudicatio et firmamentum est inveniendum. 'Nam,' inquit, 'non ut quodque dicendum est primum, ita primum animadvertendum videtur; ideo quod illa quae prima dicuntur, si vehementer velis congruere et cohaerere

ad Herennium in this passage as some believe, brazenly distorting everything. Rather he seems to be condemning that work in which he followed Hermagoras[74] for the most part and of which only the two books of *De inventione* are in existence. And so that example referring to Cicero's son and wife provides convincing proof that the *Rhetorica ad Herennium* was written by someone other than Cicero.

If we have refuted these arguments that have led several scholars to believe that the work should be attributed to Cicero, let us reveal the path that we ourselves are following. First of all, the style in its manner and content is decidedly puerile and is quite unlike the other works that Cicero composed, whether in his youth, in his prime or in his old age; it is too inelegant for Cicero himself to have written it. Consideration of style, then, seems to point to anyone at all other than Cicero as the author of this work. 8

Secondly, the order of precepts, to say nothing of differences in content within them, is unnatural and contrary to those handed down to us by Cicero himself and Quintilian and other meticulous rhetoricians, and is accordingly a clear indication that someone else and not Cicero was the author of this tract. For, to say nothing of the fact that in this work the precepts on memory and delivery are given before those on style, although style naturally takes precedence over these, it is quite alien to Cicero's organization of his material that the methods of how to begin and how to narrate should be dealt with before advice is given relating to the points at issue in a case. 9

For as Cicero himself says in the first book of *De inventione*, not only must the kind of case be considered before we begin, but we must find the point at issue, the question, the justification, the points for the court's decision, and the central argument. "For," he says, "it cannot be right to turn your attention first to what you will say first, since if you want your opening statement to cohere with and agree strongly with the main statement of the case you 10

cum causa, ex eis ducas oportet quae post dicenda sunt. Quare cum iudicatio et ea quae ad iudicationem oportet inveniri argumenta diligenti erunt artificio reperta, cura et cogitatione pertractata, tunc demum ordinandae sunt caeterae partes orationis.' Hoc idem alibi quoque praecipit Tullius nec ab hoc ordine Fabius Quintilianus recedit. Ex quo quidem aperte colligimus opusculum illud ab alio quam Cicerone fuisse conscriptum.

11 Quid quod in primo libro ubi de numero constitutionum disseritur Hermestis cuiusdam doctoris sui meminit illius operis auctor, qui nusquam Ciceronis temporibus fuisse memoratur cum de omnibus claris suorum temporum rhetoribus Cicero ipse aliquam faciat mentionem? A. praeterea Gelius totius antiquitatis diligentissimus indagator in duodecimo *Noctium Atticarum* libro scribit antiquorum neminem usque ad Augusti tempora hoc nomine barbarismo usum fuisse cum in *Rhetoricis ad Herenium* et barbarismus definiatur et soloecismus. Aut Gelium igitur falso ea memoriae commendasse aut opusculum illud Ciceronis non esse fatendum est cum ante Augusti imperium Cicero ipse Antonii rabie fuerit interemptus. Quamobrem satis superque patere arbitror *Rhetoricam ad Herenium* Ciceroni hactenus falso fuisse inscriptam.

12 Cui autem id opusculi sit attribuendum in tanta praesertim antiquorum rhetorum copia quorum nomina sine operibus extant haud facile diiudicari potest. Minime tamen id est dissimulandum quod mihi pridem cum Paduae profiterer vulgatum quidam exceperunt, Cornificium videlicet illius opusculi idcirco auctorem videri quod Fabius Quintilianus eam statuum divisionem ac quaedam alia quae in *Rhetoricis ad Herenium* leguntur Cornificio ipsi ascribit. Sed non omnia quae ad Cornificium a Fabio referuntur in

must draw its content from what is to be said later. And so when the points for the court's decision and the arguments that must be devised for the judgment of the court have been skillfully identified, and carefully and thoughtfully studied, then and only then all the other parts of the speech[75] are to be arranged in order."[76] Cicero says the same elsewhere and Quintilian also follows this same order. From this we can clearly infer that this work was composed by someone other than Cicero.

What too of the fact that in Book One when he is discussing 11 the number of Types of Issue of a case (*constitutiones*), the author of this work mentions a certain teacher, Hermestes, of whose existence in the time of Cicero there is no record,[77] although Cicero himself mentions all the famous orators that were his contemporaries? What is more, Aulus Gellius, a most industrious researcher of all antiquity, writes in Book Twelve of his *Attic Nights*[78] that none of the ancients used the word *barbarismus* up till the time of Augustus, although both *barbarismus* and *soloecismus* are defined in the *Rhetorica ad Herennium*.[79] If Gellius did not err in recording this information for posterity, we must admit that the work is not by Cicero, since, as a result of Antony's mad desire for vengeance, Cicero was murdered before Augustus came to power.[80] Therefore it is abundantly clear, I think, that the *Rhetorica ad Herennium* has been falsely attributed to Cicero right up to this time.

It cannot be easy to decide whom we should credit for this 12 work, especially given the large number of rhetoricians in antiquity that we know only by name without knowing anything of their works. Nevertheless I must in no way conceal what certain persons heard me spread abroad sometime ago when I was lecturing in Padua in the University, namely that Cornificius seemed to be the author of this work, since Quintilian ascribes to him the same division of the Types of Issues of a case (*constitutiones*) and some other features that are contained in the *Rhetorica ad Herennium*. But not everything that Quintilian refers to Cornificius can be found

libris ad Herenium inveniuntur nisi forte quis dicat alia quoque opera de facultate dicendi a Cornificio ipso fuisse conscripta.

13 Quod quidem ut verum esse potest, ita nihil impedit libros ad Herenium ab alio quam Cornificio et fortasse multo post Quintiliani tempora non solum Cornificii fuisse conscriptos. A stilo certe et compositione illorum temporum longe abesse videntur.

14 Quanquam autem nihil in tanta rerum omnium perturbatione ac potius confusione affirmare ausim, fortasse tamen nec immerito Timolaus Zenobiae e triginta Romanorum tyrannis unus id sibi opusculum vindicaret. Is namque, ut testatur Pollio Trevellius, non indiligens historicus, et grammatices et rhetorices fuit peritissimus ut summus Latinorum rhetor illis temporibus haberetur. Huic frater Herenianus natu maior fuisse memoratur qui et ipse imperium usurpavit. Sed ab Aureliano Imperatore superati et in triumphum una cum Zaenobia matre ducti principis indulgentia in Tiburti agro otiosam vitam vixerunt, ubi fortasse Timolaus Herenianum fratrem praeceptis rhetoricis instruxit ad eumque id opusculi scripsit.

15 Facile autem Timolaus, rhetor obscurus a posterioribus, in Tullium oratorum clarissimum et Herenianus in Herenium propter nominum similitudinem ab iis qui posterioribus et rudioribus seculis fuere potuit commutari. Cui namque potius libri de arte rhetorica scripti quam M. Tullio eloquentiae parenti ab imperitis rudioribusque temporum infelicitate hominibus ascribi debuerint cum pleraque alia de eadem facultate opera Tullio ipsi conscripta viderent?

in the books addressed to Herennius — although one can perhaps argue that Cornificius also wrote other works on eloquence.

While this may be true, nothing prevents the *Rhetorica* from having been composed by someone other than Cornificius, and perhaps it was written not only after the time of Cornificius but even much later than Quintilian's lifetime. It certainly seems far removed from that period in its style and the arrangement of the subject matter. 13

Although I would not dare to make a definite statement about a period when everything was in a state of confusion and unrest, perhaps it would not be amiss if Timolaus, the son of Zenobia, one of the thirty tyrants of the Romans,[81] claimed this work as his. For, as is attested by Pollio Trevellius, a most conscientious historian,[82] he was a very accomplished philologist and rhetorician, so much so that he was regarded as the greatest Latin orator of those times. He is said to have had an elder brother, Herennianus, who himself seized power. But they were overcome by the emperor Aurelian and were led in a triumph along with their mother, Zenobia. However, the indulgence of the emperor allowed them to lead a life of leisure in an estate in Tibur. This is perhaps the place where Timolaus instructed his brother Herennianus in the precepts of rhetoric and wrote the *Rhetorica* for him. 14

Because of their similarity, the names of Timolaus, a rhetorician hardly known to later generations, and Herennianus could easily have been changed into Tullius, the most famous of orators, and Herennius respectively by those who lived in later and more ignorant times. For to whom other than Cicero, the father of eloquence, ought books written on the art of rhetoric to have been attributed by men who had little knowledge and training because of the wretched nature of the times they lived in, especially when they saw that most of the other works on this same subject had been written by Cicero? 15

16 Sed ut mihi hoc verisimile videtur, ita cum nullius certa auctoritate nitamur, in medio est relinquendum ne aliquid temere affirmasse videamur. Quisquis vero illius opusculi auctor fuit minime est negligendum. Si enim diligenter ac cum eorum annotatione quae minus recte praecipiuntur expositum studiosi iuvenes edidicerint cum aliarum eloquentiae partium rudimenta tum elocutionis praecepta maxime aliquid scribere volentibus necessaria se percepisse gaudebunt. Omnes namque et verborum et sententiarum exornationes non solum definiuntur sed iis etiam illustrantur exemplis quae fere de Ciceronis orationibus sumpta ad imitationemve ipsius composita plerosque in ea detinent opinione ut libros *ad Herenium* nulli alii quam Ciceroni ascribendos putent.

17 Sed de hac quaestione satis. Quam quidem si tibi et probari et gratam esse cognovero, non parum lucri mihi fecisse videbor. Vale, nostri seculi eximium decus.

Venetiis: xiiii Calendas octobres, MCCCLXXXXI.

: IX :

Nicolaus Angelius Bucinensis ad Philippum Strozam
Pro Rhetoricis *Ciceronis* Ad Herennium.

1 Apporto tibi muneri, Philippe Stroza, *Rhetoricen* Ciceronis *ad Herennium* novam, id est recognitam, detersam, nitidam. Librariorum enim depravatione et temporum vitio Cicero in his libris a seipso

While this seems probable to me, we must leave the question open, since we do not have the certain authority of anyone to depend on. For we do not wish to seem to have made a rash pronouncement. Whoever was the author, the work itself must by no means be ignored. For if students learn by heart what is expounded in it with care and with reference to notes on less correct precepts that it contains, they will take pleasure in having learned the rudiments of every element of eloquence as well those precepts of style that are particularly necessary for aspiring writers. For all the figures of speech and figures of thought are not only defined but even illustrated by those examples that are for the most part taken from Cicero's speeches or composed in imitation of him, and this is what has led many to hold fast to the belief that the *Rhetorica ad Herennium* has to be attributed to no one other than Cicero. 16

But enough on this topic. If I discover that what I have said meets your approval and gives you pleasure, I will feel greatly enriched. Farewell, you who are the outstanding glory of our age. 17

Venice, September 18, 1491.

: IX :

Niccolò Angeli of Bucine,[83] The Authorship of the *Rhetorica ad Herennium*

(1515/16)

Niccolò Angeli of Bucine to Filippo Strozzi,[84] *in defense of Cicero's authorship of the* Rhetorica ad Herennium.

I offer you as a gift, Filippo Strozzi, a new edition of Cicero's *Rhetorica ad Herennium*, new[85] in the sense that its text has been carefully reviewed, the blemishes have been removed and it is, so to speak, sparkling clean.[86] I say this for the deficiencies in these 1

per mendas ita sensim abierat in deformitatem vix iam ut suorum plerisque agnosceretur. Incelebres vero lectionis eius quibus macularum foeditas divinae eloquentiae vultum subtraxit, titulum huius operis subdititium esse contendunt et auctoris inopes, Virginio vel Cornificio cuidam quem penitus non norunt, quod maxime rideas, levissima quadam, immo nulla coniectura pueriliter tribuunt. Sed quamobrem tam bonas dicendi rationis praeceptiones summi opificis artificio surripiant discas.

2 Primum aiunt Quintilianum cum suas *Institutiones Oratorias* crebris orationum Ciceronis et omnium eius de arte rhetorica operum exemplis confirmet, *Rhetoricos*[7] *ad Herennium* nusquam citasse, utique citaturum si Ciceronis esse scivisset; tum Plutarchum in *Ciceronis vita*, enumeratione voluminum quae Cicero reliquerit libros ad Herennium tacuisse nec Hermestem quendam, de quo in illis fit mentio inter praeceptores per quos Cicero profecerit nominasse; deinde legi quaedam in his quae *De oratore* ad Quintum fratrem libris magnopere repugnant nec esse ferendum quenquam sibi in suis scriptis dissentire. Dicendi postremo figuram multo humiliorem ac sicciorem cognosci disputant quam quae Ciceronis sublimitatem atque opulentiam referat. His tenuibus coniecturis, hoc opus a suo parente per inscitiam revulsum Cornificio aut Virginio, nec id quidem sibi si reviviscant asserturis, ridicule addicunt.

3 Verum exigui est negotii — tam est aperta veritas — horum refellere pueriles opiniones. Primo loco aiunt Ciceronis opus ideo non esse quod nusquam a Quintiliano citetur quasi sit necesse ea omnia suo auctore spoliari quae a Quintiliano non citentur. Quod si

books caused by the corrupting work of copyists and the ravages of time had gradually transformed Cicero and so disfigured him that most of his followers could scarcely recognize him. Moreover, some persons of little distinction,[87] for whom the repulsive stains of this text have destroyed the face of divine eloquence, claim that the author's name in the title of this work is supposititious. Lacking an author, they naively attribute it to a certain Virginius or Cornificius — a person about whom, most laughably, they have not even the slightest of evidence. But learn why they so cunningly strip the supreme artist of such fine precepts on the art of rhetoric.

First they say that although Quintilian frequently adduces ex- 2
amples from Cicero's speeches and all his works on rhetoric in support of what he says in his *Rhetorical Principles*, he nowhere cites the *Rhetorica ad Herennium* and he would certainly have done so if he knew that the work was by Cicero. Secondly, in his *Life of Cicero* Plutarch says nothing about the books addressed to Herennius when he lists the volumes that Cicero left behind;[88] nor does he name a certain Hermestes as one of the teachers who helped Cicero develop his skills although he is mentioned in the *Rhetorica*.[89] Thirdly, the *Rhetorica* contains some material that is greatly at odds with what is said in the *De oratore*, addressed to his brother Quintus — and it is intolerable that anyone should contradict himself in his writings! Finally, they argue that the *Rhetorica* is written in a style that is recognizably too low and dry to evoke the loftiness and richness of Cicero. On this thin evidence and in their ignorance they snatch this work from its creator and ridiculously assign it to Cornificius or Virginius, who would not claim it for themselves if they were brought back to life!

The truth is plain to see and so it is an easy task to refute 3
the puerile arguments of these men. In their first point they say that the work is not by Cicero because it is nowhere cited by Quintilian — as if all works must be stripped of their author if they are not cited by Quintilian. But if this were so, it follows that

ita est, nullius opus esse relinquitur quod nemini sua citatione Quintilianus adiudicet. Locis tamen non paucis horum librorum verbis et sententiis usus eos Ciceronis esse grandem coniecturam facit.

4 Eius enim libro primo, de elocutionis virtutibus verba haec sunt: 'Usitatis tutius utimur, nova non sine quodam periculo fingimus. Nam si recepta sunt, modicam laudem afferunt orationi; repudiata etiam in iocos exeunt. Audendum tamen, nanque, ut Cicero ait, etiam quae primo dura visa sunt usu molliuntur.' Cicero in praefatione libri quarti *Rhetoricorum* hunc sensum his verbis expressit: 'Quae enim res apud nostros non erant, earum rerum nomina non poterant esse usitata; ergo haec asperiora primo videantur necesse est.'

5 Eiusdem libro nono de verborum coloribus: 'Qui sunt qui foedera saepe ruperunt? Carthaginenses.[8] Qui sunt qui bellum crudelissime gesserunt? Carthaginenses. Qui sunt qui Italiam deformaverunt? Carthaginenses. Qui sunt qui sibi ignosci postulant? Carthaginenses.' Exemplum hoc est Ciceronis Rhetoricum quarto de complexione. Ibidem: 'Amari iucundum est si curetur ne quid insit amari. Avium dulcedo ad avium ducit.' Sic Cicero in Rhetoricis de traductione. Nec obstat quod Quintilianus subiunxerit paulo post, 'Cornificius hanc traductionem vocat.' Nam ea quae iocandi causa ferebantur in ore vulgi obvia erant exemplis pluribus scriptoribus. Plenus est hoc loco Quintilianus exemplis quibus utitur etiam Cicero de verborum figuris.

any work that Quintilian does not attribute to anyone in his citations is authorless. Despite this omission, Quintilian uses the words and ideas of the *Rhetorica* in not a few places and thereby provides good evidence that the work is by Cicero.

In his first book this is what Quintilian says when talking 4
about the virtues of expression: "It is safer for us to use well-known terms, and it is not without risk that we make up new ones. For if the latter are accepted they bring only modest praise for our mode of expression, while if repudiated they are even a source of merriment. Nevertheless, one should take the risk; for, as Cicero says, even what seemed harsh at first becomes less disagreeable with use."[90] Cicero in the preface to book four of the *Rhetorica* expressed this sentiment in the following words: "Concepts that we did not have could not have familiar terms to describe them. Accordingly, such terms must at first seem quite harsh."[91]

Quintilian in book nine on the figures of diction: "Who are 5
those who have often broken treaties? The Carthaginians. Who are those who have waged war in the most cruel fashion? The Carthaginians. Who are those who have scarred the land of Italy? The Carthaginians. Who are those who ask for pardon? The Carthaginians."[92] This example is in book four of the *Rhetorica* on the section treating *complexio*.[93] Quintilian in the same book: "It is pleasing to be loved (*amari*) if only we take care there is no bitterness (*ne quid amari*) in it. The sweetness of birds (*avium*) leads one to a remote place (*avium*)."[94] So also Cicero in the *Rhetorica* on *traductio*.[95] There is no problem in what Quintilian adds a little later: "Cornificius calls this *traductio*."[96] Expressions that were used in common parlance for humorous purposes were available as examples to several writers. In this part of his work Quintilian is full of examples which Cicero also uses in his section on figures of diction.[97]

6 Quod autem hanc *Rhetoricen* inter caetera M. Tullii volumina negant a Plutarcho enumerari, infirmissimum sane est. Quid si Plutarchi memoriam in tanto librorum numero fugit, cuius negligentia super Ciceronis rebus nemini vel mediocriter erudito obscura est? Praeteriit nanque et alia multa. Quid si consulto tacuit ne summi oratoris alia de facultate oratoria divina opera tractatu tam familiari deformaret? Quid si ea verba apud quem legerunt Plutarchum desunt? Multa enim in omnibus scriptoribus et deesse et superesse passim intellegimus; quale hoc ipsum quod aiunt de Hermeste. Nam in vetustissimis ac fidelissimis codicibus, quorum plurimos legendos summa diligentia curavimus, nullum Hermestem invenient. Leonardus enim Aretinus, summae eruditionis vir, hoc opusculum caeteris Ciceronis voluminibus procul dubio annumerat, ubi in ea re Plutarchum latinum facit. De quo id acceptum ostenditur.

7 Indignum tertio loco clamitant et nullo animo ferendum in suis scriptis sibi quenquam dissentire. Fateor ego indignum, si loco, tempore, volumine eodem sibi quisquam dissentiat aut de uniformi scientia. Hic vero non de numeris, aut de terrae mensuris, non de ratione siderum agitur sed ea de arte de qua mira est scriptorum traditionis varietas. Qua causa[9] Quintilianus se opus suum suscepisse scribit ut inter auctores tam varios quid putet sequendum doceat. Quin Peripateticis nullus est datus labor durior quam conari ne dogmatis princeps sibi ipsi in suis libris repugnare videatur.

As for their saying that this *Art of Rhetoric* is not listed by Plutarch with all the other works of Cicero, this is truly a very weak point. What if it slipped Plutarch's mind when he was dealing with such a large number of books (his carelessness on matters relating to Cicero is clear to anyone of even a modest education)? For he overlooks many other things as well. What if he deliberately said nothing about it, out of a wish not to contaminate the supreme orator's other divine rhetorical writings with a work treated in such an informal way. What if such a mention has been lost in the copy of Plutarch that these critics read?[98] For we are aware that in all writers there are omissions and suppletions everywhere. An example of this is what they say about Hermestes. They will find no mention of him in the oldest and most accurate manuscripts, a very large number of which we have read with the greatest of care.[99] In his Latin translation of Plutarch on this point Leonardo Bruni,[100] a most erudite man, includes this work with all the other writings of Cicero without any reservation at all. Thereby the *Rhetorica* is shown to have been accepted as Cicero's work. 6

For their third point these persons scream that it is shameful and intolerable for anyone to contradict himself in his writings. I admit that it is shameful if someone contradicts himself in the same passage, or in things that are written at the same time, or in the same volume, or if the contradiction relates to a discipline that deals only with straight facts. Here, however, we are not dealing with mathematics, or the measurements of the earth or with the planetary system, we are dealing with that art on which there is a marvelous variety in what writers have said about it. For this reason Quintilian writes that he has undertaken his work so that he may instruct his readers on what, in the writings of such differing authors, he thinks should be followed.[101] Indeed, the Peripatetics had no more difficult task than to strive to remove any apparent contradictions in the works of the founder of their beliefs.[102] 7

8 Quaero hoc loco an libros *De inventione* et *Partitiones* ad filium Ciceronis esse negent, quod in iis pariter multa verbis mutatis quaedam in pauciores species aut plures partita, alia ita dissidentia ab illo divino de Oratore opere legent ut utique diversa cognoscant. Alium scriptorem alio loco Cicero secutus est. Nec enim unus est ad persuadendum callis nec semita eadem sed quavis ratione quis apposite ad persuasionem dixit, is nimirum functus officio oratoris fuerit.

9 Formam postremo dicendi haud esse Ciceroni similem contendunt. Quo equidem multo sum aequior illis quam in caeteris. Ego enim ipse nonnunquam vix in his libris Ciceronis vultum agnoscebam, adeo erat vocum perturbatione, mutatione, detractatione, adiectione, omnia vitio temporum et librariorum culpa inversa et depravata nec suus orationi numerus assurgebat nec verus ille nitor plurimis in locis renidebat. At nunc opera nostra disiecta magna ex parte nebula, iam propemodum aperta est sua Ciceroni facies, iam nulla ibi figurae tenuitas aut exilitas apparet, sed nuda, venusta, pura verborum castitas, ingeniosissima ac lucidissima docendi brevitas, maxima praeceptionum virtus omnibus ingeniis praeterquam unius Ciceronis erepta ubique cernitur.

10 His opinor satis diluimus adversariorum argumentationes. Nunc adiumenta nostra confirmemus ac veritatem ipsam, quae est luce meridiana clarior, paucis tueamur. Qua in re omittimus omnem antiquitatem, cuius maiestati et in fabulosis semper fuit habita multa fides, quae sola gravissimo suo testimonio asserit

I ask at this point whether they deny that Cicero is the author of *De inventione* and the *Partitiones,* written to his son. For in them they will read, side by side, many things that are broken down into fewer or more numerous subdivisions (and differently expressed), and also other items that are so at odds with the divine work *De oratore* that these persons will acknowledge that they are quite different from each other. Cicero followed difference sources at different places. For there is no one pathway or road to the art of persuasion; no matter what method someone uses, if by appropriate choice of words he manages to persuade his listeners, that person will indeed have performed the function of an orator. 8

Finally they claim that the style of the work is unlike Cicero's. 9
In this point to be sure I am more sympathetic to them than in all their other arguments. On some occasions I myself could scarcely recognize the features of Cicero in these books. Everything had been distorted and disfigured by the ravages of time and the mistakes of scribes; words were in disorder, they were changed in form, some had been lost, others added; the rhythm of his speech could not be felt and that true elegance of his style did not shine forth in many places. Now, however, thanks to us, the fog has to a great extent been lifted and Cicero can almost recognize his own features.[103] Now thinness and sparseness of style is nowhere on view; instead, the pure untarnished charm of his diction and the brilliant and clear conciseness of his exposition are evident, and the high quality of the precepts taken from all talented predecessors in addition to those of Cicero himself can be seen everywhere.

These responses I believe have satisfactorily rebutted the argu- 10
ments of our adversaries. Now let us strengthen these props of our case and in a few words protect the actual truth, which is clearer than light at noon. In this matter we say nothing of[104] the whole of antiquity, to whose high repute much credence has always been given, even in mythical subjects. The testimony of antiquity by itself carries the greatest weight, and it claims the *Rhetorica* for

Ciceroni opus, cuius titulum ab eo acceptum servat adhuc ad nostra tempora incolumem nec in[10] tam longa saeculorum fluxura inventus est qui aut ei ademerit aut de ea re quicquam se dubitare scripserit. Dicant hoc loco isti, si possunt, quae causa hominem (quisquis ille fuit) impulerit ut titulum auctori suo ereptum Ciceroni adscripserit vel qua id ratione in tot voluminibus sparsum facere potuerit.

11 Omitto plurimos et gravissimos testes: Leonardum Aretinum, annumerantem hanc *Rhetoricen* (ut dictum est) inter alios Ciceronis libros; Trapezuntium primo *Rhetoricorum*, citantem Ciceronem ad Herennium; Priscianum libro tertio de superlativo et libro decimo de praeteritis saepius confirmantem artem suam verbis Ciceronis ad Herennium; Hieronymum, doctrina et antiquitate gravissimum et alios permultos, quorum tenui testimonio multo difficiliorem causam apud severissimos iudices tenerem.

12 Quis obsecro est tam hebes et, ut Graeci aiunt, ἀναίσθητος qui primis statim operis verbis Ciceronem non agnoscat? Cuius plurimam operam defendendis amicorum negociis periculisque versatam, multis in locis legimus, quod in praefatione *Tusculanarum* scribit et *Philippica VII* his verbis: 'Omne enim curriculum industriae nostrae in foro, in curia, in amicorum periculis propulsandis elaboratum est' et alibi saepius. Atqui pro foribus Ciceronem adstare diximus, ingredere, bone Lector, limen, circunspice, totus tibi Cicero aperta facie ad summam tegulam, nisi dissimules, passim occurrit.

13 Equidem non gravarer proferre plurimos ubique locos eisdem verbis, cum caeteris de facultate oratoria scriptis, tum praecipue de

Cicero. Having been given this ascription to Cicero, the work has kept it unscathed right up to our times. In the long passage of the centuries no one has been found who has either taken it away from him or has expressed in writing any doubts at all about this matter. Let those persons tell us at this point, if they can, what reason impelled some man or other to strip its composer of the authorship and assign the work to Cicero and let them explain how he was able to have this change spread to so many copies.

I say nothing of many important witnesses: Leonardo Bruni, 11
who includes this *Art of Rhetoric* (as it was called by him) with all the other books of Cicero; George of Trebizond, who cites "Cicero to Herennius" in book one of his *Rhetorica;*[105] Priscian[106] in book three on the superlative and book ten on the past tenses, who often backs up what he said in his *Ars* with words of Cicero to Herennius; Jerome,[107] the weightiest witness because of his erudition and antiquity; many others on the basis of whose slender testimony I would have a much more difficult case to plead before the severest of judges.

Pray tell me, who is so obtuse and, as the Greeks say, so ἀναί- 12
σθητος (unperceptive) that he would not immediately recognize Cicero from the very first words of the work. We read in many places that a great deal of his work was involved in protecting the interests of his friends and in defending them in court. He writes in the preface of the *Tusculan Disputations* and the *Seventh Philippic* as follows: "For all our energies were expended in the forum, in the Senate, in warding off the dangers to our friends"[108] and he says the same elsewhere quite often. And yet all we have said is that that Cicero is standing at the very doorway of the work, so to speak; cross the threshold, dear reader, look around, the whole Cicero meets you everywhere, his appearance clear to behold, from floor to roof, unless you pretend not to recognize him.

I would gladly adduce very many widespread common topics, 13
expressed in the same words, that can be found in all the other

Inventione libris communes ut manifestum appareat, hic familiarius perfecisse quod ibi Cicero iuvenili calore ambitiosius inchoaverat. O ridiculum hominum genus! Tantane ille istorum Cornificius verborum infelicitate laboravit ut suam artem alienis verbis vestiverit? Moturus maiores risus quam cornicula Horatiana, 'furtivis nudata coloribus,' si repetat Cicero quod ibi suum est. Nam nihil ibi relinquetur Cornificio praeter furti infamiam quod suum sit.

14 Verum ne in scyrpo nodum inveniri posse arguat defensio nostra, ipse Cicero adversus istiusmodi calumniam et plagiariorum iniurias nullius omnino patrocinio indiget; sui enim est acerrimus defensor et sibi ipse multis in locis inconvincibilis testis.

15 Nam primo ad Herennium sic scriptum reliquit: 'Adhuc quae dicta sunt, arbitror mihi constare cum caeteris artis scriptoribus nisi quia de insinuationibus nova excogitavimus quod eas soli nos praeter caeteros in tria tempora divisimus ut plane certam viam et perspicuam rationem exordiorum haberemus.' Et libro primo *De inventione*, tripartita est insinuatio, his verbis: 'insinuatione igitur utendum est cum admirabile genus causae est, hoc est, ut ante diximus, cum animus auditoris infestus est. Id autem tribus ex causis maxime fit: si aut inest in ipsa causa quaedam turpitudo aut si ab his qui ante dixerunt iam quiddam auditori persuasum videtur aut si eo tempore locus dicendi datur cum iam illi quos audire oportet defessi sunt audiendo.'

writings on rhetoric, but especially in *De inventione*. It is clear that here [in the *Rhetorica*] Cicero has brought to completion in a more intimate way what he had begun rather ambitiously in that work in the heat of youth. How ridiculous is the human race! Did that Cornificius of theirs toil with such difficulties in his choice of diction that he clothed his *Rhetorica* in someone else's words? He would provoke greater laughter than Horace's crow, "stripped of the colors it had stolen,"[109] if Cicero were to claim back what is his in the work. For all that would be left for Cornificius would be the infamy of the theft that he committed.

But lest we, in our defense of Cicero, may be arguing that a 14
knot can be found in a rush,[110] Cicero himself needs the support of no one at all to counter such quibbling and to redress the wrongs done by kidnappers. For he is the fiercest defender of himself and in many passages he himself offers incontrovertible evidence on his own behalf.

For in the first book to Herennius this is what he wrote: "In 15
what I have said up till now I think I am in agreement with all other writers on rhetoric except that we have devised some novelty on the question of subtle approaches (*insinuationes*). For we alone in contrast to all others have distinguished three occasions on which they may be used; this was to provide us with a very sure method and a lucid theory of introductions (*exordia*)."[111] In *De inventione*, book one, in the following words *insinuatio* is also divided into three parts: "We should therefore use *insinuatio* when the case is a difficult one, that is, as we have said above, when the listeners are antagonistic to us. For the most part this antagonism arises from three causes: there is something scandalous in the case itself; the listener seems to have been convinced on some point by previous speakers; the opportunity for speaking comes at a time when those who should pay attention are worn out by listening."[112]

16 Quod si se solum praeter caeteros insinuationem in tria tempora divisisse profitetur, et est insinuatio utrobique in tria tempora divisa, utriusque rhetorices eundem fuisse auctorem necesse est. Hic profecto nihil est quod quisquam amplius dubitet aut quod isti citra sui risum calumnientur.

17 Planius adhuc hoc ipsum praefatione libri quarti *Ad Herennium* facit, his verbis: 'Postremo haec quoque res nos ducit ad hanc rationem quod nomina rerum Graeca quae convertimus, ea remota sunt a consuetudine. Quae enim res apud nostros non erant, earum rerum nomina non poterant esse usitata; ergo haec asperiora primo videantur necesse est, idque fiet rei, non nostra difficultate.' Σχήματα, id est verborum sententiarumque lumina, quae Latinis vocabulis antea caruerant a se conversa esse testatur, quae et hic et in tertio *De oratore,* Romana civitate ab eo donari manifestissimum est, quod a Cicerone alius scribere nullo modo potuit. Insuper pollicetur tertii libri initio se de republica reque militari scripturum, quod utrunque postea praestitit.

18 Vereor ne prudentioribus ridear quod in sole lucernam afferre laborem, quid istorum caecitati clarius proferri potest? Libro enim primo ne quid cuiquam addubitationis reliqui faceret inquit, 'Tullius haeres meus Terentiae uxori meae xxx pondo vasorum argenteorum[11] dato, quae volet.' Quam hic calumniam isti comminiscantur equidem non video.

19 Praeterea caetera si desint argumenta, unum illud evidentissimum est quo solo claret eos libros esse nobis a Cicerone relictos; cuius si non concesserint manu,[12] aetate tamen scriptos figura in

But if he professes that he alone in contrast to all others has distinguished three occasions for the use of *insinuatio* and if this tripartite division of *insinuatio* is present in both works, the author of each rhetorical work must be the same.[113] On this point there is nothing for anyone to have further doubts about regarding the authorship, there is nothing for those persons to carp about without making themselves a laughingstock. 16

This is made clearer in the preface of the fourth book of *Ad Herennium,* where he writes the following: "Finally, this situation too has led us to this method, namely, that the names of things in Greek that we have translated into Latin are quite alien to our usage. For the names of concepts that are foreign to us could not be familiar to us. These translations must seem quite harsh to us at first. That will be a difficulty arising from the subject matter, not from me."[114] He is testifying that σχήματα (that is. figures of diction and thought), which had previously lacked Latin names, had been translated into Latin by him. Both here and in the third book of *De oratore*[115] it is quite clear that these figures were given Roman citizenship by him. In no way could anyone other than Cicero have written this. An additional point is his promise at the beginning of the third book to write about the art of war and how a state should be run;[116] he later fulfilled both these promises.[117] 17

I fear that men of good sense may be laughing at me since I am exerting myself in offering them a lantern in full sunshine.[118] What clearer evidence can be adduced to cure these fellows of their blindness? For in the first book, so that he might not leave any remaining doubt, he says, "Let my heir Tullius give my wife Terentia thirty pounds' weight of silver vessels, such as she wishes."[119] I cannot see what niggling quibble those persons can think up on this point.[120] 18

If all the other arguments fail, the following is the most obvious one and on its own makes it evident that these books were left to us by Cicero. If these fellows have not yet conceded that they were 19

iis dicendi caecis clarissimum facit. Nam si veterum monumenta repetas, triplicem praecipue doctissimorum hominum foeturam, varia[13] eloquentiae et figura et vultu, Romanis illuxisse comperies.

20 Unam Laelii et Scipionis, fere aetate qua post Livium Andronicum plurimi et poetae et oratores floruerunt summa eloquentiae gloria, de quibus Plauti, Catonis, Terentii, Lucretii superstes est adhuc illa eloquii veneranda maiestas. Alteram, omnium temporum felicissimam, Iulio et Augusto Imperatore, qua aetate clarissima oratorum et poetarum et historicorum lumina floruerunt. Tertiam sub gente Flavia Caesarea, sed tum dicendi genus mutatum animadvertimus quale est utriusque Plinii, Taciti, Suetonii, Quintiliani et reliquorum scriptorum eius aetatis. Faciem vero elocutionis huius voluminis dicendi formae, tum primae, tum tertiae foeturae dissimilem, si inspicias, cognosces, at simillimam secundae foeturae qua nascitur Cicero felicissimo dicendi generi[14] cognosces

21 Quod si hanc argumentationem tenui coniectura colligi dicas, nec quae eam de ratione dicendi praeceptionem a Cicerone ideo compositam confirmet, hoc certe vel si durissimae cervicis et inauditae pervicaciae sis, negare nullo modo potes, necesse esse operis auctorem aut ante Ciceronis tempora, aut cum Cicerone simul aut post fuisse.

22 Eum ante Ciceronis aetatem scripsisse negant exempla eorum quae proferuntur in iis libris, ut Caepionis et Lucii Cassii et aliorum quos cum Cicerone vixisse manifestissimum est. Infra Ciceronem hos libros editos non fuisse indicat non modo dicendi

written by him, the style of writing in these books makes it as
clear as can be even to those who cannot see that they were composed at a period when he lived. For when you look back at what
the ancients have left us you will discover that the Romans were
distinguished by three harvests of extremely learned men, each
one with a different style and appearance in their eloquence.[121]

One was that of Laelius and Scipio, around the time when, fol- 20
lowing Livius Andronicus, many poets and orators flourished,
evincing the most glorious eloquence. Of these the wonderfully
majestic eloquence of Plautus, Cato, Terence, and Lucretius survives to this day. The second, the richest harvest of all, was in the
time of Julius Caesar and the emperor Augustus, a period in
which there thrived the most brilliant and famous of orators, poets
and historians. The third occurred under the Flavian emperors,
but at this time we observe that the nature of the style in which
they write has changed, as can be seen in the two Plinys, Tacitus,
Suetonius, Quintilian and the other writers of the period. If you
look carefully, you will recognize that the style of writing in the
Rhetorica is quite different in its features from that of the first or
third harvests, but is very similar to that most felicitous style of
the second harvest of which Cicero is a member.

You may say that this argument is based on thin evidence and 21
does not prove that this instructional work on the art of rhetoric
was for that reason composed by Cicero. However, unless you are
extremely thickheaded and are extraordinarily stubborn, you can
certainly in no way deny the following, that the author of the *Rhetorica* lived before the time of Cicero, or at the same as Cicero, or
later than him.

That he did not live before the age of Cicero is shown by the 22
examples that are offered in these books and taken from Caepio
and Lucius Cassius and from others who, as is abundantly clear,
lived at the same time as Cicero.[122] That the books were not published later than Cicero is indicated not only by the style, which is

figura, nihil a figure secundae foeturae immutata, quam semper cum temporibus immutatam fuisse cernimus, et quod nullum ibi historiae aut exempli vestigium citra aetatem Ciceronis progreditur, sed id quod mox subiungam planum facit. Relinquitur ergo ut operis auctor cum Cicerone vixerit et eum iam grandem, id est, ubi eloquentiae splendore et multis suis scriptis universo orbi factus fuerit illustris, norit, cum Terentiam eius uxorem et liberos superiore exemplo norit.

23 Quod cum ita sit, cur in praefatione libri quarti ubi docet ad comparandam eloquentiam exempla esse sumenda a Catone, a Gracchis, a Laelio, a Scipione, Galba, Porcina, Crasso, Antonio, Ciceronem, Virgilium, Horatium, ne plures commemorem, linguae nostrae lumina utique tacet? An, si diis placet, melioribus relictis, quos sibi proponere ad imitandum oportuit, deteriores nominat? Sed agnoscant hic[15] aperte Ciceronem, qui de se, ut decuit, prudenter tacuit, et magnos poetas caeterosque scriptores qui mox a se claruerunt nosse nondum potuit.

24 Qua re garrire isti desinant et ad melioris iudicii sanitatem iam redeant nec post tot saecula, tam graves testes, firmissimas coniecturas, validissima argumenta, fraudent Ciceronem hac tantula industriae gloriola nec litem insuper de Caio Herennio intendant, quicum sibi Cicero in fine operis cognationem fuisse scribit, de quo meminit Sallustius, auctore Gellio, libro nono *Noctium Atticarum*, et *Pro Marco Caelio* Cicero scribit Lucium Herennium sibi esse familiarem.

in no way different from the style of the second group and which we note always remains constant throughout the time of the group's existence. There is also no historical reference or trace of an example that can be dated later than Cicero. What I am just about to mention makes the date plain. Our conclusion then is that the author of the work lived at the same time as Cicero and knew the orator when he was of mature age, that is, when he had become famous through the whole world because of the brilliance of his eloquence and his many writings; for he knew of his wife Terentia and his children, as the earlier example shows.

Since this is the case, when the author advises in the preface in book four that in order to acquire eloquence examples should be taken from Cato, the Gracchi, Laelius, Scipio, Galba, Porcina, Crassus, and Antonius,[123] why does he not say a single word about Cicero, Vergil, Horace, to mention only a few, the luminaries of our language? For heaven's sake, does he abandon the better models whom he ought to hold up as examples to imitate and name the inferior ones. On this point let them openly acknowledge the authorship of Cicero, who wisely said nothing about himself, as was proper, and could not yet know the great poets and all the other writers who became famous soon after him. 23

And so let those fellows give up their blabbering nonsense and let them return to the sanity of a better judgment and, after so many centuries and in light of such authoritative witnesses, the most solid evidence and very powerful arguments, let them not deprive Cicero of this glorious product of his industry. And let them not launch a case as well against Gaius Herennius, who was related to Cicero, as he writes at the end of the work.[124] According to Aulus Gellius, in book nine of his *Attic Nights*,[125] Sallust refers to him, while Cicero in his *Defense of Caelius*[126] writes that Lucius Herennius was a close friend of his.[127] 24

: X :

*Aldus on How to Assemble Your Own Bilingual Text**

In a note addressed to the reader (ANT 10 C) in his edition of Prudentius (volume 1 of the series "The Ancient Christian Poets"), Aldus explains how readers can go about assembling the unbound sheets containing the *Cantica* of the Greek patristic writer John of Damascus so that pages of the original Greek text face the corresponding pages of the Latin translation. As the explanation is hard to follow, even with a copy of the book in hand, the following comments are offered to illustrate the procedure, which might be labeled, to coin an ugly but expressive term, "interbifoliation."

The first state of the register for Aldus' 1501 Prudentius, shown overleaf, defines the structure of copies of this edition by listing the catchword of each first recto of all the bifolia, signature by signature. Its last column maps the four quires of the Greek section. But Aldus revised the register by adding a Latin translation of the Greek. The register page went through the press again to cancel column four, by means of two composite rules, and simultaneously to print a revised, bilingual, register for the four interbifoliated quires (see p. 307). (Alternating the originally listed Greek bifolia with new ones in Latin, they feature, at the center of each expanded quire, a single bifolium that mixes Latin and Greek.) Column three was lengthened, and new fourth and fifth columns were crammed under the canceled fourth.

The diagram on page 308, pertaining to the first state, shows how two sheets of quarto could have been folded twice and one nested in the other to produce a sixteen-page quire, a quarto-in-8s.

---

* The Social Sciences and Humanities Research Council of Canada supported this research. Artwork is by Brandon Besharah. Jane Carpenter and Michael Winship kindly provided bibliographical information.

REGIMEN LIBRORVM PRVDENTII.

ff
Senex fidelis
Christe graues
Legis adhuc
Connixa

gg
Ductores
Prosilit
Israel
Compositis

hh
AVRELII
Hymnus
Opifex
Nectare
Ode post

ii
Fulmen
Gemmas
Nona sum
Hymnus ad

kk
Saxum
Quas de
Inculto
Filius haud

ll
Infelix
Iam mater
Ipsa deum
Condens

mm
AVRELII
Aduersus
Motu
Frangere

nn
Et pigris
Nupta uo
Labi ho
Mobilitate

oo
Incumbe
Putas a gen
Iam quis
Ieiuniorum

pp
Aeternitatem
Vix iam
Ne morte
Quæ uera

qq
Hunc esse
Si feruor
Iudæa quem
Quicquid

rr
Viuis ac poe
Turba,
Quod fixa
Sed belze

ss
Locus ubi
Et qua
Hæc dum
Non stabu.

tt
Quam uis
Argenti &
Pendentem
Omnigeni

uu
Se'que
Credere
Laurea
Annales

xx
Templum
Sic æui
Sic hominis
Eruta,

yy
Syderibus
Hisce uiis
Aegypti per
Si stetit
Fœcundauit

hh
PROSPERI
Multa
Sicut
Duæ sunt

ii
Mittit
Turis,
Apud.
In quo

kk
Nunquam
Absque
Vnde

1 i
ΙΩΑΝΝΟΥ
οὐ πλεῖστον
στείβει
σωτηρίαν

2 i
κτείνασ
ἔφυγον
καὶ οὐκ
ἀσωίτος.

3 i
παῖδος.
ΚΟΣΜΑ
ἔπιπτα
θῶσει.

4 i
ἔλυσε.
βρέφος
υἱόν.

τέλος.

REGIMEN LIBRORVM PRVDENTII.

ff	nn	uu	1	i
Senex fidelis	Et pigris	Se'que	IΩANNOY	
Christe graues	Nupta uo	Credere	ου πλάσιον	
Legis adhuc	Labi ho	Laurea	Στεῖβει	
Connixa	Mobilitate	Annales	σαπειάν	
gg	oo	xx	2	i
Ductores	Incumbe	Templum	κτείνας	
Prosilit	Putas agen	Sic æui	ἔφυγον	
Israel	Iam quis	Sic hominis	καὶ οὐκ	
Compositis	Leinniorum	Eruta,	ἀπώλετο.	
hh	pp	yy	3	i
AVRELII	Aeternitatem	Syderibus	παῖδος·	
Hymnus	Vix iam	Hisce uiis	ΚΟΣΜΑ	
Opifex	Ne morte	Aegypti per	ἐπιπα	
Nectare	Quæ uera	Si stetit	θέσει·	
Ode post		Fœcundauit	4	i
ii	qq	hh	ἔλυσε·	
Fulmen	Hunc esse	PROSPERI	βρέφος	
Gemmas	Si semor	Multa	ἰδόν·	
Nona sum	Iudæa quem	Sicut		
Hymnus ad	Quicquid	Duæ sunt	τέλος.	
kk	rr	ii	στείβει	παῖδος
Saxum	Viuis ac poe	Mittit	noctis	nehu
Quas de	Turba,	Turis,	σαπειά	ΚΟΣ
Inculto	Quod fixa	Apud.	Preca	fidelib⁹
Filius haud	Sed belze	In quo	2 i. b	ἐπιπα
ll	ss	kk	κτείνας	nétem
Infelix	Locus ubi	Nunquam	omnes	θέσει
Iam mater	Et qua	Absque	ἔφυγον	COS.
Ipsa deum	Hæc dum	Vnde	nerati	4 i. d
Condens	Non stabu.	2. 1. 1.	καὶ οὐκ	ἔλυσε
mm	tt	IOANNIS	dicitp	crux
AVRELII	Quamuis	IOANNOY	ἀπώλ	βρέφος
Aduersus	Argenti &	Immate	o disci	ut uidit
Mom	Pendentem	ου πλά	c. 3 1	ἰδὸν ὡ
Frangere	Omnigeni	Matricem	& sup	annũti

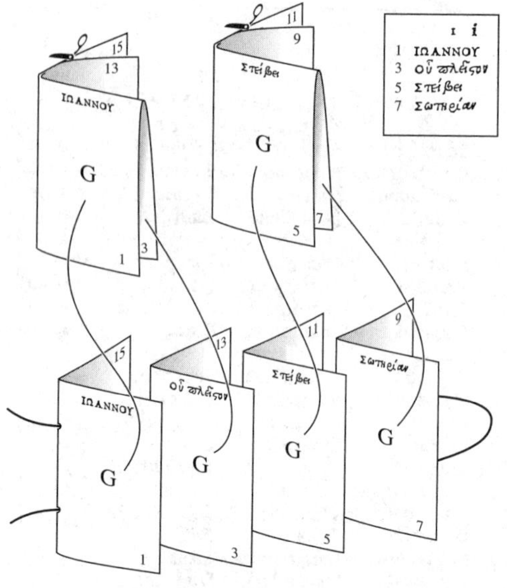

Page numbers have been supplied to clarify this structure (Aldus used none), and the appropriate catchword for the first Greek quire has been added on each recto in the fore-quire. A loop of thread indicates how to sew it—through the gutters of each bifolium. Scissors signal that the bolts at the head of the quire had to be opened for reading. (Normally, they would have been plowed off at the bindery in a single operation after the sewing of the quires together as a text block—or, later, cut open severally by the reader.)

The sheets that Aldus used for this edition were watermarked one-quarter of the way down the long axis. Thus, in this quire-in-8s format, one watermark appears straddling the gutter on bifolia 1.8 *or* 2.7 (pp. 1–2|15–16 or 3–4|13–14) and another on 3.6 *or* 4.5. (The presence of three watermarks in a quire would thus indicate

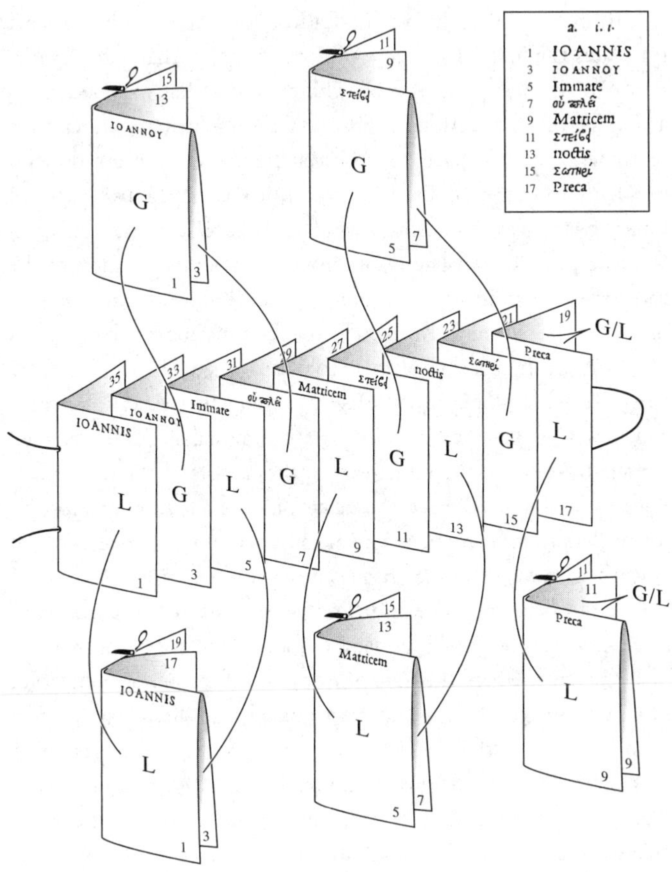

a sophisticated copy, as would watermarks appearing, say, on both 1.8 *and* 2.7.)

The diagram above shows the structure of the first Greek quire interbifoliated with the translation, which swelled to thirty-six pages, a quarto-in-18s. New page numbers apply. As before, each bifolium has been marked with the appropriate catchword.

The quire now begins with a Latin bifolium. As its latter verso translates the first Greek recto of the next quire, that second quire needs to be merely in-16s—but the one after that must be in-18s again. So much for Aldus' solution to the problematic outer faces of these expanded quires. In the center of each, a more difficult problem arose: the bifolium inserted to translate the two pages of Greek formerly at the center, which now faced its outer side, offered nothing to translate on its inner side. Aldus' solution to the threatened vacuum at the center of each bilingual quire was to begin an entirely new Greek text on the innermost verso, and to place a Latin translation of it on the facing recto (hence the "G/L" label in the last of the new sheets in the diagram). And if, as usual, this new text did not finish in the space available, Aldus directed readers to seek out the remainder in the middle of the next quire. *Quaere reliquum in medio sequentis quaternionis* is not an easy direction for readers to follow when the edition offers no page references to help them navigate these shape-shifting bilingual quires. And, if this leapfrogging text does not finish even within the current volume, as it does not in Aldus' 1504 edition of the poems of Gregory of Nazianzus, where the first printing of the gospel of Saint John in Greek breaks off in a mid-quire installment after 6:59, readers should seek it in the Latin translation of Nonnus Panopolitanus' verse paraphrase of the gospel in Greek. Aldus' 1503 catalogue advertised both. The Greek verses appeared (with no title page, epistle, or colophon), but the Latin never did.

The last of the Latin sheets shown here is imposed differently from the others, for printing by "work-and-turn": four different pages of text are *worked* on one side of this sheet, and, with the *turning* of it, printed again on the other side with the *same* text: the cutting of such a sheet in half yields two identical copies, and thus its print-run need be only half that for the other sheets. (Only one-half of this "Latin" sheet is for the composite quire in hand; the other half serves the corresponding quire of another copy.)

In a bilingual quire as laid out in the second diagram, the distribution of watermarks should proceed by the same logic as before: in the first four bifolia of Latin and Greek, we expect two bifolia to bear watermarks, one of which will be on a Latin bifolium, the other on a Greek. Perplexingly, however, preliminary investigations often find departures from this expected order, in cases where no latter-day sophistication of the volume can be suspected (as it is in a copy of Prudentius at UCLA, for example, in which a former owner brags about making up his own copy). There is no obvious way to account for all such discrepancies, but at least two plausible explanations can be imagined. One is that, in the bindery, gathering to assemble such interbifoliated quires-in-18s and in-16s demanded opening the bolts at the outset. In the production of a single interbifoliated copy, prior opening of the bolts would not have produced watermarks out of sequence. But if production of many such copies at one go began with the cutting of all the bolts in a large number of copies of each sheet *before* gathering commenced, the watermarks could easily have been rearranged. The other plausible explanation is that the purely Latin sheets could also have been imposed for work-and-turn. If they had been, one should not expect a regular pattern of watermarks among the new bifolia.

Aldus was wedded to interbifoliation. It arose as a clever and practical afterthought around 1498, when he added a Latin translation to the Musæus printed circa 1495, a quarto (*Greek Classics*, 8–11). Whether it was again an afterthought (now less clever) in Lascaris' Greek grammar, also a quarto, printed circa 1501 (*Greek Classics*, 82–89), it certainly was not in 1512, when Aldus reprinted this grammar in the same format (*Greek Classics*, 212–17). When, in 1517, two years after Aldus died, his father-in-law and partner, Andreas Asulanus, reprinted Musæus, now in-octavo, every sheet combined Greek and Latin. Interbifoliation did not survive Aldus' death.

Note on the Text and Notes

This volume is much indebted to Giovanni Orlandi's fine edition of the prefaces (see Bibliography), both for the text and for the annotation. The text of the prefaces to the ancient and the humanistic works is drawn in the first instance from Orlandi (integrating the *Aggiunte e correzioni* in 2:417–18), though I have consulted Aldine editions that were accessible to me when the Latinity was of a questionable nature. It has not always been possible to check readings or facts where some doubts arose. The textual source of the nine items in the Appendices is indicated below. The dating of the Aldine volumes is drawn from Ahmanson-Murphy and sometimes differs from that in Orlandi.

APP. I. Text drawn from an edition of the work held by the Bayerische Staatsbibliothek, 4 Inc. c. a. 1412, reproduced online in the Digitale Bibliothek (Münchener Digitalisierungs Zentrum).

APP. II. This letter was included, after Aldus' dedicatory letter to Alberto Pio, in the 1500 edition of Lucretius (ANT 2). The text is drawn from images of the letter supplied by the John Rylands Library, University of Manchester, from a copy of this edition held by that library (Aldine Collection /R 213736, Christie 34 b 1).

APP. III. De Nolhac, p. 24, no. 23.

APP. IV. Orlandi, 1:170–72.

APP. V. The text is drawn from images of the letter supplied by the John Rylands Library, University of Manchester, from a copy of the 1513 edition of Julius Caesar's *Opera* (see ANT 23) held by that library (Aldine Collection /R213171).

APP. VI. The letter appears after the two prefaces of Aldus in his *Scriptores rei rusticae*, published in May 1514 (ANT 25). The text is based on that of a copy of this edition held by the Thomas Fisher Rare Book Library, University of Toronto. A copy of this edition in the John Rylands

Library, University of Manchester, was also used, through an image of the letter kindly supplied by that library.

APP. VII. The text is taken from a copy of the 1515 Aldine edition of Lactantius held by the Thomas Fisher Rare Book Library, University of Toronto. It may also be found in Renouard, 71–72.

APP. VIII. The text of the *quaestio* given here is based on the one found in James J. Murphy and Michael Winterbottom, "Raffaele Regio's 1492 *Quaestio* doubting Cicero's Authorship of the *Rhetorica ad Herennium*: Introduction and Text," *Rhetorica* 17 (1999): 77–87. Their text is a transcription of the incunable held by the Bodleian Library, Oxford (Auct. O. 5. 10).

APP. IX. The text is based on that of the prefatory letter of Niccolò Angeli to Filippo Strozzi in a copy of his 1515/16 edition of the *Rhetorica ad Herennium* and Cicero's *De inventione* (Florence: Giunta) held by the John Rylands Library, University of Manchester (Christie 22 d 19). Images of the letter were kindly provided by that library. I also consulted the text of the letter found in the 1541 (Basel: Winter and Platter) and 1546 (Aldine) editions of Cicero's rhetorical works, copies of which are held by the Thomas Fisher Rare Book Library, University of Toronto.

Notes to the Text

ANCIENT LATIN AUTHORS

1. The text reads *de decem,* an easily understandable typographical error on the part of the printer for *de duodecim.* The text refers to the famous Twelve Tables of early Roman Law. I thank Robert Maxwell of Brigham Young University for verifying the reading *decem.*

2. I have changed *quas Latinas* of the text, which does not make sense, to *quae Latinas.* One must understand the antecedent *iis.*

3. An object for *conferre* such as *multum* seems to be needed.

4. There is no apodosis for the conditional clause. Syntax would be restored if one read *hoc* for *Quod* and attached *hoc libentius facturum te existimamus* to what precedes. There is no need, however, not to think that the text as it stands is what Aldus wrote.

5. Orlandi reads *coepissent.*

6. One expects an accusative and infinitive construction (*reliquos commentarios . . . videri*), dependent on *inferre,* similar to *extare . . . omnia.* Aldus has been careless here.

7. Aldus wrongly prints *paratam* for the correct *parata.* That this is a conjecture and not just a typographical error is suggested by the punctuation: commas are printed after *sumerent* and *scribere.* In the Aldine edition of Cicero's rhetorical works (see ANT 24), the reading at *Brutus* 262 is *parata.*

8. Aldus' Latin is faulty here. A relative pronoun (*quos*) in place of *et* would rectify the syntax.

9. Orlandi adds *est* to supply the clause with a verb.

10. Perhaps *propter quod* or *quo* should be read.

HUMANISTIC AUTHORS

1. This dactylic hexameter has a spondee in the fifth foot (*parvus*) instead of the normal dactyl. Read *parvulu(s)?*

2. The *ut-* clause lacks a verb, such as *putent.*

3. Immediately following this preface there are printed the last two of the three elegiac couplets that appear in his *Institutiones Grammaticae* of 1493 (HUM 1, §5). At the end of the volume, Aldus has reprinted the first half of section 6 of the preface of the earlier grammar (down to *labori meo*) and then the whole of section 9 (with very slight variations); this is dated to February 1501, four months earlier than the date of the preface printed here.

The volume also includes two further prefaces. One of these also appeared in the 1501 edition of Constantine Lascaris' *Grammar;* see *Greek Classics* I, Preface B, and Orlandi's apparatus to the text of this preface for the modifications in the edition of 1501. The other is the same as Preface D of Lascaris' *The Eight Parts of Speech,* also of 1501; see *Greek Classics,* 17.

APPENDICES

1. Unless *huic* (dative) is a typographical error for *hic* (nominative), Avanzi seems to have changed the syntactic structure of the sentence in midstream, substituting, for example, *sortitus est* for a verb such as *contigerunt.*

2. The feminine forms *iniquam* and (in the next line) *animadversuram* are decidedly odd. They can be explained only if some feminine noun has been omitted by accident; for example, a personification such as *Malitiam* (Maliciousness) or *Invidiam* (Envy). Otherwise, one must assume they are errors for *iniquum* and *animadversurum.* The translation reflects the latter.

3. Giocondo uses the third conjugation verb *detergo,* rare in classical Latin, where *detergeo* of the second conjugation is the norm.

4. One would expect *dies noctesque* or *die noctuque.*

5. *quam* is an insertion of Murphy and Winterbottom.

6. The Bodleian edition reads *similia,* corrected by Murphy and Winterbottom.

7. An unusual variation of the title that persists into the Basel and Venice editions.

8. *Carthaginenses* (and not *Carthaginienses*) is the spelling in the four occurrences of the word in all three editions consulted.

9. The Basel and Venice editions read *qua de causa,* which may be right.

10. The preposition is omitted in the Basel and Venice editions.

11. The Florence edition reads *argentorum,* which is replaced with the correct adjectival form in the Basel and Venice editions.

12. This is an instance of an *apo koinou* construction, with *scriptos* in the main clause having to be understood with *manu* in the preceding conditional clause.

13. All three editions read *varia,* though *variam* is attractive.

14. The Basel and Venice editions read *genere.*

15. The Basel and Venice editions read *hi,* thus supplying a subject for *agnoscant.* However, Angeli usually refers to his adversaries as *isti* and there are frequent instances of the lack of a subject. There is a similar usage of *hic* (= *hoc loco,* "on this point") at §16 above: *Hic profecto nihil est quod . . .*

Notes to the Translation

ABBREVIATIONS

Ahmanson-Murphy	*The Aldine Press. A Catalogue of the Ahmanson-Murphy Aldine Collection of Books by or Relating to the Press in the University of California, Los Angeles* (Berkeley, Los Angeles, and London: University of Caliornia Press, 2001)
ANT	Prefaces (in this volume) to works of antiquity
Barker	Nicolas Barker, "The Aldine Italic," in *Renaissance Culture*, 95–107
Caplan	[Cicero], *Rhetorica ad Herennium*, trans. Harry Caplan (Cambridge, MA: Harvard University Press [The Loeb Classical Library 403], 1954)
CCSL	*Corpus Christianorum. Series Latina* (Turnholti, 1954–)
CEBR	*Contemporaries of Erasmus: A Biographical Register of the Renaissance and Reformation*, ed. Peter G. Bietenholz and Thomas B. Deutscher, 3 vols. (Toronto: University of Toronto Press, 1985–87)
Ciceronian Controversies	*Ciceronian Controversies*, ed. JoAnn DellaNeva; trans. Brian Duvick (Cambridge, MA: Harvard University Press [ITRL 26], 2007)
CSEL	*Corpus scriptorum ecclesiasticorum latinorum* (Vienna, 1866–)
CWE	*Collected Works of Erasmus* (Toronto: University of Toronto Press, 1969–)
DBI	*Dizionario biografico degli italiani* (Rome, 1960–)

de Nolhac	Pierre de Nolhac, *Les correspondants d'Alde Manuce: matériaux nouveaux d'histoire littéraire* (1483–1514) (Torino: Bottega d'Erasmo, 1967)
Geanakoplos	Deno John Geanakoplos, *Greek Scholars in Venice* (Cambridge, MA: Harvard University Press, 1962)
GL	*Grammatici Latini*, ed. H. Keil, 7 vols. (Leipzig: Teubner, 1857–80)
Greek Classics	Aldus Manutius, *The Greek Classics*, ed. and trans. N. G. Wilson (Cambridge, MA: Harvard University Press [ITRL 70], 2015)
HUM	Prefaces (in this volume) to the editions of humanistic works
ITRL	I Tatti Renaissance Library
Lowry	Martin Lowry, *The World of Aldus Manutius: Business and Scholarship in Renaissance Venice* (Ithaca, NY; Cornell University Press, 1979)
Modern Poets	Lilio Gregorio Giraldi, *Modern Poets*, ed. and trans. John N. Grant (Cambridge, MA: Harvard University Press [ITRL 48], 2011)
New Aldine Studies	Harry George Fletcher III, *New Aldine Studies* (San Francisco: B. M. Rosenthal, 1988)
Orlandi	Giovanni Orlandi, ed. and trans., *Aldo Manuzio editore. Dediche, prefazione, note ai testi.* Introduction by Carlo Dionisotti, 2 vols. (Milan: Edizioni Il Poilifilo, 1979)
PG	J.-P. Migne, *Patrologiae cursus completus, series Graeca* (Paris, 1857–66)
Phillips	Margaret Mann Phillips, *The "Adages" of Erasmus* (Cambridge: Cambridge University Press, 1964)
PL	J.-P. Migne, *Patrologiae cursus completus, series Latina* (Paris, 1844–64)

Renaissance Culture — *Aldus Manutius and Renaissance Culture. Essays in Memory of Franklin D. Murphy* (Florence: L. S. Olschki, 1998)

Renouard — A. A. Renouard, *Annales de l'Imprimerie des Alde ou Histoire des trois Manuce*, 3rd ed., 3 vols. in 1 (Paris: L. J. Renouard, 1834)

Rizzo — S. Rizzo, *Il lessico filologica degli umanisti* (Rome: Storia e letteratura, 1973)

RLV — *Renaissance Latin Verse: An Anthology*, ed. Alessandro Perosa and John Sparrow (London: Duckworth, 1979)

Wilkins — Cicero, *De oratore libri tres*, ed. A. S. Wilkins (Oxford: Clarendon Press, 1892; repr., Georg Olms: Hildesheim, 1965)

Wilson (1977) — N. G. Wilson, "The Book-Trade in Venice, ca. 1400–1515," in *Venezia, centro di mediazione tra oriente e occidente* (secoli XV–XVI): aspetti e problemi (Florence: L. S. Olschki, 1977): 32–47

Wilson (1992) — N. G. Wilson, *From Byzantium to Italy* (London: Duckworth, 1992)

ANCIENT LATIN AUTHORS

1. Guido da Montefeltro (1472–1508) became duke of Urbino in 1488, succeeding his father, Federico III, whose patronage of artists and writers Guido continued. After leading Venice's forces in an unsuccessful expedition against Florence, Guido returned to Venice in the spring of 1499. The prefatory letter of the 1503 edition of Xenophon is also addressed to him.

2. Macrobius, *Saturnalia* 3.17.8. The immediately preceding words also paraphrase Macrobius at this point.

3. The Getae referred to in the Latin text inhabited the area around the lower Danube, near where the river enters the Black Sea, in what are now the eastern parts of Bulgaria and Romania. It is impossible to be certain where the manuscript in question was actually found by Francesco Negri

(or Negro), whose patron, Cardinal Ippolito d'Este, had sent him to northern and eastern Europe in search of manuscripts and who seems to have taken a leading part in the editing of this volume. The title of this Aldine edition states that "the books of the *Astronomica* had been recently brought to us from the shores of Scythia," and, in a dedicatory letter immediately following Aldus' letter to Alberto Pio, Negri, who taught for a time in Arad (now in Romania), says that he found it after traveling "to the furthermost dregs of Scythia" (*ad extremam Scytharum faecem*). These words suggest the provenance was extremely remote, perhaps in the outermost region of the Hungarian empire, but Negri may well have been exaggerating. For Negri see *CEBR* 3:10–11.

4. The reference is to the *editio princeps* of the *Astronomica* that appeared in 1497 (Venice: Simon Bevilacqua), although parts of the work had been printed earlier; see pp. xxviii–xxix of the Teubner edition of Kroll and Skutsch (Leipzig, 1897). The oldest manuscripts break off at 4.22.16, the rest being transmitted by *recentiores* much inferior in quality to the earlier manuscripts.

5. Firmicus, *Mathesis* 1.6.2–4.

6. Alberto Pio (1475–1531), prince of Carpi, was tutored by Aldus in his childhood for several years in the 1480s, and this forged a long-lasting bond between them, one result of which was Pio's support of the Aldine press, though this may have been more moral than financial. Given their former relationship as teacher and pupil, it is not surprising that the prefatory letter of Aldus' Latin grammar of 1493, published by Andrea Torresani in Venice (see HUM 1, below), was addressed to him. More significantly, Aldus dedicated the five volumes of the Aldine edition of Aristotle (1495–98) to him, as well as the later 1515 edition of Lucretius (see ANT 28). After periods of exile from Carpi, he finally lost the principate in 1525 and moved to France, where he died. He was engaged in a dispute with Erasmus during the last years of his life over Erasmus' alleged support and encouragement of Martin Luther. Aldus' praise of him is somewhat hyperbolic and might more realistically be applied to Pio's uncle, Giovanni Pico della Mirandola. See *CEBR* 3:86–87.

7. Girolamo Avanzi, whose dates are uncertain, though his death occurred some time after 1534, studied at Padua, where he earned a doctorate in arts and medicine and taught moral philosophy. His prime classical interest lay in textual criticism, his best-known work being his emendations on Catullus and Lucretius, though he worked on several other authors that include Ausonius and Statius, acting as editor for another Venetian printer, Iohannes Tacuinus, as well as for the Aldine press. According to Renouard (74), who does not think too highly of Avanzi ("editeur plus zélé qu' habile"), the 1515 edition of Lucretius, edited by Andrea Navagero, was far superior to this one of 1500. For Avanzi's prefatory letter to this edition and a description of the problems that faced an editor of Lucretius, see Appendix II.

8. Compare Juvenal 7.232, and Erasmus, *Adagia* 2.4.91, "As well as I know my name, or, my fingers" (*CWE* 33:234). This is a favorite proverb of Aldus, who employs it in the prefaces to Juvenal and Persius (ANT 6) and to Cicero's rhetorical works (ANT 24).

9. By the term "academy," Aldus may be simply thinking of Pio's library as an assembly of learned authors.

10. Empedocles was actually preceded by Parmenides in engaging in philosophical verse.

11. The first edition of the *Anthology* of Iohannes Stobaeus (fifth century CE), did not appear until 1535. Aldus' remarks here suggest that he had access to a manuscript of Stobaeus, and this is confirmed by Erasmus' use of Stobaeus for his 1508 Aldine edition of his *Adagia* (most of the over thirty citations from Stobaeus in the *Adagia* occur in this edition). Aldus and Erasmus worked alongside each other in Venice in the preparation of the edition; see *CWE* 33:14.

12. The syntactic connection of this sentence to what precedes has apparently been lost, even though the sense is clear.

13. The actual title of the volume is *Prudentii poetae opera* (see Ahmanson-Murphy, no. 38).

14. Daniele Clario, a native of Parma, taught Greek and Latin literature in Ragusa (modern Dubrovnik) in the school of which he was rector, for a dozen or so years. The city had close ties with Italy, and Venice in par-

ticular. Aldus dedicated his editions of Aristophanes and Demosthenes to Clario as well as the second volume of *The Christian Poets*. See J. Torbarina, *Italian Influence on the Poets of the Ragusan Republic* (London: Williams & Norgate, 1931): 23–25.

15. This description of his employees ("the plotting . . . runaway slaves") is given in Greek, but it does not seem to be an actual quotation. Though Orlandi (*ad loc.*) suggests that the use of Greek is designed to modify somewhat the intensity of Aldus' anger, it may be that Aldus wrote this insulting description of his workers in Greek to prevent them from understanding it.

16. Unrest among Aldus' employees was not uncommon. In his pamphlet of 1503 directed at the pirating presses of Lyons (*Monitum in typographos Lugdunenses*), he refers to four conspiracies against him. See Appendix IV.

17. Vergil, *Georgics* 2.272. It is also quoted in the preface to the second volume of *The Christian Poets* (ANT 10) and in that of Aldus' Latin grammar of 1501 (HUM 5).

18. The manuscript was identified by Bergman in his edition of Prudentius (*CSEL* 61:xlix) as one now in Boulogne-sur-mer in France. It is of the eleventh century and hardly merits the description of "very ancient." The eleven hundred years mentioned by Aldus refers to the span of time between Prudentius' lifetime and the date of publication — Prudentius would have been fifty-three years old in 401 CE. Although this edition is not the *editio princeps* of Prudentius (an earlier one, by a few years, had been published in Deventer), it probably had the status of one in Italy.

19. Prosper of Aquitaine (ca. 390–ca. 455) is meant; he was a historian as well as a poet.

20. These are the authors contained in volume two, which also has a few additional poems by some other poets, including Lactantius and Cyprian.

21. Printed in June 1504 with a Latin translation. See *Greek Classics*, Preface 29.

22. This was published close in date to that of the volumes of the Christian poets, without date or preface.

23. This immediately follows the preceding letter to Clario, introducing the note on the meters of Prudentius, not printed here.

24. Aldus plays on the similarity of Clario's name with the Latin *clarus* (bright/distinguished/clear).

25. This address is also placed at the beginning of the volume (f. 6v).

26. The reason for this advice to the reader is the presence in the volume of the *Cantica* (in Greek) of Saint John of Damascus. The instructions for how to combine the two quires so that the appropriate pages face each other are not very precise (they also appear in Aldus' edition of *De octo partibus orationis* by Constantine Lascaris, the date of which is either early 1501 or 1502; see *Greek Classics*, 84–87). See Appendix X for a detailed explanation.

27. This volume marks important innovations on the part of the Aldine Press on two fronts: it is the first to be printed entirely in the italic font cut by Francesco Griffo of Bologna, and it is identified by Aldus as the first of a series of such volumes containing classical literary texts ("all the best authors") in the octavo pocket-book size format. Books with this size of page were not new, but they were often devotional texts, where the smallness suited the needs of worshippers; and manuscripts with narrow pages had been used for verse in the fourteenth century, though not for the classical authors (see Barker, 105–6). In the preface to the 1514 edition of Vergil (ANT 27), Aldus says that he got the idea from the small books (that is, manuscripts) in the library of Bernardo Bembo, the famous Venetian nobleman and bibliophile. On this library, which may have contained a manuscript of Horace similar in size to the new format, written by Bartolomeo Sanvito, see Cecil H. Clough, "The Library of Bernardo and of Pietro Bembo," *The Book Collector* 33 (1984): 305–31, esp. 309 and Plate 5.

28. The reference is to the so-called *Appendix Vergiliana*, which included the *Priapea*, a collection of obscene poems to which Aldo here refers. They were printed in the 1505 edition but did not receive careful atten-

tion textually until 1517, when the Aldine Press published an edition of the *Appendix Vergiliana* on its own (see ANT 17, n. 164). The association of the pocket-size format with devotional texts may be the reason that Aldus excludes the obscene poems.

29. This preface, consisting of three Phalaecian hendecasyllabics, immediately follows preface A.

30. The font closely resembles the humanistic cursive as propounded and practiced by Pomponio Leto in Rome and reflected in Aldus' own hand. See Barker.

31. Daedalus was the skilled craftsman in Greek myth who built the labyrinth as well as wings for himself and his son, Icarus, to escape from it.

32. Identified as Francesco Griffo (1450–1518). In addition to his Greek and italic fonts, the Roman font that he cut for Pietro Bembo's *De Aetna*, published by Aldus in 1496, was very influential.

33. This is an appendix that appears after the Vergilian text.

34. See *GL* 2.357ff., where Priscian deals with the accusative plural forms of nouns of the third declension.

35. There now follows a list of homonyms that are differently accented: for example, *Venere*, the ablative case of *Venus* (where the first two vowels are short and the stress accent falls on the antepenultimate [the first] syllable), and *venere*, the third person plural of the perfect tense of the verb *venio* (where the vowel in the second syllable is long and the stress accent falls on it, the penultimate syllable). However, some examples of the differing accentuation are puzzling and merit further investigation. In his pamphlet directed at the pirated editions being printed in Lyons (see Appendix IV), he criticizes the Vergil edition for not marking accents (whether he means in this letter or in the text of the poems themselves is not clear), an indication that the subject was important to Aldus.

36. This list of five corrections to be made to the text immediately follows the address to the students relating to orthography and the use of accents. The corrections apply to *Aeneid* 1.2, 6.34, 7.464, 8.402, 9.9 (not Book 8). These are in fact five of the six suggestions made by Pietro

Crinito in a letter from Florence to Aldus dated March 21, 1500 (de Nolhac, no. 4). Crinito had seen pages of the Vergil edition that Aldus had sent to him. The date is given Florentine style, and the actual year must be 1501 in modern reckoning (in Florence the New Year began on March 25); see *New Aldine Studies*, 82.

37. Marino Sanuto (1466–1536), the famous diarist and historian, studied the classics under Giorgio Merula, in the school of San Marco in Venice, and wrote a dissertation on Ovid's *Metamorphoses*. His interests in classical Latin poetry are reflected in the dedications to him of this Aldine edition of Horace, as well as those of Catullus-Tibullus-Propertius (January 1502) and the three editions of Ovid's works (ANT 13, 14, 15). Aldus also dedicated the edition of Angelo Poliziano's *Opera* (1498) to him (HUM 3). Sanuto's own scholarly endeavors were primarily historical, often focused on his home city. His most important work was his *Diarii*, covering the period from 1496 to 1533, in fifty-eight volumes, offering invaluable information on many topics. Despite his prolific historical writings, he was never appointed official historian of the city of Venice, much to his disappointment. He entered the Venetian senate in 1498, serving as *Savio agli Ordini* from 1498 to 1501, at which point he was appointed *camerlengo* in Verona (April 6, 1501), a position that he held until September 1502. On his return he was again chosen to be a *Savio agli Ordini* (see preface to Ovid's *Heroides*, etc. of December 1502). The board of five *Savi agli Ordini* was an advisory and administrative body of the Venetian Republic.

38. Scipione Fortiguerri (1466–1515), whose humanist name was Carteromachus, a Greek translation of his Italian name, worked on several first editions of Greek authors published by the Aldine press in a ten-year period, from 1495 to 1504, and was a member of the Academy of Aldus. He was later in the service of several churchmen, including Cardinal Grimani. In his last few years, Angelo Colocci was his patron. Although he did not himself publish very much, he was much admired by Erasmus for his erudition in the *Ciceronianus* (*CWE* 28:418). He studied under Poliziano in Florence for a while, but, as Aldus implies here, he probably studied in Rome as well. See *CEBR* 2:44–45.

39. This is a close paraphrase of Juvenal 1.149, where the phrase is *omne in praecipiti vitium stetit,* literally, "every vice stands above a sheer descent," that is, every vice has reached its highest point.

40. Martial 8.3.20 (where *adgnoscat,* not *cognoscat,* is the reading in modern editions).

41. For the proverb, see the preface to Lucretius (ANT 2, n. 8).

42. Some copies of the first edition read *Benedicti* for *Leonardi,* before correction during the press run. For Marino Sanuto, see n. 37, above.

43. In addition to Girolamo Avanzi, his coeditor of Catullus, other celebrated humanists who were from Verona or were closely associated with the city include Guarino Veronese, Gaspare da Verona and Domizio Calderini (both of whom Aldus studied under in Rome), Girolamo Fracastoro, and Giovanni Giocondo. On the last-named, see the preface to Pliny's *Letters* (below, ANT 18, n. 172). Another close associate of Aldus who came from Verona was Francesco Rosetti, a member of his academy (see ANT 15, n. 147).

44. There were numerous earlier editions, the *editio princeps* appearing in 1472. This became the working text on which later editions were based. The two more important editions after this were edited by Calfurnio (Vicenza, 1481) and Antonio Partenio (1485).

45. Avanzi wrote his *Emendationes in Catullum* in 1493 and had this work published in 1495. For his editing of Catullus he used two manuscripts to correct the editions of Calfurnio and Partenio. See Julia Haig Gaisser, *Catullus and His Renaissance Readers* (Oxford: Clarendon Press, 1993) 24–65. For Avanzi, see the preface to the 1500 edition of Lucretius (ANT 2, n. 7).

46. In the Latin the syntax of the sentence is a little odd (one would expect *incubuit* rather than *incubuimus*), but the sense is clear enough.

47. To give a few examples, asterisks are added at Catullus 1.9 (*qualecumque quidem ora per virorum**), 3.10 (*pipilabat**), 3.16 (*o factum male, bellus* ille passer*), 6.12 (*nam mi praevalet ista nil tacere**), 11.11–12 (*Gallicum rhenum horribilesque* ulti- / - mosque britannos*), 10.27 (*'. . . deferri.' 'minime'**). Many of the marked passages have acquired the status of well-known *cruces,*

though some of them show how far Aldus' text is removed from what is in modern editions.

48. This seems to be a much larger print run than usual, but that Aldus meant three thousand copies of the book as a whole, and not one thousand copies of each of the three authors, is supported by Avanzi's letter in this edition, in which he too refers to the figure of three thousand with reference to the Catullan part of the volume. See *New Aldine Studies,* 100–102.

49. The several branches of the Thurzó family were all prominent in Hungary, with many of its members serving as churchmen. Sigismund Thurzó later held various bishoprics in Hungary, including (from 1505) that of Varád, where he died in 1512. He is named as bishop of Varád in the heading in the revised edition of 1512 instead of as "provost of Transylvania and royal secretary." Sigismund was secretary to Vladislav II, king of Bohemia from 1471 and then king of Hungary from 1490. In the preface to Cicero's *Letters to Atticus* of 1513 (ANT 21), Aldus refers to him as a fellow student in Ferrara under Battista Guarini.

50. Ovid, *Epistolae ex Ponto* 2.11.21–22.

51. For the letter, see Appendix III. Given the speed at which Aldus could on occasion produce editions, it is possible that Thurzó's letter, written in late December 1501, was actually the instigator of this edition of Cicero's *Ad familiares,* but Aldus may have been on the point of publishing these letters on his own volition, as he says, and had done some preparatory work.

52. György Szathmári (1457–1524) was provost of Buda until 1500, and then held several bishoprics, finally (from 1505) that of Pécs (its Latin name being *Quinqueecclesiae,* which replaces the references to Varád in the revised edition of these letters of 1512). He is referred to in the letter that Thurzó wrote to Aldus (Appendix III). According to Orlandi, he at one time raised the possibility of the publication of the poetry of Janus Pannonius by Aldus, and he may have done this through a protégé of his, István Brodarics (see *CEBR* 1:203–4).

53. Cicero's *Epistolae ad Atticum* did not appear until 1513. His rhetorical works were published in the following year.

54. See ANT 10, n. 63, below.

55. Quintilian 10.1.112.

56. The proverb occurs at Cicero, *Ad familiares* 6.3.3. See Erasmus, *Adagia* 1.2.1 (*CWE* 31:151). The singular "owl" seems to have been originally the correct form, but the proverb often appears, as in Erasmus, with this noun in the plural, "Owls to Athens."

57. Marcantonio Morosini was a member of a very prominent Venetian family. In addition to his military services to the state, he served as Venetian ambassador to Charles the Bold in 1474–75, and to Emperor Maximilian, along with Antonio Grimani, in 1495–96. His support of humanistic studies is reflected by the dedications addressed to him in works by Giorgio Merula, Girolamo Avanzi, and Sabellicus. See M. King, *Venetian Humanism in an Age of Patrician Dominance* (Princeton, NJ: Princeton University Press, 1986), 410–12.

58. The adjective *antiquus* suggests that Aldus is referring to a manuscript rather than an early printed edition. Its identity is unknown.

59. Compare Quintilian 10.1.90–91.

60. Sedulius was a Latin poet of the ninth century from Ireland; Iuvencus, from Spain, lived in the fourth century, while Arator lived in the sixth. These were the main authors of the volume, but it also included works by Lactantius and Cyprian among others.

61. The first part of this volume was printed in January 1501 as the colophon on f. hh vi r attests (see Ahmanson-Murphy, no. 58), that is, at the same time as the first volume of Christian poetry (ANT 3), but publication was delayed until the following year.

62. For Daniele Clario, see the preface to the first volume of Christian poets (ANT 3, n. 14, above).

63. The address of Aldus' printing house was *Thermae*. The building occupied by the press may have originally been a bathhouse; see *New Aldine Studies*, 60–61.

64. Horace, *Epistles* 1.68–69; Erasmus, *Adages* 2.4.20. The translation here is that of Sir Roger Mynors in *CWE* 33:200–201. The quotation oc-

curs also in the preface of Aldus' *Rudiments of Latin Grammar*, published in 1501 (HUM 5).

65. Vergil, *Georgics* 2.272. This quotation also appears in the preface to the first volume of the Christian poets (ANT 3) as well as in the Latin grammar of 1501 (see preceding note).

66. In the preface to volume one, Aldus uses the figure of eleven hundred years for the length of time that Prudentius has "lain hidden." Here the thousand years would apply to Arator, a poet from Italy of the sixth century.

67. The sentiments expressed in the second half of this sentence and in the next two echo similar thoughts in the preface to volume 1 of the Christian poets (ANT 3).

68. Little is known of Daniele Resti. We learn from the dedicatory letter to Clario in the Aldine edition of Demosthenes (1504 = *Greek Classics*, Preface 32, §7) that he was in that year serving a second term as Ragusa's ambassador to Venice. Perhaps Aldus met him in Venice during his first term in that office.

69. Giovanni Pontano, born in 1429, was active in the service of the Neapolitan court and took over the headship of the academy there after Panormita's death in 1471. He was a prolific composer in both verse and prose and wrote on social and philosophical topics. Many of his poems were didactic in nature, like the *Urania*, the *Meteora*, and *The Gardens of the Hesperides* (on arboriculture), which Aldus refers to in this preface. He died in September 1503, a year after the date of this preface. Aldus published the first part of Pontano's poetical works in 1505 (see HUM 8). The complete works, many of which were in prose, were published over a period of eight years (1505–12) in Naples under the supervision of Pietro Summonte. See *CEBR* 3:113–14.

70. Suardino Suardi, born in Bergamo, was a close friend of Pontano, who describes him as *familiaris noster* and addresses a poem from Book 2 of his *Baiae* to him (ITRL 22). He is also an interlocutor in Pontano's dialogue *Aegidius*. We have a letter sent to him by Pontano, dating from the end of December 1502, regarding the publication of his works by the Aldine Press (de Nolhac, no. 28). Pietro Summonte (see preceding note)

dedicated his edition of Pontano's *De sermone* to him. He played a prominent part in the activities of the Confraternity of the White Robes of Justice, a lay organization devoted to practicing penance and a simple lifestyle. His upright character, referred to here by Aldus, can be paralleled in an epigram of Pietro Gravina, who refers to his love of probity. He held various political positions of importance in Naples. He died in 1536 or shortly thereafter. See Camillo Minieri-Riccio, *Biografie degli accademici alfonsini* (1881; repr., Bologna, 1969), 170–73.

71. Horace, *Carmina* 1.22.1.

72. The title *Urania* means, literally, "heavenly things," the adjective from οὐρανός, the Greek word for "heaven/sky." The work consisted of five books.

73. The *Meteora* consisted of one book, while there were two books of *The Gardens of the Hesperides*. The syntax of Aldus' Latin suggests that the *Meteora* consisted of more than one book.

74. Isaeus was an Assyrian rhetorician, who came to Rome at the end of the first century CE and whose abilities in rhetoric are detailed in Pliny, *Letters* 2.3. The idea of exceeding one's reputation comes from the beginning of that letter. Isaeus is also mentioned at Juvenal 3.74.

75. This dedicatory letter was placed at the beginning of a tract on the orthography and morphology of the Greek words used by Statius.

76. Marcus Musurus (ca. 1470–1517) was one of the leading Hellenists of his day and collaborated with Aldus in the editing of several Greek authors, including Aristophanes (1498), Euripides (1504), Athenaeus and Hesychius (1514), and, most important, Plato (1513). He held chairs of Greek in Padua (1503–9) and Venice (1509–16), attracting many fine students to his lectures. He moved to Rome in 1516. See Wilson (1992): 148–56; Geanakoplos, 111–66; *CEBR* 2:472–73; *Greek Classics*, passim.

77. Vergil, *Eclogues* 1.66.

78. William Grocyn (d. 1519) was a fellow of New College, Oxford, in 1467. He was later appointed reader in divinity at Magdalen College in 1483, but then gave up the position to travel to Italy, where he spent two years, including some time in Florence with Thomas Linacre studying

under Angelo Poliziano and Demetrius Chalcondyles. He played a leading part in the teaching of humanistic studies, particularly Greek, at Oxford, until he spent more of his time in London. In his preface to the Greek section of his volume of astronomical works (ANT 1), Aldus refers to a letter Grocyn had written him (see *Greek Classics,* Appendix III). He published almost nothing, but despite this Erasmus thought highly of him. See *CEBR* 2:135–36.

79. Thomas Linacre (ca. 1460–1524) was elected Fellow of All Souls College in Oxford in 1484 but spent thirteen years in Italy (1487–99), where he studied in Florence, Rome, and Padua. His scholarly interests lay in medicine and physics, and he translated several Greek works, especially those of Galen, into Latin. For his Latin translation of the *Sphaera* of Proclus, Aldus refers to him in glowing terms in his preface to the Greek parts of his publication of astronomical works (*Greek Classics,* Preface 16). See *CEBR* 2:331–32.

80. Demetrius Chalcondyles (1423–1511) was born in Athens but came to Italy in 1449, where he studied under Theodore Gaza (1450–52) and taught Greek at Perugia. Like many others of Greek origin, he was in Cardinal Bessarion's circle in Rome and later held positions at Florence and Padua. Apart from his teaching, he edited the first edition of Homer, an edition of Isocrates' orations, and the *Suda* (the Byzantine lexicon). See *CEBR* 1:290–91.

81. The Aldine edition of Valerius Maximus was originally published shortly after this edition of Statius, in October 1502, but Aldus prepared a second printing in spring 1503 to include twenty-four examples from Book 1 of Valerius Maximus which were missing from his edition and which Iohannes Cuspinianus (Johann Spiesshaymer) sent him. See the preface to Valerius Maximus (ANT 12).

82. Asconius Pedianus was a scholar and philologist of the first century CE. Only fragments of his commentary on some speeches of Cicero survive. A commentary on the Verrine orations of Cicero is also ascribed, wrongly, to him. Of his *Elegantiae* (*Principles of Style*), nothing is known.

83. Domizio Calderini (1446–78) taught in the Studio at Rome and was one of the leading humanists of his day. His patron was Cardinal Bessa-

rion. His published commentaries on Martial and Juvenal were widely used into the sixteenth century, and records of his lectures on Silius Italicus and Suetonius have survived in manuscripts and in handwritten notes added to printed editions. He led the way in publishing a collection of learned notes on a variety of *cruces* from different authors, but only a few of his *Observationes* appeared in print. See Maurizio Campanelli, *Polemiche e filologia ai primordi della stampa. Le "Observationes" di Domizio Calderini* (Rome: Edizioni di storia e letteratura, 2001), and Domizio Calderini, *Commentary on Silius Italicus*, ed. Frances Muecke and John Dunston (Geneva: Librairie Droz, 2011), as well as *CEBR* 1:243–44.

84. Many of the works of Lorenzo Valla (ca. 1407–57), the renowned classical and theological scholar, were extremely popular and influential. These included his *Elegantiarum linguae Latinae libri sex*, on Latin style and usage, referred to here by Aldus, and his *Collatio Novi Testamenti*, a major influence on Erasmus' editions of the New Testament. See *CEBR* 3:371–75.

85. In the last few years of the fifteenth century, Aldus attempted to establish a learned academy in Venice to foster Greek studies. Although its statutes have survived (see *Greek Classics*, Appendix V), the academy never attained the status of a real institution. However, it seems to have been active in some form or other when this preface was written, since the edition of Sophocles of August 1502 bears the stamp "Venice in the Academy of Aldus of Rome." See Introduction, xxv, above.

86. This is an introduction to the list of errors, which follows the tract on orthography.

87. There now follows a list of comments and corrections.

88. Jan Lubański (d. 1520) was appointed bishop of Plock in 1497 or 1498 and bishop of Poznań in 1499. He studied at Bologna and Rome but returned to Poland in 1485. He later served on legations, including one to Venice, in the course of which Aldus' meeting with him in Padua, referred to in the letter, may have taken place. He founded a school for humanistic studies in 1519 and may well have had educational interests when Aldus met him at a much earlier date. If so, Aldus' choice of him as a dedicatee is not surprising. Raffaele Regio (see below, n. 90) dedi-

cated his translation of Plutarch's *Regum et imperatorum apophthegmata* (1508) to Lubrański.

89. The wording is reminiscent of the setting of Cicero's *De amicitia;* see 1.2 of that work.

90. Raffaele Regio (ca. 1440–1520) taught in different capacities for most of his career in Padua but became public lecturer in Latin in Venice in 1512. He is best known for refuting the attribution of *Rhetorica ad Herennium* to Cicero, though he was not the first to have doubts about it (see Appendix VIII). He also wrote commentaries on Ovid's *Metamorphoses* and Quintilian, as well as on the *Rhetorica*. For his Quintilian, see ANT 26, n. 334. See *CEBR* 3:134.

91. A rather odd detail. An example of synecdoche for "castle" or "chateau"?

92. Compare Juvenal 2.40; Erasmus, *Adagia* 1.8.89 (*CWE* 32:172–73).

93. Compare Erasmus, *Adagia* 1.2.56 (*CWE* 31:196–97), where the eloquence rather than the counsel of Nestor is the point.

94. Homer, *Iliad* 2.381–84.

95. The Latin *pietas* has a wide semantic range and often means in neo-Latin something like "devoutness," a laudable virtue in a churchman such as the addressee. It has been translated here in a broader sense.

96. Vergil, *Aeneid* 11.285–91.

97. This second prefatory letter was added when the edition of October 1502 was reissued in spring 1503 to include missing parts of the first book of Valerius Maximus. Aldus enlarged and reset the first gathering to include the material. A new title page included the following: EXEMPLA QUATUOR ET VIGINTI NUPER INVENTA ANTE CAPUT DE OMINIBUS (Twenty-four examples recently discovered before the chapter on omens). See Ahmanson-Murphy, no. 71.

98. Iohannes Cuspinianus (Johann Spiesshaymer; 1473–1529) studied at Leipzig, Würzburg, and Vienna and succeeded Conradus Celtis as professor of rhetoric and medicine in Vienna in 1508, having been appointed rector of the university there in 1500. His major scholarly work was a historical treatise, *De Caesaribus atque imperatoribus Romanis,* though he

also edited Florus and Prudentius. He served on several legations, especially to Hungary, and this may account for his knowledge of the availability of manuscripts in eastern Europe.

99. At the end of a letter from Cuspinianus to Aldus, dated December 28, 1501 (de Nolhac, no. 27), the major topic of which is the text of Avienus' translation of the Greek poem *De situ orbis* of Dionysius Periegetes, Cuspinianus added a postscript: "I send you the examples (*historiae*) that you asked for and that are missing in book one of Valerius." See *New Aldine Studies*, 109–11.

100. The lacuna occurs between *ut comperit* of 1.1.ext.4 and *Deiotaro vero regi*, which begins 1.4.ext.2. Aldus replaced the original first gathering of eight leaves by a gathering of twelve leaves (unique in size in the edition) to accommodate the new material, which came from an epitome of Valerius Maximus by Julius Paris. This material had already appeared, however, in a Mainz edition of 1471 and in an edition by Martin of Würzburg that was published in Leipzig in 1501 (see p. xii, n. 19, of the first volume of John Briscoe's Teubner edition of Valerius Maximus, published in 1998).

101. This may be someone living in Britain, which Aldus often describes as cut off from the whole world; see ANT 11, §4, above.

102. This is probably Tiberius Claudius Donatus, whose commentary survives, rather than Aelius Donatus, whose commentary on Terence has survived (in a somewhat mangled form in some parts) and who is also said to have written a commentary on Vergil (only a small part of which survives).

103. The largest surviving commentary on Vergil from antiquity has come down to us under the name of Servius, of whom little is known.

104. Marcus Valerius Probus was a scholar of high repute who probably lived in the second half of the first century CE. Little or nothing remains of his work, though a few short works, including a treatise on abbreviations, are ascribed to him. The manuscript is probably a phantom.

105. None of the works mentioned was published by Aldus.

106. This Greek term *βιβλιοτάφοι* was used earlier by Michael Apostolis; See Geanakoplos, 93, n. 81.

107. On Marino Sanuto, see the preface to the 1501 edition of Horace (ANT 5, n. 37).

108. "Many" is something of an exaggeration. Aldus dedicated to Sanuto his editions of Angelo Poliziano's *Opera* (1498), Horace (1501), and Catullus, Tibullus, Propertius (1502). However, Aldus also dedicates the other two volumes of Ovid's works to Sanuto.

109. Aldus is referring to Sanuto's help in the granting of a *privilegium* to Aldus by the Venetian senate, mentioned later in the letter.

110. The second Ottoman-Venetian war lasted from 1499 to 1503 and was marked by naval battles near territory under Venice's sway, particularly in Dalmatia and the Peloponnese.

111. Sanuto was appointed *camerlengo* of Verona in April 1501, from where he returned in September 1502. Aldus also praises this city for having produced distinguished sons, in the preface to Catullus (see ANT 7, n. 43).

112. Terence, *Eunuchus* 232–33.

113. On Aldus' attempt to establish an academy, see the preface to Statius (ANT 11, n. 85) and Introduction, xxv, above.

114. See Renouard, 504–5.

115. His cousin Marco was the son of Francesco, the elder brother of Leonardo, Marino's father.

116. A favorite expression of Aldus. It occurs, for example, in the prefaces to Lucretius (1500) and Juvenal (1501). See ANT 2, n. 8.

117. On the literary side, Maximus Planudes (ca. 1260–ca. 1305), a Byzantine grammarian and theologian, is best known for his *Greek Anthology*, but he also translated into Greek several Latin works, including Ovid's *Metamorphoses* and *Heroides*, Saint Augustine's *De trinitate*, and Cicero's *Somnium Scipionis* with Macrobius' commentary.

118. Plutarch, *Parallel Lives* 306F, 311F.

119. For Poliziano, see HUM 3, n. 27, below.

120. Poliziano, *Epigrammata Graeca* 47. Aldus has slightly altered the text, which literally translated says, "and it is no wonder if we children cherish our old mother in turn." The Greek verb *antipelargein* (to cherish in turn) is based on the Greek word for stork (*pelargos*). See Erasmus, *Adages* 1.10.1 (*CWE* 32:233–34). Poliziano's epigram appeared in the prefatory material of *The Treasury, The Cornucopia of Amalthea,* and *The Gardens of Adonis,* published by Aldus in 1496, to which Guarino Favorino of Camerino, the addressee of Poliziano's epigram, had contributed (see *Greek Classics,* Preface 6).

121. There now follows (not given here) the quotation in Greek from Aristotle, *Historia Animalium* 8 (9).615 24–27. The translator referred to is Theodore Gaza (ca. 1415–ca. 1475/76), who taught Greek in Ferrara (1447–50) and then in Rome, to where Pope Nicholas V had invited him. His Latin translations of Aristotle's scientific works were highly thought of and used extensively in Italy, when knowledge of the Greek language was limited to comparatively few. Aldus published his Greek grammar (1495) and his Latin translations of Aristotle and Theophrastus (1504); see *Greek Classics,* Prefaces 4 and 27.

122. On Sanuto, see preface to the 1501 edition of Horace (ANT 5, n. 37).

123. On his return from Verona in 1502, where he served as *camerlengo* for one year, Sanuto was reappointed to the position of *Savio agli Ordini* in September, that is, a few months before this edition appeared.

124. He means the dedicatory letters to Sanuto of the pocket-size editions of Horace, Catullus (with Tibullus and Propertius), and Ovid's *Metamorphoses.* Aldus also addresses to Sanuto the prefatory letter to the works of Poliziano (HUM 3).

125. Aldus plays on the etymology of the Greek *encheiridion,* which means "handbook" or "manual" but, literally, "something that can be held in one's hand" (Latin, *in manibus*). Aldus applies the term to his small octavo volumes.

126. This appears after the *Heroides* and before the *Amores,* introducing the three verse epistles, mentioned in the frontispiece to the volume as being the work of Sabinus (*Heroides* 16, 18, 20). Aldus here addresses the

question of the authenticity of the *Heroides*. The Ovidian authorship of several of the poems has often been questioned, in particular *Heroides* 15 (Sappho to Phaon) but especially the last six poems, which comprise three pairs of letters, the first of which is put in the mouth of a male lover, and the second of which is a response by the female to the first partner. This marks a departure from the first fifteen poems, which are all put in the mouth of a female lover and do not have a response.

127. Little is known of this poet apart from what Ovid tells us in his poems. The relevant verses are quoted by Aldus in this letter (see nn. 133 and 134).

128. Aldus gives the name as "Demophon" for the correct "Demophoon."

129. Aldus is referring to the letters of three male lovers: Paris, Leander, and Acontius (*Heroides* 16, 18, and 20). He seems to imply that these were thought, at least by some, to be the work of Sabinus, while the three responses may have been by Ovid. On the latter point he gives a different view in preface C.

130. Ovid, *Heroides* 16.39–144 in the Budé edition. These 106 verses are not to be found in the best manuscripts. They describe the judgment of Paris (see next note). Aldus goes on to say that he has removed lines 97 and 98 in this section, thus making his arithmetic correct.

131. The lines in question would then be superfluous given that that the judgment of Paris has been extensively described. However, the two lines that Aldus cites are not to be found in modern editions.

132. Ovid, *Heroides* 16.97–98.

133. Ovid, *Amores* 2.18.27–34. The lines refer to the letters identified at the beginning of this preface.

134. Ovid, *Ex Ponto* 4.16.13–16. Aldus has made a slip in assigning the poem to Book 3.

135. The title of the poem written by Sabinus, as given at *Ex Ponto* 4.16.15, is in a corrupt form. The Oxford Classical Text (1915) reads *Troesmen* (cf. *Ex Ponto* 3.9.79) but certainty seems unattainable.

136. This is to be found at the very end of the volume.

137. Ovid, *Amores* 2.18.27–34. For the full quotation, see §4 of this letter.

138. Ovid, *Heroides* 21.14. Aldus seems to be referring to everything that follows this verse. In the major manuscripts the text of the poem ends here, and this is probably what lies behind Aldus' rejection of the verses, though why he did not say so is something of a mystery.

139. Ovid, *Heroides* 2.18–19. According to the Budé edition of the *Heroides* (see apparatus *ad loc.*), these two verses, in a slightly different form from how Aldus gives them, are found in only one manuscript (Giessen, Universitätsbibliothek 66, of the fourteenth century). Is this why Aldus thought the lines were suppletions?

140. In other words, though not by Ovid, the lines are needed in the opinion of Aldus. However, his point that they are needed for reasons of syntax is hardly a valid one, as line four in the quotation can follow the first without great difficulty.

141. For Marino Sanuto, see the prefatory letter to the 1501 edition of Horace (ANT 5, n. 37).

142. Horace, *Carmina* 1.1.1.

143. Ovid, *Tristia* 2.549–50.

144. Aldus reads *subiectum* for *libratum* in modern editions, the meaning of the latter being that the earth's power of rotation keeps it balanced.

145. Ovid, *Fasti* 6.271–76. They are lacking in most manuscripts, but the similarity in the ending of verses 270 and 276 (*-et onus*) could account for their loss. Some modern editors, however, regard these verses and the two following (6.277–78) as spurious.

146. Ovid, *Fasti* 6.269–70.

147. Francesco Rosetti (or Rosetto, or Roscio) was a physician and classical scholar. He is named as one of the members of the New Academy of Aldus in its regulations (see *Greek Classics,* 293). He is referred to in the preface of the edition of Theocritus and Hesiod (1496) as having seen a manuscript containing the Greek translation of Planudes of the so-called *Disticha Catonis*.

148. These are four books of letters.

149. The renowned scholar and theologian Origen, born in Alexandria in 184 or 185 CE, was subject to accusations of heresy from fellow Christians and also suffered torture during the persecution of Christians by the emperor Decius. He was a prolific author, writing on textual criticism, biblical exegesis (to which category belong his homilies), and dogmatics. Much of his work has not survived, and some of what has come down to us is in Latin, such as the homilies in this volume published by Aldus.

150. Giles of Viterbo (1469–1532), whose birth name was Egidio Antonini, joined the Augustinian order in 1488 and became its general in 1507. He was appointed cardinal in 1517. He won renown as preacher, theologian, and scholar (he had mastered Hebrew as well as Greek and Latin) and was therefore a suitable choice of dedicatee for this volume of Origen's homilies. Whether Aldus knew him well is not known. See *CEBR* 1:64–65; also J. W. O'Malley, *Giles of Viterbo and Church Reform* (Leiden: Brill, 1968).

151. Giovanni Pico della Mirandola, Gian Francesco Pico, *Opera omnia* (Basil, 1557 and 1573; repr., Hildesheim: Olms, 1969), 1:206–7.

152. What follows is a close paraphrase of a letter of Origen, cited in Rufinus, *Liber de adulteratione librorum Origenis* (PG 17, col. 625A–C).

153. 2 Thessalonians II:1–3.

154. Marcion and Apelles were well-known heresiarchs of the second century CE.

155. Rufinus, *Liber de adulteratione librorum Origenis* (PG 17, col. 626A).

156. Ibid., col. 626C.

157. Horace, *Ars Poetica* 269, adapted to fit the syntax. The verse is also cited in the preface to the grammar of Theodore Gaza (*Greek Classics*, Preface 4).

158. Not till ten years later.

159. This appears at the end of the initial quire of the volume (ff. 3v–4r).

160. It is interesting to note that here Aldus links the handiness of his octavo editions with the italic font rather than with the pocket-book size of the pages.

161. Aldus is referring to what is now called the *Appendix Vergiliana,* though he does not make it clear which of the poems in this collection he regards as youthful endeavors of the poet and which he thinks are the work of a later date.

162. That is, the *Priapea.*

163. This appears after the *Appendix,* following the *Copa.*

164. The text of the various works in the *Appendix Vergiliana* was not to be radically changed until after Aldus' death, in the Aldine edition of 1517, when the editor, Andrea d'Asola's son, Francesco, made use of some manuscripts, including probably Vatican City, Biblioteca Apostolica Vaticana, Vat. lat. 3252, which was the property of the prominent Bembo family of Venice, and Brussels, Bibliothèque Royale 10675-6. Pietro Bembo (on whom see ANT 24, n. 262) may also have contributed to the edition as well, through his as yet unpublished dialogue *De Virgilii Culice et Terentii fabulis,* which contained the whole text of the *Culex;* see John N. Grant. "Pietro Bembo as a Textual Critic of Classical Latin Poetry: *Variae lectiones* and the Text of the *Culex.*" *Italia medioevale e umanistica* 35 (1992): 253–303, esp. 260–64. The work was not published until 1530, but most of it was probably composed some twenty-five years earlier. This was the dialogue entitled *De corruptis poetarum locis,* for which Aldus was granted a ten-year *privilegium* from the Venetian senate in March 1505.

165. Maffeo Vegio (1406/7–58) wrote a continuation of the *Aeneid* in the form of a "Book 13" (see ITRL 15), and this was frequently printed in editions of Vergil's works. Here Aldus indicates his disapproval of such action (the term *libellus* here has probably pejorative force) but claims to have been coerced to include it. One can only guess at the identity of those who pressed him (perhaps Andrea d'Asola, his father-in-law?).

166. This was the first Aldine edition in which the colophon reflected the partnership of Aldus and his father-in-law, Andrea of Asola: *In aedibus Aldi et Andreae Asulani soceri.*

167. The Mocenigo family was prominent in Venetian society, some of its member serving as doge. This Alvise Mocenigo (there were several members of the family with this first name) was elected to the Venetian

senate in 1506 and served as the Venetian ambassador to the French court in 1505–6.

168. Apart from a few fragments, the work of Pompeius Trogus, a historian who lived in the Augustan age, survives in an epitome done by Justin. Aldus inveighs against such epitomes in the preface to Festus (ANT 22).

169. It is generally, though not unanimously, agreed that a manuscript of Pliny's *Letters* now in the Pierpont Morgan Library in New York City (M. 462), consisting of only six leaves, is a fragment of the manuscript to which Aldus is referring here and the rest of which is lost. It is written in uncials and is usually dated to circa 500 CE. (If this is the manuscript to which Aldus refers, he must be thought to be exaggerating the difficulty in reading the script.) The surviving fragment contains *Letters* 2.20.13 (*-cessit ut*) to 3.5.4 (*viginti quibus*). Aldus had earlier corresponded with Janus Lascaris, when the latter was in Paris, about finding manuscripts of Pliny in France, but in a letter to Aldus of December 24, 1501 (de Nolhac, no. 24), Lascaris claims lack of time for the task. See *New Aldine Studies*, 113.

170. The Greek phrase, a Homeric formula, here in the genitive singular but also occurring in the plural, can be found at *Odyssey* 3.325; compare Hesiod, *Theogony* 46; *Homeric Hymns* 18.12, 29.8.

171. Most previous editions of Pliny's letters had lacked a central part of Book 8 (letters 3–18) and all of Book 10, though in Venice in 1502 Girolamo Avanzi of Verona had published *Epistles* 10.41–121 (modern numeration), and these were reprinted in editions done by Beroaldo the Elder (Bologna, 1503) and Cataneus (Milan, 1507).

172. Giovanni Giocondo of Verona (ca. 1433–1515) was a renowned architect and engineer, plying his professional skills in Naples, Paris (serving as "architecte royal" to Charles VIII from 1495/96 to 1506), and Venice. However, as Aldus says, he had scholarly interests as well. He put together a large collection of Latin inscriptions and was responsible for two editions of Vitruvius, *De architectura*, one published in Venice in 1511 (Iohannes Tacuinus) and the other published in 1513 in Florence by the Giunta press, the latter including an edition of Frontinus *De aquaeductibus*

urbis Romae. His Frontinus marked "a great improvement" over the first edition (Michael Reeve in *Texts and Transmission* [Oxford: Clarendon Press, 1983], 170). In addition to his contribution to this Aldine edition of Pliny, Giocondo collaborated with Aldus in preparing the 1513 editions of Caesar's *Commentarii* and Nonius Marcellus' *De compendiosa doctrina*, the latter appearing in the same volume as Perotti's *Cornucopiae*, and the 1514 edition of the *Scriptores rei rusticae*. The table of contents of the 1513 edition of Perotti's *Cornucopiae* reads: "The *Compendia* of Nonius Marcellus, in which almost a third of the work not previously printed has been added by the hard work and diligence of our dear Giocondo of Verona. He collated Nonius in France against ancient manuscripts" (see Ahmanson-Murphy, no. 115). Little is known of the first fifty years or so of Giocondo's life. See *DBI* 56 (2001): 326–38.

173. It is not clear whether Giocondo gave or sent Aldus actual manuscripts or material copied from manuscripts that he had written himself. The latter seems more likely. The printed material referred to in the rest of the sentence was probably an edition of Pliny annotated by Giocondo.

174. Pliny, *Letters* 1.1.1, where *accuratius* in Aldus' report is the reading of B and F, manuscripts that seem to descend from the ancient manuscript that Aldus talks about here. In the Oxford Classical Text, the editor, R. A. B. Mynors, gives preference to *curatius*.

175. Pliny, *Letters* 10.81.

176. Martial, *Epigrams*, Book 8, preface, and 5.8.1.

177. Tertullian, *Apologia* 2.6; Eusebius, *Historia Ecclesiastica* 3.33.1; Orosius 7.12.3. The letters to which Aldus refers are Pliny, *Letters* 10.96 and 97.

178. Pliny, *Letters* 2.13.2–3 and then 2.13.5–6.

179. Here in his quotation Aldus omits the words *malles tu quidem multos*, with no indication of his having done so. The words actually are present in the text of the letter in the Aldine edition.

180. Pliny *Letters* 10.4.1 and then 10.4.4–5.

181. Pliny, *Letters* 2.11 and 2.12.

182. Pliny, *Letters* 2.11.2.

183. Aldus offers *amissa defensione,* meaning "his defense having been unsuccessful," where modern editions read *omissa defensione,* meaning "no defense having been offered."

184. Pliny, *Letters* 10.3A.2.

185. Pliny, *Letters* 5.10. Other letters of Pliny addressed to Suetonius are 1.18, 3.8, 9.34.

186. Pliny, *Letters* 5.10.3.

187. Pliny, *Letters* 10.94.1–2.

188. Erasmus, *Adagia* 2.4.76 (*CWE* 33:229). Aldus and Erasmus worked closely together to produce the 1508 edition of the *Adagia* in September 1508, two months before the Pliny appeared. The proverb refers to those who find problems or difficulties where none exist. It occurs at Plautus, *Menaechmi* 147, and Terence, *Andria* 941. See also Appendix IX, n. 110

189. Homer, *Iliad* 2.25.

190. Homer, *Iliad* 2.205–6.

191. Eutropius 8.5.3.

192. Aldus is referring to Xenophon's *Cyropaedia,* a fictionalized biography of Cyrus the Great.

193. Cicero, *Ad Quintum* 1.1.23.

194. Scipio Africanus, referred to in Cicero *Ad Quintum* 1.1.23.

195. This work, *De viris illustribus,* is not by Pliny.

196. Suetonius, *De grammaticis et rhetoribus.*

197. Jerome, *De viris illustribus* 1.

198. Giambattista Egnazio (1478–1533) was a member of Aldus' academy and held various civic and ecclesiastical positions in Venice, where he spent most of his life. He was appointed to the public chair of Latin in Venice on the death of Raffaele Regio. As a classical scholar he is best known for his 1516 edition of the *Lives of the Caesars* (including Suetonius' *Lives,* but also extending the biographies of the *Historia Augusta* up to and including the life of Emperor Maximilian I). The first volume of the Aldine edition of the Greek Orators (April 1513) was dedicated to him. He edited the *Divine Institutions* of Lactantius in 1515, in which his prefatory

letter is a eulogy of Aldus, who had died earlier that year (see Appendix VII). He was also an executor of Aldus' will. See *CEBR* 1:424–25.

199. Aldus puns on Giocondo's Latin name by describing him as *iucundissimus*.

200. Julius Obsequens culled the prodigies recorded in Livy for his *Liber prodigiorum*. Next to nothing is known of the author, who is usually placed in the fourth century CE. The Aldine edition is the only primary source for this work. Giocondo's manuscript was lost, without any known copies having been made.

201. Geoffroy Carles, was born around 1460 of noble stock in Saluzzo, in the Piedmont region of Italy, and studied at Pavia, Bologna, and then Turin, where he earned a doctorate at the age of twenty. He served Ludovico II, the marquis of Saluzzo, in several roles. In 1499 he was named a member of the new senate in Milan that was instituted by Louis XII of France, becoming its president in 1504. He was a negotiator for the League of Cambrai against Venice and fought in the battle of Agnadello that took place a month after Aldus wrote this dedicatory letter. After the French were driven from Milan in 1512, Carles went to Grenoble, of whose parliament he had been appointed a member since 1492 by Charles VIII, and he died there in 1516. He was a patron of the arts and possessed an impressive library of books and manuscripts. See *Dictionnaire de biographie française* 7 (1956): 1154–55. For his library, see E. Pellegrin, "Les manuscripts de Geoffroy Carles, président du parliament de Dauphiné et du sénat de Milan," in *Studi di bibliofilia e di istoria in onore di Tammaro de Marinis* (Verona, 1964), 3:309–27.

202. Milan at this time was in the possession of the French, enemies of Venice. Even though Aldus was not Venetian, as a resident of that city he may have been considered to be one. The year 1506 and most of 1507 marked a lull in the publications of the Aldine press, and Aldus spent some of this time in northern Italy in search of manuscripts.

203. Maecenas, a close associate of the emperor Augustus, was a patron of several poets, most notably Vergil and Horace.

204. Francesco II Gonzaga (1466–1519).

205. That is, the ambassador of Louis XII.

206. Horace, *Satires* 2.8.

207. Aldus had already published an edition of Horace's poetry, in spring 1501, which is eight years before this new edition, not seven, as he says in the next paragraph.

208. Horace, *Odes* 1.1.2.

209. Aldus includes a collection of his philological notes in the edition. They are printed in Orlandi, 1:172–80.

210. The renowned *condottiere* Bartolomeo d'Alviano (1455–1515) was principally in the service of Venice from 1497 until his death. In addition to his military skills, he also showed interest in the new learning, giving protection and support to scholars (these included Andrea Navagero and Marcus Musurus) and attempting to found an academy at Pordenone. A month after the date of this dedication, he was to become a prisoner of war of the French after the battle of Agnadello. See *CEBR* 1:38–39.

211. Janus Lascaris (ca. 1445–1534), born in Constantinople, came to Italy soon after the fall of that city and was to play an important part in the propagation of Greek literature in Italy, through his teaching at Florence and his editions of the *Greek Anthology*, the *Hymns* of Callimachus, and four tragedies of Euripides. Aldus dedicated his edition of Sophocles (1502) to him; see *Greek Classics*, Preface 21. He entered the service of the French court in 1494 but returned to Italy on several occasions, eventually becoming the French ambassador to Venice from 1504 until 1509. He was later called to Rome by Leo X to direct the college for Greek studies there. See *CEBR* 2:292–93. Aldus corresponded with him when he was in Paris, on the matter of manuscripts of classical authors. In a letter to Aldus, mostly in Italian, and dated to December 24, 1501 (de Nolhac, no. 24), Lascaris refers to manuscripts of Terence and Pliny (probably Pliny the Younger).

212. For Giovanni Giocondo, see the preface to Pliny's *Letters* (ANT 18), n. 172.

213. Does he mean "in almost all *editions* other than this one," rather than "in almost all other manuscripts"? It is highly unlikely that Aldus consulted many manuscripts. The vulgate reading appears to be *ab optimo quoque ad minus bonum*—it is to be found, for example, in two editions

published in Leipzig (1495 and 1503) and two published in Venice (1493 and 1500).

214. Sallust, *De coniuratione Catilinae* 2.4–6.

215. Móré was secretary to Vladislav II of Hungary (ca. 1456–1516) and was that country's ambassador to Venice when Aldus wrote the preface. He was appointed bishop of Pécs in 1524 and died two years later in the battle of Mohács fighting against the Turks.

216. Filippo Beroaldo the Elder was born in 1435 in Bologna and taught there from 1472 until his death in 1505, with the exception of four years (1475 to 1479), during which he spent some time in Parma, Milan, and Paris. His commentary on Cicero's *Tusculan Disputations*, to which Aldus here refers, was published in 1496 in Bologna, though it is for his commentary on Apuleius' *Golden Ass* (1500) that he is better known. See *CEBR* 1:135; *DBI* 9 (1967): 382–84.

217. The point of this may be that Bologna attracted many fine students and for Móré to be marked out by Beroaldo indicated that he had truly exceptional talents.

218. Aldus may be thinking of writers such as Tertullian (b. ca. 160 CE).

219. Compare the similar sentiment at Cicero, *Orator* 9.31.

220. Aldus was in Ferrara in the late 1470s until 1480.

221. Sigismund Thurzó was secretary to King Vladislav II of Hungary. He was provost of the church of Transylvania and then appointed bishop of Varád in 1505. He died in 1512. Aldus dedicated his edition of Cicero's *Epistolae ad Familiares* (1502, ANT 8) to him. See also Appendix III.

222. A close paraphrase of Persius 5.51.

223. Aldus gives the beginning of Cicero, *Ad Atticum* 15.11, but then quotes from a different letter in the same book (15.27.2).

224. Cicero, *Ad Brutum* 1.18.6.

225. Cicero, *Ad Brutum* 1.16.5.

226. Cicero, *Ad Quintum fratrem* 2.14 (13).5, citing Euripides, *Suppliants* 119. Aldus has made a slip here in saying it is a letter to Brutus.

227. Vergil, *Georgics* 1.510–11.

228. Aldus published an edition of Caesar's *Commentarii* in December 1513 (see ANT 23).

229. Nepos, *Atticus* 16.2–4.

230. Aldus published an edition of Cicero's rhetorical works in 1514 (see ANT 24), but his speeches and philosophical works were not published by the Aldine press until after Aldus' death: the speeches in 1519 (in three volumes), the philosophical works in 1523 (in two volumes).

231. At this point a list of Greek passages with Latin translations is given.

232. For Marcus Musurus, see the preface to Statius (ANT 11, n. 76).

233. Vergil, *Aeneid* 11.285–86, with *Argiva* replacing *Idaea*. The Greek phrase that follows comes from Homer, *Iliad* 2.372, in a passage that Vergil is echoing. See also the preface to Valerius Maximus (ANT 12), where the same Vergilian passage is adduced. "The land of the Argives" is, of course, Greece.

234. Sextus Pompeius Festus, usually known as simply Festus, epitomized a work of Marcus Verrius Flaccus, a famous philologist of the Augustan period, entitled *De verborum significatu* (On the meaning of words). When this was done is not known. This epitome was then itself abbreviated by Paul the Deacon, in the age of Charlemagne, and it is to this that Aldus is referring.

235. In a new edition of Niccolò Perotti's encyclopedic *Cornucopiae* that Aldus published in 1513, Aldus included some works of antiquity: Varro, *De lingua Latina* and *De analogia*; Pompeius Festus, *De verborum veterum significatione*; Nonius Marcellus, *De compendiosa doctrina*. Of the ancient authors, only the work of Festus had a preface, occupying columns 1133–34. Aldus had published an edition of Perotti's work on its own in 1499 (see HUM 4).

236. Pompeius Trogus, who was alive when Augustus was emperor of Rome, wrote a *Universal History* in forty-four books. The work itself has been lost, but an epitome of the work by Marcus Junianus Justinus has come down to us. See J. C. Yardley, *Justin and Pompeious Trogus: A Study of*

the Language of Justin's Epitome *of Trogus* (Toronto: University of Toronto Press, 2003).

237. The historian Florus, possibly an elderly man by the time of Hadrian, was not the author of the *Periochae* of Livy's great historical work *Ab urbe condita*, though he was often credited as such in the Renaissance. Moreover, the *Periochae* are very brief summaries of the books of Livy's work and are different in nature from the epitomes of Trogus and Festus.

238. It is unlikely that this friend of Aldus actually possessed a copy of the original Trogus.

239. The short letter from Paulus to Charlemagne immediately follows the preface of Aldus.

240. In June 1512 Giovanni Giocondo of Verona (on whom see ANT 18, n. 172) was granted a ten-year *privilegium* by the senate of Venice for his work on several classical works; these included Caesar's *Commentaries*. Given the readiness of Aldus to thank those who helped him in his enterprises, it seems odd that he makes no mention of Giocondo in his preface here. However, he prints a letter of Giocondo in this publication (Appendix V), and this may explain the absence of any reference to Giocondo in Aldus' own preface.

The date on the first colophon is April 1513. Aldus, however, then added the colored map of Gaul, a list of place-names in Latin with their French equivalents, and two additional woodcuts. All of this was preceded by the second address to the reader (B), dated December 1513. H. George Fletcher says that the volume "is un underappreciated example of the seriousness of Aldus' scholarly practices and requirements" (*In Praise of Aldus Manutius*, 54).

241. The term *commentarii* signifies something like a collection of historical notes on events rather than a full historical account, though, in fact, Caesar's *commentarii* amount to much more than notes, as Aldus says.

242. A very close paraphrase of Hirtius' words at *Bellum Gallicum* 8, praef. 5.

243. As Hirtius did not participate in the African campaign of 46, it is hardly likely that he was the author of the *Bellum Africanum*.

244. *Bellum Gallicum* 8, praef. 2.

245. Cicero, *Brutus* 262.

246. This follows the map of Gaul, which is printed after the initial address to the reader. The lengthy explanation of the map takes up ff. A iii v–vi r. The colored map in one copy of the edition is on the front cover of *In Praise of Aldus Manutius* (see n. 240, above).

247. Caesar, *Bellum Gallicum* 1.1.1.

248. The coloring was done by hand; as a consequence, the colors vary somewhat from copy to copy. The translation of the color terms that follow has taken into account the colors in the map as illustrated on the front cover of *In Praise of Aldus* (see above, n. 240), though, to take but one example, the color of Germania there is hardly yellow. The polychrome map and its preface was dropped in the 1519 edition, being replaced by two black-and-white maps. See *New Aldine Studies*, 116–19.

249. As at Juvenal 6.120: "a tawny wig concealing her black hair."

250. Aristotle, *Sophistici Elenchi* 165a 11–14.

251. Aldus seems to be thinking of an illustrated encyclopedic work, clearly an ambitious enterprise and one that did not come to fruition.

252. There now follows a list of names in six groups, based on geographical areas, as distinguished by different colors. The six colors given here are *viridis* ("green," used to indicate the provinces of Transalpine and Cisalpine Gaul), *flavus* ("yellowish," for Germany), *ruber* ("red," for the Belgae), *luteus* ("tawny," for the Celtae), *purpureus* ("purplish," for Aquitania), and *caeruleus/caesius* ("blueish/grayish blue," for the sea and ocean).

253. Andrea Navagero (1483–1527), born into a patrician family of Venice, studied there under Sabellicus before moving on to Padua to work under the Hellenist scholar Marcus Musurus. He cooperated with Aldus on the Aldine editions of Quintilian and Vergil (both in 1514), Lucretius (1515), and this edition of Cicero's rhetorical works. He succeeded his teacher Sabellicus as librarian of the Marciana in 1516. This was after an unhappy association with Bartolomeo d'Alviano, the famous Venetian

condottiere (and the addressee of the prefatory letter to the Aldine edition of Sallust of 1509; see ANT 20), with whom he fought at the disastrous (for Venice) battle of Agnadello. He later served Venice as ambassador, first to Charles V in Spain in 1523 and then to the French court in 1526. He died in Blois a year later. Although Aldus thought highly of his poetic abilities, linking him with Vergil himself at the end of this dedicatory letter, only a small part of his poetic work has survived; see *Modern Poets* 67. See also *CEBR* 2:8–9.

254. Plato, *Letters* 358A; see also *Laws* 4.717–18.

255. Horace, *Ars Poetica* 332.

256. Vergil, *Aeneid* 1.293–94, with *clausae essent* for *claudentur.* The Vergilian verses refer to the gates of the temple of Janus, which were closed when Rome was not involved in any war.

257. Propertius 2.34.79–80.

258. Horace, *Ars Poetica* 476.

259. Horace, *Ars Poetica* 292–94.

260. A reference to the well-known myth, according to which Hercules relieved Atlas from holding up the heavens.

261. Cicero's speeches appeared in 1519 and the philosophical works in 1523.

262. Pietro Bembo (1470–1547), a member of a prominent Venetian family, edited Petrarch's *Rime* and Dante's *Commedia* for the Aldine Press (1501 and 1502, respectively), and his own *Asolani* were published by Aldus in 1505. After initially engaging in textual criticism of Latin poetry (see ANT 17, n. 164), he won more renown for his work in Italian. He went to Rome soon after Leo X was elected as pope in 1513, as one of Leo's secretaries. In his *De imitatione* (written in 1513 but not published until 1516) he espoused using Cicero as the single model for writing in Latin against the eclecticism advocated by Gianfrancesco Pico; see *Ciceronian Controversies,* 16–125. Aldus dedicated the 1514 edition of Vergil to him. For his Latin poetry, see Mary P. Chatfield, ed. and trans., *Pietro Bembo: Lyric Poetry; Etna* (Cambridge, MA: Harvard Universiy Press, 2012 [ITRL 18]).

263. Vergil, *Aeneid* 12.168.

264. Cicero, *Ad Quintum fratrem* 3.5.7.

265. Eutropius 8.5.3.

266. This does not seem to refer to what has immediately preceded—the praise of Navagero—but rather to Aldus' earlier complaint about constant interruptions of his work from visitors.

267. See the preface to Lucretius (ANT 2), n. 8.

268. Horace, *Ars poetica* 438–39. The Quintilius referred to is Quintilius Varus, a critic and friend of Horace and Vergil; see H. J. Rose, *A History of Latin Literature* (London: Methuen, 1966), 275. His death (in 24 or 23 BCE) is mourned by Horace in *Carmina* 1.24.

269. The story is told at Cicero, *De oratore* 2.75–76. Nothing else is known of Phormio, despite *ille Phormio* (*ille* being taken over from Cicero).

270. Most of this sentence is a close paraphrase of what Cicero writes at *De oratore* 2.75.

271. Cicero, *De oratore* 2.75.

272. Cicero, *De oratore* 2.76.

273. The sense of *in numerum ludere* is not altogether clear.

274. *Rhetorica ad Herennium* 3.28.

275. He is referring to examples that illustrate the principles of style. On the practices of the Greek writers whom the author of the *Rhetorica* rejects, see Caplan, liv–lv. They advocated drawing examples from the orators and poets who were most highly valued.

276. The five elements are invention, arrangement, style, memory, and delivery.

277. Cicero, *De oratore* 1.5; compare also 1.94.

278. Cicero, *Epistulae ad familiares* 6.18.4.

279. Aldus understood the Latin phrase *meum oratorem* in Cicero's letter to refer to Cicero's *De oratore*. Cicero, however, is referring to his *Orator*,

not *De oratore*, as Aldus later realized. He corrects his error in the address to the reader that follows below.

280. These were held in Rome from September 4 to 12.

281. This sentence and the part of the preceding one marked off by quotation marks are a close paraphrase of Cicero, *De oratore* 1.24.

282. Cicero, *De oratore* 1.26. The dialogue is set in the midst of the political struggle between the *optimates* and the *equites* in 91 BCE, when the tribune of the plebs, Livius Drusus, had brought forward proposals that added to the tension between these groups. These included the transferral of the judicial function of the *equites* in the courts to the senatorial order.

283. Cicero, *De oratore* 1.28.

284. Cicero, *De oratore* 1.29–30.

285. Cicero, *Epistulae ad Atticum* 4.16.3.

286. Plato, *Republic* 1.331D. Strictly speaking, Socrates had gone to the house of Polemarchus, the son of Cephalus.

287. It is odd that a technical discussion be described as "lighthearted." The reading of modern editions, in which the adjective applies to Scaevola ("jovial") and not to the discussion, restores sense.

288. Not, of course, the famous dictator, but an orator and advocate whose full name was Gaius Iulius Caesar Strabo Vopiscus. See Wilkins, 25–26.

289. The other two being style and delivery.

290. Cicero, *De oratore* 2.216.

291. Compare Cicero, *De oratore* 2.233. Roscius was a famous actor who lived at the end of the republic and was a friend of Cicero. See Erasmus, *Adagia* 4.7.69 (*CWE* 36:328–29).

292. Caesar deals with the topic of humor from sections 217 to 290 of Book 2.

293. Cicero, *De oratore* 3.17.

294. Cicero, *Orator* 12.

295. An echo of Cicero, *De optimo genere oratorum* 14. The two speeches are Aeschines' indictment of Ctesiphon and Demosthenes' response to it, the speech known as *De corona* (On the Crown).

296. Most humanists of the fifteenth and early sixteenth centuries held to the traditional view that the *Rhetorica ad Herennium* was the work of Cicero. Raffaele Regio, whom Aldus knew (see the preface to Valerius Maximus [ANT 12, n. 90]), was one of the first to question in print this attribution, in a *Quaestio* published in Venice in 1492, though written in the preceding year. It is surprising that Aldus makes no reference to him or his work. For the *Quaestio*, see Appendix VIII.

297. Cicero, *De oratore* 1.5.

298. *Rhetorica ad Herennium* 1.1.

299. *Rhetorica ad Herennium* 4.69.

300. Ibid.

301. This is to counter a possible counterargument against Aldus' contention that Cicero would have mentioned the *Rhetorica* in *De oratore* if he had composed the work after *De inventione*.

302. The point is that Jerome, Priscian, and others seem not to have entertained any doubts regarding the authorship. Jerome wrongly thought that the work that Cicero regretted having released in his youth was the *Rhetorica ad Herennium*; see his commentary on Obadiah (*PL* 25:1098; *CCSL* 76:350). Priscian refers on many occasions to Cicero as the author; see, for example, *Institutiones* 2.21 (*GL* II 96) and 10.32 (*GL* II 523). Aldus dismisses this evidence, which the defenders of Ciceronian authorship make much of, in a very casual way.

303. Horace, *Ars Poetica* 78.

304. Presumably, the Vatican Library in the palace of the popes. The manuscript has not been identified.

305. That is, for "Tullius."

306. Here Aldus is very unconvincing.

307. Ovid, *Ex Ponto* 4.11. Aldus quotes lines 1–2 and then lines 11–12.

308. Vergil, *Eclogues* 1.71–72. The text reads *en queis* for *his nos,* the reading most often adopted by modern editors.

309. Vergil, *Eclogues* 9.2–4.

310. In calling Navagero a divine poet and second only to Vergil, Aldus echoes words spoken by Menalcas to Mopsus at Vergil, *Eclogues* 5.45 and 5.49. Lilio Gregorio Giraldi also thought highly of Navagero's poetry; see *Modern Poets* 67.

311. Vergil, *Eclogues* 1.46 and 40–41 (the last two lines being adapted by Aldus).

312. Compare Terence, *Eunuchus* 1085. Aldus is fond of this image, which recalls the myth of Sisyphus, and uses the line on several occasions.

313. Vergil, *Eclogues* 1.1.

314. Vergil, *Eclogues* 1.6.

315. This is to be found on the last folio of the volume.

316. For Giovanni Giocondo, see the preface to Pliny's *Letters* (ANT 18), n. 172. A letter of Giocondo to Pope Leo X follows Aldus' address to the reader; see Appendix VI.

317. Vergil, *Georgics* 2.1.

318. Columella 3.1.1.

319. Aldus makes a slip here, printing *cura* for *cultus.*

320. Columella 8.1.1.

321. Columella 11.1.2.

322. This follows immediately after A.

323. With respect to Palladius, a table giving the length of the gnomon's shadow on the sundial on the first day of each month is given at the end of the volume.

324. Vergil, *Georgics* 1.32.

325. Matthew 27:45; Mark 15:33; Luke 23:44.

326. Martial 4.8.

327. This appears at the very end of the volume.

328. There now follows a list of corrections.

329. Giovanni Battista Ramusio (1485–1557) was born in Treviso and was a fellow student of Navagero's at Padua. He had a diplomatic and political career in Venice, his first position being secretary to Alvise Mocenigo, Venice's representative to France in 1505–6 and the addressee of the preface to Pliny's *Letters* (ANT 18). Ramusio later held positions in the Venetian senate. His scholarly interests lay in part in ethnography and geography and are reflected in his three-volume work *Delle navigazioni e viaggi*, explorers' firsthand accounts of their travels translated by Ramusio into Italian. In the second volume of this work, he included Giorgio Interiano's short treatise on the Zygians (see HUM 7).

330. On Navagero, see the prefatory letter to Cicero's rhetorical works (ANT 24, n. 253).

331. An echo of Vergil, *Georgics* 3.110, *Aeneid* 5.458.

332. Compare Vergil, *Aeneid* 1.312, 6.158.

333. J. W. Moss (*A Manual of Classical Bibliography* [London, 1825], 535) reports that the text of this Aldine edition was based on that of the Giunta 1510 edition of Quintilian, as corrected by Navagero, aided by Ramusio. If Moss is right, then the allusion to Ramusio's help in providing Aldus with manuscripts is misleading here.

334. A close reminiscence of Plautus, *Poenulus* 443–44. Aldus had an excellent textual critic of Quintilian in the person of Raffaele Regio (who delivered Aldus' funeral eulogy), but he does not appear to have made much use, if any, of him or his published work. In his *Ducenta problemata in totidem institutionis oratoriae Quintiliani depravationes* (Venice: 1492) he makes approximately 340 conjectures on the text of Quintilian, of which more than half have been accepted or can be deemed worthy of mention in the apparatus to the text. See Michael Winterbottom, "In Praise of Raphael Regius," in *Antike Rhetorik und ihre Rezeption* (Stuttgart, 1999), 99–116, who ends his essay with the following: "To read the *Problems* of Raffaele Regio, like the *Classical Papers* of A. E. Housman, is to learn by example how one should deal with a corrupt text."

335. Compare Catullus 49.2–3, 21.3, 24.3, used frequently by Aldus.

336. For Pietro Bembo, see the preface to the rhetorical works of Cicero (ANT 24, n. 262) and the preface to the Vergil of 1505 (ANT 17, n. 164).

337. Donatus, *Vita Vergilii* 36.

338. In Vergil the text read *Arcades* (Arcadians). The point of the change, if deliberate, is that both Bembo and Navagero were poets, and so devotees of the Muses, who were supposed to live in Aonia, part of Boeotia.

339. Vergil, *Eclogues* 7.4–5.

340. A reference to at least some of the items that now go under the name of *Appendix Vergiliana*, perhaps the obscene poems of the *Priapea* in particular.

341. Bernardo Bembo (1433–1519) was a prominent Venetian politician and diplomat who had amassed a vast and valuable library that contained some important manuscripts, of which the most famous may be Vatican City, Biblioteca Apostolica Vaticana, Vat. lat. 3226 of Terence, known as the *codex Bembinus* (see also note 344, below). For manuscripts in the small octavo format that Aldus says were his model, see the preface to the Vergil of 1501 (ANT 4).

342. Vergil, *Aeneid* 6.304, describing the ferryman Charon as he toils in the underworld.

343. He is referring to the Ciceronian dialogue *De senectute*, or, as Cicero entitled it, *Cato maior*, in which the main character is Cato the Elder (234–149 BCE).

344. Aldus means the shorter poems in the *Appendix Vergiliana*, not the longer items such as the *Culex*, the *Dirae*, and the *Aetna*, which he distinguishes from the *Lusus* in the preface to the Vergil of 1505. Items in the *Appendix* are present in the manuscript that is now Vatican City, Biblioteca Apostolica Vaticana, Vat. lat. 3252 of the ninth century and was in Bernardo Bembo's library. Pietro Bembo drew on it for his dialogue that focused primarily on the text of the *Culex* (see ANT 17, n. 164).

345. Aldus died before such an edition could be issued. It appeared in 1517, edited, perhaps with the help of Pietro Bembo, by Francesco d'

Asola, the son of Aldus' partner and also brother-in-law of Aldus. See ANT 17, n. 164.

346. For Alberto Pio, see the preface to the 1500 edition of Lucretius (ANT 2, n. 6). After a period of disruption, Pio was assured of possession of his principality of Carpi in 1512 by Emperor Maximilian I and held it until 1525, when he was stripped of it by the imperial general Prospero Colonna. For much of this time, however, he was in Rome, first, as mentioned here, as Maximilian's ambassador (until 1519) and then as ambassador of Francis I of France. He left Rome for Paris shortly after the sack of Rome in 1527 and died there in 1531.

347. Vergil, *Aeneid* 3.265–66.

348. On Navagero, see the preface to Cicero's rhetorical works of spring 1514, which is addressed to him and in which Aldus expresses his thanks for his assistance and his admiration for his abilities (ANT 24, n. 253). He helped Aldus in the preparation of the editions of Quintilian and Vergil, also in 1514.

349. The headings, functioning as a list of contents, are given together, *seriatim* on the pages immediately following this prefatory letter. They are preceded by the words *Quae singulis libris continentur* (The contents of each book).

350. Aldus died on February 6, 1515.

351. There is a short list of *errata* on the final page, preceded by the same words that are found in preface C of the *Scriptores rei rusticae* (ANT 25).

HUMANISTIC AUTHORS

1. This Latin grammar was published in Venice by Andrea Torresani, Aldus' future partner and father-in-law. Three other editions of the grammar were published by the Aldine Press in Aldus' lifetime, in 1501 (see HUM 5), 1508, and 1514. It was pitched at a very elementary level.

2. If "for more than six years" refers to the period from 1482 until 1489, eleven years have passed at the date of writing this preface since Aldus began his instruction of the two young noblemen, at which date one may

presume that his manual of grammar had begun to take shape. He had certainly completed an early form of a Latin grammar in 1487, as he states in a letter to Catarina Pia, the mother of Alberto and Leonello. On the Latin grammar of Aldus, see Kristian Jensen, "The Latin Grammar of Aldus Manutius and its Fortuna," in *Renaissance Culture*, 247–81. Jensen traced sixty editions of the work, which did not match in popularity other Latin grammars that were in currency.

3. Horace, *Ars poetica* 388.

4. Vergil, *Georgics* 4.176 (slightly misquoted).

5. He seems to be suggesting a Greek grammar of his own composition. He can hardly be referring to the *Erotemata* of Constantine Lascaris, which he published in early spring 1495 (see *Greek Classics*, Preface 1), since the manuscript that he used (at least in part) for this edition was not brought back from Messina by Pietro Bembo until near the end of 1494.

6. What follows is a short poem (comprising three elegiac couplets) addressed to a young boy who would be using the grammar. The last four lines (from "Young Iulus") are repeated in the 1501 edition of *Rudimenta grammaticae Latinae* (see HUM 5).

7. This is to be found at the end of the volume. It is repeated in the 1501 edition of *Rudimenta grammaticae Latinae* (see HUM 5).

8. Aldus seems to be using the term *figuris* to embrace two rather different things. For *figura* meaning "a type of style," see *Rhetorica ad Herennium* 4.11, and Caplan, 252, n. b, according to whom the use of the word to refer to "a figure of speech" originates with Quintilian; see, for example, *Institutio Oratoria* 9.1.10–12.

9. Vergil, *Georgics* 4.6–7 (the translation is that of H. R. Fairclough in the Loeb edition of the poet's works).

10. Compare Martial 1.98.2.

11. Plautus, *Aulularia* 198.

12. Compare Pliny, *Letters* 3.21.3.

13. Martial 5.81.

14. Marcus Tullius Cicero, the greatest Roman orator.

15. Compare Horace, *Ars poetica* 268–69.

16. Cicero, who was hailed as *pater patriae.*

17. The orator Demosthenes, who denounced Philip of Macedonia in the speeches known as *Philippics.*

18. Saint Augustine, who taught for several years at Carthage before journeying to Rome and was one of the Doctors of the Church.

19. Saint Jerome, whose name "Hieronymus" means "sacred name" in Greek.

20. A paraphrase of Persius 5.62. Aldus changes *nocturnis* (of the night) of Persius to *doctis* (learned).

21. The Greek word *epiphyllides* in the title means "bunches of grapes," referring to the fruit that is left over after the harvest has been cropped.

22. Vergil, *Georgics* 2.490.

23. Four of the five Aldine volumes of Aristotle had already appeared when this preface was written. The distinction made here between logic and philosophy is similar to that in Aldus' 1498 advertisement of his Greek works for sale, where the five volumes of Aristotle (1495–98) are subdivided into the first volume, listed under logic, and the remaining four, listed under philosophy; see Davies, *Aldus Manutius. Printer and Publisher of Renaissance Venice,* 21. This same distinction was already made in the prefaces to the Aristotle volumes (see preface to the second of the five; *Greek Classics,* Preface 7). Aldus had also published a volume of Greek authors (primarily Theocritus and Hesiod) in February 1496 (see *Greek Classics,* Preface 5).

24. Not a great deal is known of Maioli other than what Aldus tells us here and in the prefatory letter to the second of the five Aristotle volumes (see *Greek Classics,* Preface 7). There Aldus praises him highly and reports that Maioli had helped him by collating the text of Aristotle against the manuscripts owned by his colleague in Ferrara, Niccolò Leoniceno, the renowned physician, who, in addition to medicine, also taught mathematics and philosophy over many years in the university there. Among Maioli's pupils in Aristotelian logic at Ferrara may have been Giovanni

Pico and Alberto Pio. Aldus had published a work of Maioli's on medicine (*De gradibus medicinarum*) earlier in 1497.

25. Ercole d'Este I, Duke of Ferrara (1431–1505).

26. For Maioli's letter, see Appendix I.

27. Angelo Poliziano (1454–1494), based in Florence, was the leading humanist of his generation, perhaps sharing this accolade in the eyes of contemporaries with the Venetian Ermolao Barbaro (1453/54–94). His qualities are best exemplified by his *Miscellaneorum centuria*, a collection of learned notes on a wide range of topics, published in 1489. He made a great contribution to the practice of textual criticism, stressing the importance of the detailed study of manuscripts to establish their relationship and therefore their significance as witnesses to the text. He was learned in areas of the classics beyond the many literary authors, both Greek and Latin, on whom he lectured in the Studio in Florence, turning to philosophy and law in the last few years of his life. The bibliography on him is vast, but see A. Grafton, "On the Scholarship of Politian and Its Context," *Journal of the Warburg and Courtauld Institutes* 40 (1977): 150–88, and *CEBR* 3:106–8.

28. For Marino Sanuto, see the preface to the 1501 edition of Horace (ANT 5, n. 37).

29. *De origine, situ et magistratibus urbis Venetae*, of which the letter of dedication to the doge Agostino Barbarigo is dated 1493.

30. Marino Sanuto, *Le vite dei dogi di Venezia*.

31. Marino Sanuto, *La spedizione di Carlo VIII in Italia*.

32. A saying of Pliny the Elder, reported by Pliny the Younger at *Epistolae* 3.5.10, which Aldus cites here, almost exactly.

33. See Suetonius, *Augustus* 25.5; Gellius, *Noctes Atticae* 10.11.5. Aldus' printer's device of the dolphin and anchor, first appearing in the 1502 edition of *Poetae Christiani veteres*, was a pictorial representation of the sense of the proverb. See Erasmus, *Adagia* 2.1.1 (*CWE* 33:3–17).

34. Alessandro Sarti was a prominent Bolognese humanist; he met Poliziano in Bologna in June 1491 at the beginning of Poliziano's travels in northern Italy in search of manuscripts. Whether he ever saw him again

is uncertain. He was involved in the publication in Bologna of several works of Poliziano in the years 1491 to 1494. One of these was Poliziano's translation of Herodian, and in his letter to Andrea Magnani that prefaces the edition (*Epistolae* 4.13), Sarti is described as "a man of literary learning, devoted to me and, most importantly in my opinion, never the least bit sluggish in taking care of something for a friend." See *Angelo Poliziano, Letters, Volume 1: Books I–IV,* ed. and trans. Shane Butler (Cambridge, MA: Harvard University Press, 287 [ITRL 21]). Another of these, *Le cose vulgare* (August 1494), included the first printing of Poliziano's *Stanze per la giostra,* though this was probably printed without the knowledge of the author. For a different view of Sarti, see J. H. Cotton, "Alessandro Sarti e il Poliziano," *La Bibliofilia* 64.3 (1962): 225–46, who views him more as an opportunistic entrepreneur than the close friend of Poliziano that Aldus suggests in this letter; and indeed Lowry (118, 220) states that Sarti was responsible for inserting "complimentary but entirely spurious references to himself into Poliziano's letters and appears to have been a typical press-shark."

35. Ovid, *Tristia* 1.7.40, with *eram* being changed to *erat*. Aldus uses the same line in the prefatory letters to Perotti's *Cornucopiae* and in the poetry of Tito and Ercole Strozzi (HUM 4 and HUM 11, respectively).

36. Poliziano died in 1494, at the age of forty.

37. The Pisan codex of the *Pandects* was used by Poliziano for the first century of his *Miscellanea,* published in 1489 (chaps. 41, 77, 78, 82).

38. Since Aldus could hardly fault Poliziano on his scholarship, he seems to be referring to the manner in which Poliziano's learning was expressed. Poliziano favored an eclectic range of models for his Latinity, in contrast to the Ciceronians, who were closely identified with Roman humanists. For the exchange of letters on this topic between Poliziano and Paolo Cortesi (1465–1510) in the 1480s, see *Ciceronian Controversies,* 2–15. At the time of this publication of Poliziano's works, Cortesi was the head of one of the several academies that existed in Rome and was the leading proponent in Rome of a strict adherence to Ciceronian syle; see D'Amico, *Renaissance Humanism in Papal Rome,* 102–7; *CEBR* 1:345–46.

39. That is, from the scholastics.

40. After the resounding success of Poliziano's *Miscellaneorum centuria*, published in 1489, it was the disappearance of its sequel in the years immediately following his death in late September 1494 that most disturbed his followers. The autograph manuscript of the work, incomplete as it turned out, was not to surface until nearly five centuries had elapsed. See A. Poliziano, *Miscellaneorum centuria secunda*, ed. V. Branca—M. Pastori Stocchi (Florence: Fratelli Alinari, Istituto di Edizione Artistiche, 1972). Some of the other works mentioned here have also surfaced (see following note).

41. On these see, for example, G. Gardenal, *Il Poliziano e Suetonio: Contributo alla storia della filologia umanistica* (Florence: Olschki, 1975); V. Fera, *Una ignota* Expositio Suetoni *del Poliziano* (Messina: Centro di Studi umanistici, 1983); R. Lattanza Roselli, *La commedia antica e l'*Andria *di Terenzio* (Florence: Olschki, 1973); L. Cesarini Martinelli, *Commento inedito alle* Selve *di Stazio* (Florence: Sansoni, 1978).

42. Although the two letters of Pietro Crinito to Sarti, printed by Aldus in Book 12 (nos. 22 and 23), focus primarily on topics that Crinito knew to be in Poliziano's second century, he also refers in passing to the question of Poliziano's work being appropriated and published by others. See J. H. Cotton, "Frosino Bonini: Politian's protégé and plagiarist," *La bibliofilia* 71 (1969): 157–75.

43. Erasmus, *Adagia* 1.5.15 (*CWE* 31:332).

44. Compare Terence, *Eunuchus* 1095. The image is one that Aldus frequently uses in his prefatory letters.

45. Niccolò Perotti (1429–80) was in the service of Cardinal Bessarion in Rome and was appointed bishop of Siponto in 1458. Although he had a distinguished career as a member of the Curia, serving as papal governor in Viterbo, Spoleto, and Perugia, he never gave up his scholarly interests. He was one of the team of translators that Pope Nicholas V enlisted to translate Greek works into Latin, being responsible for the first translation of Polybius, Books 1–5 (1452–54). His Latin grammar, published in 1473, was extremely popular. He was also responsible for editions of Martial and Pliny the Elder in the same year. Other works include a tract on letter writing, *De componendis epistolis*, and a commentary on Statius.

The *Cornucopiae* was a quite different work; it started as a commentary on Book 1 of Martial but amounted to more than one thousand learned columns of small print in the 1513 edition and covered many aspects of classical philology. In the 1470s Perotti was engaged in a bitter dispute with Domizio Calderini, who had also been in the entourage of Bessarion and who published his commentary on Martial in 1474. On the dispute, see Campanelli, *Polemiche e filologia*, 13–21.

46. Perotti dedicated to his nephew his Latin grammar as well as other works, including his commentary on Statius.

47. Ovid, *Tristia* 1.7.40. Also used by Aldus in the prefatory letters to Poliziano's *Opera* (HUM 3) and the poetry of Tito and Ercole Strozzi (HUM 12).

48. This immediately follows the dedicatory letter.

49. Aldus uses the term *semipagina*, literally, "half-page." This refers to one side of a leaf. See Rizzo, 36, n. 2.

50. The *editio princeps* of the *Cornucopiae* appeared in Venice in 1489 (P. Paganini), nine years after Perotti's death.

51. It is not immediately clear whether Aldus is referring to this edition of his Latin grammar (note that the prefatory letter is dated to four months after the date of the initial publication of the work) or to the earlier edition of 1493. If we set store by titles, then the former must be true, since the 1493 edition was entitled *Institutiones grammaticae Latinae*. It seems more likely, however, that he is referring to the earlier edition, of which this new edition is an expansion; this included the addition of several texts for students to read, almost all of which were religious in nature. The presence of this amount of reading material made Aldus' grammar distinctive among other Latin grammars; see Jensen, "The Latin Grammar of Aldus Manutius and its Fortuna," in *Renaissance Culture*, 253. Aldus printed two later editions of the grammar in his lifetime, one in 1508 and the other in 1514, both in quarto. During the sixteenth century, more than sixty editions of the grammar were printed in Europe, including France, Germany, and the Netherlands, as well as Italy, but it was less popular than others on the market.

52. Pliny, *Letters* 3.5.10. Aldus cites the same passage in his preface to the *Omnia opera* of Poliziano (see HUM 3)

53. Horace, *Epistles* 1.2.69–70; Erasmus, *Adages* 2.4.20 (*CWE* 33:200–201, on which the translation offered here is based).

54. Vergil, *Georgics* 2.272. Also quoted in the preface to *The Christian Poets*, vol. 1 (ANT 3), as well as in the Erasmian adage referred to in the preceding note.

55. Juvenal 7.209–10. "They" refers to "our ancestors."

56. Quintilian, *Institutio oratoria* 1.1.9.

57. Tibullus, 1.4.17–18.

58. The word *daimon,* which in classical Greek could refer to both beneficent and maleficent beings, was linked etymologically with the adjective *daemon* (knowing); see Plato, *Cratylus* 398B.

59. It is not clear to what Aldus is referring here. Perhaps the *Ars Minor* of Donatus, or the *Doctrinale* of Alexander de Villadei, to which he alludes at the end of the next paragraph (see next note).

60. Aldus is referring to Alexander de Villadei's *Doctrinale,* an elementary Latin grammar, written in verse, that was composed about the end of the twelfth century but which was still in use in Aldus' lifetime and later, for example, in the school of Guarino, where it was the custom to commit it to memory. Lowry (63) states that 279 printed editions of this work appeared in the fifteenth and sixteenth centuries.

61. Quintilian, *Institutio oratoria* 2.5.19. Modern editions read *expositum* (clear, plain) for *expolitum* (polished).

62. Quintilian, *Institutio oratoria* 2.5.20. Modern editions read "Livius" for "Plinius."

63. See Notes to the Text, Humanistic Authors, n. 3.

64. Gianfrancesco Pico della Mirandola (1469–1533) wrote widely on religious and philosophical topics and was highly thought of by humanists in Italy and Europe. The work *De imaginatione* deals with, among other things, the power and flaws of imagination and its relationship with the intellect. For an edition of the text with accompanying English transla-

tion, see Gianfrancesco Pico della Mirandola, *On the Imagination*, ed. Harry Caplan (New Haven: Yale University Press, 1930). Aldus would have been known to Pico when he was tutor to the prince's cousins Alberto and Leonello Pio in Carpi in the 1480s. Aldus dedicated to Pico the Greek grammar of Urbano da Belluno of 1498 (*Greek Classics*, Preface 11).

65. For Alberto Pio, see ANT 2, n. 6.

66. A close paraphrase of a sentence in Pliny, *Letters* 3.21.3. Perhaps quoted from memory.

67. The grandfather of Alberto Pio was a renowned *condottiere* in the service of Francesco Sforza and later of Savoy.

68. Giovanni Pico della Mirandola (1463–94) enjoyed an outstanding reputation in Europe for his scholarship. He studied at many Italian centers of learning, such as Bologna, Ferrara, and Padua, and also spent a year in Paris (1485–86). His fame rested on his philosophical and theological works, the best-known of which was his *Conclusiones sive theses DCCCC*, later condemned by Innocent VIII. See *CEBR* 3:81–84, and *DBI* 83 (2015): 268–75.

69. Very little of the commentaries on the Psalms has survived. See E. Garin, *La cultura filosofica del rinascimento italiano*, 2nd ed. (Florence: Sansoni, 1978), 241–53.

70. Giorgio Interiano was well known in his lifetime as a Genoese merchant, traveler, and ethnographer, though few details of his life are known. He was governor of Corsica in 1496, and after his travels in the east he lived in Naples, where he was for a while the guest of Jacopo Sannazaro. He may have left Naples in 1501 when King Frederick I of Naples went into voluntary exile (accompanied by Sannazaro).

71. This work, written in a dialect that is close to contemporary Florentine, attracted attention from those who had similar interests to Interiano. A German translation by Johann Mair von Eckh (1486–1543) appeared in 1518, and Giovanni Battista Ramusio (1485–1557) included it in the second volume of his *Navigationi et viaggi*. Interiano was also known to another friend of Sannazaro, Antonio de Ferrariis Galateo (1448–1517), who refers to him in his *De situ elementorum* (written 1504–5). See

F. Crifò, W. Schweickard, "*Vita et Sito de Zychi* di Giorgio Interiano," *Zeitschrift für romanisches Philologie* 130 (2014): 160–78.

72. Jacopo Sannazaro (ca. 1457–1530) was from a prominent family of Naples and spent most of his life in that city, where he was in the service of King Ferdinand, as poet and as a member of the Neapolitan academy under Giovanni Pontano. On the latter's death, Sannazaro succeeded him as head. His most famous work in Italian was *Arcadia*, a pastoral romance (see HUM 12). Sannazaro had a reputation for constantly refining his compositions, so much so that Pontano claimed that he did not know how to lift his hand off the page (see *Modern Poets*, 17). See *CEBR* 3:193–94.

73. For Daniele Clario, see the preface to the first volume of *Poetae Christiani veteres* (ANT 3, n. 14).

74. Homer, *Odyssey* 1.1–4.

75. For Giovanni Pontano, see the preface to Statius (ANT 11, n. 69).

76. A. Politianus, *Miscellanea* §47, where Interiano is described as *homo rerum abditarum investigator experientissimus*, "a very experienced researcher of exotic subjects."

77. Strabo 2.129, 11.429–97; Pliny, *Natural History* 6.19; Stephanus *sub* Zygoi.

78. In the Caucasus to the north of the eastern end of the Black Sea.

79. Sannazaro's *Arcadia* was first printed in Venice in 1502, but it was defective in many respects. It was not published by Aldus until 1514; see HUM 12. His not inconsiderable Latin works were printed by the Aldine Press in 1535; see Iacopo Sannazaro, *Latin Poetry*, trans. M. C. J. Putnam (Cambridge, MA: Harvard University Press, 2009 [ITRL 38]).

80. For Musurus, see ANT 11, n. 76.

81. For Giovanni Pontano, see ANT 11, n. 69. Some of his short poems may be found in *RLV* 67–87.

82. Johann Kollauer (1459–1519), who received a doctorate from Bologna in 1499, joined the secretariat of Maximilian I in about 1504. As this preface shows, he supported Aldus' desire to establish an academy in Germany, a plan that Aldus had conceived several years before. In late

March 1499 Johann Reuchlin wrote to Aldus on this topic, telling him that the emperor had been too distracted by the prospect of war and by civil unrest to give attention to Reuchlin's attempt to speak on behalf of Aldus (de Nolhac, no. 14). In additional attempts to establish an academy, Aldus in 1502 used the services of Iohannes Cuspinianus (Johann Spiesshaymer, on whom see ANT 12, n. 98), rector of the university of Vienna; in late 1504 and early 1505 he used those of a Dominican Johannes Cuno of Nuremberg (see de Nolhac, no. 50); and in late 1505 he used those of Jacob Speigel, secretary to the bishop of Trieste (see de Nolhac, no. 58). All were unsuccessful.

83. Menander, *Monostichoi* 832 (present in the Aldine Theocritus). See Erasmus, *Adagia* 1.1.33 (*CWE* 31:82).

84. Little is known of this person. He was living in Italy but clearly had close contact with the imperial court. We have a short letter of his to Aldus, written in Padua (de Nolhac, no. 63).

85. Matthaus Lang (1468–1540), from Augsburg, was a prominent churchman, rising to the rank of cardinal and archbishop, but he was very active in the political arena for most of his life, serving Maximilian I, Charles V, and Ferdinand I. It is little wonder then that Aldus enlisted him along with Johann Kollauer in his attempt to found an academy in Germany. See *CEBR* 2:289.

86. The dialogue of Macro and Lepidina is in the first of four eclogues of Pontano that are also printed in this edition.

87. This appears before the *Meteora*.

88. This letter acts as the preface to the second part of the volume (f. aa i r–v).

89. For Suardino Suardi, see ANT 11, n. 70.

90. Pontano composed two books of *Hendecasyllabics*, which focused on life at Baiae. See Giovanni Gioviano Pontano, *Baiae*, trans. R. Dennis (Cambridge, MA: Harvard University Press, 2006 [ITRL 22]).

91. Literally, the Latin means "about you," which does not make sense. However, the two books of the hendecasyllabics were addressed to Sardi.

92. Pontano wrote to Sardi in March 1503, giving him instructions about the Aldine publication, including the title of the hendecasyllabics (de Nolhac, no. 28).

93. Not identified.

94. Pontano died in late summer 1503.

95. Adriano Castellesi (ca. 1461–1521) was appointed cardinal in May 1503, a year after he became bishop of Hereford in England. He spent much of his diplomatic career (from 1489) as papal collector in that country, incurring there the hostility of several English churchmen, including Cardinal Wolsey. As a result of his implication in an abortive plot to assassinate Pope Leo X, he was stripped of his cardinalship in 1518. Besides this poem on hunting (*De venatione*), he composed a poem on Julius II's conquest of Bologna (*Iter Iulii Pontificis*). In addition to his literary (and philosophical) interests, his activities extended to pedagogy in relation to the teaching of Latin, for which he published two tracts, *De sermone latino* and *De modis latine loquendi*, published near the end of his life. Lilio Gregorio Giraldi refers (without much enthusiasm) to his Latin poetry at *Modern Poets* 1.105. See *CEBR* 1:279.

96. Ascanio Maria Sforza Visconti (1455–1505), the younger brother of Ludovico Sforza, duke of Milan, was appointed cardinal deacon in 1484. He was active in papal politics and was instrumental in having Rodrigo Borgia elected pope (Alexander VI). He is addressed as *cardinalem S. Viti vicecancellarium* on the title page, and he is the protagonist of the *De venatione*.

97. The *De venatione*, composed in Phalaecian hendecasyllabics, comprises only 427 lines. Near the end of the poem, the goddess Diana addresses Ascanio Sforza, bewailing the moral decadence of the times (in 86 verses).

98. Orlandi (2:356; n. 3 to this preface) reports a quite different view of Castellesi, that of Marino Zorzi, the Venetian ambassador to the Curia. Zorzi describes Castellesi as a "duro e sinistro uomo."

99. Michele Ferno (1467–1513) was a pupil of Pomponio Leto. He edited the *Opera omnia* of Giovanni Campano in 1495 (Rome: E. Silber). Like Ascanio Sforza, he was a supporter of Alexander VI and wrote a histori-

cal account of him from the time of his election as pope in 1492. On the publication of the *De venatione,* Ferno criticized Aldus for printing the cardinal's name as "Adrianus" rather than "Hadrianus." Beroaldo the Younger refers to this in a letter of November 15, 1505 that he sent to Aldus from Rome (de Nolhac, no. 22), supporting Aldus' orthography.

100. Desiderius Erasmus, who was to become one of the leading humanists of his generation, was not yet very widely known when he went to Italy in late 1506. The Dutchman spent nearly a year there in Bologna and then wrote to Aldus on October 28, 1507 (Letter 207; *CWE* 2:129–33) to ask him if he would publish a corrected and revised edition of his Latin translation of two plays of Euripides (*Hecuba* and *Iphigeneia in Aulis*), which Josse Bade had published the year before in Paris. This edition, claimed Erasmus, was full of errors. Aldus agreed to the Dutchman's request, and the revised translation came out in December 1507 (see *Greek Classics,* Appendix IX), this being the only publication of the press in the two years 1506 and 1507. This connection with Erasmus led to Aldus taking on this new edition of the *Adagia* of Erasmus (see next note).

101. This collection of proverbs was a much expanded and more erudite version of Erasmus' *Collectanea,* published in Paris in 1500, which had 821 headings and about 950 adages. A slightly expanded edition appeared in December 1506/January 1507. The actual title of the new edition is *Three Thousands [Chiliades] of Adages and Nearly Three Hundred More,* and the number of headings is just under 3,300; see Phillips, 75. The *Collectanea* was directed primarily at students; the *Chiliades* was pitched at a much higher level and would have appealed to scholars.

102. Aldus conceals the way in which the work was actually produced, giving the impression that Erasmus delivered him a completed manuscript. Erasmus tells a different tale in *Adagia* 2.1.1, of how he and Aldus worked together over a ninth-month period from December 1507 to produce the finished volume, Erasmus composing and Aldus then transferring that material onto the printed page; see *CWE* 33:14. As for the classical works that Aldus says he has put aside, he was to publish the letters of Pliny the Younger and a volume of the Greek orators in No-

vember 1508, and four more in 1509 (Plutarch's *Moralia*, Horace, Sallust, and the second volume of the Greek orators).

103. The proverb is Erasmus, *Adages* 3.3.28 (*CWE* 34:291), where Erasmus gives an example of how it can be used; it may be addressed to someone asking him to prove the truth of an achievement of which he has been boasting. Here I take Aldus to be using the proverb to mean that he can back up the claims he has made for Erasmus' *Chiliades*, the proof lying in the qualities of the work itself, as the following proverb indicates. The original context of the proverb (an Aesopic fable) relates to someone boasting of having performed great jumps in Rhodes, and then being challenged to repeat them in a different place.

104. The proverb is Erasmus, *Adagia* 2.5.86 (*CWE* 33:279), the sense being that a man has no need of anyone else to sing his praises when his own achievements speak for themselves. The quality of the *Chiliades* justifies Aldus' claims.

105. Tito Vespasiano Strozzi (1424–1505) played a prominent part in the political life of Ferrara, holding various positions under Borso d'Este and Ercole I. Only fragments of Books 1 and 5 of his *Borsias* (a poem in praise of Borso) survive. His poetic corpus included six books of the *Eroticon*, four books of elegies (*Aeolostichon libri*) and a book of *Sermones*. See *RLV* 46–54.

Ercole Strozzi (1472–1508) was the eldest son of Tito and held the position, like his father, of Giudice dei XII Savi. He was a pupil of Aldus for a time at Carpi (around 1482), where Aldus was tutor to the sons of Leonello Pio (Alberto and Leonello). He was assassinated in June 1508, and the perpetrator has never been identified with certainty. His poetry included Latin elegies and sonnets in Italian.

106. Lucrezia Borgia (1480–1519) was the wife of Alfonso d'Este, who became duke of Ferrara in 1505 on the death of his father, Ercole I d'Este. She was greatly admired by the writers of her time, including Pietro Bembo, Ludovico Ariosto, and Ercole Strozzi. Ferrara was the main abode of Aldus from May 1509 until June 1512, when he returned to Venice, and he must have come to the attention of the duchess during that period.

107. Vergil, *Georgics* 1.510–11.

108. Only 217 lines of the *Gigantomachia* are printed in this edition.

109. Euripides, *Hecuba* 379–81. The sentiment of these verses is one of which Aldus is very fond, as he also quotes them in the prefaces to his Xenophon of 1503 (*Greek Classics*, Preface 25), with reference to Guido da Montefeltro, and to the first volume of his Greek rhetoricians of 1508 (*Greek Classics*, Preface 35), with reference to Janus Lascaris.

110. Borso d'Este (1413–71) succeeded Leonello d'Este in 1450, becoming the first to hold the title of Duke of Ferrara.

111. The *Gigantomachy* of Ercole Strozzi.

112. The Fates.

113. Compare Vergil, *Aeneid* 1.94: "O thrice and four time blessed." Aldus is referring to his assassins.

114. Ovid, *Tristia* 1.7.39–40. Also used by Aldus in the prefatory letters to Poliziano's *Opera* (HUM 3) and Perotti's *Cornucopiae* (HUM 4).

115. This epitaph, composed of iambic trimeters, is to be found at the end of the first part of the volume, which contains the poetry of Ercole Strozzi.

116. Aldus follows a convention of epitaphs on gravestones in addressing a passerby (*hospes*, here imaginary). See *Corpus Inscriptionum Latinarum* I^2 1210, 1211, 1837, 2161.

117. These are the pseudonyms of characters who feature in Tito Strozzi's *Erotica*.

118. A close adaptation of Catullus 49.2–3, 21:2–3, 24.2–3. Aldus uses it more than once.

119. There are clear echoes here and what immediately follows of Horace, *Odes* 3.30.1–5.

120. Ercole Strozzi married Barbara Torelli only thirteen days before his assassination.

121. For the doctrine of bodily resurrection see 1 Corinthians 15:35–49.

122. On Sannazaro, see the preface to Interiano's ethnographical work *The Land and Customs of the Zygians* (HUM 7, n. 72). *Arcadia*, a pastoral

romance written in verse and prose, is the most important of Sannazaro's works in Italian.

123. Girolamo Borgia (b. in 1475) studied under Pontano in Naples and then after Pontano's death in 1503 served under Bartolomeo d'Alviano, the renowned *condottiere* and addressee of the preface to the 1509 edition of Sallust (ANT 20). He went to Venice in 1507 and studied Greek under Marcus Musurus in the studio in Padua. He later took sacred orders and won the support of Alessandro Farnese (later Pope Paul III). He was a prolific Neolatin poet (hence Aldus' description of him as "highly distinguished in letters"). His lengthy prose work, *Historia de bellis Italicis,* which engaged him during most of his life, was not published. See *DBI* 12 (1970): 721–24.

124. Vergil, *Eclogues* 5.17–18, followed by a line that is Aldus' own composition. He is referring to Sannazaro's poems in dactylic hexameters, in particular to his *De partu Virginis* (published in his *Latin Poetry,* ed. Putnam [ITRL 38], 3–93).

APPENDICES

1. This is the letter to which Aldus refers in his preface to Lorenzo Maioli's *Epiphyllides,* published by the Aldine press in July 1497 (see HUM 2) and presumably written in the late spring or early summer of that year. Aldus was indebted to Maioli for his help in the production of the second volume of Aristotle that appeared in February 1497 (see *Greek Classics,* Preface 7), and Aldus may well have felt obliged to accede to Maioli's request, despite his misgivings about the work's stylistic shortcomings. However, his decision to print this letter immediately after the prefatory letter to the *Epiphyllides* may have been in part self-serving, as the first section of it was a fulsome endorsement of Aldus' achievements.

2. Maioli writes as if Aldus himself was the type-cutter of the Greek and Roman fonts used by him. Although Aldus must have been closely involved in the design of the fonts, the credit for their manufacture must go to Francesco Griffo, as Aldus acknowledges in the preface to Vergil of 1501 (ANT 4). Most of the works published by the Aldine press up to

this time were Greek; on the Roman side, Maioli is probably thinking of the attractive font used in Pietro Bembo's *De Aetna*, published in 1495.

3. Aristotle, *Rhetoric* 3.1.6.

4. See, for example, Plato, *Phaedo* 66B–67A, for the defilement of the soul by the body.

5. He means perhaps the prefatory letter that Aldus will write for the edition.

6. That is, in Ciceronian Latin; see HUM 3, n. 38.

7. Avanzi was the editor of the edition of Lucretius published by the Aldine Press in December 1500. This letter immediately followed the dedicatory letter of Aldus to Alberto Pio (see ANT 2). For Avanzi, see ANT 2, n. 7.

8. As the letter informs us, Valerio Superchio was a physician and mathematician who taught in Padua. He seems to have been involved in some capacity with editions of Ovid and Terence. His *Oratio de laudibus astronomiae* was published in 1498.

9. Asclepius, the son of Apollo and Coronis, was a renowned physician in Greek myth, even having the power to raise the dead.

10. That is, to mark out faults. See Erasmus, *Adagia* 1.5.58 (*CWE* 31:436–37); see also 1.5.91 (*CWE* 31:463).

11. The obelus was a critical mark used by Hellenistic scholars to indicate spurious lines in an author's work.

12. This is probably a reference to a famed scholar and textual critic of antiquity, Valerius Probus, "a man skilled in reading and evaluating ancient writings" (Aulus Gellius, *Noctes Atticae* 9.9.12).

13. Avanzi's *Emendationes in Catullum et Priapea* was published by Iohannes Tacuinus in 1495. Tacuinus also published Avanzi's edition of Ausonius in 1496. Tacuinus may be the distinguished man to whom Avanzi refers.

14. Virbius is the Latin equivalent of Hippolytus. A component of his cult in Aricia was the belief that Hippolytus (Virbius) was brought back to life by Artemis (Diana) because of his vow of sexual chastity. His pu-

rity evokes the recovered purity of the text of Lucretius. The phrase *meis auspiciis* reinforces the reference to ritual. In Greek myth, Asclepius (see n. 9, above) is also credited with resurrecting Hippolytus.

15. Vincenzo Querini (1478/79–1514), a member of a rich and powerful Venetian family, studied philosophy at Padua, after which he presented, as did Superchio, his doctoral dissertation in Rome in the summer of 1501. He was a close friend of Pietro Bembo at this time, who thought highly of his scholarly abilities, but they later became estranged. Querini served as Venice's ambassador to Philip, duke of Burgundy, in 1504 and then, soon afterward, to Emperor Maximilian I. Always attracted to the contemplative life and to monasticism, he entered a Camoldese hermitage in 1511. Avanzi dedicated one of his poetic works to him in 1502. See Stephen D. Bowd, *Reform Before the Reformation. Vincenzo Querini and the Religious Renaissance in Italy* (Leiden: Brill, 2002).

16. The university of Padua is meant.

17. The rest of the sentence suggests that by "mathematics" Avanzi included astronomy (which in turn included astrology).

18. Domenico Grimani (1461–1523), born into a prominent Venetian family, was appointed cardinal deacon in 1493, having served as apostolic secretary to Innocent VIII. He studied classical literature, philosophy, theology, and canon law in different centers, including Padua, where he earned a doctorate in 1487. He continued to enjoy a high reputation for his proficiency in these areas, despite his involvement in affairs of the church. He amassed a huge personal library, reputed to contain some fifteen thousand volumes. See M. J. C. Lowry, "Two Great Venetian Libraries in the Age of Aldus Manutius," *Bulletin of the John Rylands Library* 42 (1975–76): 128–66; also *CEBR* 2:132–34.

19. Rather awkwardly, no subject of the verb (*cognoscant*) is expressed.

20. The phrase "so to speak" refers to the use of the word *emaculationes*, which may be a coinage, based on the verb *emaculo*.

21. An exaggeration on Avanzi's part as far as Hebrew is concerned, though Aldus contemplated a trilingual polyglot Bible, mentioned in William Grocyn's letter of August 27, 1499 to him (see *Greek Classics*, Appendix IV). It never came to fruition, although a pair of proof sheets of

the Bible survive. See Davies, *Aldus Manutius. Printer and Publisher of Renaissance Venice,* 57 (Fig. 28). Davies dates the sheets to 1501.

22. On Alberto Pio, see the preface to Lucretius (ANT 2, n. 6).

23. If the date given here is correct, the edition of Lucretius did not appear until almost two years after this letter was written, in December 1500. Avanzi's words suggest that Aldus was in no hurry to publish the volume, but the date may be given in the Venetian style, and the year may have been actually 1500.

24. The text of the letter is taken from de Nolhac, no. 23. It is a little surprising that Aldus did not print it in the edition of Cicero's *Letters to Friends,* since it is an excellent endorsement of the Aldine Press and of the convenience of the pocket-size format.

25. For Thurzó, see the preface to Cicero, *Letters to Friends* (ANT 8, n. 49).

26. He seems to be referring to other classical authors rather than other editions of Vergil and Horace.

27. An obvious exaggeration.

28. An adaptation of Vergil, *Aeneid* 1.33, with *linguam* (language) replacing *gentem* (race).

29. Aldus refers to friction between his workers and him in the prefatory letter to the first volume of the Christian poets of January 1501 (ANT 3).

30. The edition of Vergil was the first in the pocket-book format with the italic font, appeariing in March 1501, almost exactly two years before this pamphlet. The most recent edition of those mentioned was the Lucan of April 1502. On Terence, see nn. 39–41, below.

31. This famous symbol of the Aldine Press first appeared in the second volume of *Poetae Christiani veteres* (see ANT 10).

32. See Preface C of the 1501 edition of Vergil (ANT 4).

33. Juvenal 1.13. The three following examples refer to Juvenal 1.21, 1.22, 1.23.

34. Martial *Spectacula* 3.1.

35. Martial 2.6.3. The correct reading is actually ἐσχατοκόλλιον, meaning the end of a papyrus roll.

36. Martial 2.43.1 and 2.43.16.

37. Aldus addresses a prefatory letter to Marcantonio Morosini in his edition of Lucan (ANT 9).

38. Since this letter deals primarily with errors in the Aldine edition of Lucretius of 1500, it is not surprising that the pressmen of Lyons omitted it from their pirated edition of Catullus.

39. Aldus did not live to publish an edition of Terence. However, the Aldine Press produced an edition in 1517.

40. This last point concerns the production details relating to Terence's *Woman of Andros:* "Put on at the Ludi Megalenses when M. Fulvius, Marcus Glabrio and Quintus Minutius Valerius were curule aediles." The appropriate heading would be DIDASCALIA [production notes], not *ARGUMENTUM*.

41. In many of the early editions of Terence, the plays were printed as prose. This reflects the practice in a large number of late manuscripts. Even in manuscripts where the plays were written as verse, the line breaks were often wrong, corrupting the meters. So too the versification in the better printed editions was in places defective.

42. Iambic meters are meant, and Aldus is correct in his analysis of these five lines (Terence, *Andria* 172–76).

43. *Quadrati* is another term for trochaic septenarii, but what Aldus says holds good only for the sixth and seven lines of the passage quoted. The remainder are iambic octonarii.

44. The verse breaks in these lines (Terence, *Andria* 172–83) are correct.

45. On Giovanni Giocondo, see the dedicatory letter to the 1508 edition of Pliny's *Letters* (ANT 18, n. 172).

46. Giuliano de' Medici (1479–1516) was the third son of Lorenzo de' Medici (il Magnifico) and the younger brother of Giovanni (see n. 48).

47. Lorenzo the Magnificent (1449–92) was renowned for his patronage of scholars and artists, including Poliziano, Botticelli, and Leonardo da Vinci.

48. Giovanni de' Medici (1475–1521) became Pope Leo X on March 11, 1513, just a month before this edition of Caesar's *Commentaria* appeared. His immediate appointment to the apostolic secretariat of Pietro Bembo and Jacopo Sadoleto was an indication of his support of humanistic learning. A letter of Giovanni Giocondo to Pope Leo X was included in the 1514 edition of the *Scriptores rei rusticae* (see Appendix VI).

49. The phrase comes from Pliny, *Letters* 1.8.1, and became proverbial. See Erasmus, *Adagia* 1.2.47 (*CWE* 31:189–90).

50. This letter appears after the two prefaces of Aldus in his *Scriptores rei rusticae*, published in May 1514 (ANT 25).

51. On Giocondo, see the prefatory letter to Pliny's *Letters* (ANT 18, n. 172).

52. On Pope Leo X (Giovanni de' Medici), see n. 48, above.

53. Manius (not Marcus) Curius Dentatus (d. 270 BCE) held the consulship on three occasions, in the first of which (in 290) he defeated the Sabines and Samnites. In 275 (again as consul) he repelled Pyrrhus, king of Epirus. He served as an example of Roman incorruptibility, since he refused the bribes offered him by the Samnites, preferring turnips to wealth. For his response to the Samnites reported here, Giocondo draws on Valerius Maximus 4.3.5, though the story is told elsewhere. See Erasmus, *Apophthegmata* 5.264 (*CWE* 38:534).

54. Lucius Quinctius Cincinnatus is another hero of the early Roman Republic, renowned for preferring a simple life as a farmer to political power. After obeying the call to confront the Aequi, he retired to his farm after defeating them, having held the office of dictator for a mere fifteen days. See Livy, 3.29.

55. Cicero, *De senectute* 16.55; Plutarch, *Vita Catonis maioris* 9.

56. John 15:5.

57. Compare John 15:14.

58. This eulogy of Aldus takes up most of the prefatory letter of the 1515 Aldine edition of Lactantius, addressed by Giambattista Egnazio to Antonio Trivulzio. The edition appeared just two months after the death of Aldus.

59. Giambattista Egnazio (1478–1553) spent almost his whole life in Venice, eventually being appointed to the public lectureship in Latin in 1520, on the death of Raffaele Regio. He was a member of the Neacademia established by Aldus and was executor of his will. As well as editing this volume of Lactantius, he was also responsible for editions of Aulus Gellius (later in 1514), the *Historia Augusta*, and Suetonius' *Lives of the Caesars* (1516). Aldus dedicated the first volume of the Greek orators to him (*Greek Classics*, Preface 41), not inappropriately, as he had won fame primarily through his oratory. See *CEBR* 1:424–25.

60. Antonio Trivulzio was appointed bishop of Asti in Piedmont in 1499 and again in 1509, having served as bishop of Piacenza for one year. Later he became bishop of Como, where he died in 1519.

61. This took place in March 36 CE, in the reign of the emperor Tiberius. A talking raven, owned by a cobbler, was in the habit of addressing Tiberius and the two Caesars (Germanicus and Drusus) by name. On its death at the hands of a rival cobbler, the bird was given an impressive funeral attended by a large number of the Roman populace. See Pliny, *Natural History* 10.121–23.

62. Jerome, *De viris illustribus* 80.

63. In other words, the meter of the poem was the elegiac couplet — a dactylic hexameter followed by a dactylic pentameter. One might have expected "foot" rather than "syllable," as in Simonides, *Epistles* 4.18.5, "stretch out a hand to our elegy with its limping foot," but Egnazio is thinking of the clausula of the pentameter as being one syllable shorter than that of the hexameter. His criticism seems to be that he does not think that the meter suits the subject matter. The meter of epic, the dactylic hexameter, would have been more appropriate.

64. Egnazio is probably referring to the Franciscan humanist Antonio da Rho (ca. 1398–before 1453), whose *Lactantii errata*, pointing out Lactan-

tius' theological errors, was printed with all the incunabular editions of his works. See the entry on Antonio in *DBI* 3 (1961): 574–77.

65. For Raffaele Regio, see the preface to Valerius Maximus (ANT 12, n. 90). While Regio was the first to argue the point at any length in print, doubts on the Ciceronian authorship of the *Rhetorica ad Herennium* had certainly been expressed before Regio's *Quaestio* was published in 1492. Humanists who refer to the question in some way or other include Ermolao Barbaro and Filippo Beroaldo; see Gian Carlo Alessio, "*An Rhetorica falso sit inscripta ad Herennium*. Un promemoria," *Ciceroniana. Rivista di studi ciceroniani* 11 (2000): 141–58. Giorgio Merula (1430/31–1494) may have written an unpublished tract on the topic along the same lines, perhaps around the same time as Regio; see Annalisa Belloni, "Tristano Calco e gli scritti inediti di Giorgio Merula," *Italia medievale e umanistica* 15 (1972): 283–328, esp. 299–308. It should be noted that in Angelo Decembrio's dialogue *De politia litteraria,* at 1.10, Leonello d'Este (d. 1450), one of the participants, argues briefly that Cicero was not the author of the *Rhetorica vetera,* that is, the *De inventione* (not the *Rhetorica ad Herennium*).

66. Giovanni de' Medici (1475–1521), the future Leo X, was created cardinal in 1489. He had a sound classical education from a very early age. This and the importance of the Medici family made him a suitable dedicatee for this short disquisition of Regio's, even though he was still three months short of his sixteenth birthday when Regio dated it. He also studied canon law at Pisa and served as the church's legate on several missions. His papacy (1513–21) was marked by support for humanistic learning.

67. For the source of the text, see p. 314, above.

68. Lorenzo Valla, in his *Antidotum in Facium* (3.11.29), paraphrases Cicero's words at *De oratore* 1.5, where the orator is talking of *De inventione,* a work that he regrets having let slip from his possession in his youth. Valla, like Jerome (ANT 24, n. 302, above), mistakenly thought Cicero was referring to *Rhetorica ad Herennium.* In fact, Valla explicitly attributes the *Rhetorica ad Herennium* to Cicero on several occasions. See John Monfasani, "Three Notes on Renaissance Rhetoric," *Rhetorica* 5 (1987): 107–18, esp. 112–15.

69. See n. 65, above.

70. Jerome, *Comm. in Abdiam* (*PL* 25:1098; *CCSL* 76:350).

71. Quintilian 1.4.3. Regio already drew on Quintilian's words, at the beginning of the *Quaestio*.

72. The example referred to (it occurs at 1.20) is an imaginary clause of a will. It starts *Heres meus uxori meae . . .* (My heir to my wife . . .). The manuscripts read *Tullius heres meus Terentiae uxori meae*, but *Tullius* and *Terentiae* are intrusive glosses, probably originally written in the margin of manuscripts to refer the example to Cicero himself.

73. Cicero, *De oratore* 1.5.

74. Hermagoras, a rhetorician of the second century BCE, is cited on several occasions in *De inventione* (for example, at 1.8, 12, 16).

75. Six other parts are named: exordium, narrative (*narratio*), partition (*partitio*), confirmation (*confirmatio*), refutation (*reprehensio*), peroration (*conclusio*).

76. Cicero, *De inventione* 1.19.

77. The Types of Issue are discussed at *Rhetorica ad Herennium* 1.18, where the author reports that some think that there are four types and others three, the latter being "conjectural," "legal," and "juridical." The author writes that "our teacher (*noster doctor*) thought that there were three." The name Hermestes, which is found in a few manuscripts, must have been an intrusive gloss (on "our teacher"), as Niccolò Angeli points out in his defense of Ciceronian authorship (Appendix IX, §6), when he states that the name is not found in the oldest manuscripts.

78. Aulus Gellius, *Attic Nights* 13.6.4.

79. *Rhetorica ad Herennium* 4.17. Regio may have included "soloecismus" because he knew that this word too seems not to be found in republican Latin; see *Oxford Latin Dictionary* s.v.

80. Cicero (b. 106 BCE) was murdered in 43 BCE (interestingly enough, by a centurion named Herennius, according to Plutarch) when the young Octavian, the future Augustus, had just come on the scene after the assassination of Julius Caesar.

81. A suspect series of thirty tyrants appearing in the *Historia Augusta* who were supposed to be claimants to the throne during the reign of Gallienus (sole emperor from 260–268 CE, after sharing power with his father from 253 to 260).

82. Flavius Vopiscus, *Divus Aurelianus* 27–28, 30.

83. Niccolò Angeli was born in 1448 in Bucine in Tuscany. He studied at Siena and then moved to Florence, where he taught Greek and Latin literature. He also worked as an editor and corrector for the Giunta Press, being responsible for many volumes, including editions of Plautus (1514), Quintilian (1515), and Cicero (1515). He also wrote many of the prefaces for the editions that the Giunta press produced. The last dateable edition by him is of Priscian's *De syntaxi* of 1529. The date of his death is not known. See *DBI* 3 (1961): 199–200. It was in his edition of *Rhetorica ad Herennium* and Cicero's *De inventione* of 1515/16 that this defense of the Ciceronian authorship of the *Rhetorica ad Herennium* first appeared; see catalog item no. 89 in William A. Pettas, *The Giunti of Florence. A Renaissance Printing and Publishing Family* (New Castle, DE: Oak Knoll Press, 2013). It was regularly printed in sixteenth-century editions of Cicero. A much longer and more virulent attack on those who denied Ciceronian authorship was made by Marino Becichemo, a fierce rival of Raffaele Regio, in 1500 or early 1501; see John O. Ward, "Quintilian and the Rhetorical Revolution of the Middle Ages," *Rhetorica: A Journal of the History of Rhetoric* 13 (1995): 231–84, esp. 234–51. Becichemo's tirade is often printed alongside Angeli's defense in editions of Cicero.

84. Filippo Strozzi the Younger (1489–1538), the famous banker and condottiere of Florence. His alliance with the Medici family through his marriage to Clarice de'Medici, the niece of Pope Leo X, is referred to at the end of the letter.

85. Angeli is playing on the practice, common in the Renaissance period, according to which the *Rhetorica ad Herennium* was often termed *Rhetorica nova,* "The New Rhetoric," as opposed to the *De inventione,* which was termed *Rhetorica vetus,* "The Old Rhetoric."

86. This sentence was dropped in later editions of Cicero's rhetorical works that included the letter as a defense of Ciceronian authorship of

the *Rhetorica ad Herennium*. This is the case with the Basel edition of 1541 and the Aldine Venice edition of 1546. As a result, some minor adjustments were made to the opening sentence, which is identical in both. It begins *Librariorum quidem depravatione, Philippe Stroza*.

87. The Latin here is difficult and idiosyncratic. Word order suggests that *lectionis eius* should depend on *incelebres*, but what that means ("persons unfamiliar with this text"?) is not clear. I have translated as if *lectionis eius* depends on *maculis* in the relative clause and assumed an extreme example of hyperbaton (cf. *vix iam ut* for *ut vix iam* in the preceding sentence). One assumes that Angeli would have known of the Aldine edition of Cicero's rhetorical works of March 1514, in which Aldus argues against Ciceronian authorship (ANT 24 §§32–43).

88. It is true that in his Latin biography of Cicero, the *Cicero novus* (1413), based partly on Plutarch, Bruni gives a list of all of the orator's works, and this includes the *Rhetorica ad Herennium* (though he says this contains five books). However, there is no such listing in the Greek manuscripts of Plutarch. Angeli's point, then, carries no weight. See n. 98, below.

89. The name appears in some manuscripts at *Rhetorica ad Herennium* 1.18, but this is a gloss on *noster doctor* (our teacher) that has been incorporated into the text. The name is absent from modern editions.

90. Quintilian 1.5.71–72. Compare Cicero, *De natura deorum* 1.95.

91. *Rhetorica ad Herennium* 4.10.

92. Quintilian 9.3.31.

93. *Rhetorica ad Herennium* 4.20. *Complexio* is a figure of diction that uses both antistrophe and epanaphora, figures in which words are repeated at the beginning or end of expressions. In the Loeb edition, Caplan translates *complexio* as "interlacing."

94. Quintilian 9.3.69–70.

95. The first instance occurs at *Rhetorica ad Herennium* 4.21, as an example of *traductio*. The second can be found at 4.29, as an example of paronomasia (*adnominatio*), the figure that the first example more accurately illustrates.

96. Quintilian 9.3.71.

97. An exaggeration. Compare Quintilian 9.3.72 and *Rhetorica ad Herennium* 4.30; Quintilian 9.3.38 and *Rhetorica ad Herennium* 4.40.

98. Angeli seems to be arguing that there may have been manuscripts of Plutarch in which the *Rhetorica* was included in a list of the works of Cicero, one such manuscript being the exemplar for what he wrongly takes to be Leonardo Bruni's Latin translation of Plutarch, which Angeli adduces (but see n. 88, above).

99. This is a good point that negates one of the arguments of Raffaele Regio in his *Quaestio* (§11).

100. Leonardo Bruni (1370–1444) served as chancellor of Florence for many years up to his death. He translated several of Plutarch's *Lives,* as well as Plato, Aristotle, and Demosthenes. He is best remembered for his historical works; see Gary Ianziti, *Writing History in Renaissance Italy: Leonardo Bruni and the Uses of the Past* (Cambridge, MA: Harvard University Press, 2012).

101. Quintilian, 1, prooemium 2–3.

102. That is, Aristotle.

103. He is clearly referring to his own edition of the *Rhetorica ad Herennium,* which follows this prefatory letter.

104. A common rhetorical figure, termed *praeteritio* or (as at *Rhetorica ad Herennium* 4.37) *occultatio,* which "occurs when we say that we are passing by, or do not know, or refuse to say that which precisely now we are saying" (see Caplan, 320, note, and 312). Angeli uses it again in the next paragraph, when referring to authorities who credit the work to Cicero, and especially at the end of the letter (not printed here), where he lists the qualities and achievements of Filippo Strozzi and his family.

105. George of Trebizond, *Rhetoricorum libri quinque,* ed. Luc Deitz (Hildesheim: Olms, 2006), 21–22. George of Trebizond frequently refers to Cicero as the author of the *Rhetorica ad Herennium.* See John Monfasani, ed., *Collectanea Trapezuntiana. Texts, Documents and Bibliographies of George of Trebizond* (Binghamton, NY: Renaissance Society of America, 1984), 229, 394, and index (sub *Auctor ad Herennium*), on p. 823.

106. Priscian, *Institutiones* 2.21 (*GL* II 96) and 10.32 (*GL* II 523).

107. Jerome, *Comm. in Abdiam* (*PL* 25:1098; *CCSL* 76:350).

108. Cicero, *Philippics* 7.7; *Tusculan Disputations* 1.1.

109. Horace, *Epistles* 1.3.19

110. In other words, that he is going to unnecessary excesses in the arguments he has adduced to defend Ciceronian authorship. Compare Erasmus, *Adagia* 2.4.76 (*CWE* 33:229): "You seek a knot in a rush used to be said to a meticulous and overconscientious or fussy man, who would raise scruples where there was no reason to hesitate." Another interpretation would be that Angeli is referring to the possibility that his own arguments are failing to persuade.

111. *Rhetorica ad Herennium* 1.16.

112. *De inventione* 1.23.

113. This is probably the best of what evidence there is for Ciceronian authorship, even if it is in no way decisive; see Caplan, xxix–xxx.

114. *Rhetorica ad Herennium* 4.10.

115. Compare Cicero, *De oratore* 3.202–5.

116. *Rhetorica ad Herennium* 3.3.

117. Cicero's *De republica* fits the latter. For the former, Angeli is probably thinking of a handbook on military tactics, *De re militari*, by Vegetius, a writer of the late fourth century. This circulated under the name of Modestus, but was sometimes printed in editions of Cicero's works. This gave rise to the belief that Cicero was the author.

118. That is, in trying to establish by argument something that is quite obvious. Compare Erasmus *Adagia* 2.5.6 ("You use a lantern at midday") and 2.5.7 ("To hold a candle to the sun") in *CWE* 33:245.

119. *Rhetorica ad Herennium* 1.20. The names are interpolations. See Appendix VIII, n. 72.

120. But see the argument that Raffaele Regio makes on this point in APP VIII §7.

121. The three periods are roughly: (1) the second century BCE, though Lucretius lived later; (2) circa 90 BCE to 14 CE (when Augustus died); (3) the late first century CE to the early second.

122. Quintus Servilius Caepio (d. 91 BCE) is referred to at *Rhetorica ad Herennium* 1.21, 2.17; Lucius Licinius Crassus (140–91 BCE), who was the leading orator of his generation (see Wilkins, 8–13) at 4.2, 4.5, 4.7. Since Cicero was born in 106, both were actually of the previous generation.

123. *Rhetorica ad Herennium* 4.7. These orators date from the early second century BCE (Cato) to the early first BCE (Antonius and Crassus). See Caplan, 244, n. a.

124. *Rhetorica ad Herennium* 4.69.

125. Aulus Gellius, *Noctes Atticae* 10 (not 9).20.10.

126. Cicero, *Pro Caelio* 25.

127. Here ends Angeli's arguments in favor of Ciceronian authorship. The letter continues, however, concluding with fulsome praise of Filippo Strozzi and his family and a reference to his marriage to Clarice de' Medici.

Concordance

Grant	Ahmanson-Murphy	Orlandi	Renouard 1834
ANT 1	34	XVII	p. 20, no. 3
ANT 2	37	XXI	p. 23, no. 1
ANT 3	38	XXII	p. 24, no. 1
ANT 4	39	XXVII	p. 27, no. 3
ANT 5	41	XXIX	p. 27, no. 4
ANT 6	44	XXXI	p. 29, no. 6
ANT 7	52	XXXIII	p. 39, no. 16
ANT 8	55	XXXV	p. 33, no. 2
ANT 9	56	XXXVI	p. 33, no. 3
ANT 10	58	XXIII	p. 39, no. 17
ANT 11	61	XXXIX	p. 35, no. 7
ANT 12	65	XLII	p. 36, no. 10
ANT 13	66	XLIII	p. 37, no. 12
ANT 14	67	XLIV	p. 37, no. 13
ANT 15	68	XLV	p. 38, no. 14
ANT 16	72	XLVII	p. 44, no. 11
ANT 17	94	LXI	p. 50, no. 7
ANT 18	100	LXIV	p. 53, no. 3
ANT 19	102	LXVII	p. 56, no. 2
ANT 20	103	LXVIII	p. 57, no. 3
ANT 21	113	LXXVII	p. 61, no. 3
ANT 22	115	LXXX	p. 63, no. 6
ANT 23	117	LXXIV	p. 60, no. 1
ANT 24	120	LXXXII	p. 65, no. 1
ANT 25	121	LXXXIII	p. 66, no. 2
ANT 26	124	LXXXVI	p. 68, no. 5

Grant	Ahmanson-Murphy	Orlandi	Renouard 1834
ANT 27	127	LXXXIX	p. 68, no. 8
ANT 28	130	XC	p. 74, no. 11
HUM 1	—	pp. 165–66	—
HUM 2	13	X	p. 14, no. 11
HUM 3	26	XV	p. 17, no. 4
HUM 4	32	XVIII	p. 19, no. 2
HUM 5	42	XXV	p. 31, no. 9
HUM 6	40	XXVIII	p. 32, no. 11
HUM 7	64	XLI	p. 36, no. 9
HUM 8	91	LVII	p. 49, no. 4
HUM 9	92	LIX	p. 49, no. 5
HUM 10	98	LXIII	p. 53, no. 2
HUM 11	110	LXXIII	p. 65, no. 10
HUM 12	126	LXXXVIII	p. 68, no. 7

Bibliography

EDITIONS

Aldus Manutius. *The Greek Classics*. Edited and translated by N. G. Wilson. Cambridge, MA: Harvard University Press, 2015.

Orlandi, Giovanni, ed. and trans. *Aldo Manuzio editore. Dediche, prefazione, note ai testi*. Introduction by Carlo Dionisotti. 2 vols. Milan: Edizioni Il Polifilo, 1979.

Nolhac, Pierre de. *Les correspondants d'Alde Manuce: matériaux nouveaux d'histoire littéraire* (1483–1514). Torino: Bottega d'Erasmo, 1967.

CATALOGUES

The Aldine Press. A Catalogue of the Ahmanson-Murphy Aldine Collection of Books by or relating to the Press in the University of California, Los Angeles. Berkeley: University of California Press, 2001.

Fletcher, Harry George, III. *In Praise of Aldus Manutius. A Quincentenary Exhibition*. New York: Pierpont Morgan Library, 1995.

In Aedibus Aldi. The Legacy of Aldus Manutius and His Press. Edited by P. J. Angerhofer, M. A. A. Maxwell, R. L. Maxwell, with P. Barrios. Provo, UT: Brigham Young University, 1995.

Kallendorf, Craig, and Maria X. Wells. *Aldine Press Books at the Harry R. Ransom Humanities Research Center, The University of Texas. A Descriptive Catalogue*. Austin: University of Texas, 1998.

Renouard, Antoine Augustin. *Annales de l'Imprimerie des Alde ou Histoire des trois Manuce*. 3rd ed. 3 vols. in one. Paris: L. J. Renouard, 1834. Reprint, New Castle, DE: Oak Knoll Books, 1991.

LITERATURE

Aldus Manutius and Renaissance Culture. Essays in Memory of Franklin D. Murphy. Edited by David S. Zeidberg, with Fiorella G. Superbi. Florence: L. S. Olschki, 1998.

Barker, Nicolas. "The Italic Script." In *Aldus Manutius and the Development of Greek Script and Type in the Fifteenth Century*, 109–18. 2nd ed. New York: Fordham University Press, 1992. Slightly revised version, under the title, "The Aldine Italic," in *Renaissance Culture* (see Abbreviations), 95–107.

D'Amico, John F. *Renaissance Humanism in Papal Rome: Humanists and Churchmen on the Eve of the Reformation*. Baltimore: John Hopkins University Press, 1983.

Davies, Martin. *Aldus Manutius. Printer and Publisher of Renaissance Venice*. Tempe, AZ: Arizona Center for Medieval and Renaissance Studies, 1999.

Dionisotti, Carlo. *Aldo Manuzio, umanista e editore*. Milan: Il Polifilo, 1995.

Fletcher, Harry George, III. *New Aldine Studies. Documentary Essays on the Life and Work of Aldus Manutius*. San Francisco: B. M. Rosenthal, 1988.

Geanakoplos, Deno John. *Greek Scholars in Venice*. Cambridge, MA: Harvard University Press, 1962.

Infelise, Mario. "Manuzio, Aldo, Il Vecchio." In *Dizionario biografico degli italiani* 69 (2007): 236–45.

Kenney, E. J. *The Classical Text. Aspects of Editing in the Age of the Printed Book*. Berkeley: University of California Press, 1974.

Lowry, Martin. *The World of Aldus Manutius: Business and Scholarship in Renaissance Venice*. Ithaca, NY: Cornell Univesity Press, 1979.

Richardson, Brian. *Printing, Writers and Readers in Renaissance Italy*. Cambridge: Cambridge University Press, 1999.

Wardrop, James. *The Script of Humanism. Some Aspects of Humanistic Script, 1460–1560*. Oxford: Clarendon Press, 1963.

Wilson, N. G. *From Byzantium to Italy*. London: Duckworth, 1992.

Index

For classical and humanist authors, see also under Aldine Press editions.

Publication of this volume has been made possible by

The Myron and Sheila Gilmore Publication Fund at I Tatti
The Robert Lehman Endowment Fund
The Jean-François Malle Scholarly Programs and Publications Fund
The Andrew W. Mellon Scholarly Publications Fund
The Craig and Barbara Smyth Fund
for Scholarly Programs and Publications
The Lila Wallace–Reader's Digest Endowment Fund
The Malcolm Wiener Fund for Scholarly Programs and Publications